MICKEY AND WILLIE

MANTLE AND MAYS—

The Parallel Lives of
Baseball's Golden Age

MICKEY

AND

WILLIE

ALLEN BARRA

CROWN
ARCHETYPE
NEW YORK

Library of Congress Cataloging-in-Publication Data
Barra, Allen.
Mickey and Willie : Mantle and Mays, the parallel lives of baseball's
golden age / Allen Barra.
p.   cm.
Summary: "Culturally, Mickey Mantle and Willie Mays were light-years apart.
Yet they were nearly the same age and almost the same size, and they came to
New York at the same time. They possessed virtually the same talents and played the
same position. They were both products of generations of baseball-playing families,
for whom the game was the only escape from a lifetime of brutal manual labor.
Both were nearly crushed by the weight of the outsized expectations placed on them,
first by their families and later by America. Both lived secret lives far different from
those their fans knew. What their fans also didn't know was that the two men
shared a close personal friendship—and that each was the only man who could truly
understand the other's experience." —Provided by publisher.
Includes bibliographical references and index.
1. Mantle, Mickey, 1931–1995. 2. Mays, Willie, 1931– 3. Baseball players—
United States—Biography. I. Title.
GV865.A1B3239   2013
796.3570922—dc23
[B]   2012013345

ISBN 978-0-307-71648-4
eISBN 978-0-307-71650-7

Printed in the United States of America

Book design by Barbara Sturman
Jacket design by Nupoor Gordon
Front jacket photography © Herb Scharfman/Sports Imagery/Getty Images

2 4 6 8 10 9 7 5 3 1

First Edition

To my father,

ALFRED BARRA,

who loved Mickey but worshipped Willie

Whatever you do, don't God-up these guys.

— Red Smith's advice to a young sportswriter

I have seen the boys of summer in their ruin.

— Dylan Thomas

What's the use of being a boy
    if you're going to grow up to be a man?

— Frank Merriwell

I used to dream how good it would be to be
Willie Mays or Mickey Mantle.

— Reggie Jackson

Contents

Preface

I didn't cry when my father died, but I held back tears on August 13, 1995, when I heard that Mickey Mantle was gone. My father would have understood. He once told me he had not cried when *his* father died, but I recall him weeping uncontrollably when Joe Louis passed away in 1981. Several friends have told me they had similar reactions to the deaths of their fathers and their sports heroes.

Many times over the years I've thought about this, and I've come to the conclusion that if we don't weep over losing our fathers, it might be because we do not yet comprehend the magnitude of our loss. But when the favorite athletes of our youth are proven to be mortal, we experience a sudden jolt; we know then that not only is our youth gone, but our youthful dreams as well.

Mantle's death ended a dream I had nourished for years that I could sit Mickey and Willie down together for a long interview, a hope I'd had since I had seen them interview each other in 1968 in *Esquire*. I was scheduled to interview them both for *Inside Sports* in 1983 when they had been banished from baseball by Commissioner Bowie Kuhn, but I couldn't get them together. Mantle was polite but exceedingly hungover and, to my staggering disappointment, seemed to have no memory of or even interest in the things I wanted to discuss, like his 1958 barnstorming tour with Willie or his appearance in Birmingham to promote his Mickey Mantle's Country Cookin' restaurant in 1970, where he autographed a *Sport* magazine with his picture on the cover and gave me ten minutes of interview time for my school paper. Mays was distracted and in the same ill humor he was in every one of the five times I had attempted to interview him.

The idea for this book — to try to trace their remarkably parallel lives — came later and must be credited largely to Charles Einstein. Charlie and I first met in 1996, when I was working with the *Newark Star-Ledger* and realized that a man named Charles Einstein was covering lounge acts in Atlantic City for the paper. I asked the sports editor if it could possibly be the same Charlie Einstein who had written *Willie's Time*, published in 1979 and perhaps the finest book about a professional athlete that I had ever read. Indeed it was the legendary Charlie Einstein — sportswriter, novelist, screenwriter (I had seen his documentary *A Man Called Mays* only once but could repeat entire chunks of it verbatim), editor, son of the radio comic Harry Parke (better known as Parkyarkarkus, or "park your carcass"), and half brother to both the comic Super Dave Osborne and the comedian-actor-director Albert Brooks.*

Over the next few years, in person, in long phone sessions, and through several letters, Charlie told me of a Willie Mays I not only had never known but had never dreamt of — a man with a huge capacity for kindness and generosity, but given to dark moods and desperation, a man who had never entirely come to terms with his own fame or his place in the world after baseball. He also told me how much Willie liked and admired Mickey and about their personal rivalries on the ball field, on the golf course, and even at the pool table.

The more people I sought out who knew Mickey and Willie, such as the greatest of all baseball writers, Roger Kahn, and George Lois, the innovative advertising genius who befriended them both, the more I had a picture of two men who had never entirely grown

---

*Charlie's history fascinated me. After a successful career as a sportswriter, mostly covering the New York Giants and Willie Mays (with whom he had collaborated on several books), he moved to Arizona in the mid-1950s and then got a job covering the Giants when they moved to the Bay Area in 1958. In the late 1970s, after his wife died, he moved back east, to a small town in southern New Jersey called — swear to God — Mays Landing.

up and who seemed just a bit bewildered that the world had passed them by while leaving them as famous as they had been in their playing days.

I began retracing their lives to a past dimly remembered but still strongly felt by those of us who lived through it. To me, and I firmly believe to millions of other Americans, Mickey and Willie signify a simpler time. Not, as purveyors of nostalgia would have us believe, a more innocent time, but a simpler time. Their images, if not their personal lives, reflect an America to be found now only in old baseball cards, yellowing newspapers, and moldy sports magazines — and in the memories of fans like me. It's an America I hope to revive in these pages before it passes altogether.

MICKEY AND WILLIE

Introduction

My First Game Was Better Than Yours

E very baseball fan has a "my first game" story, but mine is better than yours. My first ball game was at Yankee Stadium, and I saw Mickey Mantle and Willie Mays play.

Until I saw that game, it had not occurred to me that Mickey Mantle and Willie Mays could actually play baseball on the same field. That they did in 1961 was an accident of scheduling. Both the Yankees and Giants had a break before road trips, and the team owners agreed to an exhibition game to replace the annual Mayor's Trophy Classic that had been played for years between the Yankees and either the New York Giants or Brooklyn Dodgers, the proceeds going to city charities. (Since the Giants and Dodgers moved to the West Coast in 1958, there had been no game.)

When the game was set, the New York press went wild. The theme was Willie Mays's "return" to New York since the Giants had moved to San Francisco three years earlier. Actually, Willie had played in

New York twice since then: in a 1958 postseason exhibition that pitted Willie Mays's National League All-Stars against Mickey Mantle's American League All-Stars at Yankee Stadium, and again at the second All-Star Game in 1960, when Willie demolished Whitey Ford in front of the home crowd in the Bronx.

Nonetheless, Yankee Stadium was in a frenzy on that early summer day when we took our seats. I don't recall if the game was a sellout; it certainly seemed that way to me. The crowd's spirits were dampened a bit when the threat of rain canceled a pregame home run contest between Mays and Orlando Cepeda (who would go on to lead the NL in home runs that season) and Mantle and Roger Maris (who would, of course, break Babe Ruth's record of sixty home runs that season). But the disappointment was forgotten when the game began.

I had my first experience with goose bumps when the PA man — surely it was Bob Sheppard, the ghostly voice of the Yankees, though I did not know this at the time — announced, "Now batting . . . for the San Francisco Giants . . . number twenty-four . . . Wil-lie . . ." The roar of the crowd was like a wave hitting the shore, drowning out the rest of his name.

Many years later, Charles Einstein sent me his account of the game. Describing the crowd as Mays came out of the dugout, he wrote, "An unbroken, throat-swelling peal of adulation sprang from the hearts of Giants-starved New Yorkers. It rolled and volleyed off the great tiering of this triple-decked palace and against the vague outline of the Bronx County Courthouse, looming in the gray-black mist out beyond the huge scoreboard in right-centerfield.

"They rocked and tottered and shouted and stamped and sang. It was joy and love and welcome, and you never heard a cascade of sound quite like it." And in the hundreds of games I've attended since, I've never heard it again.

Mickey Mantle, some said, was a forgotten idol that night. He was not forgotten by me. He woke up Yankee fans with a towering two-run homer into the right-field seats, delivered from the left side of the plate. My father and I, sitting over the third-base dugout, had a perfect view. It was my first major league home run, and it was everything I had hoped it would be. I could hear the distinctive crack of the bat and could easily follow the trajectory of the ball as the thousands in the stands rose to watch its flight.

I cannot tell you who was pitching — and anyway, the only pitcher I knew then was Whitey Ford. I think the pitchers were minor leaguers brought up for the game. Neither can I recall what anyone else on the Yankees did at bat. I do, though, have one sharp recollection of Mantle after his home run swing: he shot out of the batter's box down to first base as if he did not know the ball was going over the wall. (And how could he not have?) After crossing first base, he slowed into a home run trot with his head down. I would later learn that this was typical of Mickey after a home run; he didn't want anyone to think he was showing up the opposing pitcher — even a minor leaguer like the guy pitching for the Giants.

Willie Mays walked his first time up, drawing boos from the crowd, which shocked me. How could anyone *boo* Willie Mays? My father explained that they were booing the Yankee pitcher who hadn't given Willie anything good to hit. Mays, playing to the crowd, attempted to steal second; the Yankees catcher, who I later learned was Johnny Blanchard — both Elston Howard and Yogi Berra had the day off — muffed the pitch, allowing Willie to slide in uncontested. No matter that there wasn't a close throw — Willie lost his cap about two-thirds of the way down the base path to second, and that's what we had all come to see.

The second time up — I'm sure it was the fourth inning and Willie's second and last plate appearance — he lunged into a pitch and smashed a hard bouncer between second and third, scoring two runs that proved to be decisive.

The fans bellowed their approval in the fifth when Willie made a basket catch of a medium-range fly ball and fired home in time to prevent a runner from scoring; he couldn't have satisfied us more if he'd thrown out the runner at the plate.

If there was a disappointing note to an otherwise perfect day, it was that both Mickey and Willie were out of the game after the fifth inning. There wasn't anyone else on either the Yankees or Giants who I was remotely interested in, though I also had great affection for Yogi and Whitey. The Giants had Cepeda and Juan Marichal, but I knew nothing about them at the time. Nor did I yet understand who Roger Maris was and what significance he would bring to the 1961 season.

I got to see Mickey and Willie, and nothing else mattered.

I suppose the seed that would become this book was planted that afternoon, though it could have also been the year before, when my father brought home four packs of Topps baseball cards. Now, you're either going to believe this or you aren't — and I realize I'm testing my credibility and your credulity — but in either the first or second pack I opened, I got both Mickey Mantle and Willie Mays All-Star cards. I understand now that this was more than just a case of incredible luck; the way Topps packaged cards back then was supposed to guarantee that things like that didn't happen. If it did, kids who were happy with what they got in a few packs might not buy more. (I know I was more than satisfied with what I got. Every card I possibly could have wanted was in that one pack. Who cared about Dick Groat or Brooks Robinson or Mike McCormick?)

I admit that it's entirely possible, perhaps even likely, that I did not get both cards in the same pack; I can only swear that that's how I remember it. At any rate, I have the cards to this day, and if I'm wrong and they weren't in the same pack, the odds of getting the Mantle and Mays cards in just four packs was still astronomical. But I got them.

The smell of the stick of bubblegum under Mickey's card lasted for years. Every time I picked the card up, it gave off such an evocative aroma that I understood how the taste of a cookie could inspire Proust to write seven volumes. On the day Mickey died in 1995, I was at the New York Giants training camp working on a story. Later that afternoon, when I returned home, I went upstairs and dug out the card and sniffed it. All traces of the scent of bubblegum had vanished.

On the day in 1960 when my father gave me the four packs of

cards, some neighbors came over for a beer. One or two of them suggested that Mays and Mantle would someday be regarded as the greatest two players of all time. Len O'Sullivan, our next-door neighbor,
told me, "They might be the two greatest players ever!" Jim O'Kane,
who lived around the corner, said, emphasizing the point with his
finger, "They are the only two guys in the game who can do it *all*."
(I didn't know what "all" meant back then; I had some vague idea that
it meant they could also take a turn at pitching.)

Listening to my father and his friends debate the relative merits of
Mantle and Mays was my introduction to sports guy talk and my first
experience with baseball analysis. I knew the names of other professional athletes; I knew that Joe Louis, Rocky Marciano, and Sugar
Ray Robinson had been champion boxers at some time in the recent
past, and I knew that Johnny Unitas was a great football player. I knew
that Wilt Chamberlain was a basketball player who had set some sort
of scoring record. But Mickey Mantle and Willie Mays were the only
two professional athletes whose names I heard mentioned in super-
market lines or in restaurants or in a New York subway. They were
the only two I heard discussed at backyard barbecues. I wasn't old
enough to yet understand the hopes and dreams that post–World
War II America had invested in them. It quickly became clear to me,
though, that Mickey and Willie were symbols of something much
more important than just baseball, and that in the America I was
growing up in baseball was much more than just a game.

In our house, much of this feeling was tied to Mays. I remember my father talking about Willie Mays as if there were something
very important at stake in his success, something I vaguely understood as a hope for integration and equality — though no one I knew
had any real notion that blacks could achieve equality with whites
in society. (My father, like all children of immigrants, was raised to
believe in the New Deal; by the 1950s, he had become a moderate
Republican — pretty much like Willie himself, I came to understand.)

The first picture I ever tacked to my bedroom wall was of the
two smiling young sluggers at their first meeting in the 1951 World

Series. (You can see it in the first photo section of this book.) Willie was twenty, and Mickey would be twenty in another sixteen days. How splendid they were — I would have sold my soul to be either one of them. Though I never articulated it, the thought in the back of my mind was always, *What a great country we are to have heroes like Mickey and Willie!*

In 1961 *Sport* magazine held a contest, "Who's the Greatest, Mickey or Willie?" With my mother's help, I addressed and stamped the envelopes and stuffed the ballot box with ten votes for each of them. The first baseball magazine I remember owning was a special edition put together by the editors of *Sport* devoted entirely to Mickey and Willie. I can still feel the rush of pure joy when I spotted it at the newsstand. I bought three copies, carefully preserved two, which I own to this day, and cut up the third to lovingly paste the photos in a scrapbook.

One day in the spring of 1963, after finishing up my paper route, I stopped for a Coke at Whelan's Drugstore on Route 9 in Old Bridge, New Jersey. There I spotted a Mickey Mantle–Willie Mays "Zippee" ball — a Wiffle ball with Mickey and Willie's picture on the package. As it turned out, I didn't have money for both the Coke and the ball; I skipped the Coke. I took thousands of swings at Wiffle balls while fantasizing that I was Mickey or Willie, but I hit only generic Wiffle balls. The Mickey Mantle–Willie Mays "Zippee" ball package remains unopened to this day.

For making the honor roll at St. Thomas Aquinas Elementary School, my parents bought me Mickey Mantle and Willie Mays Hartland statues. Mickey's was a perfect replica of his crouching left-handed batting stance; Willie was re-created making his famous "basket catch." When my daughter was ready for college, I considered selling them on eBay for $500. At the last moment, a scholarship saved me countless sleepless nights.*

---

* My Mickey Mantle Hartland has a couple of minor scratches on his left forearm from falling over. My mother suggested the cause was "Mickey's bad left knee," but

I tried to become a switch-hitter in stickball and Wiffle ball to imitate Mickey and taught myself to lunge at the ball when batting right-handed to look like Willie. I tried, with miserable results, to basket-catch fly balls, and when rounding the bases after a home run — something I didn't get a lot of practice at — I put my head down like Mickey so as not to show up the pitcher. (My father told me that he would always catch me looking up to see where the ball landed.)

When I recall gazing at the beaming, boyish faces on their bubblegum cards, or waking up every morning to see that 1951 picture on my wall, I wonder if Mickey and Willie ever truly understood how much they meant to so many. When that picture was taken, I now believe, they were as happy as they would ever be. Many years after I first stuck the photo on my wall, I learned that it was taken on October 4, perhaps two hours before the first game of the 1951 World Series. The next day Willie hit a fly ball to right-center; Mickey, running to make the play, caught his cleats in an exposed drain and tore up his knee, altering the entire course of his career. He wound up in the hospital alongside his father, who collapsed while watching his stricken son, and they would watch the rest of the World Series on television from adjacent hospital beds.

There was no inkling among the press and fans that Mutt Mantle had only a short time to live, that Mickey would spiral into an unending cycle of alcohol abuse, or that Willie's anxieties would result in lifelong stomach pain, fainting spells, and nervous exhaustion. Though it is now mostly forgotten, the two greatest players of the

---

my father saw that the problem was that Mickey's left shoe was uneven on the bottom. He thought about gluing something to the bottom of the shoe to even it out, but decided against it. "You might want to sell this someday," he said, "so don't put any glue or anything else on it." He fixed the problem with a tiny sliver of cardboard instead.

My father's suggestion that I might want to sell the statue someday struck me as absurd at the time. It never occurred to me when I was a kid that any of my treasures would increase in value over the years or that I would ever sell them for any price. (I did sell my Dick Groat and Luis Aparicio Hartlands and gave the money to my daughter.)

1950s and 1960s, the men who would be remembered as the most popular players of their time, would also endure horrible, and to us inexplicable, booing from their hometown fans.

Money problems, marital discord, and alienation from their own children were all unknown to the young men who posed side by side that day. With all respect to Roger Kahn (and Dylan Thomas), it was Mickey and Willie, not the 1950s Dodgers, who were truly the boys of summer. And though I, like much of America, tried to look the other way over the next forty-some years when it came to their frailties, I would finally come to see them in their ruin.

I don't know that anyone's ever calculated this, but I wouldn't be surprised to find that Mickey Mantle and Willie Mays, in that order, are the two most written-about players in baseball history, or at least two of the top three, along with Babe Ruth. The year 2010 saw the publication of a thick and well-researched biography of Willie, *Willie Mays: The Life, the Legend,* by James Hirsch, and there are count- less shorter lives of Willie, several autobiographies and memoirs, and a superb life-and-times account, *Willie's Time,* by Charles Einstein that, in my opinion, stands as the best thing ever written about him. Also published in 2010 was Jane Leavy's Mantle biography, *The Last Boy: Mickey Mantle and the End of America's Childhood,* the most detailed of the nine versions of his life. There are also six volumes of autobiography, memoirs, and recollections, as well as numerous books by fans and collections of letters to and from Mickey, that have been published since his death.

And yet, it seems to me that there has always been one major element missing from the many books on Mantle or Mays: each other. Though they are and always will be linked in the minds of millions, I don't think it's ever been noted exactly how much they had in common and how each man's image reflected the other. The similarities in their lives were uncanny. Both were children of the Great Depression, born in 1931. They were almost the same size (about five-foot-eleven and 185 pounds, at least early in their careers);

Mantle had a bit more muscle, and for most of his playing career probably outweighed Willie by five to ten pounds.

Both were heralded as phenoms when they arrived in New York in 1951 after brief but legendary minor league careers. (If integration had come along a couple of years earlier, they probably would have played against each other as minor leaguers.) Both started out playing for Hall of Fame managers, Mantle for Casey Stengel and Willie for Leo Durocher. Both played stickball in the streets of New York with kids (though only Willie was lucky enough to have TV cameras record the games). The burden of expectation caused each of them to break down in tears before his first season was over.

Mickey exploded on the national scene in 1953 when he hit the first "tape measure" home run, and Willie the next year when he made the most famous catch in World Series and probably baseball history. In 1958 and 1959, they barnstormed against each other with specially selected All-Star teams.

Together they defined baseball in the 1950s and through the mid-1960s. Both made the covers of *Time* and *Life*, and they were the subjects of popular songs. In the 1960s, they were often pictured together on the covers of baseball magazines, including some devoted entirely to them. They were paired off on television on the popular show *Home Run Derby*, did commercials and endorsements together, and appeared together on numerous TV shows. Together they created nostalgia and the autograph and memorabilia craze. Finally, in the early 1980s, they were both banned from baseball by Commissioner Bowie Kuhn for doing public relations work for Atlantic City casinos.

They had exactly the same talents — everyone who saw them observed that no other players in the big leagues possessed their astonishing combinations of power and speed. And despite Willie's far greater durability, they were, in terms of effectiveness on the field, remarkably similar. Both batted over .300 ten times and hit over 50 home runs in a season twice. *Total Baseball: The Official Encyclopedia of Major League Baseball* ranks Mays as the best player in the NL from 1954, the year he returned from the Army, through 1965, except 1959, when he ranked fourth. (For the 1956 and 1961 seasons, he shared the top spot with Henry Aaron.) Mantle was *Total Baseball*'s best player in the AL every year from 1955 through 1962; he was also ranked second in 1952 and fourth in 1954. (Mantle was surely poised to top *Total Baseball*'s ranking in 1963, when he batted .314 but was limited to just sixty-five games by injuries.)

In every season from 1954 through 1965, Mickey and Willie were selected for the All-Star teams. From 1951 through 1964, the Yankees or the Giants were in every World Series except in 1959. Their fortunes in the World Series and All-Star Games contrasted oddly. Mays was the ultimate All-Star, hitting .307 in twenty-four games, producing 29 RBIs and runs scored, while Mantle hit just .233 in sixteen All-Star Games without a single home run. But in twenty World Series games, Mays managed just .239 without a single home run; in sixty-five games, Mantle set the all-time World Series home run mark with 18.

That Mickey and Willie were the most dominant players of that period isn't simply a myth built up by worshipful New York sportswriters — it's a fact. The ultimate question isn't "Were they the greatest of their time?" but "Which of them was the greatest?" (That's a subject I explore in detail in Appendix A.)

Both were consummate all-around athletes who excelled at basketball and football in high school. Reversing the stereotype, Willie was a great passing quarterback at Fairfield Industrial High School in Westfield, Alabama; at the same time, Mickey was a dazzling running back at Commerce High in Commerce, Oklahoma. If circumstances had been different, they might have ended up playing for the two greatest college football coaches of their era: Willie for Bear Bryant, then at Kentucky — Bryant had been hugely impressed when he saw Willie play baseball for the Black Barons at Rickwood Field — and Mickey for Bud Wilkinson at Oklahoma.

They were both natural center fielders, but both played other positions when they were young. Mantle spent more time at shortstop than Willie, but neither of them ever quite got the hang of it. Willie began his rookie season in center field; Mickey began his rookie year in right field while Joe DiMaggio struggled through his final season, and in 1952 Mickey became the Yankees' starting center fielder. Both had great throwing arms and were told during their early careers that they had a shot to make it as a pitcher.

Mickey and Willie both idolized Joe DiMaggio. Both loved Westerns and, as boys, dreamed of growing up to be cowboys. Their lives were dominated by their fathers, who saw baseball as a way for their sons to escape a life of brutal manual labor. For Cat Mays it was the steel mills, for Mutt Mantle the hellish zinc mines. By the time Mickey and Willie graduated from high school, both their mothers had almost disappeared from the narratives of their lives.

It was often said of both that they were "born to play ball." Whether or not that was true, they were certainly bred to the game. Cat began rolling a ball to his son while Willie was still an infant. Mutt began to throw to his son as soon as Mickey could hold a broom handle.

Both men were southerners. (New York sportswriters were fond of labeling Mickey a cowboy, a westerner — he did, after all, once ride a horse to school — but Mickey regarded himself as a southerner and often said so.) The Mantles and the Mayses were living, breathing Americana. The Mantles were what John Steinbeck's Joad family might have been had they chosen to stay and scrape a living out of the harsh Oklahoma earth rather than emigrate to California. Willie's folks were the country cousins of the Younger family in Lorraine Hansberry's great play, *A Raisin in the Sun*; they resisted the lure of northern cities like Chicago and stayed near their roots.

They were both the products of two generations of ball-playing men, and both honed their skills through competition with industrial leaguers. Though neither of them was actually a member of an industrial league team, their fathers, uncles, and close friends played industrial ball, and Mickey and Willie played with and against them. Mantle and Mays were probably the last products of the great age of industrial league baseball that died out a few years after World War II.

Neither man ever truly understood how to manage money. Mantle envied Willie's salary; Willie was notoriously jealous of Mantle's income from commercials and endorsements.

Needless to say, in spite of all these similarities, there were enormous cultural differences. Mickey grew up listening to country stars such as Bob Wills and His Texas Playboys; his favorite singer was Hank Williams. Willie and his family listened to country blues singers like Amos Millburn, the more sophisticated R&B sounds of Louis Jordan, and even jazz artists like Billie Holiday and Nat King Cole. The one singer both men enjoyed was Bing Crosby.

The Mantle clan was large and closely knit; Mays came from a broken home. Mickey's father drove him relentlessly toward baseball; Willie's father helped him along and let him find the way to baseball on his own.

Mickey drank prodigiously and recklessly from an early age; Willie got sick on his first taste of alcohol and never touched it again. Mantle, though he remained married to his high school sweetheart for decades, led a sex life that was an unreported scandal. Mays, in contrast, was never the subject of rumors of promiscuity; his first marriage, to an older, more sophisticated woman, went badly. He had no biological children and, if the journalists who knew him are to be trusted, seldom saw his adopted son after his divorce.

One Mantle biographer, writing seven years after his death, concluded that "Mickey Mantle, like most heroes, was a construction; he was not real. He was all that America wanted itself to be, and he was also all that America feared it could never be."[1] Surely, it would be no stretch to say the same thing of Willie Mays. In his mammoth one-volume history of the decade, *The Fifties*, David Halberstam wrote that "Willie Mays seemed to be the model for the new supremely gifted black athlete. . . . He showed that the new-age black athlete had both power and speed. . . . [Mays was] a new kind of athlete being showcased, a player who, in contrast to most white superstars of the past, was both powerful *and* fast."[2] At the same time Mays was at his peak, there was a supremely gifted *white* athlete named

Mantle who had at least as much power and speed. Bob Costas says, "There was one thing about Mantle that screamed out 'The Natural.' He was a God-made ballplayer."[3] Surely the same God made Willie Mays.

"Today," Arnold Hano, one of Willie's first biographers, wrote in 1965, "players are as skilled as most stars of the past, but something is lacking. Call it color, call it magic, but you call for it in vain. Except for Willie Mays. Oh, there are a few others. Mickey Mantle has always brought his own sense of excitement to the game."[4] He most certainly did, and who, at their peak, could have denied that Mantle's "own sense of excitement" was a brand quite similar to Willie's?

Though their names are melded in the minds of three generations of American sports fans and their careers ran along uncannily parallel lines, they are still, oddly, segregated. Indeed, for most of their playing careers the realities of American life dictated that they be segregated. It wasn't until the early 1960s that they could meet together at restaurants and nightclubs in most parts of the country, and even then not in the Deep South. And it wasn't until the 1970s that they began to appear together regularly at card shows, in commercials, and on television shows.

Mantle and Mays were friends, probably as close as it was possible for a white man and a black man to be at that time. In any event, their work schedules didn't allow them to see each other more than a couple of times a year. Always, the newspapers kept one apprised of what the other was doing. "We kept an eye on each other, Willie and me. I was always aware of him," Mantle remarked. "I'd go long periods without seeing him," Mays said after Mantle died, "but I couldn't go for two days without hearing about him. It was like we were never far apart."

Mickey and Willie — they were given boys' names that they never grew out of. The private lives of both men revealed that they were ill equipped for life after baseball, a fact that those of us who loved them found almost impossible to understand. How, though, could we have understood? From our perspective, what could have been better than being Mickey Mantle or Willie Mays? Even after baseball, what better life could a fan imagine than being Mickey Mantle or Willie Mays?

"In some ways," Roger Kahn told me, "I believe they knew each other better than anyone else knew them. They were the only two men in America who understood the experience they had both been through."

1

Fathers and Sons

If a scientific research team were to conduct an exhaustive study of the ideal places, times, and conditions for breeding the perfect baseball player, they'd surely come up with something very close to Westfield, Alabama, in the heart of Birmingham's steel industry, or the mining district of Commerce, Oklahoma.

Thousands of southern blacks left their homes during the Depression and moved to industrial cities in the North, but in Westfield, Alabama, William Howard "Cat" Mays chose to stay home. Grueling as the work in the local steel mills was, Cat understood that the promise of a better life in towns like Gary, Indiana, Flint, Michigan, and Pittsburgh, Pennsylvania, was remote. He stayed in Alabama. At the same time, countless families from Oklahoma and adjoining states made the decision to abandon everything and make the hazardous trek to California; their stories would be told in prose by John Steinbeck and in song by Woody Guthrie. No one spoke for Elvin Charles "Mutt" Mantle, who chose to keep his family in Oklahoma, taking jobs as a road grader, tenant farmer, and, finally, miner to put food on the table.

For both Cat Mays and Mutt Mantle, the main recreation — practically the only one — was baseball, specifically the industrial league baseball organized by their companies. They raised their boys in a baseball culture. No fathers ever guided their sons toward professional baseball with more single-mindedness than Cat and Mutt. Both men saw baseball as a way to get their sons out of those small towns, out of the mills and mines, although they guided them in very different ways. And once Mickey and Willie left, neither ever lived in his hometown again.

Willie Howard Mays — why he was not named William like his father has never been explained — was born in Westfield on May 6, 1931. There's no monument or plaque to mark the spot; little of the Westfield that Willie knew remains standing today. A pamphlet printed by the Birmingham Chamber of Commerce in the 1960s called it a "village," which is inaccurate — Westfield was never a village or a town, but a community of neighborhoods populated by black working-class families whose lifeline was the steel mills in nearby Fairfield. Virtually all the houses were of the type called "shotgun" — it was said that you could fire a shotgun at the front door and the pellets would go out the back door.* They were built and owned by mills such as the Tennessee Cast Iron and Railroad Company (TCI), the great subcorporation of U.S. Steel, officially to "benefit" the workers but in reality to maintain their dependence on their employers.†

The larger town of Fairfield provided necessary services — such as schools — to the small nearby communities like Westfield. Fairfield was born in 1910, the same year that nearby Rickwood Field opened,

---

* This was because the shotgun houses were usually three to five rooms in a row with no hallways and sometimes no doors between them.
† "Oh, the boss man high with TCI," ran the lyric from a popular song of the 1930s.

and it was a planned community from the start, the result of U.S. Steel's purchase of TCI.*

Years later in his autobiography, Jackie Robinson, criticizing Willie for his lack of involvement in the civil rights movement, would remind Mays of his roots: "I hope Willie hasn't forgotten his shotgun house in Birmingham slums, wind-whistling through its clapboards, as he sits in his $85,000 mansion in San Francisco's fashionable Forest Hills, or the concentration camp atmosphere of the Shacktown of his boyhood."[1]

The house Willie grew up in was fairly standard for families of black steelworkers, and not terribly unlike those of most white steelworkers in the Birmingham area. In fact, it was not a great deal different from the house of a zinc miner in Commerce, Oklahoma, where Mickey Mantle grew up. Some might have rated the Mays home as superior: an early Mays biography describes the house he grew up in as "middle class."[2] It's doubtful anyone would have said that to describe the Mantles' house in Commerce; Cat's family had little money, but his house had electricity, which the Mantle home did not.

Today some of the neighborhoods in and around Westfield are in ruin. All that's left of most of the original company houses is their foundations. The population has been shrinking steadily for decades, from perhaps 5,000 when Willie was born to just over 1,100 in 1990 and under 1,000 today. The steel industry that sustained these communities began deserting the Birmingham area in the late 1970s, and the industrial baseball leagues that produced Willie Mays were gone at least two decades before that.

The black population of Alabama yielded many fine baseball players, among them perhaps the game's greatest pitcher, Satchel

---

* The town was first named Corey, after the president of U.S. Steel, William E. Corey; the name was quickly dropped when Corey was caught in a New York hotel with a showgirl from the Copacabana, an incident that made headlines from New York down to Birmingham. Asked to rename the town, the company's new president thought that his hometown of Fairfield, Connecticut, deserved a namesake.

Paige; the leading home run hitter of the twentieth century, Henry Aaron; and arguably the greatest all-around player in the game's history, Willie Mays. The greatest concentration of black baseball talent in the country was in the South, and in the South no state produced as many Negro League players as Alabama; in Alabama the preponderance of talent came from the industrial leagues of the Birmingham area.

Mays grew up in a baseball tradition that was more than half a century old when he was born. Baseball had been introduced to the Deep South after 1865 by Confederate soldiers who had learned the game either from their Union captors in prison camps or during breaks when men from the two armies would get together for some R&R before they resumed slaughtering one another. How the game came to be popular with southern blacks is a subject on which historians are split. Some say that free blacks learned it from their former masters. Others suggest that black soldiers in the Union Army, who numbered perhaps 200,000, picked it up from their white comrades. Yet a third possibility is that blacks watched white men play, then went home and played it themselves. It's likely that all three factors had a role.

The father of black ball in Alabama was a man named Charles Isam Taylor, who went to Birmingham from South Carolina in 1904. A veteran of the U.S. Army and the Spanish-American War, Taylor worked his way through Clark College in Atlanta, where he helped organize the school's first baseball team. For four years, Taylor made a living by staging and promoting (and sometimes playing in) baseball games for Birmingham's black fans. In 1910, realizing that there was more money to be made above the Mason-Dixon Line (where black teams could be matched against white teams), Taylor moved his team to the industrial town of West Baden, Indiana. The fans were heart-broken, and at least one black newspaper, the *Birmingham Reporter*, continued to print items about their games, passing on information about the local lads who were playing ball so far from home. From there, Taylor fades into obscurity, but his brainchild of using the industrial leagues as a talent farm for a professional league lived on and flourished.

If there was one progressive aspect to the steel and coal barons who dominated Birmingham industry, it was that they saw the value of sponsoring baseball teams among the black as well as the white workforces. Baseball provided great exercise and improved morale enormously, and shirts with company names and logos proved to be cheap but effective advertising.

Lorenzo "Piper" Davis, the most important figure in Birmingham black ball history, was Willie Mays's mentor and first manager. He told me in 1987, "There is a lot to be said about the way the companies treated us. It was the closest thing a black man could get to a square deal. They paid for bats and gloves and uniforms, and they even paid for our travel expenses to go play other company teams."[3]

Davis, of course, was speaking of a time in the late 1930s and early 1940s when the Birmingham steel industry, shaking off the Depression, was booming again, but from the years before World War I until the early 1950s, when a combination of factors ranging from the civil rights struggle to televised major league baseball eroded support for both the Negro Leagues and white minor leagues, Birmingham could lay claim to being the baseball capital of the South.

Allen Harvey Woodward, known to his friends for reasons no one can remember as "Rick," was one of the big reasons. Rick was the son of steel baron Joseph Hersey Woodward and, despite his father's indifference, was an enthusiastic supporter of Woodward Iron's company team. In 1909 he made a daring move — supervising the construction of the first steel-and-concrete ballpark in the South. Rickwood Field, named in a radio contest and combining the owner's nickname with the first part of his last name, became the home of a team called the Birmingham Barons, named for the coal and steel magnates who ran Birmingham. It would also be home, beginning in the early 1920s, to the Black Barons, who played on alternate Sundays and other days when the white team was traveling.

Rickwood Field opened on August 18, 1910. It was largely modeled after Shibe Park in Philadelphia, home of Connie Mack's champion A's — Mack himself came to Birmingham to advise Woodward on construction details — while also incorporating elements of Pitts-burgh's Forbes Field and Cincinnati's Crosley Field (still known in 1910 as "Palace of the Fans"), ballparks that Willie Mays would still be performing in more than half a century later. Rickwood, which stands today as the oldest ballpark in the country, was for decades the crown jewel of southern baseball. It was as if history wanted to provide Willie Mays with a worthy stage from which to launch his legend.*

Willie Mays would become the favorite ballplayer of New York's liberal-leaning sportswriters, but there was a conservative streak in him that the writers never acknowledged. He came by it naturally enough. His father was named for William Howard Taft, who was president in 1912, the year Cat was born. Many blacks in Alabama, like blacks throughout the South, supported the racially progressive Republican Party of Abraham Lincoln, Teddy Roosevelt, and William Howard Taft. When the party turned more conservative, they contin-ued to support it if only because most of the local political machines were controlled by white Democrats.

Birmingham after World War II would become one of the hotbeds of black civil rights activism, particularly when black GIs returned from the war. But there were pockets of the black population outside the city who did not easily understand or quickly respond to the call for civil rights. Willie Mays was raised in such neighborhoods, first in Westfield and then later a few miles away in Fairfield. When Willie was born, most black families in Westfield and the surrounding areas

---

* In 1931, the year Willie was born, Rickwood was the site of Game 1 of the Dixie World Series between the Southern Association's Birmingham Barons and the Texas League's Houston Buffaloes, in which Ray Caldwell, a forty-three-year veteran, outpitched Jay Hanna "Dizzy" Dean 1–0, in a duel that many called "the greatest game ever played." The radio announcer was Eugene "Bull" Connor, later to become infamous as Birming-ham's public safety commissioner during the civil rights years. Also at the game — or so he said — was Charles "Charlie O" Finley, future owner of the Birmingham A's and the major league Oakland A's, against whom Willie would end his major league career. Finley claimed he was the Barons' batboy at the Caldwell-Dean duel.

didn't have roots there. They had come there for jobs in the mills and foundries, which had sprung up only in the late 1890s. Black mine and mill workers came to enjoy a certain autonomy and created a life for themselves less dehumanizing than was possible in much of Georgia, Louisiana, Mississippi, and even South Alabama, where there weren't many opportunities for blacks other than picking cotton, lumber sharecropping, and truck farming.

Because of the steel and coal industry, most of the black communities to the south and west of Birmingham were more or less self-sufficient and in most ways independent of the city. They had schools, churches, restaurants, and even movie theaters that were black-owned and -operated (though the movie houses got the films only after they had run in the white theaters). On Saturday afternoons, when there was a nickel to spare, young Willie would see the B-movie Westerns he loved so much and get to fantasize that he too would someday be a cowboy like Hoot Gibson, Gene Autry, Roy Rogers, or Johnny Mack Brown, who had been a football star at the University of Alabama in the mid-1920s and became a national celebrity when the Crimson Tide won the 1926 Rose Bowl. At the same time, Mickey Mantle sat in all-white theaters in Commerce, Oklahoma, thrilling to the same celluloid cowboys, including Oklahoma's own Tom Mix.

Willie's father Cat — or sometimes "Kitty Cat" (or "Kat" with a "K" in early writings on Willie) — was, in the words of Charles Einstein, "a small bouncy, Buddha-tummied figure."[4] His nickname came from his reflexes — his teammates always admired the way he broke immediately in the right direction on fly balls — and the way he sprang out of the batter's box on bunts. William Howard Mays learned his baseball from his father, Walter, who had been a sharecropper in Tuscaloosa and was a pretty fair country pitcher. "It went from him through me," said Cat, "and to the third generation, my own son. And they say the third generation is it."[5]

During Willie's formative years, Cat worked in the "spike and bolt" shop of TCI and starred for its company team, just one of several organized teams he played for before and after the war. "I'd play for anybody who'd give you money," he told Charles Einstein, "because every time somebody came to get me to play baseball, I'd say, 'I can't go, man — I got something to do,' and he'd say, 'Come on, man, I'll give you $2.50.' Sometimes when things was bad, you'd have to go for ten cent [sic] a game. And for that money you learned baseball. You know, I used to study the pitchers when I got on first base 'cause I could bunt my way on, and if I got on first base it was like getting a double. And to me, from second base to third base was much easier than from first to second."[6]

Sometime in 1930, Cat, maybe while picking up some spending money on a traveling ball team, met Annie Satterwhite. Annie was sixteen when Willie was born, but she and Cat never married. Her mother had been dead for several years, and sometime before that her father had abandoned the family. Not much is known about Annie, and Willie talked little about her in his adult years. Shortly after his birth, he was given over to the women he would call his aunts, his mother's younger sisters: Sarah, thirteen, and Ernestine — or "Steen," as Willie called her — just nine.

Or at least that's the story Willie told numerous writers. The truth may be a great deal stranger. Willie never addressed the question of why his mother, who settled down near Westfield after she married a man named Frank McMorris, never brought him to live with her. Moreover, the true identities of Ernestine and Sarah have never been established. In the earliest books on Willie, the girls are said to be Annie's younger sisters, as they are in James Hirsch's massive 2010 biography: "As a baby, he was given to his mother's two younger sisters, 13-year-old Sarah and 9-year-old Ernestine, who were his principal caretakers and who called him 'Junior.' " Sarah was "the most important female figure in the boy's life, a role she played even after Willie left Alabama to play for the Giants." The makeshift family, writes Hirsch, "expanded to include two more children born out of wedlock, one from Sarah and one from Ernestine. Both women later married, Sarah to Cat's cousin, Edgar May, who at some point lost the 's' on his last name (or perhaps Cat Mays's family added the 's'). Sarah May ended up raising her sister's son while married to his father's cousin."[7]

In 1988, however, Willie told a different story to journalist Lou Sahadi. In *Say Hey*, Sarah and Ernestine are not identified as Annie's sisters, or even as being sisters at all, but simply as "two young girls in the neighborhood" who were orphaned and "moved" into the house by Cat to take care of young Willie.[8] How Cat would have gotten the authority to move underage girls into a house — and exactly whose house it was — has never been explained or even addressed. Was this different version due to Willie's faulty memory or to Sahadi's misunderstanding? Surely Sahadi had access to Hano's and Einstein's texts, in which Willie clearly says that the girls were his aunts. Even more of a mystery is why Hirsch, in his far more comprehensive book, doesn't mention this discrepancy.

One person in Willie's life to whom he was definitely not related but whom he called "Uncle" was a man named Otis Brooks. Brooks was not mentioned in Mays literature until *Say Hey* was published in 1988. Willie remembered, "He was from Mobile, and when we moved to Fairfield, he helped out around the house. . . . Fortunately, he helped me out all the time. Whenever any of my chores took away from playing baseball or any of the other sports I played, like football or basketball, he'd cover for me. He was the first person who ever said to me, 'Willie, you're going to be a ball player.' " When Sarah would tell Willie to wash the dishes, "Otis would give me a wink. I knew he'd do them for me. Sarah, meanwhile, hovered over me all the time, making sure that I went to school every day and always finding chores for me — chopping firewood, cleaning up the yard — that Otis ended up doing. If it hadn't have been for Otis, I wouldn't have had time to play ball as much as I did."[9] It was the first but far from the last time in his life that Willie Mays would be fortunate enough to find someone to do his chores for him.

One wonders how such a young family got by in the early years of the Depression. There was little money and just two underage girls — one of them just nine years old when they moved in — to do the cooking, cleaning, and child care. How did they pay the bills? When the girls became old enough to work, the combination of their earnings, Cat's income — he did a little better as the decade went on and a New Deal stimulus package stoked up the steel industry — and the extra money from semipro ball must have improved their situation considerably. In or around 1941, Cat moved them out of the company-owned house in Westfield to a larger home in Fairfield in a neighborhood called "The Heights." It had always been his father's dream, Willie said, to own his own house.

Cat wasn't around much between his job, playing ball, and, after the war, working as a porter for the Pullman Company on the sleeping cars that ran between Detroit and Birmingham — mostly hooked to the legendary Wabash Cannonball.* But he never deserted the family; he always sent money back and came home as often as he could.

With Cat so often absent, if Sarah and Ernestine had not been mature and caring well beyond their years, it's likely that Willie would have drifted into juvenile delinquency and not have graduated from Fairfield Industrial High School. Cat never pushed Willie into baseball — he didn't have to. Willie loved to play. One of the first stories told about little Willie is the famous tale of his father rolling a ball to the toddler and Willie rolling it back, bursting into tears when his father stopped. In a story cut from the same cloth, Mickey's

---

* The famous train and the city had a long love affair that began in 1871 with the establishment of Birmingham at the crossing of the Alabama & Chattanooga and South and North Atlantic Railroads. The first version of the song about the train, "The Great Rock Island Route," was written by a man named J. A. Roff in 1882. The song then was published with its famous name, "Wabash Cannon Ball," in 1904, with the author listed as William Kindt. Over the decades, there were several popular versions, one by the grandparents of country music, the Carter Family, in 1932, and of course the most famous one, recorded in 1936 by Roy Acuff. In Chuck Berry's up-tempo rock-and-roll version, "Promised Land," a broken-down Greyhound bus leaves him stranded in downtown Birmingham; he then takes the Midnight Flier, another famous train, to New Orleans.

mother would say that Mutt dropped baseballs into their son's crib and tried to get the infant to hold them in his tiny hands; at one time, she said, there were so many baseballs in the crib that the baby "was practically rolling around on ball bearings."[10]

Cat and Willie played ball together constantly — at the age of five, one biographer claimed, Willie had regular afternoon catches with his father on the steel mill's field. By the time Willie was six, Cat once told a writer, "I'd come home from work and catch him across the street on the diamond alone, playing by himself. "[11] If no pals were around, Willie would go to the empty lot, toss the ball up into the air, smack it, tear around the bases, slide home, jog out to pick up the ball, then start the routine again.

When he was around ten, Willie moved up to pickup games, playing sometimes with Cat's pals from the industrial league and with some of his own friends. His first ball field was a makeshift diamond staked out from the corner of a football field at Sixty-Third Street and Court F in Fairfield, today an empty lot just a couple of base-ball throws from a few crumbling buildings that are the remains of Willie's old high school. Later, in his early teens, he would pick up pocket change by playing second base on the Gray Sox, a local semi-pro team that featured his dad in center field.

The ball field at Sixty-Third Street and Court F wasn't much, but it was big league compared to the scruffy patch of ground on which Mickey Mantle first learned baseball. There were numerous other makeshift fields around Commerce, but some of them were too dangerous for kids to play on because of the sinkholes that would suddenly appear when a tunnel caved in. Mickey liked to joke that a person could walk the twenty or so miles from Commerce to Joplin completely underground. Perhaps he wasn't joking.

Not all the fields were hazardous, but none of them were bargains. One summer, Mickey remembered, "we claimed a spot near an abandoned mine shaft. It made a perfect baseball field, smooth and firm. The foul lines were laid out with a stick and we used old gunnysacks for bases, nailing them to the ground. One bad feature, though, was the outfield. An endless plain of alkali. You couldn't see a ditch or a fence or anything that would slow the ball. I guess it's the main reason why I became an infielder. I hated chasing after base hits when they slipped past and rolled halfway to the next town before I could flag them down." The games on that field lasted until a northern wind blew in and hurled gray clouds of dust at their eyes. "End of game. We'd cough all the way home."[12]

"In Commerce," said Mickey in one of his several memoirs, "when I was five or six, there was a battered tin barn that leaned close to our house" — at 319 South Quincy Street, as anyone in Commerce today will tell you — "and I spent countless hours there, hitting tennis balls* off the roof or onto the trees of the adjoining lot. Dad would pitch to me right-handed and I'd bat lefty; Grandpa pitched lefty and I'd bat righty. That's how they taught me to switch-hit. Every once in a while I'd hit one over the house. Often as not, the next pitch would knock me down. Wherever I'd hit 'em, my brothers Roy and Ray would chase them."[13]

The Mantles were said to have come to Oklahoma from Missouri. Spavinaw, where Mickey was born, was just a few miles from the Missouri state line in the heart of Cherokee country. Elvin Mantle — the name was spelled "Elvan" on his driver's license and "Elven" on his birth certificate and, finally, on his tombstone† — was called "Mutt" as long as anyone could remember, and he was. There was English, Dutch, German, and perhaps some other blood in the Mantle veins. We do know, thanks to the family historian, Harold Mantle, that Mutt's English ancestors worked mines around Brierley Hill and iron smelters near Birmingham, England, in the early 1800s, some 130

---

* One wonders where Mickey would have gotten so many tennis balls. What he probably meant were the cheap, tough rubber Spaldeens that were popular all over the country and a particular favorite of inner-city kids playing stickball in the street.

† To further confuse matters, the middle name of Mickey's youngest brother, Larry, was Elven.

years before Willie Mays's father worked in the iron smelters of Birmingham, Alabama, a city named for its English progenitor.

Mickey also proudly claimed some Cherokee blood from his mother's side, though that has never been substantiated and might have been wishful thinking on his part. "As a small boy living in Commerce," he said in *The Mick*, "I heard many stories about the Cherokees, the Chickasaws, the Creeks, and the other Oklahoma tribes, stories told mostly by my dad's friends." As an adult, Mickey loved to tell stories about his encounters with the Oklahoma Indian tribes, and when he came to the Yankees he was delighted to find that his teammate Allie Reynolds had Oklahoma Muscogee (Creek) Indian blood. The history of the Oklahoma Indians, particularly the Cherokee, was one of the few subjects about which Mantle displayed any social awareness. "Years later," he told Herb Gluck, meaning after he graduated from high school, "reading up on Indian history, I began to understand more. Until then it never occurred to me that the Indians made a forced march from southern prison camps, that hundreds died of starvation during the journey into Oklahoma. Their Trail of Tears. They didn't teach that in school."*[14]

Cat Mays was nineteen when Willie was born; Mutt was nineteen when he became a father. Willie's mother, though, was just sixteen, while Lovell Richardson, Mutt's wife, was twenty-seven. Like Willie, Mickey had a grandfather, Charlie (from whom his middle name came), who was a left-handed pitcher. Like Cat, Mutt was a pretty good ballplayer on industrial teams who also picked up some extra money playing semipro ball.

Like Willie, Mickey thought his dad was good enough to have played professional ball if he had had the chance. Mickey would

---

*However, a St. Louis native, Robert Mantle, researched the genealogical history of the family and offers at least one possible piece of evidence for Indian blood in the family: while many white settlers moving down into Oklahoma Territory were attacked by Indians, the Mantles were spared because riding in their wagons were two Indian women who had married Mantle men. Or so he claimed from the record left by a wagonmaster.

watch him play on weekends, driving from Commerce to see Mutt and his pals play for Spavinaw and other groups that were little more than pickup teams in and around Mayes County. "I sat in the stands, thinking he was Pepper Martin, Mickey Cochrane and Dizzy Dean all rolled into a single package. I mean, he ran, pitched, fielded most any position, batted both ways, hit for distance, had a shotgun arm, and threw strikes. I thought he was the best damn ballplayer in the territory. Only the professional scouts never saw him play."[15] Mickey's evaluation might not have been objective; his friend Nick Ferguson thought that Mutt was only an average player, and so did Mickey's younger cousin, Jim Richardson. But they did not see Mutt play till he was over thirty, well past his physical prime and after years of backbreaking hard labor. A pitcher from the Tri-State League, Harry Daniels, told John G. Hall, "The reason guys like Mutt never had a chance to develop their game was there was very little equipment and very few organized teams where the youth of his generation could learn to play the game."[16] The black mill workers in Birmingham's industrial areas were better equipped to play baseball than the white miners of northeastern Oklahoma.

In Willie's memory, his father deserved to be placed on the same kind of pedestal. Mays recalled to Charles Einstein the praise he received from Piper Davis: " 'You got the greatest instinctive jump on a ball I ever saw, except for maybe Joe D. [DiMaggio] or his brother Vince.' 'Sounds like I'm pretty good,' Willie cracked. 'Only one better,' Davis said. 'Your old man. Know the difference, Buck?* You don't pounce. You're a grabber. The old man though — that's why we called him Kitty-Kat — now *he* knew how to pounce! I've seen you on

---

* "Buck" was the short version of Willie's nickname, "Buck-Duck." Willie claimed never to know the origin of the term, which Arnold Hano referred to as "unfortunate and derogatory." Buck was a common nickname for young African American males. Some players who knew Willie thought the "Duck" part might have had something to do with the shape of his posterior. Willie once offered a different explanation to a sportswriter: "It's 'cause I used to dodge back and forth, duck so quick when I was running" (Hano, *Willie Mays*, p. 37). Willie thought that the first to call him Buck was his boyhood friend Charley Willis, whom he called "Cool."

the bases. Passed ball, no more than three feet away, and you *explode*. Explode, that's the word for it. Better than Jackie [Robinson], better than anybody. But, Buck, you don't *pounce*. You just never learned how.' "[17]*

Whatever the two fathers' real skill levels, it's certainly true that circumstances gave neither of them a chance to test themselves in the big leagues — Cat because of segregation, Mutt because he had a family to support before his eighteenth birthday and never got out of the Oklahoma mines. But both knew the game from top to bottom, thanks to the tough and spirited competition of the industrial leagues, and they taught their sons to play the same way.

In about half a century, baseball would evolve into a sport in which parents would groom their kids from grade school to perfect a single skill or play a single position. Willie Mays and Mickey Mantle were all-around players because that was how their fathers played the game.

---

*Arnold Hano, echoing Piper Davis, wrote, "No ballplayer is as likely to explode at any given moment in any of a half-dozen ways as is Willie Mays." He also wrote, "Mays does not glide; he scampers. When he runs the bases, he runs with head over his shoulder, looking behind him for the ball" (Hano, *Willie Mays*, p. 15).

2

Bred to Play Ball

To call Willie Mays and Mickey Mantle "natural" ballplayers would be an insult to their years of practice and preparation. To New York sportswriters in 1951, Willie Mays seemed to have been born to play center field, but it wasn't until his early teens that he began to understand that his talents were best suited to the position. "By the time you get to high school varsity play," he recalled in his first memoir, "you should be stationed where you play best. If you're not, it's not the end of the world, but if you go on in baseball from there, somebody is going to have to come along and make you over. Sometimes this 'making over' doesn't even take place till the player actually reaches the big leagues. You all can think of players who came up at one position — Mickey Mantle was one — only to be shifted to another."[1]

Cat Mays allowed Willie the freedom to find his position, while Mutt Mantle, probably assuming that a switch-hitting slugger who could play a key infield position would be much sought after, tried to mold Mickey into a shortstop. Cat instinctively understood about his son what Mutt did not about his: even when possessed of great speed and a terrific throwing arm, a heavily muscled young man might be better suited to outfield rather than infield play.*

Cat's more relaxed attitude about his son's position was representative of the two fathers' attitudes about their sons' skills. Cat played baseball with Willie to encourage him; Mutt drove Mickey to play with a purpose that bordered on obsession, though Mickey's childhood pals insisted that Mutt was a patient teacher and not a slave driver.

There was a yawning chasm between the two fathers' baseball dreams for their sons. For blacks living in the Birmingham area, a solid job in a steel mill (or perhaps as a railroad porter) was nearly as attractive as the life of a professional Negro League baseball player — that is, viewed over a lifetime. In the 1930s, thanks to the Roosevelt administration, which pumped millions of dollars in stimulus money into the devastated Birmingham steel industry, a black man stood a very good chance of having a job that could support a family for all his working life and, if he could play baseball, an opportunity to pick up some side money. For Mickey, professional baseball, even at the minor league level, offered prospects for a far better life than the dirty, backbreaking, and dangerous zinc mines, where, it was said, "miners breathed death."

Mays entered the world of organized baseball through a side door. When he was only nine, just before World War II began, he accompanied Cat on road trips with the United Steelworkers' CIO semipro team; Cat was the leadoff hitter and center fielder. After one game, Willie was amazed to find that his father actually got paid for playing baseball. "That seemed to me just about the nicest idea anyone ever thought up."[2] By the time Mays found this out, Mantle knew that his father's intention for him was to remove the "semi" in front of the

---

*Perhaps it was because Mickey didn't pack on the layers of muscle until his later high school years that Mutt thought he would develop into a slender, wiry man, much like Mutt himself.

"pro." Willie played ball for fun and pocket money; Mickey played because he wanted to be a big league ballplayer.

When Willie was a boy, integration of the major leagues was just a dream. A black player could make some decent money playing ball, but only a handful of superstars, Satchel Paige most prominent among them, had any leverage when it came to making his own deals or jumping to another team. For most, Negro League ball was an extremely dubious proposition that promised nothing beyond a few years of high life. To Oscar Charleston, Cool Papa Bell, Josh Gibson, or even Birmingham's own Piper Davis, baseball was a mean, tough living that took a man away from home for long periods of time (and often took away his home life altogether). Life in the Negro Leagues meant hours of travel in brutal summer heat on buses with no air conditioning and being denied service in most restaurants and hotels.

Willie, noticing that his father had done well for himself at TCI, indicated that he didn't think that life was so bad; Cat, with a wary eye, advised him, "Once you get into the mill, you never get out."[3] This hadn't occurred to Willie. While the steel mills paid a better wage than most black men in the South could expect, a job there didn't offer the opportunity for prosperity, which was what some young black men were beginning to think about in a changing America. Cat encouraged Willie to play baseball for fun with the hope that it might, just might, offer him a way out of life in the mills.

For Mickey, it was also fun to play baseball, at least the kind of baseball played at picnics with mining people and their families and with his friends. But as he would recall to Herb Gluck, "All through my early childhood Dad kept drumming it in: 'Practice, practice, practice.' Which I did, attacking each pitch, whether it was thrown underhand, sideways, or over the top. . . . Dad worked with me every day. I was hitting them pretty good from the right side. But Dad also wanted me to bat lefty, which I hated. When it got dark and supper was ready, Dad would turn me around, from righty to lefty. 'Your belly can wait,' he'd say. Then he'd start pitching again."[4]

Hank Bauer, who was Mantle's teammate for years and saw Mays

play many times, nailed down the biggest difference in their playing styles. "Yeah, Willie made some plays that Mickey wouldn't have
made. And Mickey, who I think was maybe a step faster than Willie,
caught a fly ball now and then that even Willie wouldn't have gotten to. The big difference was in the way they were perceived. Willie
made all the hard plays look easy, and Mickey made all the hard plays
look hard."[5] For Willie baseball was mostly play, while for Mickey
baseball was mostly practice.

Both were daddy's boys. Willie spent little time with his mother,
though he was fond of telling sportswriters stories he had heard
about her. "My mother was a wonderful athlete," he told Charlie Einstein, "a star runner who held a couple of women's track records in
that part of the country."[6]*

Mickey loved Lovell, and by holding the family together and
keeping everyone clothed and fed, she was as big a factor in his baseball development as Mutt. She knew the game too. Like millions of
American housewives in the 1930s and 1940s, she learned it from
listening to the radio. She understood baseball terms and was familiar with the players' strengths and weaknesses. Sitting in the stands,
she yelled louder for her boys than Mutt did. According to Mickey's
childhood friend Nick Ferguson, when he stayed for supper at the
Mantles' house the topic of conversation at the table was that afternoon's St. Louis Cardinals game. (Most of the Cardinals and Browns
games then were still played in daylight.) Mrs. Mantle, he said, while
doing her housework, listened to the Cardinals radio broadcast and
then recapped the game for the family over their evening meal.

---

* In 1961, Mays went for a complete physical at Mt. Zion Hospital in San Francisco,
where a doctor attempted to attach a suction cup to his back for a vector cardiograph.
The suction cup wouldn't hold. "What's the problem?" Willie asked. The problem,
the doctor told him, was that Mays had no fat on his back to create the suction: "All
you got for a back is one continuous muscle." Willie's father must have been an athlete, the doctor commented. "My mother too," Willie informed him. "Well," said the
doctor, "I guess that explains that" (Mays, *My Life In and Out of Baseball*, p. 41).

By no surviving account, though, was she a demonstrative mother. Some of Mickey's children would recall her as mean; Merlyn Mantle's recollection of her mother-in-law was that she was "not a warm or openly affectionate woman, but she was a tireless and protective mother. She had seven children, two by a first marriage, and I never saw anyone do as much laundry." Merlyn's folks were town people; the Mantles, she noted, "lived in the country and didn't yet have electricity."[7]

Curiously for a southern family living in a small town, the Mantles were not a religious family. There were four churches in Commerce, all Protestant, but the family did not belong to any of them, though Mickey said that he had been inside all of them for the weddings of friends and family. None of the Mantles, he said, "took religion seriously. I suppose it was my dad's influence. He used to say, 'Religion doesn't necessarily make you good. As long as your heart is in the right place and you don't hurt anyone, I think you'll go to heaven — if there is one.' "[8]

If Mutt doubted the existence of God, at least a benevolent God, it was certainly understandable. When Mickey was thirteen, Mutt sold the much-loved house on South Quincy Street and bought a farm, thinking that moving away from the mines might improve his own father's health. But Charlie, who had contracted Hodgkin's disease (which probably had little or nothing to do with conditions in the mines, though Mutt did not know this), deteriorated quickly, and the first left-handed pitcher Mickey ever faced soon died. The disease overtook Charlie so quickly that it shocked Mutt and Mickey. "He died shortly after we moved," Mickey later recalled. "I never forgot that moment, standing beside the casket with my little twin brothers, Ray and Roy, the three of us looking down on him and my father whispering, 'Say good-bye to Grandpa.' I was just a kid then. I didn't understand death and sickness very well. Even now I don't remember the order of events from that time in my life. It just seemed that all my relatives were dying around me."[9] A little less than three years later, his uncle Tunney died of stomach cancer at age thirty-four, and shortly after, Uncle Emmett died of what appeared to be Hodgkin's. Mickey's fatalistic attitude toward life was set at an early age.

For at least a while, though, life on the farm seemed idyllic. Mickey got to pretend he was a cowboy when he rode a horse to school* — which was closer than Willie ever came to being a cowboy.

When Mutt could scrape together the cash, there were outings to a ballpark. On one, the family had the sensational luck to see a minor league game between Joplin and Springfield that featured a much-heralded young left-handed slugger from Pennsylvania who hit from a low, crouching stance. "See that guy?" Mutt, a superb judge of talent, asked his son. "He's going to be a major league star." The twenty-one-year-old in question, soon to be called up to the St. Louis Cardinals for a legendary twenty-two-season career, was Stan Musial. On another trip, Mickey and his brothers got to spend an entire weekend in St. Louis watching the Cardinals on Saturday night and then again in a Sunday doubleheader. "To me," Mickey said in reflection, "this was like a journey to the Big Rock Candy Mountain."[10] When having breakfast at the Fairgrounds Hotel, where many of the players from both teams stayed, they would often recognize the Cardinals and some of their opponents in street clothes. If Mickey had any inclination to ask for a player's autograph, Mutt quickly squashed it; ballplayers were people too, he told his son, and they had a right to privacy like anyone else. Mutt's attitude made a big impression on his son and might explain why, in later years, he was often standoffish to fans he thought were too aggressive.

Nick Ferguson, one of Mickey's pals, told writer David Falkner, "We all had a happy childhood, I think. Nobody had any great expec-

---

* The name of Mickey's horse was Tony. Though history has not recorded who it was named after, in all likelihood it was an homage to the hugely popular Western film star Tom Mix's champion horse Tony. Mix was Mickey's first big cowboy movie idol. Born in Pennsylvania, he found fame in Oklahoma working for the Wild West shows and then appearing in early silent Westerns produced by the Miller brothers of Oklahoma's enormous 101 Ranch.

tations. We didn't have much, but we'd play all day long . . . either baseball, football or basketball."[11] But Nick didn't have the pressure on him to excel that Mick had. Merlyn, who was to bear the brunt of Mickey's reckless immaturity, was always sympathetic to the forces that shaped her husband's psyche: "The early pressure on Mickey to play ball and his self-imposed desire to play it better than anyone caused real emotional problems for him. A lot of the conflicts in him later had their roots in those years. Mick wet his bed until he was 16 years old . . . it is important, I think, in understanding what he went through, and how much he wanted to please his dad. This is what the pressure that wanting that approval did to him."[12] The bed-wetting didn't stop until Mickey played his first season in Class-D ball at Independence, Missouri, in 1949.*

The Tom Sawyer–like life Mickey led at the farm didn't last for long. When he was fourteen, a devastating rainstorm caused the Neosho River to flood the Mantle farm. The crops were lost, which meant the farm was also lost. There was only one way for Mutt to feed his family: return to the mines.

The family was forced to downscale their already hardscrabble existence. They moved into a dilapidated house closer to town in a village called Whitebird, where Lovell had to boil water on a wood-burning stove for bathing; more than forty years later Mickey still remembered that they bathed in a number 3 zinc tub.[13] There weren't enough rooms for all the kids; Mickey shared a bedroom with his parents and his younger sister, Barbara. The winters were miserable. "Bleak, gray, the fields covered with frost," Mickey told Herb Gluck, adding details that could have come from a Depression-era novel. "Some nights those winds whistled through little cracks in the wall so fierce they'd lift the linoleum right off the floor. You had to be

---

* In 1970, Mickey appeared on *The Dick Cavett Show* and admitted, in front of millions and in particular fellow guest Paul Simon, that he had a bed-wetting problem through his high school years. Simon, who grew up idolizing Mickey, was stunned. Mickey was equally stunned to learn that the "Where have you gone, Joe DiMaggio?" line from "Mrs. Robinson" was originally "Where have you gone, Mickey Mantle?" but Simon couldn't work it into enough syllables to fill out the line.

careful or you'd step on the rising billows and crack the linoleum."[14] Amazingly, despite the hardships, Mickey could not recall a single time that Mutt and Lovell had a serious argument.

Lovell whipped her sons and daughter into line and saw that they behaved like good Christians, but with practically no talk of religion in the house, the closest thing to Sunday worship was the passion the boys showed at picnics for getting a baseball game going. Nearly half a century later, Mickey would remember what those Sundays were like. "You'd see the dust coming up on the road and dozens of old cars honking by. What a sight! They formed a circle around the field. Picnic baskets, egg crates, and whatnot would be dragged out of the back seats, pints of whiskey in back pockets, too; everybody laughing and hollering, then settling down to watch us play, so attentive, so respectful, you'd think they were actually paying their way into a World Series."[15]

Sundays and baseball were something Mickey and Willie had in common. On most Sundays, company baseball teams were playing, and often the players' sons, if they were old enough, were allowed to play with their fathers. On every other Sunday, the Black Barons played in beautiful Rickwood Field. Even during the Depression years, it was a time for dressing up in one's best outfits, the women in their most fetching hats, and going to the ballpark. During the 1940s, a well-known black preacher, the appropriately named Rev. John W. Goodgame of the Sixth Avenue Baptist Church, spoke for blacks all over the city and probably for whites as well when, after services every baseball Sunday, he told his congregation, "Well, I'm going to the ball game."

For both Mickey and Willie, the springs and summers of their youth were opportunities for pickup games. No other sport was seriously considered. Everyone showed up on the fields to play baseball. But there was one significant difference between Mays's experience and Mantle's. Mickey never saw a black person at his games. He did not play against a black until his late appearances in the minor leagues.

When Willie and his friends showed up on sandlots, there were often white kids hanging around waiting for someone with a ball or bat. "And it didn't matter to me whether I played with white kids or black. I never understood why an issue was made of who I played with. . . . I never recall trouble. . . . We played football against the white kids, and we thought nothing of it. Neither the blacks nor the whites. It was the grownups who got upset. If they saw black kids playing on the same team with white kids, they'd call the cops, and the cops would make us stop. I never got into a fight that was started because of racism; to me, it was the adults who caused the problems."[16]

Bob Veale, who was four years younger than Willie and who would star, after a stint in the Negro Leagues, for the Pittsburgh Pirates, had similar recollections. "We didn't know as kids we were breaking segregation laws. We just thought we were playing baseball. I had white friends, kids I played ball with all the time. We weren't thinking about integrating anything. We were just playing baseball."[17]

It can be said with some accuracy that Willie Mays grew up without a sense of the racial tensions that from the 1950s through the mid-1960s would reach critical mass in the Birmingham area. Westfield and Fairfield were different from other Birmingham suburbs. Fairfield, for instance, had white neighborhoods as well as black, and though they were strictly segregated, the citizens lived near one another in relative harmony, probably because most of the adult men worked alongside one another at the steel mills. Piper Davis would remember getting along well with several of his white fellow workers, if only because during their breaks they could talk about baseball. Blacks were allowed in Rickwood Field to see the white Barons play, though they were confined to an area in the right-field bleachers screened off with chicken wire called the "Negro bleachers." This was common for most minor league ballparks in the South. What was not common was that at Rickwood, on the Sundays when the Black Barons played, white fans would often crowd into the same area to watch the best players in the Negro Leagues. Baseball was the closest thing Birmingham had to a common denominator between blacks and whites. During coffee and Coca-Cola breaks, workers of both races could gab about the soaring shots that Babe Ruth, Lou Gehrig, and Joe DiMaggio hit over the fences or how Satchel Paige befuddled hitters with his notorious "hesitation" pitch.

Mutt and Mickey had to drive hundreds of miles in stifling heat to see Hall of Fame ballplayers at Sportsman's Park in St. Louis; Cat and Willie merely had to take a thirty-minute ride on a crosstown bus to do the same.*

As in the Mantle home, there was little if any religious orthodoxy in the Mays house. Ernestine and Sarah took care of Willie and kept him in school. Sarah was probably the closest thing Willie had in his formative years to a full-time mother. There was only one thing missing: like Lovell Mantle, she was not an affectionate person. She made sure Willie was well cared for and took a personal interest in his schoolwork and athletics, but with a busy household to run, she gave him little personal attention. Amateur psychologists would later conjecture that Mays's choice in women was an attempt at finding a mother figure.

As Willie grew into his teens, his skill at sports and his ebullient charm made him a favorite with the girls at Fairfield Industrial. Friends recall only one real attachment, to a pretty girl named Minnie Hansberry, but when Willie left Fairfield for professional baseball he never mentioned her again.

In at least one important respect, Sarah, Ernestine, and Willie's mother, Annie, succeeded admirably: they kept their boy out of trouble. There are virtually no accounts of juvenile gangs in the Westfield of the 1930s. The men were steelworkers — tough, independent,

---

*As an adult, Willie confessed to having slipped into several white Barons games. "I'd sneak into the games of the Birmingham club of the Southern Association, and the thing that thrilled me most was that they were the only team in the league that was allowed to wear white uniforms. Everybody else had to wear gray." Young Willie didn't realize that the visiting teams all wore gray and that the Barons' home uniforms, which were the only ones he saw them play in, were white (Mays, *My Life In and Out of Baseball*, p. 60).

and self-reliant — and did not allow delinquency to gain a foothold in their neighborhoods. Cat wasn't always there, but he made his presence felt. Like Mutt Mantle, Cat Mays smoked heavily, enjoyed cards, and occasionally drank to excess. But he saw that Willie did not indulge in any of these activities.

One day, driving down a Westfield street heading toward home, Cat spotted Willie and a pal taking a puff on a cigarette and sipping from something in a paper bag. Calmly, he stopped the car, told Willie to get in, and took him home. He told his son that if he wanted to smoke he could, and handed him a cigarette. Willie took a long drag and started coughing. Cat made him finish the cigarette — or in another account, a White Owl cigar. He then made his son drink a glass of bourbon. Willie got so sick that he didn't recover until the next day. Except for taking a sip of champagne in the New York Giants' locker room after winning the 1954 World Series, there are no eyewitness accounts of Willie Mays ever drinking liquor. Willie's only known vice — one his father not only regarded as harmless but taught him — was pool, a game that, as several Giants teammates would one day discover to their chagrin, he mastered.

The women did their part to keep the children on the straight and narrow: they were fed well and made to go to school and behave respectfully toward their elders, even if, in Willie's case, his aunts were only a few years older than he was.* But except for the occasional funeral or on Easter, there was no churchgoing.

After Annie Satterwhite married Frank McMorris, a plumber, she would have ten more children with him. They settled in a small community named Powderly, just a few miles from her son. She made an effort to see Willie as often as possible and exerted a surprisingly strong influence on him. Later Willie would remember Annie as "a

---

* "Willie Mays is Negro," wrote Arnold Hano in 1965, "a southern Negro on top of that, and a product of an early broken home — all of which shows why social workers gray easily. Mays ought to have ended up in a novel about a zip-gun toting heroin-hipped no goodnik. He is instead a non-drink, non-smoke, reasonably well-acclimated young man whose major neurosis is that he is overly aggressive to a pitched baseball" (Hano, *Willie Mays*, p. 36).

good lady" who would slip a quarter into his hand whenever she saw him and who often invited him over to the McMorris home to play with his half brothers and sisters. At the same time Lovell was attending Mickey's high school baseball and football games in Commerce, Annie was cheering Willie on from the stands of Fairfield Industrial. "My mom had a mouth," Mays told his most recent biographer, James Hirsch, "and she didn't back up." She shared at least one other characteristic with Lovell Mantle — according to one of Willie's half brothers, "Not one of the kids talked back to her."[18]

Despite the economic hardships in both the Mantle and Mays households, it would be wrong to say that they weren't happy homes. At any rate, both men insisted, time and again, that their childhoods were happy. There was usually some change left over for the comic books both boys loved to read. Mickey would ride his bike to the Commerce News to check out the latest adventures of Superman, Batman, and, starting in 1941, America's favorite teenager, Archie Andrews, of Riverdale, USA. Willie loved the superheroes too, though his favorite comics were Westerns bought at Doc Pomran's Drugstore.

Neither boy went hungry. Willie, who usually had more money to spend than his friends, related that at school, "when we had our lunch period . . . we'd head for the grocery store. I'd buy lunch meat, a couple of big loaves of bread, tomatoes, mayonnaise, and some cake, and pretty soon 10 or 12 of us would be sitting down to lunch in an empty lot."[19] Willie bought all this, or so he recalled, with the $10 that Sarah or Steen would sometimes leave on his dresser. Ten dollars sounds like an awful lot of money for the time and place, but a child's memory can easily remember one dollar as ten.

On Saturdays, Mickey and his pals found a great hangout at the Black Cat Café, where the 25-cent special might include cheeseburgers, chili, and soft drinks. When both boys were a little older, one of their favorite pastimes was pool. Willie, Charley, and their friends liked to play at Big Tony's in Fairfield; Mickey, Nick Ferguson, and their pals played in the backroom of the Black Cat. Both Mays and Mantle had the same problem: the proprietors wouldn't let them play until 4:00 P.M. to make sure they weren't cutting school and invariably began to shoo them out around 5:30 when the men — sometimes including Cat and Mutt — got off work from the mills and mines.

The high school years, as Willie once put it, "were also the days of the pool hall. I always thought pool playing had a bad rap. In the movies, you'd always see wise guys and gangsters shooting pool between drags of a cigarette as they discussed some heist." At Big Tony's, it wasn't like that. In fact, Tony was given to lecturing the boys about the importance of getting an education. And after the rap, "he very often let us play for free over one of the old, torn tables in the back of the room."[20] Mantle, wrote one biographer, "was something of a pool shark; his game was eight-ball, and his friends said he earned more than enough for pocket money."[21]

The women of both the Mantle and Mays homes loved music, and the music they loved was the music Mickey and Willie grew up on. The Mantles listened almost exclusively to country music. John G. Hall, an Oklahoma historian and friend of the Mantle family, has identified the radio stations most widely listened to by folks in the Mantles' corner of the state: KGLC in Miami, Oklahoma; KVOO in Tulsa; KOAM in Pittsburg, Kansas; KGGF in Coffeyville, Kansas; and KFSB in Joplin, Missouri. "The nation's big 50,000-watt clear channel stations," wrote Hall, "didn't bombard the paint off the garage doors until after sundown. Entertainers in the mid-part of the 20th century used their radio shows to reach a wide audience. Then they would parlay that 'fame' by playing at dances throughout the towns and villages of the Midwest. Most of the dance bands went out on Saturdays to play an evening benefit at some municipal building or high school."[22]

Jimmie Rodgers, known as "The Blue Yodeler" and "The Singing Brakeman," had died of tuberculosis in 1933, but his records were still enormously popular all over the South and played on every radio station throughout the decade. Perhaps the most popular artists of the day were Bob Wills and His Texas Playboys, who started out in Fort Worth and built up a huge following in the late 1930s in the

Midwest and the Southwest. They were an unorthodox country band that started out as a fiddle group and, as they evolved, added brass instruments and even drums. Wills, a big fan of black blues and jazz, incorporated numerous licks and riffs from black music into the band's repertoire. The Playboys' style and instruments angered the country music purists in Nashville, but that meant nothing to the thousands of miners in Oklahoma who were happy to tune in to any clear channel stations, particularly Tulsa's KVOO, to hear such standards as "Faded Love" and "San Antonio Rose." These were the songs that Mickey heard more on the radio than any other, both at home and in the car.

The music Willie grew up to was both more varied and more sophisticated. Black Birmingham in the 1930s offered a rich cornucopia of music, ranging from country blues singers to the urban R&B sounds of Louis Jordan and even jazz artists such as Billie Holiday, Count Basie, and Duke Ellington — who often played dates in Birmingham's black clubs in the Fourth Avenue District. In addition, it's likely that Willie, as a boy, spent more time listening to popular white mainstream radio than Mickey. "My oldest memory," he told Charles Einstein, "is singing the words of a popular song. Not really a cowboy song, more a popular song that was a takeoff on a cowboy song." The song was probably Johnny Mercer's "I'm an Old Cowhand" sung by Bing Crosby. Four-year-old Willie loved to yell "Yippee-i-oh-ky-ay" until members of his family were ready to throw him out the door. "You going to be a singer when you grow up?" his aunt Sarah asked. "No," said Willie. "A cowboy. A singing cowboy." "We'll call you Bing," she said.[23] He memorized the words to all manner of popular songs that came over the family radio, "a great piece of furniture in my aunt Sarah's house in Fairfield. I will never forget that radio." *[24]

The radio was Mickey's main connection to major league baseball. Mutt was a lifelong Cardinals and Stan Musial fan, which made Mickey one too. But while Mickey was restricted to listening to their

---

*Around 1960, Mays recalled, he saw the same model radio in the window of a secondhand furniture store in Cincinnati and went inside to stare at it.

games on the radio, Willie saw most of his professional heroes in the flesh. By the time Willie was in high school in 1944, he had seen Satchel Paige and Josh Gibson and many of the greats of black ball on trips to Rickwood Field with his dad.* Mickey and Willie shared at least one common baseball fantasy: both emulated the batting stances of Musial and Ted Williams, whom they knew primarily from pictures in the newspaper and from the newsreels that were shown before their beloved Westerns. Over time, Willie gave up trying to bat left-handed. Both boys, though, continued to try to swing like Joe DiMaggio.

DiMaggio was something else. He had burst onto the national scene in 1936, when Mickey and Willie were five, hitting .323 and driving in 125 runs his rookie year. The next season he led the American League with 46 home runs. When Mickey and Willie were growing up, it seemed as if the Yankees won the World Series every year. In fact, they very nearly did, taking four straight from 1936 to 1939 and fielding perhaps the most dominant team in baseball history. They won in 1941 too, the year DiMaggio electrified the country by hitting safely in fifty-six consecutive games. Willie was ten years old that year and still listening to cowboy songs on Aunt Sarah's radio. But he heard some other things on that radio as well. "The news of Joe DiMaggio's record-setting 56-game hitting streak. That's when I stopped wanting to be a cowboy." When he played ball with his friend Charley Willis, Willie told him to "call me DiMag." "You crazy?" Charley asked. "I mean it," Willie told him. "That's my new name." That meant, Charley told him, that Willie would have to change his position from the infield to center field. "I don't care about center field," Willie told him, "just so long as I hit like him."[25]

At the same time, Mickey Mantle watched newsreels of

---

*When Willie was five or six, his father would pull an old joke on him at the ballpark, "announcing he was a magician, and when he said, 'Stand up,' everybody in the place would stand up, and when he said, 'Sit down,' everybody would sit down. I didn't learn about the seventh inning stretch till long after that" (Mays, *My Life In and Out of Baseball*, p. 60).

DiMaggio at the local movie house, always shown before his beloved Westerns. "We didn't know what the word 'cool' meant back then," Mickey recalled, "but I knew what it looked like. Without actually saying 'cool,' I thought to myself, 'That guy's the coolest ballplayer I've ever seen.' "[26]

DiMaggio was also hailed as baseball's first "complete" player — someone who excelled at all facets of the game: hitting consistently and with power, running the bases, covering ground in the field, and throwing. In fact, there had been a few such players before him, among them Honus Wagner, who had played from 1897 to 1917. Wagner was a fantastic fielder, mostly at shortstop, won eight batting crowns, and led the National League in stolen bases five times and in slugging percentage six times — but no one knew what slugging percentage was in Wagner's day, so he wasn't perceived as a great power hitter. In DiMaggio's time, stolen bases weren't as big a part of the game — at least not in the all-white big leagues — and only people who watched DiMaggio play on a regular basis realized what a swift and daring base runner he was. Nonetheless, anyone who followed baseball in newspapers or on the radio knew him as the guy who could do it all.

Mickey tried to copy DiMaggio's batting style. "It just didn't work for me," Mantle told Dick Young. "I struck out too much trying to use that kind of open stance. So I finally changed — crouched lower in the box, leaned back, tried to offer less of a target to the pitcher, and still struck out a lot. It just amazed me when I reached the big leagues to find out that Joe, standing in the batter's box with his legs far apart, standing straight up, hardly ever struck out."[27]

According to Charley Willis, when he and Willie played catch, Willie would "play DiMaggio." Charley would lob the ball far over Willie's head, and Willie, playing shallower each time in DiMaggio's fashion, would race back to pull the ball down. The 1954 World Series was won on the playing fields of Fairfield, Alabama.

Like Mickey, Willie had been mesmerized by pictures of DiMaggio in the newspapers and by watching him on sports newsreels, and he carefully copied DiMaggio's wide-open, legs-apart batting stance — a stance that Mays, who when fully grown was three inches shorter than DiMaggio, would seem to have been ill suited for. But Willie made it work for him, as he did playing outfield like Joe. Occasionally someone might hit one over your head, he knew, but you gave up more runs by routinely letting singles drop in front of you. Anyway, if you couldn't play shallow and run down a ball hit over your head, you weren't a center fielder.

3

No Other Enjoyment

In later years it was common for baseball writers to say that it was Mays who kept Mantle from being the greatest player ever, in reference to the fly ball Willie hit in the 1951 World Series that caused Mickey to tear up his knee. But Mickey's injury problems began in high school, many years before his encounter with Willie Mays, and they started with football.

In retrospect, it seems as if baseball had no rival for the love of either Mantle or Mays, that there was no other possible career in sports for either to pursue. That was true, at least, in the 1930s and 1940s, when they were boys. At around five-foot-eleven, they were both too short to seriously think about professional basketball, no matter how dazzling they were on the hardwoods, and the National Football League didn't emerge as a competitor to Major League Baseball until the late 1950s. Besides, the odds were hugely against Willie Mays from Westfield, Alabama, getting a football scholarship at a major college power in the late 1940s. But both loved football, and in the recollections of those who saw them, if conditions had been right in the late 1940s, football might well have been the first sport for both.

Willie's coach at Fairfield Industrial, Jim McWilliams, called him "the greatest forward passer I ever saw," and one of the local black papers compared him to Harry Gilmer, the fabled University of Alabama quarterback who starred for the Crimson Tide from 1944 to 1947.

When Willie was thirteen, Sarah asked Cat what his plans were for his son. "What's he going to do? Work in the mill like you?" "No," said Cat, "he's going to college." How, Sarah wondered, was Willie going to get into college? "Play football," Cat replied. "He'll go to Pittsburgh." "They don't take 'em up there," Sarah replied. "Sure they do. What's the matter? You don't read the papers?" "They take 'em," Sarah said, "from around Pittsburgh. Ain't nobody in Pittsburgh heard of Alabama." "You crazy?" Cat shot back. "Pittsburgh plays Alabama."[1]

Almost every sports fan in Alabama, black and white, had been football-conscious, if not -crazy, since the mid-1920s, when the University of Alabama started sending teams to the Rose Bowl. Even black kids would, when playing pickup football games, pretend to be Crimson Tide heroes—Johnny Mack Brown, Dixie Walker, or the great Don Hutson (who played on the opposite end of the line from his friend Paul "Bear" Bryant). Black high school football players dreamed of a time when they would get their chance to play for the Tide, but no one had any realistic idea of when that would be.

Black communities all through the South were excited by the news in 1939 that UCLA had four black players on their football team, including an All-American named Jackie Robinson. How long, they wondered, could it possibly be before the Alabama team would have black players? A few years later, there was some excitement in Westfield and Fairfield in the spring of 1943, when it was announced that Alabama had scheduled a game with the University of Pittsburgh on the Panthers' home field. Because of the steel-industry connections, several black steelworkers had found good jobs in the Pittsburgh area, and some had sons who were playing baseball and football for the University of Pittsburgh. To everyone's disappointment, Alabama, like many colleges, didn't field a team that year because of the war. But the thought stayed in Cat Mays's head that Willie might be good enough to get a football scholarship somewhere.

Football was a different game in the 1940s from what it would become in the 1960s, when substitution rules were eliminated. In the high school football world of young Willie and Mickey, you weren't just a quarterback or a running back or a linebacker—you played on offense and defense, you blocked and tackled, and you often had to placekick or punt as well.

And Mays, of course, could do it all. On offense he played quarterback and sometimes fullback, passing the ball out of both positions. The play calling wasn't particularly sophisticated, but it seems there was much more passing than in the average white high school or even college game today. Willie once described his play calling as "You run here and you run there, and don't stop, because I'll get the ball to you." Mays's hands seemed to have been designed to grip and spiral a football. His arm was so strong, he could throw without winding up—"Quick release, they'd call it now."[2]

Like Alabama's Harry Gilmer, Mays was famous for his "jump pass," where he'd head into the line, stop a couple of yards short of scrimmage, leap, and fire. On one memorable day in his senior year, he threw five touchdowns in a 55–0 Fairfield win over Parker High School, Birmingham's largest black high school. In another dazzling performance, he threw a 70-yard touchdown pass against Booker T. Washington High School in Pensacola, Florida, and then, according to a school history, ran for the extra point that tied the game.*

Willie often punted, producing 60-yarders, and, on kickoffs, sent the ball out of the end zone. How much Willie loved football was demonstrated by a story he liked to tell. When he was thirteen, probably a year before he started high school, he climbed a tree to watch

---

* Somebody must have gotten the story wrong; if Mays ran for a conversion, it would have been worth two points.

a Fairfield game because he couldn't afford a ticket. When Fairfield scored a touchdown, he started clapping, fell out of the tree, and broke his leg. In another version of the story, it was his arm that he broke, and it was watching a Miles College game to see one of his first sports idols, a man named Cat Brown, with whom he would later share the infield in semi-pro ball.

Football allowed Willie to showcase his skills. But he quickly discovered its drawbacks when Charley Willis, blocking for Willie on an end run, was knocked down and got his hand stepped on, breaking two fingers. Charley missed the rest of the season. "So I started going more for basketball."[3]

"I had my baseball," Mickey said, "and I loved football, too."[4]

Oklahoma was almost as much of a hotbed of football fanaticism as Alabama, and every high school boy who played the game dreamed of going to the University of Oklahoma and leading the Sooners to victory over Texas in their annual clash. Mickey caught the football bug in his freshman year, though Mutt Mantle refused to let him play. By his sophomore year, his dad finally gave in to his pleading. Mutt was a big football fan himself, but he had seen too many young men sustain knee, head, and arm injuries that ruined them for other sports. His worst fear was that something would happen on the football field to derail the glorious future Mickey was certain to have in baseball.

Like Willie, Mickey's high school coaches recalled him with nothing but praise. "In my opinion," said John Lungo, one of the first coaches in the state to install the new T-formation, "baseball was Mickey's second-best sport. He was the best high school football player I ever saw."[5] Alan Woolard, Mickey's first football coach, was just as impressed.*

Mickey's speed dazzled his coaches, and though he was only

---

*Woolard, regarded by some Commerce football watchers as "too good for the school," turned out in fact to be just that. He went on to coach in bigger schools in Oklahoma and in his hometown, Lawrence, Kansas, where he became a mentor to quarterback John Hadl. Hadl played seventeen years for four teams in the American and National Football Leagues, eleven of them with San Diego, and threw a career 244 touchdown passes.

about 150 pounds, he was tough and determined, a natural running back. In addition to his speed and power, the combination of which was often too much for Commerce's opponents to contain, he had terrific hands. Like Willie, he was an outstanding kicker; his teammates recall that he was equally adept at placekicking with or without shoes. One friend, Joe Barker, reflected that as good a runner as Mickey was, "I think the greatest asset that he had . . . was his punting ability. He could easily have been a punter in professional football."[6]

Football wasn't a terribly sophisticated game in white high schools in the 1940s. There weren't many passes thrown, but Mantle created huge excitement just by taking a short pass in the backfield. He seemed capable of breaking for a long touchdown every time he laid hands on the ball. Researcher John G. Hall located some microfilm from the 1947 *Miami News-Record* in which the highlights of one game read: "Mickey Mantle broke loose and ran 65 yards to the 1-yard line before he was tackled. Mantle then plunged over to score. Mantle plunged off-tackle for six yards to score after recovering a Fairland Owl fumble." (Mickey, like Willie, played linebacker on defense.) In Mickey's senior year, 1948, the Commerce High Tigers lost their first three games, but the "Commerce Comet," as he was known, scored ten touchdowns.

Mickey's reputation as a football player was such that after the Oklahoma Sooners won the national championship, the Sooners' assistant coach—and former star quarterback—Darrell Royal was dispatched to Commerce to court Mickey as one of the state's brightest football prospects. Mickey made a trip to Norman for a guided tour of the campus. Long after he was a New York Yankee star, he liked to tell a story that came out of the trip. At a golf tournament years later, Mickey was again introduced to Royal, by then head coach at the University of Texas. "You don't remember me, do you?" asked Mickey. Royal said he did not. Mickey told him about his recruiting trip in 1948. Royal admitted he didn't remember but explained, "You weren't Mickey Mantle then."

An extra point to the story: In 1970, after winning the national

title as head coach of the Texas Longhorns, Royal traveled to Tuscaloosa, Alabama, to teach Bear Bryant and the Crimson Tide coaching staff the intricacies of the new wishbone offense. Mantle was in
Alabama to promote his Mickey Mantle's Country Cookin' restaurant
in Birmingham and drove over to Tuscaloosa to visit his old football
pals Bryant and Royal. He reminded the Texas coach of their second
meeting; this time Royal remembered the story, "Yeah, " he laughed.
"I said you weren't Mickey Mantle then." "Well," Mickey said with a
sigh, "I guess I'm not Mickey Mantle anymore."[7]

For Mutt and Mickey, the possibility of a football scholarship was
merely a backup in case Mickey wasn't offered a baseball contract.
But in the pre-Jackie Robinson era, Cat and Willie couldn't possibly
think that a lucrative major league baseball contract was in Willie's
future. Had a football scholarship at a good school been a realistic
possibility, it's likely that the Mayses would have jumped at it before
Willie committed to a Negro League team.

"It would appear," wrote an early Mays biographer, that around the
age of thirteen "football was the boy's greatest love." But the injury
sustained by his friend Charley opened Willie's eyes to the danger of
football. "I've never minded physical contact," he told Charles Einstein, "in the sense of being afraid of it—except with a catcher named
Foiles, who used to play for Pittsburgh, and man, don't go sliding into
him. He was built like a brick wall. But I'm not one of those people
who gets some special kick out of [contact] either."*

After witnessing Charlie's injury, Willie quickly shifted his focus
from football to round ball. As a sophomore forward in 1946, he led
all-black high school players in Jefferson County in scoring and took
Fairfield Industrial to a state championship. Had Mays been a couple
of years older, he could have done what his future Black Barons manager Piper Davis and several other baseball players from the industrial

---

* Hank Foiles played eleven seasons, from 1953 to 1964, four of them with the Pirates,
and appeared in 608 games. He is unremembered today except as the man Willie
Mays didn't want to run into.

teams did: played semi-pro basketball. Davis played with the Harlem Globetrotters for four years, alternating basketball with Black Barons baseball.* Davis was very grateful for the $50 a game he could make playing for the Globetrotters.

Cat, though, saw from the start there was no future for his son in basketball. Aside from the Globetrotters, there were no professional opportunities for black men in the game, especially if they had trouble topping out a little under six feet. In his own way, Cat Mays was as single-minded as Mutt Mantle. If his son had a future as a professional in any sport, it was going to be baseball.

As it was played by white kids in Mantle's Oklahoma, basketball was a more static and conservative game than the one played by black kids in Birmingham high schools. At the time, the white game was accurately described by one sports historian as "very much station-to-station, played below the rim. A player who scored in double figures, 10 to 12 points, was often a team's."[8] The strategy was to constantly pass the ball around and around from player to player until someone was open for a shot—always a two-handed shot.

If you had the right players, though, the game could be played much differently. Commerce had one such player.

Mickey's coach, Frank Bruce, was the first in his area to implement the fast-break game. Mickey's pal Bill Moseley was the team's center, and Mantle, a hot-shot guard—a point guard, actually, years before anyone used that phrase—didn't hesitate to drive straight for the hoop if a defender challenged him. In one game, Moseley recalled, Mickey scored more than 30 points, a remarkable total for that era. It might have been interesting to see what would have happened if, in 1945 or 1946, Commerce High and Fairfield Industrial had gotten together for a game.

⚾   ⚾

* A man named Bob Welch, who did promotion for the white Barons of the Southern Association, knew Abe Saperstein, the founder and owner of the Globetrotters, and made the connection for Piper.

It wasn't true, then, as Mickey was to say years later, that he had "no other enjoyment than baseball."[9] Or, as Willie said, "The game [baseball] was everything to me."[10] It was probably true that both boys had no other enjoyment than sports. Most of their waking hours, when they weren't in school, were spent playing baseball, football, or basketball, or daydreaming about them. "All the time my algebra teacher was saying 'X equals how much?'" Willie told a writer shortly after arriving in New York, "I was thinking about the next ball game."[11] At about the same time, Mickey was thinking much the same way. "At Commerce High, I'd sit in class listening to the teacher, but half the time I would gaze out the window and see myself scoring sensational touchdowns." He was not, he admitted, a very good student, but "I passed my classes. I took easy subjects—home economics, shop, gym, and so forth—and staggered through the rest." He recalled with fondness an English teacher named Mrs. Jacoby who had him memorize Joyce Kilmer's "Trees."* "I didn't get it quite right in class. But after school she let me catch a glimpse of the page over her shoulder while I recited to the empty classroom."[12]

Teachers had no such ambitions for Willie or his classmates. Instead, Fairfield Industrial trained Willie for a job as a launderer. "I never became a cleaner or a presser," he said, looking back on his high school years. "Don't laugh. That was a big job for most young boys back then, back in the late 1940s, in that part of the South. Let's face it, there just weren't that many other opportunities for a young black kid living in the Deep South almost twenty years before the coming of the Civil Rights movement."[13]

When he was grown, Willie could remember having only one actual job, washing dishes in a Birmingham café, "Folks treated me

---

* Surprisingly for someone who read little besides comic books, Mickey was one of the editors of his school newspaper, *Tiger Chat*, probably because "I knew so much about sports." The teacher, a Mrs. Aldene Campbell, had enough confidence to send him to a competition for high school journalism students in Miami (Oklahoma). To both their surprise, Mickey came in second. At graduation, Mrs. Campbell gushed, "I always knew you could do it if you tried." Mickey never found out whether she meant "trying to be a ballplayer or journalist."

grade-A," he said, "but I quit after one week." As Willie phrased it, "Working wasn't for me." Mickey had numerous odd jobs, including some hard, nasty work in a cemetery, and, of course, a steady round of chores both at Quincy Street and later on the farm and in Whitebird, the most tedious of which was shucking corn. (There was no Uncle Otis around to wash dishes and chop wood for Mickey.) But for the most part, "All I did: play, play, play"—mostly baseball.[14]

At one time or another, both boys played just about every position. Mutt made Mickey play catcher, a position he hated and that seems, in retrospect, a curious choice, considering not only how frequently catchers are injured but also that it was such an obvious waste of Mickey's incredible speed. Nonetheless, it showed him baseball as it looked from behind the plate—the only position on the diamond where one can see every player without turning one's head. (So sure did Mickey become of his ability to perform a catcher's tasks that he once challenged Yogi Berra to let him call the pitches from centerfield when Whitey Ford was on the mound. The strain was too great, though, and he gave up pitch-calling after just one inning.)

According to his friends, Mickey, while playing second base for the championship-winning Gabby Street League team from Douthat, could not only bat but throw left-handed, at least to toss a ball around. Nick Ferguson thought, "He coulda thrown left-handed for real if he had to." Mantle had by far the strongest arm on nearly all the teams he played on, and many who saw him in his teenage years thought he could have made it as a pitcher. In addition to a humming fastball that he could throw with excellent control, Mickey developed a specialty pitch, a knuckleball. No one knows who taught it to him or how he mastered it, but it was a skill he maintained over his entire professional career.

Years later, while with the Independence Kansas Class-D team in the Kansas-Oklahoma-Missouri (KOM) League, Mickey broke a teammate's nose throwing a knuckleball. On the team bus headed for a game, Mantle was demonstrating the proper grip; when they arrived at the ballpark, Lou Skizas, a third baseman, crouched down in the catcher's position and said, "OK, let's see it, kid." According to Mickey, "I uncorked the knuckleball, struck him right in the nose, and sent him tumbling. He was out cold for two or three minutes." Skizas was rushed to the infirmary, "He had a broken nose and missed three days of baseball. Matter of fact, he still has a permanent lump on his nose."[15] (In 1956, Mantle's kunckleball claimed a second victim when, while having a catch with teammate Norm Siebern, he unleashed a floater that smashed into Siebern's nose, costing him two days of practice.)*

Willie, like Mickey, had terrific hands and seemed to have promise as a shortstop. According to one account, though, he gave it up when he threw so hard to first base he almost broke the fielder's hand. (Though this story sounds apocryphal, it may well be true. Piper Davis once told me that black kids in the 1930s and 1940s often played with gloves "where there was so little padding that you often had to stuff a rag or something in it just to keep your hand from getting broke.") When he was a young teenager, Willie's throwing arm was already legendary in the Fairfield area, and like Mickey it looked as if he could have made it as a pitcher. He liked pitching for the same reason he liked playing quarterback in football: he got to be the center of attention and could showcase his skills. He apparently gave up pitching for a couple of reasons. The first was dizzy spells. One summer day when he was fourteen, he pitched a complete game against an industrial team and hit a walk-off home run for the victory. As he slid across home plate—there were no fences on the field—he almost fainted. Cat carried him into the shade and gave him a drink of water, and the spell passed, but the dizziness would come back again and again over the years. No medical reason has ever been offered for why such a magnificent physical specimen as Willie Mays suffered from

---

* He once told me in an interview, "One of the few things I really wanted to do as a big-leaguer that I never got the chance to do was throw a few pitches in a real game. I always thought that someday, when we had clinched the pennant early and were ahead in a game, say 9–0, that I'd have the guts to ask Casey to let me pitch. But I never did. Man, I'd a loved to have gotten two strikes on somebody and then come in with a knuckleball."

recurring dizzy spells; perhaps, said some who had watched him over the years, it was simply a side product of the exuberance with which he played the game.

The fainting spells implanted in Willie's mind the idea that pitching might be too taxing for him, but a stronger reason for his decision to focus on the outfield was voiced by his father. Cat reminded him, "If you pitch, you can't play every day."[16] It isn't recorded, but Mutt no doubt said something similar to Mickey.

One thing that Willie always had more of than Mickey was luck— relative, of course, to what a black youth born in Alabama during the Depression and growing up without a mother or father at home could expect. Football was good to Willie, either that or he got out of it before it could turn bad. He was never seriously injured while playing the game, if one discounts falling out a tree while watching a football game and breaking a leg (or perhaps an arm).

Technically, Mickey Mantle wasn't injured playing football, either. He was injured during practice. In his freshman year, Mickey got a simple kick in the shin. Some biographers have said it occurred during a game, but Mickey, recounting the incident to Herb Gluck, said it happened during practice: "One day we were practicing, and I was carrying the ball when a tackler kicked me on the left shin. Bill Moseley and the coach helped me off the field. The coach said it looked like a sprain. That night my mother soaked the ankle in a bucket of hot water." By the next morning, his temperature had climbed to 104 and his ankle had swollen horribly.

The vast majority of ankle injuries on a football field are shrugged off and the player can be back in the lineup in a couple of days. But Mickey never had that kind of luck. His father drove him to nearby Pitcher General Hospital, where the family doctor diagnosed the injury as superficial. Because of the fever, though, the doctor determined that the ankle should be lanced. No one seemed to understand how bad the infection was. For the next two weeks, Mickey endured a regimen of peroxide, sulfur, liniments, and compresses, but nothing reduced the swelling. Mutt and Lovell shook their heads and wondered what fate had befallen their son. Every morning Lovell, after packing the rest of the kids off to school, walked nearly a mile to catch the northeast Oklahoma bus from Whitebird to visit Mickey at the hospital; when Mutt got off work at the mines, he drove his wreck of a 1935 LaSalle to the hospital to relieve his wife, who returned home to fix dinner.

To his parents' horror, Mickey was diagnosed with osteomyelitis; the doctors said that amputating the leg was a strong possibility if not a likelihood. Lovell was adamant: under no circumstances would they take Mickey's leg. Immediately after hearing the diagnosis, Lovell went to a lawyer in nearby Miami and got Mickey transferred to the Crippled Children's Hospital in Oklahoma City. The move was essential, but it involved the swallowing of a great deal of pride: the Crippled Children's Hospital was a charity hospital for patients too poor to go elsewhere. The family made the grim three-and-a-half hour drive from Pitcher to Oklahoma City, Mutt all the time at the wheel, chain smoking and brooding, despairing that his beloved son would ever walk again, let alone fulfill his promise in baseball.

But finally, Mickey did have some luck after all. The year 1946 was when penicillin was making its way into hospitals in the bigger cities, and Mickey was given an injection every three hours for several days. His ankle showed immediate improvement, and after a few days, the mood in Mickey's hospital room lighted considerably. Early in October, father and son were euphoric over the combination of Mickey's recovery and the St. Louis Cardinals' victory in the World Series. Mutt and Mickey let out a collective yelp in the eighth inning of the final game when Enos "Country" Slaughter made his daring dash from first to home to score the winning run against the Red Sox. Slaughter, Musial, and the Cardinals were the world champions. It seemed like an omen. Three days later, his arms around half-brother Theodore, Mickey walked out of the hospital. By the next spring, he was practicing with the football team.

One change that his friends noticed immediately was how much bigger Mickey looked in the few months after his hospital stay. He'd weighed around 130 pounds when he went in and lost, or so friends and family thought, about 15 pounds, but he had gained all that weight back and then some. By the spring of 1947 he looked both bigger and stronger. "I don't know what they were giving him," Nick Ferguson recalled for David Falkner. Ferguson advanced the amazing thought that "He [Mickey, that is] thought maybe it was steroids, but I have no idea what it was. But he claimed that's what pumped him up to 160 pounds."[17] Where such advanced steroids would have come from at an Oklahoma City hospital in 1946 isn't known.

Ferguson kept some photographs of the Commerce football team while they were in high school. Though he missed the 1946 season, Mantle was included at his coach's insistence. In the 1947 team photo, Nick estimates Mickey looks to weigh about 165 pounds, all of the added weight pure muscle. No friend, teammate, or relative remembers him lifting a single weight.

B oys will be boys. When he was thirteen, Willie and his pals were on their way to a ball game, riding in the back of a truck owned by Stephenson's Dry Cleaners. The driver was a member of their group, Herman Boykin, who, since he was only fourteen, had no business behind the wheel. The boys were riding with the back doors open and decided to have some fun by making faces at the driver of a truck behind them. After a couple of minutes, the man lost his temper, sped up, cut in front of them, and stopped short, nearly driving them off the road. Herman quickly figured out what had happened, and when they arrived at the field, raised his truck's dumper, rudely depositing Willie and the other players on the ground.

Around the same time, Mickey got into serious trouble—or at least as serious as trouble got for school boys in Commerce, Oklahoma, in 1944—by embarrassing Patty McCall and her girlfriends. Miss McCall had invited Mickey, Bill Moseley, and a couple more of Mickey's friends to her house for some Cokes and 7-Ups while listening to the radio. Mickey, Bill, and the others developed a bad case of fumble-itis; unaccountably, they kept dropping things on the floor so Patty and the others girls would have to bend over and pick them up. The boys would then take the opportunity to look up their skirts. Patty told her folks, and her parents told the principal, who thought that the boys were not too old for a good paddling. Mickey knew he got off easy: Lovell never found out.

As early as their high school years, it was obvious that their hometowns were incapable of holding Mickey and Willie. Back then, Mantle noted in his 1987 memoir, "There wasn't very much of anything going on for teenagers in Commerce. The main drag was only a few blocks, one end to the other; the City Hall, the volunteer fire department, the Black Cat Café, a bank, a movie house, one motel, a handful of stores . . ."* The Black Cat Café was just about the only place in Commerce that could pass for a "hot spot." One local historian called it "One of the few all-night eateries between Kansas City and Tulsa."[18] Called by one Oklahoma newspaper "a conspicuous place on U.S. 66," it was a gathering point for celebrities who happened to be passing through, including folk humorist Will Rogers, cowboy film star Buck Jones, and musicians such as Bob Wills and his Texas Playboys. Given that Mutt often went to the Black Cat, it's likely that it was the place where father and son had their first beer together—either there or at one of the other bars popular with Mutt and other miners, including JJ Café, Killa Bar (a pun on "killed a bear," as the original pioneers often had to do), the A-D Bar, and Finch's.

Legally, Oklahoma was dry, though bars were allowed to sell "near beer" with an alcoholic content of 3.2 percent ("real" beer was anywhere from 4 to 6 percent). Of course, the Black Cat and all the other Commerce taverns served the genuine stuff as well. Nick Fer-

---

* Oklahoman John G. Hall told me, "The only incident of note that happened in Commerce was when the outlaws Bonnie and Clyde stopped there in April, 1934, after killing two highway patrolmen in Texas."

guson recalled, "Everyone knew when a raid was coming. The police would notify 'em so the real booze would get put away, get put all under the bar . . . as soon as the sheriffs or the deputies or whoever would leave, well, they'd bring out the booze again. It was all payoffs back then, you know, everything got taken care of."[19]

Mickey was good-looking and, because of his athletic prowess, extremely popular. Painfully bashful and without much money, though, he had little social life. In a large room above the bank, there were Saturday-night "Teentown" dances, but they were tame affairs, especially for a boy as awkward at dancing as Mickey. One night in his senior year, his friends persuaded a pretty girl named Claudine Sanders to ask him for a dance. Mickey gave a nervous yes, but he was mortified: his face was "red as a beet, and she kept rubbing her body against mine" while his pals looked on and laughed. "Goddamn!" he thought to himself, "If I ever get away from here, I'll never dance again!"[20]

Given Willie's distaste for alcoholic beverages, he and Cat may not ever have shared a beer, but by the time Willie had reached his late teens, he and his father did frequent some of the same establishments, most of them located along Fourth Avenue North in downtown Birmingham. Fifty-seven years after moving away forever, Willie still had fond memories of the area: "Man," he remembered in an interview with journalist Paul Hemphill, "you could find whatever you were looking for. It was the place where me and my friends headed whenever we had money. During the day, the Fourth Avenue area was a swirl of activity." Willie Patterson, a fine third baseman for the Black Barons in the 1940s, recalled, "You had the Carver Theatre, and the Frolic, the Famous and the Champion. On that corner, they sold records. Anything you want, you can get on Fourth Avenue. Watches, anything you want . . ."[21]

Ballplayers, many of them from the several industrial-league teams but especially the Black Barons, were treated like kings in the Fourth Avenue district. Players from out of town stayed at the Rush

Hotel on North Eighteenth Street, just a good baseball heave from the center of the bustling black business district. The hotel was owned by Joe Rush, who also owned the Black Barons.

It was an area few whites knew firsthand. A *Birmingham News* article from 1936 described it: "The Frolic Theatre's bright lights twinkle, and the Harlem Cafe beckons—where dark-skinned and dapper city boys and lanky cotton hands from the 'Black Belt' gape . . . a paradise of barbecue stands and pool rooms, of soft drink parlors and barbershops . . . the Mecca for cooks and chauffeurs on Thursday night, a heaven for miners and mill workers on Saturday night. . . .

"Many white men have seen Eighteenth Street. Only a few know it. No white man understands it."[22]

The hottest spot in black Birmingham was Bob's Savoy—or "Little Savoy" Café—at 411 North Seventeenth, owned by a New York native, Bob Williams, and named for the Savoy Ballroom in Harlem. Williams had come to Birmingham during the early years of the Depression and used his New York contacts to keep a steady stream of black celebrities frequenting his club whenever they went on tour in the Deep South. The musicians included Duke Ellington and Count Basie; sports celebrities such as Jackie Robinson and champion fighters Joe Louis and Sugar Ray Robinson were also known to stop by.*

Like the Black Cat in Commerce, the Little Savoy was known for being open 24 hours a day (though some recall that on Sundays it didn't open until after church services let out). The upstairs was for eating: "Chicken–Steaks–Dinners–Short Orders–Drinks–Smokes" read the ads that appeared in the *Birmingham Times* and other black papers. Downstairs was for drinking and shooting pool, and though Bob's bartenders were careful not to sell beer to teenagers, schoolboys

---

* Willie Patterson also recalled that Cab Calloway and Lionel Hampton also played at Bob's, sometimes to white audiences. "See," he told Birmingham historian Chris Fullerton, "what they did then, they would play that evening, they'd play for the whites. At night the whites that sat there had to go upstairs . . . the Negroes came downstairs."[23]

(especially those like Willie, who had fathers well known as ballplayers) were often tolerated on summer afternoons when school was out and allowed to drink Cokes, Dr Pepper, and Royal Crown Cola while they shot pool.

In a few short years Willie would be in New York and would see the original Savoy Ballroom in Harlem.

For every father who raises his son to be an athlete, there's a moment at which he realizes, often with a shock, that his son has surpassed him. Mutt Mantle's realization came sooner than Cat Mays's did.

Mickey's younger brother, Ray, recalled an incident when he, his twin brother, Roy; Mickey; and Mutt were in the car, and his father and older brother began some good-natured needling about who was the fastest. Mutt pulled over to the side of the road and took off his shoes to race his son. Mickey left Mutt in his dust. (Ray didn't mention whether Mickey removed his shoes too.)

For Cat Mays, the moment came when Willie was around sixteen, and playing in a game between TCI and another factory team whose name Willie could not remember—though he did remember what happened in the second inning of the game. Cat was in center, Willie in left. An opposing batter hit a sinking line drive between left and centerfield. Father and son both went for the ball; Cat yelled, "All right, all right, let me take it!" But Willie saw that the ball was sinking and cut in front of his dad to make a shoestring catch. "I knew," he told Charles Einstein nearly twenty years later, "that I'd shown him up. And he knew it. I never apologized to him for making the play. He never apologized to me for trying to call me off. We both wanted the same thing—to get away from the situation where I had to play side by side in the same outfield with my own father.

"Because even the great Kitty-Kat was beginning to slow down, the same as his own son will slow down, and the only things worse than being shown up by youth is being shown up by your own flesh and blood.

"Because then you got to pretend you like it."

It was the last time the Mays men would ever play together.

"All I had to do was let him have that baseball for himself, out there that twilight in left-centerfield. I could have said: 'Take it, it's yours!

"But I didn't, and I can't buy it back."[24]

4

Pass-the-Hat

On April 15, 1947, Jackie Robinson made his major league debut at Ebbets Field, Brooklyn, against the Boston Braves. The landmark event scarcely caused a ripple in Commerce, Oklahoma.

"You have to remember, growing up in Oklahoma I scarcely saw a black man," Mickey said. "I knew I wanted to play major league baseball, but it didn't seem at the time that what Jackie Robinson had done was going to make much difference in my life."[1] At age fifteen, it was just beginning to dawn on Mickey that he would get a shot at the big leagues, but in his wildest dreams he would not have believed that in little more than five years' time he would be playing against Jackie Robinson in the World Series, and that Jackie would walk over to the Yankees' locker room to congratulate him on a great game.

In Birmingham, at least in black Birmingham, the news was electric. Willie said in reflection, "It was the first time most baseball fans had heard of Robinson"—which was probably not true considering how much publicity Robinson had been receiving since Branch

Rickey had signed him for the Dodgers organization more than a year before. "But we all knew who Jackie was. In fact, to us black ball players it seemed like a bigger breakthrough when, in 1946, he signed to play the Dodgers farm team in Montreal. That was organized ball. I mean, forget about the majors. No Negroes . . . had ever been in the minor leagues, had ever played any organized ball."

If there had been any doubt, Willie decided at that moment that cleaning and pressing would not be his life's work: "I didn't have any heroes who folded underwear in a laundry."[2]

To twenty-nine-year-old Lorenzo "Piper" Davis, one of the best all-around players in the Negro Leagues, the news of Robinson's signing was bittersweet. His instincts told him that major league owners were not going to be offering jobs to dozens of black veterans like himself. They would be looking for young phenoms — perhaps like the son of his friend Cat Mays.

Piper Davis would soon become a key figure in Willie's early development as a ballplayer. He was also the major force in black baseball in Alabama, and probably in all of the South. Davis was a great player, manager, talent scout, leader, and, after his playing days were over, oral historian of the game in Birmingham from the earliest days of the industrial leagues to the sad fading of the Negro Leagues in the late 1940s.

The son of a coal miner, Davis, as a boy, was obsessed with baseball. Like many young black fans in the 1920s and 1930s, he simply accepted segregation as an ugly fact and followed the fortunes of both white and black teams. He kept up with the white Barons by listening to the popular radio broadcasts of Eugene "Bull" Connor, who, by the time Piper was managing the Black Barons, would be the key figure in enforcing segregation in Birmingham. In a 1987 interview, Davis told me that his greatest thrill as a boy was seeing the 1931 Dixie Series duel between the Houston Buffaloes' Dizzy Dean and the Barons' Ray Caldwell at Rickwood Field. "I got my name," he explained, "from the town where I was born, in 1917, Piper, Alabama . . . I don't think you would find it on a map even today. It was a little coal-mining town. There weren't but a couple hundred people there after World War I, and I bet there aren't many more than that now."[*3] Piper attended Alabama State University for a year on what he called a "partial" scholarship, playing baseball and basketball, and thanks to the Harlem Globetrotters' Abe Saperstein, he made some money playing semipro basketball. In 1947, at age thirty-one, he was both player and manager for the Birmingham Black Barons.

Davis played so much baseball as a boy that by the time he was in grade school he was already looking at the game as a profession. "I remember that in the heart of the Depression, about 1935, we were living in Fairfield — that's real close to where Willie grew up — I played with an industrial team, TCI, a pipe and valve company and the same team Cat Mays played for. . . . There weren't any Little League or Babe Ruth teams back then, and most of us — not just the black boys but most of the white boys, too — learned to play organized ball on company teams. Willie did, and when I met Mickey Mantle in Birmingham in 1967 when the Yankees came down for an exhibition game, he told me he learned his ball on a company team, too, for a mining company." The most important connection Piper made in industrial baseball was Cat Mays.

In the summer of 1947, Willie was making good pocket money playing semipro ball. Mickey, at the same time, was on the cusp of organized baseball playing second base for the nearby town of Miami, a semipro amateur team. The difference between Mays's and Mantle's teams was that Mickey's was organized: under an arrangement in which the players were not paid salaries — so that they officially remained "amateurs" — they were guaranteed a portion of the ticket money to cover expenses. With Willie's team, it was strictly pass-the-hat, so the players got to take home a little cash.

---

[*] Willie Mays once told me that the name of Davis's hometown was "Piper-Coleanor." He was sure of it, he said, and all the players on the Black Barons knew that to be the name of the town. I haven't been able to find any other reference to Coleanor or what it means.

The Miami team was the first organized ball Mickey had played since the Gabby Street Pee Wee League in 1942, and it gave him the opportunity to play the first really challenging baseball of his life.* It was also the first time that he wasn't playing with his boyhood pals, and the first time he had faced players more experienced than he was. Some of Mantle's teammates and many of his opponents in semipro were good enough to play for the Miami Owls, a team in the KOM League, so named because they were the first team in the area to play night ball. For the first time in his life, Mickey had to put up with arrogant, more experienced jocks. Some of the older Miami players, or so the story goes, would grab Mickey's glove and toss it over the outfield fence. Mickey trained his dog (again, so the story goes) to crawl under the fence and fetch his glove — surely as Tom Sawyer's dog would have done.

While playing for Miami, Mickey met Barney Barnett, manager of the Baxter Springs Whiz Kids, a semipro team. Mantle would recall Barnett as "a big old Irishman with a bald head, shiny red nose, and perpetual grin on his face. He loved kids, loved the game." He had an endearing habit of calling everyone "honey" or "hon." A friend of Mantle's remarked years later, "Can you imagine him calling Mickey 'honey'?"[4]

During a game against Baxter, Barney watched Mickey smash line-drive doubles from both the right and left side of the plate and, after taking a relay throw from right field, gun down a runner at home. Barnett, who had put in several years in mines as a ground boss, had

---

*Neither Mickey nor Willie played much high school baseball, which didn't get much coverage in the local presses in Alabama and Oklahoma. Most of the games were played during the summer when the kids weren't at school, and in the fall football dominated. The level of competition in high school simply wasn't good enough to attract players of Mantle's or Mays's ability. Mickey's cousin Max recalled that nearly every time he saw Mickey bat for the Commerce Tigers he was walked.

The 1945 Commerce High School yearbook had Mantle listed among the baseball players for that season, but no accounts have been found of Mickey having played for the team that year. He probably tried out for the team and then changed his mind.

seen Mutt and Mickey's Uncle Tunney play for the Whitebird Mining team and knew the boy came from good baseball stock. Knowing something special when he saw it, he asked Mickey to join his Whiz Kids for the next season. Mickey didn't hesitate to say yes.

The league Barnett's team played in (and which he'd helped start) was a cut above the baseball Mantle had been playing. Everyone knew that, through Barney's connections, the Whiz Kids of Baxter Springs attracted scouts from professional baseball. There had been much talk when a player Barney had coached, Sherman Lollar, was signed by the Cleveland Indians back in 1943, and by 1946 Lollar had made his debut with the Indians.* Mickey knew the team was an important stepping-stone for him. As Dave Newkirk, a local boy, told John G. Hall, "The Whiz Kids were a way of life during those years. More of us wanted to play baseball for Baxter Springs than play football for Notre Dame."[5]

On July 20, 1947, Mickey took his first at-bat in a Whiz Kids uniform. (If he had played for Barnett the previous year, when Barney outfitted his boys in uniforms purchased from the New York Yankees, he'd have been wearing Yankee pinstripes.) Barnett's plan for Mickey was to turn him into a shortstop, but Mantle was not yet ready to play the position for the Whiz Kids — he would in fact never be ready — so Barney put him in left field. It was an inauspicious debut; he had just one single in five at-bats. Mantle played just three more games with the Whiz Kids that season and went hitless in his last nine at-bats, giving him an .056 batting average his first year. However, largely because of his reputation, he was asked to play in the Cardinal Junior League's all-star game on August 1. He didn't start, but he got into the game in the late innings, batted twice, and had a single, a hard shot between the shortstop and third

---

* He would go on to play eighteen seasons in major league ball, twelve with the White Sox, and be chosen for nine All-Star teams. Many thought that if not for Yogi Berra, Lollar would have been regarded as the best catcher in the American League in the late 1940s and through the 1950s.

baseman. The third baseman, from Liberty, Missouri, was future St. Louis Cardinal Ken Boyer.*

Mickey was discouraged; Barnett was not. The big leagues, Barney told Mickey, "may seem a million miles from here and out of reach for everyone, but if you work real hard, they won't be out of reach for you."[6]

I n late August, when the season was over, Barney invited Mickey to join the Whiz Kids on their annual outing to see the Cardinals play in St. Louis, even though he had played only four games with them. Mickey drove there with Harry Wells, a man he had worked for, digging graves and erecting tombstones in a cemetery — backbreaking work, though some say that's where Mickey developed his powerful back and shoulder muscles. Wells bought a red Mercury convertible and drove Mantle and three other Whiz Kids — Billy Johnson, Buddy Ball, and Jim Canega — to St. Louis for the game. Mickey vividly recalled "persuading Harry to put the top down. It was colder than Siberia, and Harry's shivering at the wheel while the three of us are in the back seat, laughing our heads off. At the same time other cars are darting to avoid us because we're chewing these big wads of bubble gum, then taking them out of our mouths and throwing them at the windshields of cars coming from the opposite direction on the old narrow highway going into St. Louis."[7]

When they arrived at Sportsman's Park, they saw something they had never seen outside any professional baseball stadium: lines of black fans waiting for tickets. The Cardinals would be playing the Brooklyn Dodgers that afternoon, and black fans had come to see Jackie Robinson. Just as they were in Rickwood Field in Birmingham, blacks were segregated at Sportsman's Park, made to sit in the left-field bleachers. The only difference was that in St. Louis there was

---

* Two years later Ken and Mickey would sign their first professional contracts; twelve years later Ken's brother Cletis would become Mickey's teammate on the New York Yankees, and in 1964 Ken, the NL's MVP, would lead the Cardinals to the World Series against Clete and Mickey.

no chicken wire to separate black and white. Integration was moving along in baby steps.

The visiting Oklahomans were impressed by Jackie Robinson's hustle and speed, particularly on a foul pop that Robinson, playing first base, nearly crashed into the dugout to grab. But afterward, when they rehashed the game, there was nothing said about the fact that, for the first time, they had seen an integrated baseball game. Mickey, not quite seventeen, would mumble to his friends that he was opposed to integration; the prejudice would fade away in less than a year.

In 1948 the Commerce Comet took off. In one game — no one remembers the exact date — Mickey slammed a ball to right field in Baxter Springs' Kiwanis Park that landed in the Spring River, a blow of around 480 feet — or at any rate, that's the story everyone told. One can practically trace the birth of the Mickey Mantle legend from that titanic home run. The only problem is that no one has ever been found who actually claims to have been there. A batboy named Guy Crow, who was later tracked down by researchers, said that Mantle did hit a ball that far in batting practice one day, "but it went in the river on one bounce."[8] Rex Heavin, another former Whiz Kid, later claimed that while he was pitching for the Baxter Springs Cubs, a sort of minor league farm team for the Whiz Kids, Mantle hit a ball off him during a night game that reached the river on one bounce. Whatever ball Mickey hit in that period, whether it reached the river on a fly or a bounce, it must have been prodigious.

Mickey most certainly did *not* do what he said he did in his Hall of Fame induction speech in 1974: "I hit three home runs that day — a couple of them went into the river, one right-handed and one left-handed."[9] As the man says in the film *The Man Who Shot Liberty Valance*, "When the legend becomes fact, print the legend." John G. Hall, after examining all of the accounts, concludes, "At least one of the ageing witnesses claimed the ball bounced into Spring River into the mouth of a giant catfish, which then swam down the Mississippi to the Gulf of Mexico and deposited the ball into the silt, where it produced hundreds of similar stories"*[10] And all those stories, at one time or another, found their way into magazines and newspapers.

There is something Tom Sawyer—ish about hitting a baseball into a river, which is probably why Mantle remembered that accomplishment rather than the better-documented feat of June 13 when he hit three colossal home runs against the Columbus (Kansas) Lions in their home park. Perhaps, too, Mantle chose to forget that game because the Whiz Kids ended up losing in the tenth inning. Those who were there, however, remember not only Mickey's performance but what happened after. After the final home run, a Baxter fan, according to local legend, pulled off his hat and started passing it around the crowd, and by the time it came back around it contained nearly $75. To put that in perspective, that was almost what Mutt Mantle earned in a month of hard work in the mines. Some of those who were there later told historians that the amount was $54—still nothing to sneeze at. When they gave it to him, Mickey later said, it was more money than he'd ever seen at one time in his life.

As would later happen with Willie Mays, the combination of money and baseball got Mickey into hot water with high school authorities. Word spread quickly of Mickey's windfall, and the Oklahoma High School Activities Association notified Mutt that his son had, by accepting the cash, forfeited his amateur status and would be barred from playing high school sports. Mutt was forced to go to the state capital, Oklahoma City, to straighten matters out. The association relented, on the condition that the money be returned — an absurd request considering how difficult it would have been to round up all the spectators and ask them how much they had each chipped in. Mutt agreed, and Barney Barnett started a campaign and raised enough money to make restitution — or at least said that he did. Nick

---

* According to Baxter Springs legend, the spot where Mantle hit the mammoth home run — or home runs — can be located just a few feet from a sign on the local Civil War tour that reads: ON OCTOBER 8, 1864, WILLIAM QUANTRILL, WITH 300 GUERILLA REBEL TROOPS, FORDED SPRING RIVER NEARBY TO ATTACK FT. BLAIR.

Ferguson later said, "Mickey got to keep the money, but Barney made it look good on paper."[11]

Cat Mays got Willie started as a ballplayer; Piper Davis made him into a *professional* ballplayer. Precisely when that process started isn't clear. In Mays's 1988 memoir, he said that, in 1947, "my education as a baseball player took on a new dimension under Piper. He taught me two key lessons, one about fielding and the other about hitting."[12] Davis taught him that when playing the outfield he should charge a ball hit through the infield, especially with a runner on second base; this would enable him to get momentum on throws to home. He told Willie not to try to throw the ball home on a line but to bounce it, as the ball would pick up speed when it skipped off the ground. Mays soon found that his enormous hands made it easier for him than most other outfielders to bare-hand a ball hit on the ground, which saved him a split second in firing home. The hitting tip Davis gave Willie helped correct his stance: turn more toward the pitcher and stand straighter, Davis said, instead of turning his shoulder toward home plate when he crouched down. He could see the ball better by opening up his batting stance.

Piper also gave Willie some solid off-field advice: to always dress well and take pride in his appearance (which he demanded of all his players). "If you're looking good," he told his young charge, "the girls will look at you. And if you're looking decent, you don't have to talk as much."[13]

But when exactly did Piper teach Willie these things? Though Piper knew Willie through his association with Cat, there is no recorded evidence that he worked with him before Willie joined the Black Barons — and when was that? To hear Mays tell the story, the process began when he bumped into Piper at a Chattanooga hotel in 1947. But in a 1987 interview, Piper Davis told me, "I first coached Willie in 1948 when he was just seventeen. I'd already heard about him from the guys who had played with him and against him in pick-up ballgames. It was in Chattanooga that I met him, and he was still in high school."[14]

Whose memory was faulty — Willie's or Piper's? James Hirsch, Mays's most recent and most comprehensive biographer, places the momentous Chattanooga meeting in 1948. Accepting the year as 1948 makes it easier to piece the rest of the story together.

Sometime in the summer of 1948, the Black Barons were in Chattanooga for a game with the Black Lookouts.* While leaving the Martin Hotel for the ballpark, Piper saw a familiar young face. "Boy," he said, startled to see Cat Mays's boy Willie, who had just finished tenth grade, in the hotel lobby, "what are you doing up here?" "Playing for the Grays," Willie told him. That got Piper angry. "You know, if they catch you playing out here you won't be able to play high-school sports." Willie told Piper he didn't care. While his friends and classmates were sweating it out with part-time summer jobs making perhaps $8 or at best $10 a week, "I was making about a hundred dollars a month."[15]

Or at least that's the version Willie told his biographers for many years, but the story doesn't add up. The team Willie claimed to be playing for, the Fairfield Gray Sox, did play out of town occasionally, but they were a community sandlot team. And Willie wasn't staying at the Martin Hotel on a sandlot team's pass-the-hat change. Nor would Piper Davis have cared if Willie was just playing sandlot ball.

But if he wasn't playing for a sandlot team, what was Willie doing in Chattanooga? James Hirsch doesn't mention Willie's playing for the Gray Sox in the summer of 1948, but says Mays was playing for Beck Shepherd's semipro Chattanooga Choo-Choos. The Choo-Choos were part of the Negro Southern League, definitely a cut above sandlot ball, although not up to the level of the Black Barons' Negro American League. Choo-Choos players weren't paid regularly,

---

* Most teams in the Negro American League were named after the white team in their city; Birmingham's white team was the Barons, the black team the Black Barons. In Atlanta, the Southern Association's white team was the Crackers, the NAL team the Black Crackers. In Chattanooga it was the Lookouts and the Black Lookouts.

but the team did sell tickets, and the players were paid through a combination of gate receipts and pass-the-hat. Playing for a team at that level would almost certainly have ended the seventeen-year-old's amateur status if anyone back in Birmingham heard about it. If so — and that explanation is the only one that fits all the known facts — then Willie was fibbing to Piper Davis, and Davis knew it.

The truly odd thing is that Willie would maintain the lie long after high school. In fact, he maintained it for decades, telling journalists and biographers that he was in Chattanooga playing for a traveling sandlot team when in fact he was playing semipro ball. As late as 1988, he was still telling it to Lou Sahadi — as if it was still important to him that Piper, who died shortly before the book came out, never know he had lied to him.

Willie was most certainly making good money playing ball, but he wasn't being truthful as to how he was doing it. He didn't want to offend his teachers and friends at Fairfield Industrial, but between high school football and basketball and semipro baseball, it was no contest. He liked being the center of attention at high school football and basketball games, but the money he made playing baseball made him even more the center of attention at school. He could dress a little sharper, always had money for dates, and was happy to lend a dollar here or there to a pal in need.

Willie Mays had known Piper Davis for years and idolized him. Piper had played with Willie's dad on the TCI's industrial league team and was at least as good as Kitty Cat — some thought Davis was even better. Davis, after all, was everything Willie hoped to be — a professional baseball player and a big local celebrity. And now the coming of Jackie Robinson had opened Willie's eyes to the possibility of becoming a great deal more than that. On that day in Chattanooga when Piper saw the teenager in the hotel lobby, Willie told Piper that he wanted to be a Black Baron, that it was something he had dreamed of his whole life. Piper nodded and smiled, assuming that the sight of Willie wearing the "B" cap of the Birmingham Black Barons was inevitable. (The Black Barons' distinctive Triple-B in old English letters, prized by Negro League fans today, was adopted by the team in 1948.)

All through his professional life, Willie had extraordinarily good luck. His association with Piper Davis was a case in point; a better mentor and a better manager could not have been found. Davis knew a blue-chipper when he saw one, but he was wary of giving Willie a tryout because he didn't want to draw flak for recruiting a high school student. A week after Piper bumped into Willie in Chattanooga, he saw him again in Atlanta, where the Black Barons were scheduled to play the Black Crackers. *Well*, thought Davis, *that settles it. Cat and Willie have decided that Willie's going to make money playing baseball whether his school approves or not.* Piper told Willie to have Cat call him when he got back to Birmingham.

Cat called Piper, who told him there had to be one hard-and-fast rule: if Willie played for the Black Barons, he had to drop high school sports. Davis told Willie to be at Rickwood Field at noon the next Sunday, July 4, when the Black Barons were scheduled to play a doubleheader against the Cleveland Buckeyes. Willie got there half an hour early. There were no new uniforms. He was given a worn jersey and pants. He tried them on in the clubhouse and found that they were too big, but thought better of complaining. On the back was a number that would become the answer to a popular trivia question: 21, Willie Mays's first number in professional baseball.

Willie had no way of knowing that he was lucky to even be allowed to dress in the clubhouse. That season, Barons owner Gus Jebeles had brought in Eddie Glennon, a dynamic Irishman from Philadelphia, to be the team's general manager. Glennon understood that integration was good for baseball and instituted a policy for treating the Black Barons with respect — a policy that included allowing them to change in the clubhouse. Prior to Glennon, the Black Barons had to change at home, in hotels, or on the team bus on the way to and from the ballpark.

A jittery Willie took ribbing from the older players (and they were all older, many as much as ten to twelve years older). Black veterans, like their white counterparts, loved to tease rookies. They knocked his cap off his head and flung his glove around the clubhouse and on the field. (Unlike Mickey, Willie had no trained dog to do his fetching.) In his first Negro League game, he never left the bench, nor did he say a word to anyone. Davis gave him no special attention except to put a hand on his shoulder in the first inning and tell him to watch what was going on. The team's spirits were high after a victory in the first game, but Willie sat there, glum and silent, wondering when he would be a part of it all. A half hour before the second game, as the players sat in the clubhouse drinking sodas from ice-filled coolers, Davis quietly put his hand on Willie's shoulder and told him he'd be starting. Nearly sixty years later, Mays sat in Rickwood Field and described to me how he felt: "A few months earlier my dad had said to Piper Davis, 'Willie wants to be Joe DiMaggio, but he hasn't learned to hit a curve ball.' Piper just smiled and said, 'Oh, he'll learn.' After Piper told me I was going to play, I sat there thinking to myself, 'Well, now we're going to see if I can hit a curve ball.' "[16]

When one of the veterans discovered that "that little boy" would be starting in left field, he openly questioned Piper's judgment; Davis quietly asserted his authority and told him that Willie would be starting.

Mays's first at-bat as a professional was against Chet Brewer, an experienced right-hander who began his career with the Kansas City Monarchs in 1925 at age seventeen — exactly Willie's age as he stood in the batter's box. Mays, in his first professional game, wasn't overwhelming. He was merely trying to get good wood on the ball and establish his swing against more experienced pitchers. He got two hits in his first game, both singles — one an opposite-field blooper, the other a line drive. Piper Davis was justified in front of his team. After the game, he offered Willie the only contract he would get before becoming the property of the New York Giants — a handshake from Piper Davis and an agreement to pay him $250 a month plus a $50 bonus for every month he hit over .300. Willie failed to earn that bonus, but soon that would be irrelevant.

Although Mays was, as Piper Davis liked to say, "the greatest natural ballplayer I've ever seen," what his father had told Davis turned out not to be a joke. Willie couldn't hit a curveball. He would bat just .262 in twenty-eight games for the Black Barons that season. No one expected much more; in fact, young Mays delivered much more than was anticipated. No one thought Willie would hit professional pitching right away. As his teammate Jimmy Zapp put it, "No one is born with the ability to hit a curveball. That comes with experience."[17]

Willie played with a flare and exuberance that was unusual even for a league where entertainment was essential to survival. The Negro Leagues received no financial help from the major leagues, nor were their games, except for a few teams in big cities, broadcast on radio. They survived on ticket sales, which meant that baseball wasn't just a matter of winning, it was a matter of winning while looking good. Willie had not yet mastered the technique of running out from under his cap, and he wouldn't start using his signature basket catch until years later when he was in the Army. But fans loved the way he lunged into a pitch and the force with which his huge wrists and powerful forearms could send line drives into the outfield gaps.

Though he was not yet an accomplished base stealer, his wide sweeping turns at first base and his daring when going from first to third, or second to home, ignited crowds. In the field, the hours of shagging fly balls paid off. Piper had no intention of letting such a magnificent arm go idle in the infield; he put Willie in left, where he seemed to cover both his position and a large chunk of center field as well, and the fans held their breath in anticipation when he zoned in on a fly ball and a runner on third prepared to tag up.

Things went smoothly with the Black Barons until school started in the early fall. No one had taken notice of Willie's having played ball for pass-the-hat money, nor had anyone found out about his brief foray into semipro ball. (It's possible that, like many other black play-

Mickey at age fourteen.
His father, Mutt, had already
been making him practice
his baseball skills for years.
PERSONAL COLLECTION OF THE
MANTLE FAMILY

Thirteen-year-old Willie in 1944.
Even at this age he was playing
ball with his father's industrial
league pals. BIRMINGHAM PUBLIC
LIBRARY

Fairfield, Alabama, the town where Willie went to school, was a planned
community for employees of U.S. Steel. BIRMINGHAM PUBLIC LIBRARY

Mickey, right, stands with his father, Mutt, on the porch of the Mantle family home at 319 North Quincy Street in Commerce. This was taken after the 1950 season; the house had been spruced up a bit with money Mickey brought home from playing for Joplin. NATIONAL BASEBALL HALL OF FAME, COOPERSTOWN, N.Y.

Jackie Robinson once referred to Willie's boyhood home in Westfield, Alabama, as "clapboard and windblown." Actually, it wasn't bad—better-looking, in fact, than the Mantles' home in Oklahoma. BIRMINGHAM PUBLIC LIBRARY

Mickey the Joplin Miner in 1950, playing Class C ball. Between the time this photo was taken and Mickey's debut with the Yankees the following year, he put on perhaps twenty pounds of hard muscle. CORBIS

Above left: Willie at age seventeen in 1948, playing for the Birmingham Barons of the Negro League. MEMPHIS AND SHELBY COUNTY ROOM, MEMPHIS PUBLIC LIBRARY & INFORMATION CENTER. *Right:* Willie early in 1951 with the Minneapolis Millers, just before he was called up to the New York Giants. Later in the season, Mickey played in Minneapolis and was told of the amazing young black ballplayer who had been there just a few months earlier. SPORT MEDIA GROUP

SUCH A ONE IS *Willie*

This caricature of Willie appeared in the *Minneapolis Tribune* the day after it was announced that Mays had been called up to the parent team in New York. Willie was such a hit in the Twin Cities that there was an uproar among the fans when they learned he was leaving. Giants owner Horace Stoneham took out an ad in the paper apologizing to them but also reminding them, "It would be most unfair to deprive him of the opportunity he earned with his play."

ARTIST: MURRAY OLDERMAN

Mickey with Tom Greenwade. Perhaps to avoid friction, Mickey perpetuated the myth that Greenwade "discovered" him. What Greenwade actually did was cheat the Mantle family out of thousands of dollars that Mickey should have received in bonus money.

PHOTOGRAPHER UNKNOWN

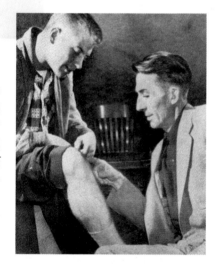

"Taste, taste. You'll hit homers with this." Hank Bauer introduces nineteen-year-old Mickey to the glories of New York delicatessen food at the Stage Deli. Bauer and Mickey shared an apartment above the legendary deli. The server is co-owner Max Asnas.

ERNEST SISTO/NEW YORK TIMES/REDUX

One of the most famous photos of Willie Mays ever taken, playing stickball with kids in the streets of Harlem. Mickey also played stickball in the street with kids, but there were no cameras around to preserve the moment.

NATIONAL BASEBALL HALL OF FAME, COOPERSTOWN, N.Y.

"And over there's where Ted Williams hit one ten rows deep . . ." Casey shows Mickey the fine points of Griffith Stadium in Washington on Mickey's first road trip. SPORT MEDIA GROUP

Leo Durocher shows his new center fielder around Shibe Park in Philadelphia. Leo would owe his posthumous 1994 election to the Hall of Fame in large part to having managed Willie Mays.

A River Ran Between Them. Old Yankee Stadium is on the right; the Polo Grounds, the home of the Giants and later the expansion New York Mets, on the left. From the grandstands of the Polo Grounds you could see Yankee Stadium in the distance.

Mickey and Willie met before Game 1 of the 1951 World Series at Yankee Stadium. Some unknown photographer thought to ask the two young New York phenoms to pose together.

"What's the matter, kid?" Joe DiMaggio asks his fallen rookie teammate. In the first game of the 1951 Series, Willie Mays lofted a fly ball into right-center. Mickey stepped on an open drainpipe as he raced for the ball and tore up a knee that had already been ravaged by osteomyelitis. An injury caused by a negligent groundskeeper—or Willie Mays?—prevented Mickey from being the greatest player who ever lived. SPORT MEDIA GROUP

Mickey returned to the zinc mines of Commerce after the 1951 season. That's Mutt to the left; in the center, also wearing a miner's helmet, is Cliff Mapes, who had worn number 7 before Mickey in the Yankees lineup. It isn't known what Mapes was doing in Commerce. CORBIS/BETTMANN

Willie points out his name on the bat to his father, William Howard "Cat" Mays. Manager Herman Franks is in the middle. AP/WIDE WORLD PHOTOS

Top: Perhaps no ballplayer had an easier time in military service during the Korean War than Willie. He would later admit he wasn't particularly proud of his nearly two years in uniform, most of it spent playing baseball. Mantle, meanwhile, was vilified by fans and press for having been rejected for service. SPORT MEDIA GROUP

Center: The Mantle boys play cards while Mutt, seated, and Lovell look on. Apparently sister Barbara was not invited. SPORT MEDIA GROUP

Bottom: Willie's stepbrothers and stepsisters back in Fairfield admire a gift from Willie—a new record player. Willie's mother, Annie, is absent from the picture, suggesting that it might have been taken after her death in 1953. INTERNATIONAL NEWS PHOTOS/CORBIS

ers, Willie had used aliases while playing on the road.) The Black Barons, though, weren't just another team. They were the pride of black Birmingham, the best-known black sports team in the entire South. There was no way Willie could play for them without detection. "My playing for the Barons," he said in his memoir, "created an uproar at Fairfield Industrial. The principal, E. J. Oliver,* didn't like it at all — and neither did my classmates. They felt I was letting them down. I was not permitted to play any high-school athletics while I was getting paid by the Barons. The kids at school felt I had sold them out, but look at the chance I had been given — to play baseball, and to get paid for doing it."[18]

Though some would characterize his actions as selfish, Mays was absolutely correct. A chance like the one he'd been given — a chance he had earned — came along once in a lifetime. Willie did not owe Fairfield Industrial or anyone else the benefit of his athletic talent and hard work.

Principal Oliver called a meeting with Cat and Aunt Sarah. Oliver, who had graduated from the Tuskegee Institute with honors, was adamant on the subjects of tradition, discipline, and the value of education, but he was also a very practical man, and he had no intention of killing a golden calf. He wanted to hear from Willie's guardians that Willie was serious about receiving his diploma. That established, a deal was worked out: Willie could not travel with the Black Barons, but would be allowed to play in home games; in return — and this was really what Oliver was aiming for — Willie would play football, the big revenue sport in every Alabama high school, white and black.

And so, with the deal worked out between Willie's father and Fairfield Industrial, the last obstacle that could have kept Willie Mays from becoming the greatest all-around baseball player in history was removed. Even the restrictions that Principal Oliver had demanded on road travel would soon be overlooked. It was as if fate itself was rooting for Willie Mays.

---

* In two earlier memoirs, Willie refers to his principal as E. T. Oliver.

5

A Dream Come True

While Willie Mays was becoming a professional, Mickey Mantle was scraping by. Early one morning after a Whiz Kids game, Mickey and Nick Ferguson bumped into a couple of teammates, Rex Heavin and his brother Charlie (aka "Frog"), who were poking around under the wooden grandstands looking for the same thing: loot. The word took in a lot of territory. It could be baseballs that had not been recovered by ball shaggers (Barney would pay up to 50 cents for each usable ball brought back to him), cans or bottles that could be returned for two-cent deposits, loose change that had fallen from spectators' pockets (a "jitney," as a nickel was called, was highly prized), or anything else that might be of value. On one scavenger hunt a new Rawlings glove was found, on another a $5 bill. When one of the boys was hard up, another was happy to loan him a jitney or two. Within a year, Mickey would be loaning out jitneys and have enough left over to buy himself a car.

During a break near the end of the 1948 Whiz Kids season, Mutt took Mickey and Nick to a tryout camp for the St. Louis Browns in Pittsburgh, Kansas. After the long drive, the Oklahomans were hugely disappointed when it rained all day. What Mickey could not know at the time was that he had been dealt a major break: given the Browns' desperation, they might have signed the soon-to-be seventeen-year-old on the spot and tied him up for the rest of his major league career.

The 1948 Whiz Kids were loaded. One group of players formed a virtual team within a team — Barney called them the Barney Barnett All-Stars. Barney matched them against the best teams he could find, including semipro clubs and, on some occasions, college teams. In a game against Northeastern Oklahoma Junior College, Mickey, hitting against a right-handed pitcher named Max Buzzard, a prospect of the New York Yankees, belted a long home run over the right-field wall in the first inning. In the third inning, he came up to bat again against Buzzard, this time hitting from the right side. (Mutt had advised Mickey to occasionally bat right-handed against right-handed pitchers if only to keep in practice, there being so few southpaws around.) He drove it well over the left-field wall.

These were good times for Mickey. He was maturing quickly, and his eye-hand coordination was so good that he was a match for even older, experienced pitchers.

Willie found the pitchers in his league a little tougher. For one thing, Negro League pitchers were meaner. They had to be — they were professionals. Pitchers were far less likely to knock hitters down at a college or semipro level — they simply weren't as hungry as the professionals, especially black professionals.

Chet Brewer, for instance. Willie had gotten two hits off the right-hander in his first game with the Black Barons, and Brewer got his revenge when he faced Willie again. Making no pretense of brushing him back, Brewer simply fired a fastball right into Mays's left arm. The teenager crumpled to the ground; he would recall that as the hardest he had ever been hit up to that time. Piper Davis knew this was a situation Willie would have to learn to deal with as he moved on up, especially in the big leagues. Kneeling down in the batter's box, he found his young prodigy on the verge of tears. He quietly asked Willie if he could see first base. Willie said yes; Piper asked him to point to it, which Willie did. Piper then told him to go there, steal second, and then third. Willie rattled Brewer by proceeding to do exactly as his manager had told him. He then scored on a fly ball. When he returned to the dugout, Davis told him *that's* how you handle a pitcher.

Even Piper Davis, though, couldn't prepare Willie for the great Satchel Paige. In a game against Paige's Kansas City Monarchs, Mays dazzled the crowd by throwing out two base runners, one at third base and another at home. The Monarchs' manager, Buck O'Neil, decided he'd seen enough; on a single to center field, he held up the runner at third, yelling for all to hear, "Whoa, whoa, that man's got a shotgun!"[1] But that's not what Willie remembered best about that game. Like every other player in the Negro Leagues, he regarded Satchel as a walking legend: "The man was the most interesting player I had ever come up against. He stood six-four"—actually, most accounts list Paige at about six-five—"and weighed about 170 pounds. . . . He was about 40 when the Indians brought him up as a rookie [in 1948], but he was no rookie to me. He showed me the darnedest stuff I ever saw, along with some of the screwiest motions and combinations of different speeds. Old Satchel could really drive you crazy."[2]

Paige's famous arsenal, in addition to a multispeed fastball, included a screwball, a knuckleball, and several kinds of curves, any one of which might be thrown from his famous "hesitation pitch" windup: he would stop with his foot high in the air and keep the batter waiting, and then, as Mays remembered, the ball would suddenly appear and the batter would be swinging well in front of it.

Satchel thought that an age advantage of nearly a quarter of a century would allow him to sneak a fastball by Willie the first time up. Mays surprised him, smashing a double down the left-field line. While Willie was dusting himself off at second base, Paige took several steps toward him and said to the bewildered teenager, "That's it, kid." What he meant was: no more fastballs. Willie recalled that Paige got him out the next time on curveballs. Biographers before and after would say that those were the only two times the two Hall of Famers faced each other; Mays remembered facing Satchel two other times. Whoever is right, after that first double Willie Mays never got another hit off Satchel Paige.

For Negro League veterans, as most of the Black Barons were, baseball was closer to hard work than fun. To Willie, even during the toughest times, it was an adventure. When leaving Birmingham, the bus would often pick the players up in front of Bob's Savoy Café. In his first memoir, *Born to Play Ball*, Willie recalled that Piper Davis, whatever his relationship with the players, was a stickler for professionalism: the bus waited five minutes and then left, whether you were on it or not. Once Willie got so involved in a pool match that he forgot what time it was, and when he heard the final horn, he threw down his pool cue and came running out of the café. "Hey, you can't leave me behind!" he shouted. "I'm a pro ballplayer!" In another version of the story, Willie missed the bus and had to grab a cab and catch up with the team a few miles out of town. Both versions end with Willie learning the same lesson: he never missed the team bus again.

The team bus was no bargain. It had no air conditioning and seated just twenty-two people, which at least made it big enough to carry the entire team: the Black Barons, like most Negro League teams, usually had just sixteen players. This is why so many of them were skilled at different positions and in different aspects of the game. There were practically no specialists, no platoon players, no utility infielders, no closers. Every player knew every other player intimately; to talk to the surviving players today is to experience a world of solidarity unknown to modern athletes.

Georgia-born Bill Greason, a World War II combat veteran and for the last fifty years a respected pastor in Birmingham, recalled it this way: "Road travel was hot and usually uncomfortable — most guys brought their equipment and suitcases onto the bus. The food wasn't always good because you had to take what you could find at midnight when you were on the road, and you couldn't always find places that would serve blacks, even through the back door of the restaurant or hotel." Sometimes the players were forced to eat out of paper bags or stop at a grocery store for bread and sandwich provisions. "And there were a lot of white people around who still didn't know that black men had fought in the war. That's the kind of life it was in 1948. But it was all made tolerable by the fact that the baseball was good and that you were playing it with men who you knew well and respected, and you were playing it for people who really appreciated the game and the fact that you had come so far to play for them."

For Willie, the long bus rides "gave me a chance to learn, and to dream about big-league baseball. All the guys on the bus had played against the big names and had been in the big stadiums. Johnny Britton, our third baseman, would always take a newspaper with him and study the sports pages. He would keep me up to date on what my hero, DiMaggio, was doing."[3]

On the road they played in different cities nearly every night: in Kansas City, home of their hated rivals, the Monarchs, in all the major cities of the South — Atlanta, Memphis, Nashville, Little Rock, and New Orleans, a big favorite as there were always good places to eat — and even in Chicago and New York. While Mickey was playing in sandlots and, if he was lucky, in minor league ballparks in Oklahoma, Kansas, and Missouri, Willie was getting the big league view in Chicago's Comiskey Park and, on one thrilling trip, the Polo Grounds in Harlem. The old Black Barons bus huffed and puffed, but got the job done.

On a trip to St. Louis, Willie and some teammates decided to go to Sportsman's Park to see Jackie Robinson and the Brooklyn Dodgers play the Cardinals, and Willie got a firsthand glimpse of one of Mickey's idols, Stan Musial. Willie, then a professional with the Birmingham Black Barons, could have been one of the black patrons standing in line to purchase tickets on the morning Mickey and his Whiz Kid pals showed up at Sportsman's Park to see the game.

In 1958, while riding a bus from New York to Syracuse, where Mickey Mantle's All-Stars would play a barnstorming game against Willie Mays's All-Stars, Mickey and Willie would joke about who had to play under the worse conditions and whose team bus, the Black Barons' or the one Mickey's Joplin Miners rode in, was tougher to ride in. "To hear them," recalled Rich Ashburn, the Phillies' All-Star outfielder who played on Willie's team, "you'd think they both had to get out and push the buses down the road themselves."*[4] (Actually, on more than one occasion, both Mickey and Willie *did* have to push buses down backcountry roads.) Mickey's team, though, had it over Willie's in one very important way: when they stopped at a restaurant, the team got out to eat instead of having to bring food out the back door and eat on the bus.

How good were the 1948 Black Barons? They had four players — shortstop Artie Wilson, who batted .402 for the season and won his second NAL batting title, pitcher Bill Greason, Piper Davis, and Willie Mays — who were signed by the big leagues. As Piper suspected, he, Greason, and Wilson, as well as several other Negro League veterans, were signed merely as window dressing to make it look as if major league teams were willing to integrate. None of them ever got a fair shot; Wilson, well over thirty by the time he got to play in the minor leagues, only got a brief shot in the bigs with the New York Giants.

The Black Barons went on to win the Negro American League pennant that year by beating Buck O'Neil's Kansas City Monarchs, four games to three. The Monarchs featured such stars as Luke Easter, a classic case of the waste of Negro League talent. In 1949,

---

*Willie neglected to mention to Mickey that in 1949 the Black Barons, having won the Negro American League pennant the year before, had made enough money to buy a new bus with air conditioning and reclining seats.

when he was thirty-four, he got his big league shot with the Cleveland Indians, playing in 21 games that year. He would play just 470 games with the Indians over the next five seasons, posting some terrific numbers: in 1950 he had 28 home runs and drove in 107 runs. The next season he hit 27 home runs and 103 RBIs, and 31 and 97, respectively, the year after that. Given his level of performance in his midthirties, it's likely that Easter would have been All-Star and possibly Hall of Fame material had he had a chance to play in the majors while in his physical prime. As much could be said for Artie Wilson and possibly Bill Greason as well.

Overall, Mays thought the talent level in the Negro Leagues in the short time he played there was at least on par with Triple-A in what Piper Davis referred to as "white folks' ball."

Willie made a big contribution to the pennant series against the Monarchs in Game 2, singling home the tying run in the ninth inning. The Barons won in the eleventh. In the World Series, though, against the Negro National League champion Homestead Grays, the Barons again played their role of the Brooklyn Dodgers to the Grays' New York Yankees. The Grays had beaten the Black Barons in 1942 and 1943 and won the 1948 series four games to one. Once again, Willie's contributions were few but memorable. In Game 2, he crashed into the center-field fence to take away an extra-base hit; he also nailed Buck O'Neil at second base on a terrific one-hop throw. Then, with two out in the ninth, he singled up the middle to win the game in his team's only victory.

But there was an autumnal flavor to the Negro League postseason that year. Integration was coming to Major League Baseball — and with it the end of black baseball. The previous year, eleven weeks after Jackie Robinson broke baseball's color barrier with the Dodgers, Larry Doby had become the first black player in the American League. Satchel Paige, Roy Campanella, and Monte Irvin — future Hall of Famers all — were headed for the big leagues, and interest in the Negro Leagues would soon decline with a swiftness that amazed those who had fought so hard for organized black ball. Over the coming years, the attention of black America shifted dramatically from the Negro Leagues to the major leagues; in many black newspapers the only question of interest regarding the major stars became how soon they would be playing in the American and National Leagues. Franchises folded without their biggest gate attractions; some leagues went to a playoff system in which the winner of the first half of the season played the winner of the second half, but it was no substitute for the Black Barons playing the Kansas City Monarchs.* Within a decade, all traces of the once-proud Negro Leagues had vanished. The year 1948 marked the last Negro League World Series, and within three years the fabled Homestead Grays, the proudest name in the Negro Leagues, would cease to exist.

As the Negro Leagues declined, their hottest young prospect blossomed. In 1949 Willie batted .311 in seventy-nine games and became one of the few remaining stars in the league. On June 1,† he finally assumed the position at which he would achieve baseball immortality. Norman Robinson, the Black Barons center fielder, broke his leg, and Piper immediately shifted Willie from left to center. When Robinson came back, Davis put him in left field and left Willie in center. "Willie can go get it, and Willie can bring it back," his manager was fond of saying. [5]

How good were the 1949 Whiz Kids? In late May, Mickey Mantle played his first game ever against black ballplayers at Baxter Springs. The *Joplin Globe* reported: "Baxter Boys Defeat Coffeyville Boosters, a Negro Team, 13–6."[6] The Boosters were a semipro pickup team that included several Negro League veterans, but sadly, the names of the team members were never recorded. Presumably there

---

* Most black ball historians are in agreement that fans considered the Negro League World Series second in importance to the All-Star Games, where they could see the best players from all over the country in a single game.

† In his 1988 autobiography, Mays said this occurred in 1948, but that would have been impossible, as he did not make his Birmingham Black Barons debut until July 4 of that year.

were several players whom Willie Mays had played against on the road with the Black Barons. Three days after the game in Baxter Springs, the Whiz Kids played the Boosters again at Forest Park and won 8–2. The *Coffeyville Daily Journal* reported that "Mantle, the slickest looking kid ballplayer seen on the local pond in the post-war era, slashed a line drive home run down the right field line in the seventh."[7] John G. Hall, the authoritative historian of the KOM League, remarks that "the two wins came as a shock to all baseball experts in Southeast Kansas, who hadn't thought the Whiz Kids were that good."[8]

In later years, stories about the men who claimed to have discovered Mickey Mantle and Willie Mays would practically become a light industry. Most of them were nonsense. Mickey and Willie, the two most naturally talented players of their time, were so well coached and prepared that by the time they were in their late teens it wasn't a question of *who* would discover them but *when*. One might just as well say that Mutt Mantle and Cat Mays "discovered" their sons; one might just as well say that Mickey and Willie discovered themselves.

In Mickey's case, at least one thing can be stated with certainty: the popular story that Tom Greenwade discovered him is false. All Greenwade did was sign him, and for a great deal less money than Mickey could have gotten from other scouts working for other organizations.*

That the Greenwade-Mantle myth has lasted so long can be attributed in large part to Mickey himself. In his 1987 memoir, he said: "Then came a significant event, a milestone in my life. In 1948, at the age of seventeen, my sole ambition was to play professional ball. The where and how meant little, only the chance. Well, there's such a thing as luck, and some of it rubbed off on me when Tom Greenwade came down the road from Springfield, Missouri, to scout prospects

---

* Greenwade had been a minor league manager and pitcher and had worked for both the St. Louis Browns and Brooklyn Dodgers, reporting to Branch Rickey in both organizations. Greenwade had some part in the signing of Roy Campanella and possibly Jackie Robinson from the Negro Leagues.

for the Yankee farm system. He was at the Baxter Springs ballpark, evaluating a kid named Billy Johnson, our third baseman. I wasn't on Greenwade's list, but whatever he saw in Billy, he apparently found something more to his liking after watching me switch-hit a couple of home runs into the river on one bounce."

Perhaps Mantle told the story this way because it was the way he had been reading it in magazine articles for years — some of them written by Greenwade himself. As Mickey recalled it, a cloud-burst interrupted the game, and during the delay his father brought Greenwade — "a really old guy with a nice friendly smile" — to meet him. "How would you like to play for the Yankees?" Greenwade asked. Mickey was speechless. Greenwade said he couldn't talk "officially" — Mickey's word — because he was still in high school, but told him not to sign with anyone else and he'd be back the day Mickey graduated. On the way home from the game, dreams of the St. Louis Cardinals vanished as an excited Mutt envisioned his oldest son playing in Yankee Stadium, walking in the footsteps of Babe Ruth (who was quite ill and would die within a few days of Greenwade's meeting with Mutt and Mickey), Lou Gehrig, and, perhaps most thrilling of all, Joe DiMaggio, the most famous ballplayer at the time. "No question," said Mutt, "we oughta wait on Greenwade."[9]

The months, however, dragged on with no word from Green-wade. It's possible that father and son did not fully understand that there were rules that strictly prohibited an agent or representative of a professional team from even approaching a high school student. Anyone caught in violation of the rules would automatically lose all negotiating rights with the prospect. In fact, Greenwade was jeopardizing his position just by shaking hands with Mickey at the Baxter Springs park. Was Greenwade assuming that Mutt was so desperate to get a professional contract for his son that he would be blinded by the dream of Yankee pinstripes? What followed would indicate that was the case.

However, long before Greenwade saw Mantle at Baxter Springs, Barney Barnett had been pushing buttons on all his connections.

Several scouts had dropped by to see Mickey, but none of them had been terribly impressed. Why exactly? The most obvious reason is that Mickey was just sixteen at the time. Another is that they saw him playing out of position. By the time he was sixteen, Willie Mays had decided that center field would be his position; one wonders how good a center fielder Mantle might have been had he made a similar decision. In 1947 he simply did not have the footwork or agility to be a middle infielder; in fact, he never would.

The scouts who saw him play simply did not have the imagination to see that Mantle was a naturally gifted outfielder. And there was another reason, one that would cloud the perception of Mickey's ability throughout his career: he struck out a lot, too much by the standards of the great stars of his day. Joe DiMaggio, for instance, struck out just twenty-four times in 1946 and thirty-two times in 1947. In contrast, Mantle would, when he reached the major leagues, sometimes strike out that many times *per month*. What no one was paying close attention to in 1947 (and indeed would not throughout Mickey's career) was how often he managed to reach base despite those strikeouts and how few times he grounded into double plays.

One scout, a man named "Runt" Marr who worked for the Cardinals organization, had talked with Mutt and Mickey, thus breaking all existing rules, but shied away on the question of bonus money. He told father and son he'd get back to them, but they never heard from him again.

A scout whom Mantle did impress was Hugh Alexander, who lived in Oklahoma City and worked for the Cleveland Indians. Alexander had never been much of a player — his entire career was seven games for the Indians in 1937 — but he was a superb judge of talent and made his name in Oklahoma by signing Allie "Big Chief" Reynolds, a legend in the state who became a mainstay in the Yankees' five consecutive pennant winners from 1949 to 1953. "Uncle Hughie," as he was called, drove over to Commerce on a tip, probably from Barnett, and did the right thing: he checked in with Mickey's high school principal, Bentley Baker. But for some reason that has never been discovered, Baker discouraged Alexander, telling him that Commerce High did not have a baseball team for Mickey to play on.

This was not true, of course, though Mickey spent very little time with the team the school did have. Baker certainly knew of Mickey's incredible athletic ability on the football field and basketball court, and he had read in the local papers about Mantle's growing reputation as a sandlot baseball player. Further, Principal Baker told the scout that Mickey had bad legs from an injury sustained during football practice — true to a point, but Mantle had recovered from that, and Baker knew it. Alexander drove back to Oklahoma City in a funk. In later years, he would wonder why Mickey's high school principal had intentionally steered him away.

Why, in fact, did Baker sabotage Mickey's chance with a professional scout? Perhaps like Willie's Principal Oliver at Fairfield Industrial, Baker was protecting what he thought were his school's best interests. Oliver had made a deal with the Birmingham Black Barons that allowed Willie to be paid for playing baseball and still play other sports for the school — just not baseball, which Willie didn't want to play for the school anyway. If, though, a professional baseball scout had signed Mickey, Baker would have lost him entirely. The rules were lax in black high schools, but the line between amateur and professional was more strictly enforced in white high schools. Had Mickey signed a pro contract, he would have been ineligible to participate in the school's biggest revenue-producing sport, football.

The date of Mickey's high school graduation was May 27, but he did not attend — Baker gave him permission to skip the commencement exercises so he could play a game with the Whiz Kids that Greenwade would attend. This suggests yet another reason that Baker had discouraged Alexander, namely, some sort of arrangement he had with Greenwade. Sometime between Greenwade's meeting Mutt and Mickey in 1948 and the boy's 1949 commencement, Greenwade, in defiance of the rules, must have been in touch. Apparently, Greenwade was impressed enough by what he saw on the twenty-seventh to invite father and son to a Yankee tryout camp in Branson, Missouri, sometime in June.

Whatever Mickey's shortcomings when major league scouts first saw him as a sixteen-year-old, by 1949 he was so impressive that by all rights there should have been a swarm of scouts at his commencement, bidding for his services. Yet, somehow, some way, by May 27 all possible competition from major league teams had vanished, and the Yankees had a clear path. Despite all Barney Barnett's major league contacts and all his players who had signed contracts for other major league farm systems, no other scout showed up to talk to Mickey, Barney's crown jewel, on the day he was eligible.

Surely the Mantles knew a lot more about Greenwade's machinations than they ever told. Why didn't Mickey say more about the peculiar circumstances of his signing in his later books? Possibly because he didn't want to embarrass Greenwade, who, by the time he died in 1986 (the year Mickey was working on his first memoir with Herb Gluck), had built much of his reputation around discovering the rough diamond from the Oklahoma sticks.

What has never been explained in Greenwade's account is how Lee MacPhail, the general manager of the Yankees' Triple-A farm team in Kansas City — and also their Midwest farm director* — would have authorized a contract for Mantle and given Greenwade money to take the Mantles to Branson if Greenwade had seen so little of Mickey on the field. According to researcher John Hall, the man who tipped Greenwade about Mantle was Johnny Sturm, a former Yankee player turned minor league manager. Sturm was a mere footnote in the history of the Yankees; he didn't make it to the major leagues until 1941, when he was twenty-five years old, and he got into 124 games and batted just .239. The war and military service ended his hopes of being a career professional ballplayer, but he knew

---

* Also son of Yankees team president Larry MacPhail, who was fired — or quit, according to which source you read — for a drunken display at the team party after the Yankees won the 1947 World Series.

talent and quickly got a job with the Yankees scouting the talent-rich Kansas-Oklahoma-Missouri area. He later said that he was aware of Mickey's enormous potential before Greenwade and certainly knew him by the time he became manager of the Joplin Miners in 1948.

According to his account, Sturm passed word to Mantle through a friend, an umpire who had seen Mickey play up close, that he would like him to try out for the minors early in the 1949 season. (Exactly why a minor league manager like Sturm could ask a high school player like Mickey to come to a tryout, and a major league scout such as Greenwade wasn't supposed to even approach him, isn't clear. But it was common practice in the Kansas-Oklahoma-Missouri region for high school kids to try out for minor league teams.) Mutt and Mickey drove to Joplin — Sturm seemed to remember that it was the Tuesday before Mickey's graduation — and Sturm watched while Mickey took practice swings from both the left and right side. Sturm recalled Mutt saying, "I have waited for this for seventeen years. It is a dream come true." (Sturm later said, "That is the gospel truth. Mutt uttered those words.") Sturm then tried Mickey out at shortstop and noticed that he fielded grounders in the hole with a slight limp. When Mickey's osteomyelitis was explained, Sturm suggested that he consider the outfield full-time, since base runners were bound to take advantage of his condition.

Unless Sturm was a liar, it's likely he was the one who spurred Lee MacPhail into moving aggressively to sign Mantle, and that MacPhail sent Greenwade to see Mickey at Sturm's passionate recommendation. Sturm also claimed that he urged Mickey to "hide out until I get my team [the Miners] back to Joplin." Sturm knew that a pal of his, Joe Becker, an ace scout for the Boston Red Sox, was hot on the trail after seeing Mickey play several games. He told MacPhail to move quickly before Boston beat them out. With a single move, Johnny Sturm quite possibly saved Mickey Mantle for the Yankees. If not for the combination of Sturm's fast thinking and Boston's sluggishness in yielding to the inevitability of integration, the Red Sox could have had Ted Williams, Willie Mays, and Mickey Mantle playing in the same outfield through the 1950s.

Johnny Sturm added one more not so minor detail that, if true, completely explodes the Greenwade myth. He said that his call to MacPhail angered Greenwade, who told him, "I've seen that kid, and he ain't worth a shit." Sturm claimed that he told Greenwade flat out that if he didn't sign Mantle, somebody else would — soon — and that the Yankees would be sorry.

In later accounts, particularly Greenwade's, Sturm's name was completely dropped from the Mantle signing story. Many years after the fact, Sturm wrote Mickey a letter reminding him about his part in Mickey's coming to the Yankees organization. He never got a reply, but in 1966, at Yankee Stadium, Mantle came up to him and said, "John, I owe you a hell of a lot."[10] But twenty years later, when working on his memoirs, Mickey had again forgotten Johnny Sturm, who went unmentioned and uncredited.

Greenwade did not sign Mantle on the night he graduated, as Mickey later said he remembered. In fact, it was not until June 13, after the tryout camp, that Mutt and Mickey signed the contract. One thing Mickey did remember, though, was that immediately after an exhibition game in Branson, Greenwade told Mutt that the Yankees were having doubts about "little Mickey," because of his inconsistent play at shortstop and lack of height. (The latter criticism is particularly silly, since Mantle was several inches taller than the man who was playing shortstop for the Yankees, Phil Rizzuto.) Despite what he told Mutt and Mickey, Greenwade would later tell *The Sporting News* that when he first saw Mantle, "I knew he was going to be one of the all-time greats. The first time I saw Mantle I knew how Paul Krichell felt when he first saw Lou Gehrig."[11]

Despite Mickey's shortcomings, Greenwade wanted to offer him a contract. After perhaps fifteen minutes of negotiation — and at this point father and son were desperate, as they had no other offers to fall back on — they agreed to $400 for Mickey to finish the season with the Yankees' minor league club at Independence, Kansas, with a signing bonus of $1,100. Mickey said that when the first figure was announced his father winced and truthfully pointed out that his son could make as much playing Sunday ball and working at the mines on weekdays — he would have earned 87½ cents an hour in the mines and perhaps $15 for every Sunday game. Shamelessly, Greenwade took out a pencil and pad of paper and pretended to be doing serious figuring. Wasn't that about $1,500, he asked? Mickey recalled the bonus as "the old ballyhoo — a foxy move to get around the possibility of having to offer a heckofa lot more."[12]

How much more? An idea of what Mantle might have been worth on the open market can be gauged by the case of Jim Baumer. Though it wasn't public knowledge at the time, just a couple of months before Mickey signed his contract, Baumer, also a power-hitting short-stop and an Oklahoma boy, signed with the Chicago White Sox for $50,000. Baumer played just eighteen games in the major leagues and batted .206. By that standard, a pretty good case could be made for Mickey Mantle as the greatest bargain in baseball history. And Willie Mays wasn't far behind.

By the end of summer, about two months after Mantle signed with the Yankees, the black baseball world from north to south, east to west, was alive with the news that a young black player from Birmingham named Willie Mays would soon be signed by a major league team. It's likely that there was even more buzz in major league circles for Willie than for Mickey. Several teams had gathered reports on Willie. The Boston Braves had *two* scouts with notebooks full of observations on Mays: Henry Jenkins, also the Braves' farm director, and Bill Maughn, who lived in Cullman, Alabama, about forty miles north of Birmingham. (An odd home base for a man who scouted black ballplayers, especially considering that as late as 1963, when the civil rights movement was in full swing, there was a sign at the town's entrance that read: NIGGER, DON'T LET THE SUN SET ON YOUR HEAD IN THIS TOWN.)

Maughn, though, not only liked Mays as a player, but would do him an enormous favor.

At Maughn's insistence, the Braves had petitioned the commissioner of baseball, Albert "Happy" Chandler, for permission to approach Willie while he was still in high school — after all, they reasoned, he was already playing for money. They were prepared to offer $7,500 to Black Barons owner Tom Hayes for Willie's contract. Maughn later told Jenkins — early in May, a few weeks before Willie graduated from Fairfield Industrial — that Willie was "the best stand-out prospect in the nation. When I say he could even pitch for my money, I am not fooling, as he is the fastest human being throwing from 60 feet, 6 inches that I have ever seen."[13]

Maughn ultimately decided not to offer Willie a deal, thanks to a report from yet another Braves scout who, after watching Mays play a doubleheader at Rickwood, concluded that he couldn't hit a major league curveball — a strange criticism of a kid who had not yet been given a chance to hit a curveball against a white minor leaguer. If the Braves' front office had listened to Maughn, Boston — or rather, Milwaukee, where the Braves would move in 1953, and then Atlanta, where they relocated in 1966 — might have enjoyed the spectacular fortune of having Willie Mays and Henry Aaron playing their entire careers alongside each other.

As it turned out, the Braves weren't the only Boston team interested in Mays. Eddie Glennon, the (white) Barons general manager, had seen Willie play several times at Rickwood Field and used his connection with the Red Sox — the Barons were part of their system — to let the parent team know about Willie. Despite Glennon's enthusiasm, the Red Sox balked after showing some initial interest. (Their best scout, George Digby, called Mays "the greatest prospect I ever saw."[14]) They had just signed Willie's Black Barons manager, Piper Davis, to a minor league contract, but Davis was never given a shot at the big leagues. It would be ten more years before the Red Sox fielded a black player.

It was at a high school all-star game in Atlanta that Braves scout Bill Maughn finally did Willie that huge favor: he told Eddie Montague, a scout for the New York Giants, what a fantastic prospect Willie was. New York was certainly the best city a young black man from the South could hope to play in, and in fact the Giants were one of the few in either league that would sign more than two black players at a time. (Giants owner Horace Stoneham had already authorized the signing of Hank Thompson and Monte Irvin.)

Montague and another Giants scout, Bill Harris, later went to Birmingham to check out the Black Barons' power-hitting first baseman, Alonzo Perry. Harris, whom Maughn had convinced to watch Willie's turn in batting practice, later said, "My eyes almost popped out of my head when I saw a young colored boy swing the bat with great speed and power and with hands that had the quickness of a young Joe Louis throwing punches." He also had occasion to see Mays throw during fielding practice and watch him run the bases during the game, after which he concluded, "This was the greatest young ballplayer I had ever seen in my life."[15]

Either Montague or Harris, or both, phoned Jack Schwarz, director of the Giants' farm system, and told him to forget about Perry. "Don't ask any questions," they told Schwarz. "Just go get [Mays]."

The most exciting possibility of all, the one that would quicken the blood of New York baseball fans for years whenever the subject was mentioned, was that the New York Yankees were also interested in Willie Mays. In 1949, well before Willie's graduation, GM George Weiss had sent a scout, Bill McCorry, to give him a report. According to Roger Kahn, who would soon be writing about both Mantle and Mays in New York, McCorry was about the last man who should have been sent to watch a black team in Alabama. He was disdainful of the Negro Leagues, regarding their players as not at the level of even the low white minor leagues. His evaluation was that Willie "couldn't hit a curve ball"—which was pretty much code for "young and black."[16]

In retrospect, one wonders why Weiss, who had no interest in signing black players and who acquired a few for the Yankees' minor league system only to trade them away, bothered to send a scout at all.

Nonetheless, what might have been is almost too glorious for Yankees fans to contemplate: with Mickey as the driving force, the Yankees won pennants every year from 1951 through 1964 except in 1954 and 1959. In 1959 the Yankees finished third, fifteen games behind the first-place Chicago White Sox, and that kind of gap was probably beyond even Willie Mays's talents. But in 1954 Mays was the best player in baseball and would win both the National League batting title and the Most Valuable Player Award. And that year the Yankees had their best record under Casey Stengel, winning 103 games, but still finished eight games behind the Cleveland Indians. It's not far from the realm of possibility that if Willie had been in pinstripes that season, New York could have made up that differ- ence by winning just four more games against Cleveland. If that had happened, the Yanks would have won thirteen pennants in fourteen seasons.

Win or no win, Willie and Mickey would have been far and away and without question the most spectacular pair of teammates ever to play baseball.

Despite many teams' reluctance to bid on a black player, Willie Mays would have been signed to a major league team before Mickey Mantle if he had not still been in high school. A minor mys- tery in Willie's life is why it took him until 1950 to graduate. He was an average student, and Sarah and Ernestine saw that he went to school. Whatever classes he might have missed, and for whatever reason, he made them up in time to graduate on May 31. It's also not known why he then went unsigned for nearly three weeks when, as the leading local black paper, the *Birmingham World*, reported, the Braves, Red Sox, Brooklyn Dodgers, and Cleveland Indians (owned by Bill Veeck, who had already signed Satchel Paige, Larry Doby, and Luke Easter) were "hot on the trail of center fielder Willie Mays."[17]

The only wonder is that there weren't more. There's just one reason that seems to make sense: many major league teams were still skittish about signing black players, and those that weren't, such as the Dodgers, Indians, and Giants, had already signed their "quota."

The Giants broke rank first. The day after the *World* story ran, Montague drove to Tuscaloosa to meet the Black Barons' bus as they arrived for a game. He walked up to Willie and asked if he could speak to him in private. Willie, wide-eyed, said sure. Montague then asked him if he would like to play professional baseball — ignoring the obvious fact that Willie was *already* playing professional baseball. Willie's immediate answer was "Yes, sir." Montague told Mays that he would speak to the team's owner about his contract. A surprised Willie replied, "What contract?"[18] Montague, his pulse racing, told Willie he would have an offer for him early the next day; he knew he had to move fast because he had already seen a Dodgers scout in Tuscaloosa, obviously there to try to sign Mays for Brooklyn.

The next morning, bright and early, Montague called Aunt Sarah and asked bluntly how much it would take to get Willie to sign with the Giants — $5,000, she answered. The scout quickly called his boss, Jack Schwarz, who told him to go for it. Montague drove like a man possessed to the Mays house, where, at four in the afternoon, Cat, off work from the mill, was waiting. They negotiated for a few minutes. Montague got Cat and Sarah to agree to $4,000, but with a $250-a-month salary. In the course of conversation, it came out that the Giants were going to pay Black Barons owner Tom Hayes $10,000 for the rights to Willie. Cat was indignant, and rightfully so: why were the Giants paying Hayes, who had no contract with Willie, $6,000 more than they were paying Willie? Montague's reply was weak: "He might sue us later, and we don't want any trouble." The truth probably had more to do with wanting to stay on good terms with the Black Barons for future prospects, but whatever the reason, it was clear that the Giants were willing to invest a cool $14,000 in Willie Mays. That wasn't much considering what the Giants got, but for Willie it sure beat what Mickey Mantle had signed for almost exactly a year earlier.

Willie signed with the Giants on June 21. Aunt Sarah divided the money, giving Cat $250, keeping $750 for the household, and leaving Willie $3,000.

Like Mickey, Willie immediately bought a car — a shiny, brand-new Mercury. (Mickey's car was secondhand, a bullet-nosed 1947 Fleetline Chevy with a vacuum shift.)* And also like Mickey, Willie would miss a high school function for a baseball game. On June 23, while Fairfield Industrial seniors went to their prom (where, he would later be told, his friends slow-danced to "Till I Waltz Again with You" and "On Top of Old Smokey" before they began jitterbugging), Willie Mays boarded a train at Birmingham's Terminal Station for a new and unknown world in Sioux City, Iowa, supplied with an enormous bag of sandwiches from Aunt Sarah that he was too nervous to eat. Though Willie would return to Birmingham several times over the years, he would almost never see the old neighborhood in Fairfield again.

About four in the morning, the train made a brief stop in Joplin, Missouri, home of Joe Becker Stadium, built just three years after Rickwood Field in Birmingham. Satchel Paige, Josh Gibson, Cool Papa Bell, and other great Negro Leaguers had played barnstorming games there, though Willie was too young to have played with them. The ballpark's lights were still on from the previous night's game between the Carthage Cubs and the Joplin Miners, which had featured a slugging shortstop named Mickey Mantle.

---

* In his early memoirs, Willie was fond of pointing out that when he left New York after the World Series to go home to Alabama, he had not yet learned to drive; he was in fact helping foster his image as an amiable schoolboy. It wasn't until his 1988 autobiography that he boasted of the convertible he bought with his bonus money.

6

"This Is Your Chance"

One day near the end of June 1949, Mutt Mantle and his old-est son, not yet eighteen years old, drove the nearly three hours from Commerce to Independence, Kansas, the home of the Yankees' Class-D club in that region. Mickey would talk about how scared and homesick he was, telling Herb Gluck, "I had an empty feeling in my stomach. I was in strange surroundings, didn't know where I'd sleep or take my meals, and Dad wasn't going to be around anymore."[1]

Mickey could not have known at the time that it was not Com-merce he was homesick for, it was his father. He would be back in Commerce in the fall, but after that he would visit his hometown as seldom as possible. Except for a handful of friends, he felt no attrac-tion for it; since he had been old enough to walk, the only things that held any emotional attachment for him were his family and baseball. And at least, in Independence, he still had baseball.

When they arrived in Independence that day in June, Mutt and

Mickey went to the Darby Hotel and knocked on the door of Harry Craft, the manager of the Independence Yankees. Craft was shaving, but wiped his face clean and shook hands. Mickey's first impression was not good. Craft struck him as aloof, which was almost certainly because he was comparing him to Mutt and Barney Barnett, the only two figures of authority he had ever really known. Craft was a professional, a company man, and he was also Mickey's introduction to the world of big-time professional baseball. Though Mickey could not know it at the time, he had a friend in Harry Craft. Craft was the closest thing young Mickey would have to the kind of mentor that Willie Mays had in Piper Davis.

Born in the little town of Ellisville, Mississippi, Craft had been a ballplayer himself — and not a bad one. In the Southern League one year he hit .341 and played several games at Rickwood Field in Birmingham. He played parts of six seasons in the National League, all with Cincinnati, beginning in 1937 when he was twenty-two. He made the All-Star team in 1939 and 1940, but he was never a star, though he had a reputation as a fine outfielder. (In 1940 he led NL outfielders in fielding percentage at .997.) His career was interrupted by military service in 1942, but that probably worked out well for him, since he had hit just .249 with 10 home runs in 1941 and didn't figure to get much better.

Harry's big professional break came when, out of the service, he managed to get a job in the Yankees organization. He knew young talent when he saw it, and he knew how to nurture it. The Yankees proved to be his ticket to a career in baseball; after his playing days were over, he would manage in the minors and for seven years in the big leagues with three different teams.

As the three men stood in Craft's hotel room, Mutt shook Mickey's hand and mumbled, "This is your chance, son, take care of yourself and give 'em hell." Mickey started to tear up; Craft, sensing that this was a good moment to jump in, put his hand on the teenager's shoulder and told him that they had a decent bunch of kids there, most of them around Mickey's age, and that he would enjoy playing there, adding, "Just keep your nose clean."[2]

Things quickly loosened up. It didn't take Mickey long to realize that he was surrounded by a bunch of boys with backgrounds similar to his own who were pretty much in the same situation he was in. "It seemed more like high school" than professional baseball. "Somebody always had a car. We'd pile in and shoot over to Pop's Place, our big social hangout, near the busiest corner in town."[3] It also didn't take Mickey long to latch on to a potential troublemaker, a third baseman named Lou Skizas, a skirt chaser, card player, and free spirit. "The nervous Greek" Mickey called Skizas, who was a pre-1950s hipster from the streets and alleys of Chicago. One of Mickey's Commerce pals who paid him a visit in Independence would later size up Skizas perfectly: "He was a poor man's Billy Martin."[4]

Under Skizas's addle-brained influence, Mickey lapsed back into adolescent behavior such as waging water-gun fights and throwing food on the team bus; Craft shook his head and clenched his jaw muscles. After a couple of years in the minors, he had already seen enough antics like this to last a lifetime, and he knew to let them roll off his back. Craft tolerated the boys' rambunctiousness because they played good ball. They won at home and they won on the road. Traveling on the team bus, Mickey would pass through Bartlesville (to play the Pirates), Carthage (the Cubs), Shanute (the Athletics), Pittsburgh (the Browns), Iola (the Indians), and Ponca City (the Dodgers). Mickey would remember the roads they traveled as "long dusty roads with stopovers only to get out and have a bite, take a piss, and climb right back again."[5]

Craft tried to work with Mickey at shortstop but didn't make much progress. Mantle never did quite learn to plant his feet right and get balance when he threw, and with his powerful arm the ball often wound up in the stands behind the first baseman. (Legend has it that a chicken-wire screen was installed on the right-field side of the stands in the Independence home park to keep spectators from being injured.) The manager had more success with Mickey's hitting. He couldn't get him to cut down on his swing — no one would ever succeed at doing that, not even Casey Stengel — but he did preach to him the importance of waiting for the right pitch. On the bases, Craft taught Mickey to run with his head down and watch how outfielders played balls hit in the gaps; see, he told Mickey, how good they are at hitting their cutoff man on long throws. The experience, combined with Mickey's dazzling speed, began to make him a smart, aggressive base runner. For Mickey to go from first to third or second to home on just about any single was soon taken as a given.

And as Piper Davis had done with Willie, Craft gave Mickey sound advice on off-the-field behavior. Steve Kraly, Mickey's room-mate at Independence, thought that Craft was "actually like a father to us . . . he taught us what baseball was really like in the minors. He made us think about what to look forward to if we moved up, he made us think about the game, getting yourself prepared to play better base-ball, moving up to better leagues, better traveling, better living."[6]

At the plate, Mantle, not used to the tougher pitching of the Kansas-Oklahoma-Missouri League, was slow out of the gate. After the first week, he began to have serious doubts and actually thought of going back home. He was, in his words, "wound tight, overanxious — sometimes after a strikeout, feeling frustrated and mad at myself, I'd trot off the field and let loose a vicious kick at a dugout water cooler."After striking out twice against Independence's arch-rival, Carthage, Mickey began what was to become his career-long battle with water coolers, kicking one so hard that a stream of cold water had his teammates jumping out of the dugout. For the rest of his stay with the Yankees, they called him "King of the Broken Water Coolers."[7]

But he matured and finished the season at .313, just two points higher than Willie Mays had hit the same year playing at a similar level of competition against Negro League pitching. In a key game against the Carthage Cubs in front of a sellout crowd, Mickey came up in the ninth inning with the score tied and belted a long drive to center field; Bill Hornsby, son of the great Rogers Hornsby,* chased the ball deep into the center-field pocket, lost it in the lights, and by the time he was able to peg it back into the field Mickey had wowed the crowd by wheeling around the bases and scoring the winning run with an inside-the-park homer.

Nothing stood in Independence's way that season. These were kids who intended to play ball for the New York Yankees; they were good, and they knew it. And as the season progressed, they knew it even more. They ended up winning the KOM pro league with a smashing victory over the Pittsburgh Browns. Mickey's confidence was building, and with it his expectations. When the team bus pulled back into Independence that night, the Yankees were expecting some kind of victory celebration, but it was late, and the townspeople hadn't yet gotten the news. The streets were dark and quiet. Harry Craft looked around and told his boys to have their own party, right there in the streets, which they proceeded to do. Mickey remembered that Lou Skizas scrambled to the top of the bus and began howling Hank Williams's great tune, "Long Gone Lonesome Blues," which Mickey said was "my favorite country song at that time."†

The locals began to walk outside to see what all the fuss was about, and Dan Peters, a policeman, began to climb the bus to pull Skizas down. Craft, who knew Peters, put his hand on his shoulder and told him that his boys had just brought glory to Independence by winning the KOM League championship. (Peters hadn't heard.) The manager diverted the policeman with a beer.

Though he couldn't see it right away, Mickey was swiftly moving out of the world of his boyhood. Some of the Independence Yankees' games were played in the same towns he knew as a Whiz Kid; in Miami, family and friends came out to watch him play, including Nick Ferguson. Earlier in the season, Mickey had told Nick and

---

* Incorrectly identified by Mickey many times in later years as "Rogers Hornsby Jr."
† But it must have been a different song by Mickey's favorite country singer. Paul Hemphill's 2005 biography *Lovesick Blues: The Life of Hank Williams* lists the song as a 1950 release.

another pal, Donnie Dodd, to come up and visit him in Independence, trying to convince them to try out for the Yankees. He was sure that Harry Craft would give them a look if they made the trip. Ferguson and Dodd did take a bus up to Independence and hung out with Mickey, but both shied away from a tryout. They had decided on other career paths. Mickey began to realize that he could never go home again.

But he did go home again, for a while, after his first pro season ended. On his first night back, he surprised Lovell by leaving a stack of tens and twenties — an eye-popping $290 in cash — on the breakfast table. It seemed like nothing about Commerce had changed in the few months he had been away, but everything had changed for him. Mickey didn't enjoy playing the celebrity and aw-shucks-ed his way through stories about what professional ball was really like and what it felt like to win the league's championship. He spent a few days hunting quail with his pals around Whitebird and on weeknights drove the Fleetline Chevy into Commerce to see a Gene Autry Western or a cops-and-robbers flick. On Friday nights he took in football games with his friends. He was not, though, in a position to take it easy for the rest of the year, and neither was his family. Mutt was now a ground boss for the Blue Goose Number One mine and was earning a respectable $75 a week. He found Mickey some odd jobs — most of them, fortunately, aboveground — running errands and assisting the electricians. His weekly pay was just under $35, actually a slight increase over what the New York Yankees, the richest team in the major leagues, paid him for finishing the season with their farm team.

There was also some time for girls. Earlier in the year, while still in high school, he had fallen for a pretty blond-haired, freckled-face girl named Jeanette Holmes, who had the added attraction of a willingness to do his homework. But the relationship between Miss Holmes and Mick Charles (which, his friends say, is what he was calling himself at the time) didn't go beyond the exchange of a class ring.

(Jeannette would later tell David Falkner that "I always wanted his baseball jacket. I would have liked to get that from him."[8]) A classmate, Ivan Shouse, set up a date for him with a friend of his sister, a pretty girl named Merlyn Johnson, whom he had met when she was a cheerleader. They were both so shy that on their first date they mostly listened to their friends talk and laugh, saying little to each other.

In November, the Mantles received a stunning postcard — Mickey was to report to the local draft board for a physical. Father and son looked at each other and shook their heads — life had blindsided them, and it looked as if Mickey's booming baseball career could be sidetracked indefinitely. A few weeks later, before Christmas, Mickey would get one of the few genuine breaks he ever had when the draft board declared him 4-F because of the osteomyelitis that had nearly cost him a leg three years earlier. That break, though, like nearly all the breaks Mickey ever got, was qualified. Within a couple of years, that classification would bring him so much public scorn that he would wonder if it had been a break at all.

The holidays passed, spring came, and the promotion that Mutt and Mickey expected did indeed happen. In the spring of 1950, the Yankees assigned Mickey to their huge minor league facilities in the Ozarks, the same place Tom Greenwade had taken him and Mutt the previous June. This time Mickey knew exactly where he would be going when the season started — the Class-C Joplin Miners of the Western Association. There was only one logical step from there, and that was the New York Yankees.

At exactly the same time, New York Giants owner Horace Stoneham was deciding where to send his nineteen-year-old phenom from the Negro Leagues, Willie Mays. The Giants had affiliates in Sioux City of the Western League, and Stoneham and his staff agreed that the level of competition there would be perfect preparation for Willie. At the last moment, though, Stoneham got word from some Giants coaches familiar with the Western Association that there were not yet any black players in the league. The owner thought it over and decided the Giants would find a farm team better suited to Mays, even though he was already on his way to Iowa. Willie said, "But I never got to Sioux City. Racial prejudice actually kept me from my first job with a white team. The Giants hoped I could play Class-A ball there, very important in my development, they figured. But Sioux City was not the place for me at that moment." An incident involving the attempted burial of an Indian in an all-white cemetery had given Sioux City a bad name around the country. Willie had never heard of anything like that happening before, but "then again, I had never played outside the Negro League, either."[9] (Willie, of course, meant "Leagues.") So secure and isolated had Mays's life been in Fairfield that the full force of racial bigotry didn't hit him until he *left* Alabama.

So the slowness with which the major leagues integrated its farm systems kept Mickey and Willie from playing against each other in the minor leagues. "To have had Mays and Mantle in the same league at nearly the same age," wrote a minor league historian, "would have been remarkable."[10]

The Giants, nothing if not paternal, decided it would be better to keep Willie closer to home, meaning closer to New York, where they could keep an eye on him. It was determined that their Trenton farm team in the Interstate League would be ideal, so Mays was diverted to New Jersey. It was all the same to him where he played, but he had one objection to Trenton: the league was Class-B. No one could ever really be certain how the Negro Leagues stacked up to the different levels of the white minor leagues, but the Barons, Willie told Charlie Einstein, played better baseball than he saw at Trenton (and probably baseball as good as he later saw in Triple-A). "No one really got to know how good the players were in the Negro League since the press" — meaning, of course, the white press — "never covered the games. But I knew it was an experience I would never forget. I was so much richer from it. I didn't realize that my leaving was another nail in the coffin of all-black baseball."[11] Willie might have been giving himself too much credit — black ball would have been doomed even if Mays and other black stars had not moved on. Willie's departure from the Black Barons, though, was a severe blow. In the spring of 1950, he was far from the best-known black player in the country and far from the biggest star to emerge from black ball. But he was one thing that Jackie Robinson, Roy Campanella, Satchel Paige, Larry Doby, and Monte Irvin were not — young. The major leagues, not yet taking a chance on young black talent, were purchasing only established stars. Willie Mays had the entire category of "budding young black superstar" all to himself. It was the main reason he would hit the major leagues with such enormous impact a year later.

It might have been better for Willie if his first exposure to a virtually all-white minor league had been in New Jersey. Instead, he was sent to meet up with his new team in Hagerstown, Maryland, where the Trenton Giants were scheduled to play. It didn't take Willie long to realize that he was below the Mason-Dixon Line again. In Washington and Baltimore, he could stay in any hotel he could afford, but in Hagerstown, about seventy miles northwest of Washington, he couldn't sleep in the same place as the rest of the team, and the moment he came out of the clubhouse he heard the first taunt he'd ever heard in baseball: "Who's that nigger walking out on the field?" On the phone later with his father, Willie told him of the racial slurs; Cat advised him to turn the other cheek. Willie told him he had no intention of turning his cheek. Cat simply told him that such things weren't going to stop right away and he had to learn not to let a few hate-filled people destroy his concentration. Though Willie later insisted that he hadn't let it get to him, he didn't get a hit the entire four-game series; as he later put it, he started his professional baseball career, "0–4 Maryland."

Nonetheless, his first experience in what was still "white folks' ball" was not a bad one. When he stepped off the train in Hagerstown, he was the first black player in the Interstate League, and the man who greeted him, a pitcher from Brooklyn named Ed Monahan, was white. He was the first adult white ballplayer Mays had ever met. At the park he met his manager, Chick Genovese, a gregarious Italian American who greeted him warmly. Practically the first thing he told Willie was that he would be the team's starting center fielder. Chick had been a prospect in the Red Sox system, but his path to the big leagues was blocked by the brother of Willie's idol, Dom DiMaggio. Genovese was good-hearted and sympathetic. He understood that the nineteen-year-old was trying too hard. He encouraged him to just relax and enjoy the game and good things would come. Willie did relax, and soon he was enjoying baseball again.

When the Giants got back to Trenton, Willie went on a tear and finished the year hitting .353, the highest batting average in the league. Because he played in only 81 games and batted just 306 times, he wasn't eligible for the league's batting title. But one statistic bowled over the Giants' scouts who watched him play: in just half a season, he led the league with 17 assists in the outfield. He also boosted attendance at Trenton's Dunn Field, and whenever a runner took off from first or second on a single, the crowd would rise in unison in expectation of a spectacular gun-down by Mays to third or home.

There was only one sour note to the whole season. During a day game in Harrisburg, Pennsylvania, Willie collapsed with stomach pains and had to leave the park in an ambulance. He was given a clean bill of health a few hours later, but his stomach problems were the first signs of anxiety attacks that would plague him for the rest of his career.

A less serious problem in his first season in the minor leagues was that he couldn't remember the names of his teammates. They knew his name but usually referred to him as "Popeye" because of his forearms. The nickname might have stuck except that Willie himself invented a catchier one, "Say Hey!," which was what he said whenever he wanted to get someone's attention. His teammates chuckled when they heard the expression, and sportswriters soon caught on.

The 1950 season ended on a definite up note. Genovese shook hands with him and said, "Willie, you're going to make a lot of money one day. I hope I helped you."[12]

When Mickey Mantle reported to the Joplin Miners for the 1950 season, his teammates noticed a remarkable physical change. Steve Kraly recalled that "the year before he was like 160, 165; then at Joplin he was all filled out, the way everyone knew him later."[13] Not quite, but the eighteen-year-old weighed between 175 and 180, all of it hard-packed. His teammates immediately noticed how the muscle translated into power during batting practice; the previous season Mickey had hit just seven home runs, not a bad figure considering how cavernous most of the minor league ballparks were. (When major league GMs reviewed the power statistics of minor league players, they wanted to be certain that they were legitimate.) Now, instead of merely hitting the ball ten or twelve feet over the fence, he was smashing the drives into the light towers beyond the fences.

Local legend has it that there was an orphanage approximately one hundred feet beyond the right-field fence of Joplin's Joe Becker Stadium and the kids would sometimes hold up signs from the windows that read MICK, HIT IT HERE. On at least a couple of occasions, he did.* Henry DeBardelaben, a stadium attendant at Joplin, had sold peanuts at Sportsman's Park in 1928 when the Yankees beat the Cardinals in the World Series. He remembered one of Babe Ruth's three home runs in that series as the longest ball he had ever seen hit. Mantle, he said, hit them at least as far as the Babe. The

---

* Joe Becker Stadium in Joplin is very nearly as historic as Birmingham's Rickwood Field. Like Rickwood, Joe Becker saw numerous appearances from the great stars of the Negro Leagues — Satchel Paige, Josh Gibson, and Cool Papa Bell played there many times on barnstorming tours. The foundation for the park was built in 1913, three years after Rickwood opened, and was called Miners Park. It was later renamed Joe Becker, to honor a well-known umpire, scout, and business manager for the team. The stadium has survived numerous fires; in the 1970s it was rebuilt in retro style with hand-painted signs in the outfield. In 2004 it hosted the USA Baseball Tournament of Stars.

difference was that in 1928 the Babe was thirty-three; in the spring of 1950 Mickey Mantle was not yet nineteen.

The Miners, though Class-C, had several talented players destined for the big leagues and were probably as talented as a good Triple-A team. They tore the league apart, and Mickey terrified opposing pitchers, hovering near .400 for most of the season and finally settling on .383. Mutt, in what was probably the best year of his life, came to many of the Miners games and critiqued his son's performance. By the end of the year, when Mickey told his dad his batting average, Mutt told him flat-out, "You could have hit .400." The remark should not be taken the wrong way: it wasn't that Mickey couldn't do anything to please his father, but that Mutt was simply trying to exhort his son to always try for perfection — and he was succeeding. He was also there to give his son a stern reprimand when Mickey lost what was sometimes an uncontrollable temper. With Mutt in attendance, Mickey did begin to show some maturity. Water coolers all over the Western League breathed sighs of relief.

It might also have been the happiest year of Mickey's life. He was still playing against older players, but now he was dominating them, excelling not only at bat but on the bases as well. And Joplin, with a population of more than 40,000, was the closest thing to a big city Mickey had ever known. The nights after home games were a dizzying flurry of beer and burgers, pool and pinball, and free movies. (The local movie houses liked to give tickets to the Joplin players and watch the patrons squeal when they recognized them, as if they were in the presence of movie stars.) All that and free steaks too: one of the city's best steakhouses gave a free dinner to every Miner who hit a home run, and Mickey became popular by taking a couple of teammates with him, splitting the cost among them. It was a veritable taste of what was to come in the big leagues.

And if all this wasn't enough, Mickey and his teammates would load up ice chests with beer and go "frogging." While one "frogger" transfixed an amphibian in a flashlight beam, another would sneak up from behind and grab it. Sadly, Mickey had to give up this pastime when he went to New York.

Shortly before the end of the season, Harry Craft brought Mickey news that stunned him. While Mickey sat in the team bus, Craft walked over and quietly informed him that next season he would be managing in Beaumont, Texas, and he certainly would love to have Mickey play for him there. But, Craft added, he did not think he would have the privilege: the New York Yankees wanted Mickey to report to the parent team.* It took Mickey a full minute to comprehend what he had just heard.

The swiftness with which the next events unfolded seemed unreal. Since Mickey had started high school, it had seemed as if his baseball dream was moving at a snail's pace. Now things were happening so quickly that his head was spinning. At the end of the season, Mickey was on a train bound for St. Louis, where he would be joining the Yankees as a nonroster player. Two days later, on September 17, 1950, he was in St. Louis, where a friendly but distant Yankee representative met him, helped him with his bags, and settled him into the team hotel — so this was what it was like to be part of a major league team. The two then caught a cab for Sportsman's Park. Mickey had been to the ballpark many times with his dad and brothers to see the Cardinals play. Now he was seeing it from the inside. Alone in the locker room — the team was out on the field practicing — Mantle quietly put on his first Yankee uniform (the road gray, not the famous pinstripes) and was comforted by the fact that it fit so well. In fact, it was the first uniform he had ever worn that seemed to have been made just for him. The number 6 was on the back.

As he walked through the concrete passageway out onto the field, he could not imagine that any ballplayer could ever be more frightened and awed than he was. This was the home field that Dizzy Dean,

---

* Craft had sent a glowing report to Lee MacPhail, outlining all of Mantle's considerable strengths and his only real weakness, his still-erratic play at shortstop. His natural position, Craft said, was probably center field.

Ducky Medwick, Enos "Country" Slaughter, and Stan Musial had played on. He instantly recognized the first player he saw, the diminutive shortstop Phil Rizzuto. Rizzuto glanced at him but said nothing, knowing that the Yankees had thoughts of replacing him at shortstop with the teenage phenom. Phil had had his best season in 1950, and in a few months would earn the league's Most Valuable Player Award. But he knew that in the big leagues no job was ever secure for long. Mickey watched Rizzuto's breathtaking dexterity in the field, though, and knew in his heart that whomever he replaced, it wouldn't be Rizzuto. He stood, silent and alone, by the batting cage. All the Yankees were to remember of Mantle from that St. Louis trip was that he and another rookie, a former college football star turned power-hitting first baseman named Bill Skowron, put on a terrific display during batting practice. The veterans, trying to be nonchalant, pretended not to notice. But they noticed.

A reporter approached Rizzuto as he walked off the field and asked him what he thought of the Yankees' new shortstop. "I dunno," Rizzuto said with a smile on his face. "He looks a little big for a shortstop, doesn't he?"[14]

The first thing Mantle noticed was how efficiently the Yankees went about their business. No one spoke to him at all except for one man whose greeting jarred him back to reality. "How ya doin'?" Mickey heard behind him. He turned to find a short, stocky, jovial, broad-faced man whom he recognized from the newsreels and newspapers. Yogi Berra, a native of St. Louis who would be playing in front of friends and family that day, shook his hand, and Mickey Mantle began to feel like a real Yankee.

Mantle, not on the roster, did not play that day, nor in any of the season's remaining games. (The Yankees would win the AL pennant and sweep the NL champ Philadelphia Phillies in four games in the World Series.) The trip was intended to orient Mickey to the team, to give him a chance to meet his teammates and to show him the routine. But he scarcely spoke to anyone. A slim, young left-handed pitcher, a native New Yorker named Edward Ford, remembered seeing him sitting in front of a locker but didn't talk to him. Whitey, as he would soon be called, was all brass on the outside, but inside he was as full of butterflies as Mickey. Ford would recall to Joe Durso that he met Mickey in the company of a pitcher, Bob Weisler (who would go on to pitch in seventy games over six seasons for the Yankees and Senators), but Whitey could remember practically nothing else. "He stayed with us a week, and I don't think I spoke to him once during that time. Except to say *hello*. And I know he didn't speak to me once during that time. Except to *grunt*. He was very shy."[15]

Back in the locker room, Mantle watched some of the veteran players joking with reporters, terrified at the thought that he might have to say something to a newspaperman. Then he saw Joe DiMaggio, who had come in early from practice and was already showered and dressed really well — to Mantle, he looked like he had stepped out of a magazine ad. No one spoke to Joe. Teammates, reporters, and clubhouse attendants seemed to part in front of him as he walked through. Mantle was even more terrified at the thought of talking to the Yankee Clipper than to a reporter. He needn't have worried; Joe DiMaggio scarcely knew that Mickey Mantle existed.

It all passed quickly, as if in a short dream. A few days later, the season was over and he was back in Commerce. As if to underline the grim reality of what Mickey faced if he did not succeed, Mutt once again had gotten him a job in the Blue Goose mine. Mickey could not help but notice that his father was moving more slowly than usual and taking longer breaks. But every time he got into a conversation with one of his friends. Mutt would mention that Mickey was "a personal friend" of Joe DiMaggio.

Before Mickey returned home, the Yankees flew him not to Florida but to Phoenix, Arizona. (The Yankees had agreed to trade spring training sites with the New York Giants; co-owner Del Webb, who lived in Phoenix, wanted to show off his world champion baseball team to friends in California.) It was Mickey's first plane ride; he was not the least apprehensive and found the experience exhilarating, particularly the dinner he was served during the flight. Mickey would be attending a special instructional camp for the Yankees' top prospects that accelerated young players' maturity by having them work out with seasoned veterans. No one would say it in so many words, but though Mickey was only nineteen, Lee MacPhail wanted him ready for the 1951 season. Mickey did not know this, and he wished he knew whether he would be spending the next season in Texas with Harry Craft or in Binghamton, New York, instead of in the Bronx with the New York Yankees.

Back in Commerce, Mickey followed the sports pages and waited to hear from the parent team. He couldn't help noticing that the war in Korea was heating up and wondering if it still might affect him in some way. He took Merlyn Johnson to the movies; Mutt, though not Lovell, was hinting that she might be the right girl for Mickey to settle down with.

Early in 1951 Mickey heard from the team: he was to report to Phoenix — immediately. Baffled as to how they expected him to do so, he did nothing. A couple of days later, he received an indignant call from the Yankees' front office — why was he not in Phoenix? Was he holding out on them? Because, Mickey stammered, he couldn't afford a train ticket. They quickly wired him expense money. The next day Mutt cranked up the LaSalle, Lovell, as Willie's aunt had done, packed a paper bag full of sandwiches, and the family began a long, almost silent drive to Oklahoma City, where Mickey would catch the Heartland Express to Phoenix. In the station, "I kept swallowing hard and drinking more water than I ever needed before. I turned to the steps to the train, took my suitcase in my hand, and tried to say goodbye to my mother and father. I was just about able to speak. I got on the train, looked for a seat by the window where I could see my parents, and tried forlornly to wave at them as they waved to me. The train began to roll at last, and then the sobs rose up and choked me." For an hour, as the Heartland sped through the Oklahoma countryside, Mickey sat with his fist in his mouth, trying to hold back tears. "What a jerk I felt like!" This time there would be no support group to help him, no friends to visit and hang out with him. Mutt would not be in the stands to watch him play.

After the Trenton Giants ended their season, Willie went home and got a workout in baseball fundamentals at least as rigorous as anything the Yankees put Mickey Mantle through. He joined a team of professionals Piper Davis had put together for a barnstorming tour, and two of the best players, Hank Thompson and Monte Irvin, would soon be Willie's teammates on the New York Giants. They played several games against integrated teams whose rosters included the Brooklyn Dodgers' Pee Wee Reese, Gil Hodges, and Jackie Robinson, who also acted as manager. Willie had several opportunities to talk to Jackie but shied away nearly every time.

They played around Florida and in New Orleans, though not in Birmingham, where section 597 of the 1944 Code of Alabama (first passed in 1944 and reaffirmed in 1951) strictly prohibited whites and blacks from participating together in any game or sporting event, up to and including "dice and cards."

In the fall, confident and brimming with optimism for the following year, Willie and Cat sat together at Bob's Little Savoy Café while Cat's pals listened with rapt attention to Willie's stories about playing professional ball in the North. Occasionally he would take a Fairfield girl to a football game at the old high school, where students and teachers had gotten past the resentment of the year before when it looked as if he might have to give up high school football for the Black Barons. Like Mickey in Commerce, Willie was a small-town celebrity; in fact, his name had spread outside the black community, and sometimes he was mentioned in the white papers, such as the *Birmingham News*. The only question seemed to be how soon he would be playing for the New York Giants. Horace Stoneham and his front office wanted Willie to jump just one more hurdle: their Triple-A affiliate in the American Association, the Minneapolis Millers. While waiting for Minneapolis to thaw, Willie boarded a train heading south to Florida.

In Sanford, Florida, at nine in the morning, he walked out onto the field to prepare for a game between the Millers and another Giants minor league team based in Ottawa, Canada. The first words he heard were from the bellowing voice of a middle-aged white man in a Giants uniform: "Hey, kid, what are you gonna show me today?" It was Willie's introduction to Leo Durocher — "Mr. Leo," as Willie would call him for the rest of his life. The Giants were to play the St. Louis Cardinals that day at their Lakeland training camp, but their manager (Durocher) and owner (Stoneham) had driven over for the express purpose of watching Willie play. Leo cheerfully informed Willie that Chick had given him a glowing report: "He thinks you're the greatest he ever saw." Willie asked him what the report said. "It said," Durocher told him with a loud laugh, "that your hat keeps flying off." That was strange, Mays remembered thinking. "I had never noticed that it did."[16]

Mays blistered Triple-A pitching in the spring, and sharp from his barnstorming the previous fall, he also stunned some veteran Giants pitchers, such as Larry Jansen and Sal Maglie, in exhibition games. (Maglie, known as "The Barber" for not being afraid to put the ball under a batter's chin, on more than one occasion considered setting the Giants' prize prospect on the seat of his pants, but thought better of it when he remembered that his boss, Horace Stoneham, was in the stands.) At the end of spring, the Millers' manager, Tommy Heath, called Willie into his office and told him pretty much what he already knew — namely, that Willie would be going back with the Millers. He also told Willie, as Harry Craft had told Mickey the previous summer, that he didn't think his stay in the minors would be long. "Boy, that raised my spirits and kept them that way all the way from Florida to Minneapolis."

There was some question about Mays's power. Everyone was impressed by the *thwack!* sound when Willie made contact with the ball, but so far, at every level from the Black Barons to the Millers' spring camp, he had not put many over the fence. But Durocher wasn't in doubt — given the frequency with which Mays hit the ball, he told Horace Stoneham, and the power he packed into that swing, the balls would soon be leaving the field. In Willie's last spring training game, he lunged at a low curveball — the kind that dismissive scouts kept saying he couldn't hit — and sent it far over the left-field fence. In fact, said some observers, the ball cleared some railroad tracks outside the ballpark. It was later estimated that the ball traveled 450 feet before hitting dirt. Durocher, having personally investigated the length of the blast, went back to report to Stoneham in the stands. In the seventh inning, to Willie's dismay, the Giants owner and manager got up to leave. Mays was at the point of tears: What had he done wrong? Should he have tried to impress them by taking an extra base? Or perhaps he should have hit the cutoff man instead of gunning a runner down at the plate? After the game, he sat in front of his locker, "so tired I couldn't even shake my head. I felt like a raw rookie who had just flunked his only chance."[17]

Though he could not have known it at the time, Willie needn't have worried. Durocher and Stoneham had simply left the park because they had seen what they needed to see.

7

"You're Going to Eat Steak"

I n the spring of 1951, Willie Mays moved from Florida to Minnesota. Nothing could have seemed more alien to Willie at that point in his life than the city of Minneapolis. There were a couple of black players on the Millers, but on most days there were more black people in the home team dugout than the stands.

For all that, Horace Stoneham could not have taken better care of his budding superstar. It would have been hard to imagine a city in the United States in 1951 with less racial tension than Minneapolis, and even harder to imagine a manager more congenial than Tommy Heath. Born in Akron, Colorado, in 1913, Heath had had a spotty major league career. He had played 134 games at catcher for the St. Louis Browns from 1935 to 1938, batting just .230, then parlayed his smarts and experience into a professional career as a coach, scout, and manager. He had led the Millers to a pennant the previous season.

The Millers called Tommy "The Round Man" for the 215-plus pounds he packed on a five-ten frame. Heath pretended not to hear them and chuckled. Willie regarded him as "a deep thinker, and a very good student of the game. I learned how to think baseball when he was around."

Mays was the first black player Heath had ever worked with; Willie found him to be "very fair, something I appreciated as a kid trying to play among men."[1] Much to his surprise, Willie also found the fans and the local press congenial. In fact, a couple of Twin Cities writers who had seen him play in Florida had already been beating the drum, leading Millers fans, who were as passionate about their team as fans in big league cities, to pack the stadium for opening day.

An excited Willie opened his eyes early in the morning on the first day of the season and was startled by the glare coming from his window: for only the second time in his life he gazed at a landscape covered with snow. He shook his head and crawled back into bed. Two hours later, a mildly indignant Heath rang his room: Why wasn't he at the ballpark, his manager wanted to know. Mays was dumbfounded. How can you play baseball in the snow? Heath patiently explained that it was a problem the Millers were used to — a helicopter had been brought in to blow the snow away. Hurry up and get to the park, he told his new player. As Willie dressed, he wondered, "Did Piper Davis ever play in any snow?"[2]

Snow, it turned out, was no impediment to greatness. In that first game, Mays electrified the crowd by slamming a long home run over the center-field wall and hitting a double — actually, a bloop single that Mays turned into a two-bagger when the center and right fielders couldn't decide fast enough who was going to field the ball. The crowd was delighted; this was the kind of play some of them had seen when Negro League teams barnstormed through Minneapolis. The next day Willie Mays became the first black athlete since Joe Louis to have his picture on the local sports pages.

Willie started out red-hot in the cold weather, collecting twelve hits in his first week. The fans loved him. He was everything they'd heard about and more, and after only a few games he became a celebrity in the city. Since there were practically no black-owned restaurants in Minneapolis, he had little trouble eating with most of his white teammates. He also found that doors, literally, were opening to him. Like Mickey, Willie often went to the movies by himself, usually to see a Western. Back in Florida he still had to use a side entrance. "I didn't care," he later recalled. "I was having a good spring, just counting the days until we'd break camp and start a new season."[3] Now, for the first time, he had the experience of buying a ticket and walking through the front door like a full-fledged American citizen.

One of his teammates on the Millers was the great Ray Dandridge, who at age thirty-eight was playing out his career as a professional player. "You got a great chance," Dandridge told Willie. "When I played in the black leagues, we were barnstorming most of the time. Sometimes I played three games in one day. We made about $35 a week and ate hamburger. You're going to eat steak, and you're going to make a lot of money. You just have to keep it clean and be a good boy."[4]

Dandridge was one of the many Negro League veterans who helped young Mays learn the ropes in professional ball. In Dandridge's case, he knew that mentoring Willie would be his last achievement in a career that had made him one of the greatest of Negro League stars. Monte Irvin later said, "Ray Dandridge was fantastic. Best I've ever seen at third. I saw all the greats — Brooks [Robinson], Graig [Nettles] — but I've never seen a better third baseman than Dandridge."[5]

There may not have *ever* been a better third baseman. The first black player for the Millers, Dandridge hit .362 in 1949 and was voted — at age thirty-six — the American Association Rookie of the Year. In 1950 he was voted the league's Most Valuable Player. The New York Giants' Sal Maglie, who had seen him play in Mexico, begged the Giants owners to bring him up to the parent club. The word came back that Dandridge was simply too old. "We could have won the pennant," Maglie would later insist. "I know damn well with Dandridge playing third, we'd have won that pennant in 1950."[6]

He probably could have helped the Giants in 1951 as well, though that year New York had a slugger who, like Dandridge, could play third base or outfield. But in 1951 the Giants already had their unofficial quota of black players, so Bobby Thomson was playing on the parent team while Ray Dandridge was hitting .324 on the farm club.*

Triple-A baseball in the late 1940s and early 1950s was a rough, sometimes brutal game filled with hungry youngsters and grizzled veterans, all clawing for a shot at the big leagues. A young black man in a predominantly white league was a particularly inviting target. At a game in Louisville, a six-foot-five right-hander named Joe Atkins threw Mays two consecutive pitches up and in. Willie was used to close pitches from his short stint with the Black Barons, but to get two in a row violated the unwritten rules — it was a stunt Atkins would not have dared to pull had the game been played in Minneapolis, where the fans would have been waiting for him outside the ballpark after the game.

Heath had no intention of giving an opposing pitcher a free shot at Willie. Charging from the dugout, he looked as if he was ready to run out to the mound and take on Atkins despite the height disadvantage. Wisely, he allowed his coaches to catch up and restrain him, but not before he let the Louisville pitcher know, in no uncertain terms, that if he threw another pitch like the previous one he wouldn't stop at the foul line. Willie recalled his manager's gesture fondly. "Once again I found someone who was willing to stick up for me, and I never forgot him. He could have taken it easy on himself and let the other teams try to screw up a rookie as they did with every new kid. But he seemed to be especially protective of me."[7]

Willie probably did not understand that he was being given pref-

---

* In March 1987 Dandridge, at his home in Palm Bay, Florida, picked up his phone and was told he had been voted into the Hall of Fame. It took him a few seconds to realize the call was not a joke. Finally, he muttered a quiet "Thank you" and burst into tears.

erential treatment; Heath was surely under orders from Stoneham not to let their prize prospect get manhandled.

During the Yankees' 1951 spring training, Casey Stengel had pretty much avoided all contact with the rookies, but it was quickly brought to his attention that the kid who had the fastest time of anyone in camp on the sprints was also hitting monstrous home runs — from both sides of the plate. Stengel made it from the veterans' field to where the rookies were playing in time to see Mickey, batting left-handed, slam the ball a good forty to fifty feet over the right-field fence. As Mickey, head down, rounded first base heading for second, Stengel jumped out on the field, waving a bat to get his coaches' attention. "What's his name?" he shouted to them. "Mantle?" "Mickey Mantle in spring training, 1951?" remarked his teammate Gil McDougald. "Let me put it this way: it was like watching a young, blond god."[8]

Although he was turning heads with his performance, Mantle was under more pressure than he had ever thought was possible. The pressure came from every conceivable source — from his father, who thought that marrying Merlyn Johnson would settle him down; from the U.S. government, which was having second thoughts about his draft status; and from the New York press, which was turning him into the inheritor of the Babe Ruth–Lou Gehrig–Joe DiMaggio legend before he had taken a single at-bat in a major league game.

In a preseason exhibition game on the University of Southern California campus, Mickey jump-started his own myth, which, when sent out over the wires by both New York and southern California sportswriters, became instant legend. In that game, Mantle hit two home runs, a triple, and a single, and one of the homers carried so far over the fence — some estimated it had gone 500 feet — that the USC students went into a state of delirium. Afterward, a crowd of students estimated in the hundreds clogged the locker-room exit, cheering and demanding autographs.

Another blond athletic god who was at the USC athletic facility that day was in awe. In a year, Frank Gifford would become, to many New York Giants fans, the Mickey Mantle of pro football (or as close to it as any player could be in what was then a second-rate professional sport). He was on the adjoining field at practice when people came running out from the baseball stadium to look for the ball Mantle hit. "It was electric," said Gifford. "It was as if something heroic had just happened. Student, coaches, everyone was buzzing."*[9]

In another game on the California junket, against the White Sox, Mickey gave the writers fodder for yet another blizzard of newspaper stories. Catching a fly ball in medium right field, Mantle set, cocked, and fired the ball on a line to Yogi Berra, who was standing a foot in front of home plate. Berra caught it chest high — it was almost as if Mickey had thrown a fastball from the pitcher's mound. "I couldn't believe it at first," Yogi recalled. "The ball hit my glove so hard it was like catching an Allie Reynolds fastball. All we had heard about and all we had seen so far was Mickey's power, that and how lousy he was as a shortstop. No one told us he had an arm like that. I was so surprised by his throw I almost forgot to tag the runner" — who was still out by a good six feet.[10]

Yankees coach Tommy Henrich, who had been a terrific outfielder — a five-time All-Star — had been working hard to convert Mantle from shortstop to the outfield, giving him a crash course in skills that Willie Mays had learned from his father and Piper Davis years before, namely, how to pivot, turn, and throw on balls hit to his right, and how to judge balls that were slicing away from him.

Henrich recalled in detail fifty-six years later the play in which all his instruction came together: "Jim Busby was the runner at third base. He was pretty fast, and I figured that given the depth at which

---

* Gifford was the most popular athlete on the Southern Cal campus, but on this day he was upstaged by Mantle. In later years, Gifford would be critical of Mickey and berate the press for making a hero out of someone with such a sordid private life — ironic considering that Gifford would eventually endure his own sex scandal. It's possible his resentment began that day in 1951 when Mickey Mantle, not Frank Gifford, was BMOC at Southern Cal.

Mickey would catch the ball, Jim had about a 90 percent chance of scoring. From the moment Mickey moved in to catch the ball, I could see his motions were perfect, that he was doing it exactly the way we had practiced it. He already had his momentum shifted forward at the catch, brought his glove down, and had the ball in his throwing hand while he was stepping forward. His follow-through was flawless."

Henrich also remembered one detail that Berra did not: "Busby was such a dead duck he actually tried to stop and looked as if he was going to head back to third base." Henrich said he had seen every great outfielder in the major leagues in his time, from the Cardinals' Terry Moore to the Dodgers' Carl Furillo to his own teammate Joe DiMaggio to Willie Mays. Mantle's throw, he insisted, "was the greatest I ever saw an outfielder make, *ever*. When I saw that throw, I thought, *This kid isn't going to just be a great slugger, he's going to be a great all-around player.*"[11]

Johnny Hopp, who dressed alongside Mantle all during the spring, told his teammate, whom he nicknamed "The Champ," "You're going to make a million dollars out of this game." Mickey just grinned. As Hopp later recalled, "He just did everything you'd ever want to see on a ballfield. The home runs were only part of it. Casey said one time that the kid runs so fast that he doesn't even bend the grass when he steps on it."[12]

Mantle had so much talent that everyone seemed to forget he was a nineteen-year-old with only a few spring training games beyond the Class-C level. Yankee GM Lee MacPhail, whose ecstatic quotes continually poured gasoline onto the Mantle bonfire in the spring of 1951, later insisted that he was not engaging in hyperbole. "No one knew what would happen on a major league field," he said later, "but Mantle had more ability than Gehrig, Ruth, anybody. He could hit with Ruth's power, and Ruth never hit from both sides of the plate like Mantle. Ruth had a great arm, but so did Mantle." Every day, MacPhail remembered, he'd say to himself, "He's the guy who's gonna be the solution for us — and he just about was. We all believed that."[13] The problem for which the Yankees needed a "solution" was, of course, how they were going to replace Joe DiMaggio when he retired.

All through Willie Mays's career, whenever an obstacle appeared in his path, it magically seemed to vanish. The rapid demise of the Negro Leagues after Willie's championship season with the Black Barons in 1948 didn't hurt him at all because, thanks to his father and Piper Davis, he was ready to make the leap to the big leagues. And through some spectacular luck — beginning with the fact that Jackie Robinson had already broken the color barrier — he signed with exactly the right organization in exactly the right city that could help shield him from the still-powerful influence of Jim Crow. Mickey Mantle's career, in contrast, seemed to run along an opposite course: every time skies were overpoweringly bright, storm clouds quickly gathered. And even as the hype generated by the Yankees' front office made Mickey prematurely famous in the spring of 1951, the draft board, reacting to that hype, was compelled to reexamine his status.

World War II hadn't made much of an intrusion into the worlds of either Mickey or Willie. In movie theaters they saw newsreels and films about American victories; their fathers were excused from military service because of their mill and mine work and also their numerous dependents. Now, both Mantle and Mays were quickly becoming aware that their country was involved in a bloody police action on the Korean peninsula. And for Mantle, the fan mail and press were beginning to get nasty. Scarcely anyone who saw Mickey in photographs or in person could believe he was anything but a marvelous physical specimen of young American manhood. How, asked sportswriters who hadn't the slightest notion what osteomyelitis was, could Mickey Mantle not qualify for military service? (One writer even made a snide comment to the effect that, after all, a bone disease in his leg shouldn't keep Mantle out of the service since he would not be required to kick anyone in Korea.)

It didn't help that the Yankees' front office intervened directly to ask the Oklahoma draft board to give Mickey another physical;

to many it seemed like influential New York interests were trying to manipulate Mantle's status. But the draft board didn't need the Yankees or anyone else to tell them what a second examination made obvious: osteomyelitis, even in a state of remission, automatically designated Mickey 4-F.

The sporting press could have prevented much of the ugliness to come by simply pointing out that Mickey had no say in the matter and would not have been accepted in the armed forces even if he volunteered. Instead, the stigma would plague him through the entire decade and result in more hate mail, booing, and bad feelings than had ever been directed at an athlete.

All during spring training, Casey Stengel delighted in showing Mickey off to reporters. Attendance for the spring exhibitions had been just under 279,000, a record largely set because of the curiosity surrounding Mickey, who batted .402 with nine home runs. The Yankees' last exhibition series had been capped off against the Dodgers in Brooklyn, where every New York writer could see him firsthand. Before the first game, Stengel walked Mickey out to the outfield of Ebbets Field to instruct him on the angles a ball might take on a ricochet off the concrete barrier, giving the rookie the benefit of his own experience in the Dodgers' park. Mantle was astonished to learn that Casey had played major league ball. Stengel, chuckling, later recounted the story to the beat reporters. "Boy never saw concrete before," he told them.[14] Mickey had four hits in the final exhibition game, including a long home run, stole two bases, and threw a runner out at third base; some of the press were now predicting he could take DiMaggio's place right then.

The press coverage at times bordered on the hysterical. In the April 15 edition of a small circulation paper, the New York Compass, Stan Isaacs, later to become one of the city's most popular sportswriters, wryly noted, "Since the start of spring training, the typewriter keys of the training camps have been pounding out one name to the people back home. No matter what paper you read, or what day, you will get Mickey Mantle, more Mickey Mantle and still more Mickey Mantle. Never in the history of baseball has the game known the wonder to equal this Yankee rookie. Every day there's some other glorious phrase as the baseball writers outdo themselves in attempts to describe the antics of this wonder."[15]

In regular foot races in camp, Mickey outran his teammates by such wide margins that he embarrassed them. He was repeatedly clocked running from home plate to first base: he was 3.0 seconds from the left side and 3.1 from the right side. It was almost a consensus among sportswriters that no other player in the big leagues was that fast. At least not yet — Willie Mays had not yet been called up to the Giants. "Whenever the black players heard that Mickey Mantle was the fastest man in baseball," Monte Irvin says, "we always said, 'Yeah, maybe. The fastest *white* man.' I would have loved to have seen a race between Mickey and Willie when they were that age." Who, I once asked Irvin, did he think would have won? He paused. "Mickey, maybe to first base, even from the right side of the plate. Willie by maybe a quarter-step goin' from first to second."[16] In a 1987 interview Piper Davis pretty much agreed with Irvin's assessment: "Willie might have lost a race to first base by half a step to Mickey. But I saw them both play. Willie, of course, a lot more than Mickey. But I saw Mickey a couple of times and he was a human streak. But I don't believe he could *turn* as fast as Willie. I don't believe anyone could go from first to third or second to home faster than Willie."[17]

Myths began to spring up around Mickey, and some of them survive to this day. One was that he was a terrible shortstop. Though he often looked bad at short, a check of minor league fielding records reveals that Mantle was no worse than most of his contemporaries. In 1949, for instance, Mickey committed 47 errors in 89 games, but given the condition of the pebble-strewn fields the young men played on and the poor lighting in most of the ballparks, that was about par for the course. Another shortstop, Dwayne Melvin, who played for Miami, made 71 errors in just six more games than Mickey; still another, Sal Nardello, a shortstop for Pittsburgh, had 75 muffs in 118 games for the same .886 fielding percentage as Mickey.

One problem with his play at shortstop was discovered by Yankee coach Frank Crosetti, who had played more than 1,500 games at the position for New York from 1932 to 1948. After watching Mantle mis-play a ground ball he had easily caught up to, Crosetti asked to see his glove. "Where'd you get this piece of shit?" he asked. Mickey mum-bled that the glove had been a Christmas gift from his father — it was the Marty Marion glove Mutt had given his son years before. The cost had been a whopping $22, nearly one-third of Mutt Mantle's weekly salary. It was not a piece of shit, as Crosetti called it; it was a fine piece of craftsmanship for a semipro player. But it was not the kind of tool needed for the big leagues. The next morning, when Mickey walked out onto the practice field, Crosetti shoved a brand-new major league fielder's mitt in his stomach; it was understood, though he never told Mickey, that Frank had paid for it himself. Mickey put the Marty Marion model away and later brought it back to Commerce.

The truth is that the Yankees wanted Mantle in the lineup *now* and in Phil Rizzuto they had not only a capable shortstop but one who had walked off with the 1950 American League MVP Award. It was Joe DiMaggio in center field who needed replacing. A story often repeated in early Mantle biographies was that GM George Weiss was reluctant to commit to Mantle, but Stengel talked him into it. Lee MacPhail told David Falkner that this was not true. "Once we made an outfielder out of him, the decision to jump him to the Yankees was really simple."[18] Mickey's speed and throwing arm made it logical to send him to the outfield, especially after Henrich began working with him.

It was significant that the man who played outfield so many years beside Henrich did not help Mickey; Joe DiMaggio, perhaps resent-ful that a nineteen-year-old had been anointed as his successor, said nothing to encourage the painfully shy rookie. There may have been another reason for DiMaggio's reticence: he despised Casey Stengel, who did not kowtow to him. DiMaggio did a slow burn every time he picked up the paper and saw another quote from Casey on Mantle's potential. Of course, Joe wasn't aloof only with Mickey. He kept a distance from all the Yankee players and generally traveled alone to and from games in a cab. Just about the only man in the organization with the nerve to prick DiMaggio's ego was the Yankees' longtime clubhouse manager, Pete Sheehy. Once, the story goes, Sheehy was asked by DiMaggio to examine what he thought was a bruise on his backside, where he had been hit with a pitch. Was there something there? There was, replied Sheehy. "It's from all those people kissing your ass."[19]

As spring training drew to a close, the publicity began to overwhelm Mickey, who receded into a shell. After the last game with the Dodgers, Stengel told his players that they would be attending the wedding of their hotshot young left-hander, Edward Charles "Whitey" Ford, who'd had a sensational 9–1 record during the Yankees' pennant drive the previous season and was home on furlough from the Army. The reception was at an Irish bar in Queens. Mickey was so shy that he stayed on the bus during the entire affair. Afterward, Ford and his bride joined the team on the bus, where he shook hands with a red-faced Mantle. Whitey's first impression of Mickey was uncharitable: "I thought, 'What a hayseed!' "[20] Their relationship on and off the field would soon improve.

The Yanks were scheduled to open the season against the Washington Senators. Mickey and some of the other rookies, who had spent the last couple of days getting special instruction in camp, flew to Washington to join the team. They were looking forward to meeting President Harry Truman, who was scheduled to throw out the opening day first pitch, but a three-day rain spoiled the trip. After the rained-out games, the team boarded their handsome private train car for the trip back to New York. Casey walked Mickey down the aisles, passing players he had been reading about in the papers, veterans of the last two world championship Yankee teams. Allie Reynolds, a fellow Oklahoman, stood up from his game of cards and shook hands; Yogi Berra, number two in the AL's MVP race the previous season, smiled and patted him on the arm. Others wondered what whistle-stop town the kid had come from. Mickey was overwhelmed by the splendid dining car — each booth had stained-glass dividers, and the lamps were curved Art Deco glass. It seemed to be designed to introduce him to the good life in New York. Mickey was literally thousands of miles and, it seemed, decades away from the lonely train journey he had taken from Oklahoma to Phoenix only the year before. Settling into a plush booth, he finally blurted out to Casey what had been on his mind since he had arrived in Washington: did the Yankees intend to put him in the lineup or would they be sending him to a minor league team for more seasoning? Stengel told him with a nod, "I think you'll stay with us. When we get back there, just be quiet, and I'll do the talking."[21]

The Yankees organization provided no safety net for the rookie. Luckily for the teenager, a Yankee veteran, Henry Albert "Hank" Bauer, took an interest in him. Bauer looked as if he had been sent from central casting to play the tough Marine veteran that he in fact was. By the time Mantle arrived, Hank was in his third season with the Yankees; he chafed at Stengel's use of him as a platoon player, but he was proud to be a Yankee and could not deny the results: batting against mostly left-handed pitching, he hit .320 in 1950 and collected his second consecutive World Series ring. "I sympathized with Mickey before I ever met him," Bauer said. "I thought all that draft dodger stuff was phony. I knew that there was no way the armed forces were going to take him with that bone disease, and it burned me that so many guys in the press who never served were suddenly getting all patriotic about Mickey not going. Like he had a choice."[22]

When the team returned to New York, Bauer noticed Mickey for the first time as the rookie got off the train at Penn Station. One glance told him there was a lot of work to be done: "He was wearing pants with cuffs that were rolled up, white socks, and, I think, Hush Puppy shoes. We were expected to travel dressed in a suit and tie. Mickey stood out like a farmer in a roomful of Madison Avenue ad execs; he had some kind of tweed jacket and a tie that had — I'm just guessing from memory, but I think there was a peacock painted on it."[23] Bauer walked up to Mickey, slapped him on the shoulder, and introduced himself. He was the first Yankee besides Yogi Berra to offer Mickey any personal attention.

Early the next day Bauer took Mickey to Eisenberg & Eisenberg, the store of choice for fashion-minded New York men for more than half a century. Joe DiMaggio shopped there, as did most of the other Yankees. Hank bought Mickey two sharkskin suits and some accessories. "I don't remember what kind of tie I bought him," Bauer said, "but it was a heck of a lot more sophisticated than the one with the peacock."

The self-proclaimed hick and pool shark from Commerce, Oklahoma, proved to be a quick study. "Those Broadway lights," he recalled thirty-five years later, "the neon glowing, hamburgers sizzling behind plate-glass windows, a carnival atmosphere with Dixieland sounds floating up from the basement steps on 52nd Street. I couldn't avoid the newsstand dailies. Big black headlines, grisly headlines, a murder a day. This is how it looked to a nineteen-year-old kid from Oklahoma. But I was starting to like the excitement of the big city."[24]

He moved into a midtown apartment over the Stage Delicatessen with Bauer and Johnny Hopp (who were both known to put away a couple of beers after the game — but no one had to teach Mickey how to do that). The deli was owned by brothers Max and Hymie Asnas, who looked after Mickey with great affection. The older brother, Max, got Mantle to try matzo-ball soup: "Taste, taste, you'll hit homers with this." Hymie saw to it that Mickey finished every meal with a hunk of cheesecake. "It was so good," Mickey recalled. "I ate just about every meal there." "You keep eating here," Hymie promised him, "and pretty soon you can change your last name from Mantle to Mendel." Mickey certainly did change: no doubt aided by regular meals at the Stage Deli, he rapidly put on weight, which on his body translated into muscle. Over the coming months, he would enjoy the company of a swarm of TV and nightclub stars who also dined regularly at the deli and were thrilled to be in the company of America's most celebrated young baseball player: Joey Bishop, Larry Storch, Buddy Hackett, and others all flabbergasted Mickey by asking for his autograph. One afternoon before a night game with the Cleveland Indians, Mickey went to the Stage Barber Shop, next door to the deli, and discovered that the man in the barber chair next to him was bandleader Harry James. A baseball nut, James recognized Mickey first; Mantle wasn't sure who James was until he shook hands and introduced himself. James urged Mantle to drop by and visit him and his wife, Betty Grable, if he was ever in Vegas — they'd play a few holes at the Desert Inn golf course. A couple of years later, Mickey, Whitey Ford, and their wives took the Jameses up on the invitation and had dinner at their home. "They were very nice to us," Mickey recalled.[25]

Just as in his father's wildest dreams, Mickey would soon have New York at his feet. But first he had to deliver.

Early in the afternoon of April 17, Mickey Mantle walked up to the lineup sheet posted on the locker-room wall and saw that he would be playing right field and batting third behind the team's other spring phenom, Jackie Jensen,* and Rizzuto, and in front of DiMaggio and Berra. In the dugout, Mantle stared silently into the cavernous stands of Yankee Stadium, filled with more than 44,000 people. Berra, standing beside him, said, "Hey, what kind of Opening Day crowd is this? There's no people here." It took Mickey a moment to realize Yogi was joking. Pitching coach "Milkman Jim" Turner asked him, "How many people watched you play in Joplin last year?" The rookie thought around 50,000 total. Turner pointed out that almost as many people would see him that day. Mickey was speechless. He gulped when Turner added, "And most of them came to see what you look like."

---

* Jensen had been a football star at the University of California and was a good enough baseball player to beat out Mickey for the 1958 MVP Award.

Stengel noticed a hole in the sole of one of Mantle's cleats and pointed it out to sportswriter Red Smith, who had not seen Mickey play in the spring. Smith whispered, "Who is he?" "He's that kid of mine," Stengel replied. "That's Mantle?" "Yeah, I asked him didn't he have better shoes, and he said he had a new pair, but they were a little too big." "He's waiting," said Smith, "for an important occasion to wear the new ones."[26]

Fate wasted no time in introducing Mickey to the big leagues: the Yankees' opponent that day was the Boston Red Sox. Just after batting practice, Ted Williams came over to shake hands with DiMaggio. Joe did not think to introduce the greatest hitter in baseball to the Yankees' much-publicized rookie, so Williams took it upon himself. "You must be Mick," said Williams with a grin, extending his hand. Mantle mumbled something in reply; later neither he nor Williams could remember what it was.

A few minutes later, the Yankees' Vic Raschi threw the first pitch, and Mickey's dream became reality. After Raschi retired the order in the top half of the first, Mantle stood in the box and, batting right-handed, took his first big league pitch from Bill Wight, an undistinguished left-hander who would finish 7–7 that season. Forgetting to hold the label on the bat toward his face so he could read it, Mickey shattered his bat, hitting a weak infield grounder. On his second trip to the plate, he popped up to second base. In the sixth inning, with runners on first and third and no outs and Wight still in the game, Mantle started to walk up to the plate. Waiting on deck, DiMaggio, who scarcely spoke to him off the field, stopped him, put a hand on his shoulder, and whispered some words of encouragement to his teenage teammate. Mickey nodded, stepped into the box, and proceeded to stroke a liner over shortstop Johnny Pesky's head for his first major league hit and first run batted in. The Yankees won 5–0.

His opening day jitters relieved, Mantle went on a tear and began to treat major league pitchers the same way he had treated those in the Western Association. The next day he batted in two more runs. Two days later, he went 3-for-5. On May 1, playing in his first road game, he made a Chicago White Sox pitcher named Randy Gumperd the answer to a trivia question: who did Mickey Mantle hit his first big league home run off of? Batting left-handed, he drove the ball over the White Sox bullpen, an estimated 450 feet from home plate. A Chicago fan, no doubt anticipating the memorabilia boom that Mickey would eventually inspire, retrieved the ball and later traded it to Mickey for a dozen autographed baseballs. By mid-May, he was among the American League leaders in home runs, RBIs, and runs scored. He was Cinderella with no coach in sight.

Cinderella, though, was lonely. He soon moved from the apartment over the Stage Deli to the Concourse Plaza Hotel, on 161st Street in the Bronx, just a couple of blocks from Yankee Stadium. Over the years the Concourse had become a home away from home for many Yankees and their families; Babe Ruth had a famous three-bedroom suite there in the 1920s.* Mickey's room, though, was small. At night, he recalled, "without a roommate and almost nobody to talk to, I'd usually sit around reading the sports pages or simply stare at the walls. And there were times when the world of baseball seemed so far off, no longer the game I loved and knew as a boy." Mickey's memories painted a scene out of an Edward Hopper painting. In the Bronx summer nights he would hear "the el trains roaring overhead, wondering where all the people were going to and coming from. Then the diners, the cafeterias, the greasy spoon restaurants . . . leaning forlornly over a cup of coffee and listening to the strange New York accents, to guys in dungarees and leather jackets bunched together at the counter, arguing baseball. I'd walk back to the hotel, head down, lost in thought."[27]

One day when he had nothing else to do, Mickey stopped to watch some kids playing stickball. The kids coaxed him into the game and gave him a stick-bat. Stephen Swid, who was one of them, later recalled Mickey's first at-bat: "Each sewer [manhole cover] was 90

---

* The exterior of the venerable old hotel still stands; it is now a home for the elderly, after an extensive renovation. It can be seen in its faded splendor in scenes from John Cassavetes's 1980 film *Gloria*.

feet apart. I was a two-and-a-half sewer guy, not bad at all. A really big hitter would be a three-sewer guy." "He swung and missed, swung and missed again. . . . A few more swings, a few more misses. Finally he connected. Boom! It was the deepest shot any of us ever saw, more than four sewers. That was it. The news spread all over the neighborhood and throughout the Bronx. Mickey Mantle was a four-sewer man."[28]

In a couple of years, some forty blocks farther downtown, another four-sewer man would thrill the street kids. Newspaper photos of Willie Mays playing stickball in the streets would charm sports fans all over the country, but Mickey's exploits would for years be known only to the handful of kids who played with him in 1951.

Meanwhile, at Yankee Stadium the cheers could be deafening, but he soon discovered how cruel some New York fans could be. "I'd hear their shouts coming from the right field stands, guys screaming at the top of their lungs. Boos and catcalls, curses — 'Go back to Oklahoma, you big bum!' "[29] The draft dodger label just wouldn't go away.

While Mickey Mantle was making national headlines tearing up American League pitching, Willie Mays was a local hero in Minneapolis, astonishing Western Association managers by hitting everything their pitchers threw at him — even when those pitchers threw, literally, at him. In a sixteen-game home stand at Nicollet Park, Mays was knocked down at least nine times and hit four times, sending his manager and teammates into fits of rage. Willie responded to the knockdowns the way a future big leaguer was supposed to: in the sixteen games, he had 38 hits in 63 at-bats for an irrational batting average of .608.

In a road game in September against Louisville, he made a play that stuck in the memory of everyone who saw it. A Louisville outfielder named Taft "Taffy" Wright, a nine-year major league veteran with a career batting average of .311, was playing out his professional career in the minors; he smashed a ball deep into center that looked as if it was headed for the flag pole. Jim Piersall, assigned by the Boston Red Sox to finish out the season in Louisville,* recalled the play this way: "Taffy hit a really good shot to the deepest part of the park. The only question was whether or not the ball would clear the fence, which was very high in that part of the park, or bounce off the top for a double or triple. No one thought it had a chance to be caught. When I replay in my memory what Willie did it still doesn't seem real. Remember that movie where Fred Astaire walked up a wall? Well, that's what it looked to me like Willie did. He caught his spikes on something — a board, a cement block, I don't know — and then took another step up. I swear, it looked like he was walking up the wall. He caught the damn thing about a foot from the top, turned like a cat, and jumped back down. He made kind of a lazy throw back into the infield. Taffy, meanwhile, slid into second base, got up, and began dusting himself off. Then he took a lead off second base. The umpire tapped him on the shoulder and told him he was out. Taffy was bewildered. 'He didn't catch that ball!' he was yelling. 'He couldn't have caught that ball!' We started yelling from the dugout, 'Taffy, he did catch it! He really did!' But Taffy didn't believe us. He thought we were kidding him. He wouldn't leave the field. Our manager, Pinky Higgins, had to come out on the field and break the news that he was out. I still remember him trotting off the field shaking his head and looking at Willie in center field, his hands on his knees and a big grin on his face."[30]

The *Minneapolis Star*'s Bob Beebe, the first baseball writer to cover Willie after he left Birmingham, recounted that nearly thirty

---

* Piersall had spent the first 121 games of the season playing for the Birmingham Barons, wowing the fans at Willie's old ballpark, Rickwood Field. Many rated him as equal or superior to Mays as an outfielder. Alf Van Hoose, a columnist for the *Birmingham News* and the official scorer for the Black Barons' games, saw both of them play and wrote a column on the debate that caused a minor uproar in the sports pages of both black and white papers. According to Van Hoose, Mays and Piersall were about equal in the ability to run down balls hit over their head and in having the range to cover ground in all parts of the outfield. Piersall was rated slightly better at getting a fast break on a ball, while Mays had a slight edge in hustle, alertness, and throwing.

years later he bumped into Taffy Wright in Orlando, Florida, and asked him if he remembered the play. Wright did. "That little son of a bitch never did catch the ball. How could he catch that?"[31]

For fans in most of the cities in the Western Association, Willie Mays was the first famous black ballplayer they had ever seen. By the time the Millers made their second road trip, the racial epithets began to fade away, replaced by cheers. Willie became a celebrity, but Jim Crow was still alive and well in many of the towns on the circuit, if not in Minneapolis itself; Willie often had to enter movie theaters from the side door and sit in the balcony.

One night in Sioux City, Iowa, he went to see a Western — he would later recall that the film starred Tyrone Power, so it was probably *Rawhide*, which was released about that time — when, about halfway through, the movie was stopped and the house lights went on. He was startled a second time when the manager came onstage and called out, "If Willie Mays is in the audience, would he please call his manager at the hotel?"

Mays's first reaction when he heard the theater manager's announcement was a natural one: he thought Cat or someone else in his family had had an accident or was ill. He took a cab back to the team's hotel — one of the nicer things about playing in Minneapolis was that all the players could stay in the same hotel — and knocked on Heath's door. Heath looked at Willie with a sad smile. "I just got off the phone with New York," he told him. "Let me be the first to congratulate you." Willie was dumbfounded. "What for?" "The Giants," Heath replied, "want you right away." Willie wanted to know on whose authority. "Leo's," Heath informed him.

In deciding to promote Willie, the New York Giants were going by much more than just Willie's batting average or even Tommy Heath's opinion. They had dispatched a scout, Hank DeBerry, to Minneapolis to monitor his progress. DeBerry's report was an unqualified rave: "Sensational. Is the outstanding player on the Minneapolis club and probably in all the minor leagues for that matter. . . . Hits all pitches and hits to all fields. Hits the ball where it is pitched as good as any player seen in many days. Everything he does is sensational. He has made the most spectacular catches. Runs and throws with the best of them. . . . Slides hard, plays hard. He is sensational and just about as popular with local fans as he can be — a real favorite." Leo Durocher paid close attention to one line in particular: the scout noted that the Louisville pitchers knocked Mays down several times, "but it seemed to have no effect on him at all." If Durocher had any doubts about Willie's toughness, the report eased his mind.

DeBerry did concede that Willie had a few flaws: "He ran a bit with his head down. There may have been a few times when his manager needed a rope." This remark probably meant that Willie was a bit too free on the bases, ready to steal in almost any situation or to try to take an extra base on a ball hit in the gap. But on the whole, "this player is the best prospect in America." DeBerry, like most seasoned scouts, was not given to overstatement. When he called Willie the best prospect in America, he was fully aware of a young man named Mantle who had just begun to play for the New York Yankees.

About four months after he scouted Willie, DeBerry died of a heart attack. Roger Kahn, who knew him, said, "I'll bet Hank thought his evaluation of Willie Mays was the culmination of a life's work."[32]

After hearing the news from Heath, the Giants' prize prospect hesitated for a moment, then told his manager to call Durocher back — he didn't want to go. It was Heath's turn to be dumbfounded. How could any young player feel that way, he wanted to know. Willie went through a litany of reasons: he was happy in Minneapolis and wanted to help the Millers win the pennant. Most of all, he still didn't think he was ready to hit big league pitching. And there was another reason that wasn't known until years later. "Willie had a girlfriend there," said Charlie Einstein. "There weren't a lot of black girls in Minneapolis at that time, but most of them were rabid baseball fans. He met a very nice girl at the ballpark and came very close to getting serious with her. I always wondered what became of her."[33]

Back in New York, Mickey was also in the process of finding himself a girl, but definitely not one he'd be bringing home to mother.

Heath, of course, knew that Mays's response would be unacceptable to Durocher. What the hell, Durocher asked, did he mean that he wasn't coming to New York? Willie hadn't heard such forceful language from a baseball man since he was a teenager and Piper Davis had straightened him out. But he still insisted that he couldn't handle major league pitchers. "What are you hitting now?" Durocher asked him. ".477." "Well, do you think you could hit 2 fucking 55 for me?" Willie swallowed hard and mumbled, "I think so." "Okay, then," the manager told him. "Quit costing the ball club money with long-distance phone calls and join the team."

Heath's young outfielder hung up the phone and quietly told his former manager he had been called up. Heath shook his hand and wished him all the best. Three days later, in the Sunday *Minneapolis Tribune*, there was a special ad placed by Horace Stoneham written to the Twin Cities' desolate fandom: "We feel that Minneapolis baseball fans, who have so enthusiastically supported the Minneapolis club, are entitled to an explanation for the player deal that on Friday transferred Outfielder Willie Mays from the Millers to the New York Giants. We appreciate his worth to the Millers, but in all fairness, Mays himself must be a factor in these considerations. On the record of performance since the American Association season started, Mays is entitled to this promotion and the chance to prove that he can play major league baseball." Stoneham added that the Giants would do their best to give the Millers' fans a winning team, but the fans knew that no matter who the parent club sent them, they would never have another Willie Mays.

The Millers traveled to Sioux City, where Ray Dandridge, who had told Willie that soon he would be eating steak, walked into the clubhouse and heard the news that Mays was on his way to the big leagues. Dandridge packed the belongings Willie had left behind so they could be sent on to him in New York. The veteran had mixed emotions — he was thrilled for the young man, but full of anxiety about his own future. He was hitting over .360 at the time and would finish the season at .338. Would the Giants be calling him up as well? In his heart, he knew the truth: he'd never be getting that call. He was thirty-seven, and his time had passed. For Willie — and Mickey — it was just about to begin.*

---

*There was an even more bitter irony connected to Mays's ascension to the big leagues, though Willie did not realize it until he had been with the team for a few days. The Giants had to release someone from their roster to make room for the rookie. The player they let go was the great Artie Wilson, Willie's teammate and mentor with the Black Barons, the last man to hit over .400 in organized baseball. Wilson, who was thirty, had played in just nineteen games for the Giants, mostly as a pinch-hitter and late-innings defensive replacement. He moved to the West Coast and played for ten more seasons in the Pacific Coast League, but never again got a shot at the majors.

8

"Is That Mickey and Willie?"

T om Hanks may have thought there was no crying in baseball, but as the summer of 1951 approached, the sport's two most highly prized rookies were weeping.

Major league pitchers are a community within a community, and word quickly got around that nineteen-year-old Mickey Mantle had weaknesses. From the right side it was high fastballs, slightly up out of the strike zone, which for some unexplained reason he simply couldn't lay off. From the left side it was low outside curves or other breaking pitches. Mickey began striking out — in bunches.

Mantle's shyness had, up to this point, masked a ferocious temper. After striking out six times in a doubleheader in June, he began assaulting water coolers again, a serious enough offense when committed at Yankee Stadium, but downright unacceptable when it occurred in other ballparks around the league. After fanning twice against the St. Louis Browns, Mickey destroyed the cooler in the visitors' dugout, much to the amusement of Hank Bauer and Yogi Berra, who did not truly understand how frustrated their new phenom was.

Yogi thought he could lighten the atmosphere with a joke. "Why are you so nervous?" he asked Mickey. Mantle mumbled that he wasn't. "Then how come you're wearing your jock strap outside of your uniform?" Yogi said with a grin. Mantle actually glanced down to see if it was true.[1]

Bill Veeck, who had just become principal owner of the Browns (after selling off his interest in the Cleveland Indians in 1950), called George Weiss in New York and suggested that the Yankees, with all their money, should pay for the water cooler Mickey had demolished. Weiss chuckled good-naturedly. Veeck wasn't kidding.

Mantle did not learn quickly from his early failures, but simply gritted his teeth and swung harder. He was pushing himself to the point of emotional strain to fulfill Mutt's dream. Stengel began to lose patience with Mickey, not because he was striking out but because he was swinging at bad pitches. Casey was right about the bad pitches, but raised in an era when making contact with the ball was the hitter's primary job, he did not understand — as many would not understand for decades — that the new game in baseball was power and that every home run Mantle hit was well worth the two or three strikeouts that it cost. But then, in the late spring of 1951, Mantle had also stopped hitting home runs.

Allie Reynolds tried to tell him about the virtue of choosing the right pitch to hit, of getting ahead in the count and forcing the pitcher to throw him something he could drive. It wasn't that Mantle paid no attention to Reynolds, but that he was too young to translate Reynolds's good advice into action. As Hank Bauer put it, "In the summer of 1951 we could see that Mickey wasn't ready for the big leagues." But, said Bauer, "it was just as obvious that in a short time he was going to be very ready."[2]

When Mickey Mantle came to New York, he was an unpolished hick. Willie Mays, who had already been to New York and played exhibition games in the Polo Grounds with the Black Barons, headed for the big city having actually seen some of America. Mickey arrived in the city in a suit that looked like it came from a road company of *L'il Abner*; Willie had been given grooming tips by several vets and, at least in comparison to Mantle, looked as if he had stepped out of a production of *Guys and Dolls* (which, starring Robert Alda, was one of Broadway's biggest smashes in 1951). On the plane, Willie put his cap and glove (practically all he'd had a chance to grab before leaving the Millers) on the seat next to him. A stewardess asked him with a smile, "Are you Jackie Robinson?" Willie beamed and said no, but he was going to play for the New York Giants and would soon be playing baseball against Jackie. When he arrived in Manhattan on May 25, the Giants were playing under .500 ball and were so far behind the Brooklyn Dodgers that Mays couldn't help but wonder, "What do the Giants need me for?"[3]

After a cab ride from LaGuardia to the Giants' front office, an ebullient Mays shook hands with Doc Bowman, the Giants' trainer, and Eddie Brannick, New York's traveling secretary, who presented him with his contract. Without hesitation, Willie, his hand shaking with excitement, signed for $5,000. Brannick put his hand on his new player's shoulder and hurried him out the door for the train ride to Philadelphia, where the Giants were playing the Phillies.

Bowman went out of his way to make Willie feel that the team was looking out for his interests — Monte Irvin, he told Willie, was going to be his roommate. Irvin, like Mays, had been born in Alabama, although he'd grown up in Orange, New Jersey, right outside Newark. He was twelve years older than Mays and knew him from barnstorming exhibitions, games Willie recalled fondly because he had made more money from them than he had playing for the Giants' farm team in Trenton.

Mays's first connection to his big league team involved none of the anxiety that Mantle had experienced. When he got to the team's hotel in Philadelphia and knocked on his door, he was greeted with "Hi ya, roomie. Does Skip know you're here?" A smiling Irvin brought him to Durocher's room; it was the first time in Willie's life he had seen a hotel suite. His eye took a quick inventory:

> This was only a weekend series, but the closet was stuffed with his clothes and shoes. Leo definitely liked the finer things in life.
>
> "Glad to see you, son," he said. "Glad you're hitting four seventy-seven."
>
> He might have made players nervous with his style, but he made me relaxed right away. I see now what he did. He buttered me up.[4]

At Shibe Park, Mays was surprised to find the Giants clubhouse quiet — but when you're in fifth place, he reasoned, there wasn't too much to talk about. His locker was next to Irvin's. He looked inside and saw for the first time the shirt with the number millions of baseball fans around the world would come to associate with him, 24. "Son," Durocher told him, "you're batting third and playing centerfield." Willie was dazzled. "That sounded to me like something DiMaggio might be doing. . . . You don't put a man up third unless you think he's your best all-around player. In centerfield — I guess of all the fielding positions on a team — that has always been the one filled by a player who can lead the team, take charge, make plays. I just couldn't believe this was happening to me."[5]

Willie walked out on the field and was surprised to find that Shibe Park, home of the Phillies and the A's, the oldest steel-and-concrete ballpark in America, looked like a larger version of Rickwood Field, where he had made his professional debut. In fact, as described earlier, Shibe had been a model for Rickwood, and Philadelphia A's owner and manager Connie Mack had visited Birmingham to help lay out the park. Now it was as if all of baseball was conspiring to help Willie hit the big leagues in style.

He felt loose. In batting practice, Willie slammed balls to all fields, including several into the seats. When he walked out of the cage, Durocher was there to hug him and tell him how happy he was to have him there. Players on both teams, Leo said, had stopped to watch him in awe as he took his swings. Unlike Mickey, Willie had not yet made headlines except in minor league parks, but among big league teams the word was out.

Thirty minutes later, he stepped into a major league batter's box for the first time and faced Bubba Church, a right-hander who had been born in Birmingham just a few miles from Willie's home. He got one decent pitch to hit and fouled it into the right-field stands. On the fourth pitch, looking for something to pull, he took a curveball on the outside corner for strike three. Chagrined, he dragged his bat back to the dugout, where his teammates grinned and said, "Welcome to the big leagues!" He was 0-for-4 the rest of the afternoon, without a single hard-hit ball, but the Giants won.

The next day, a Saturday, Willie was really welcomed to the big leagues when he had to face Robin Roberts, a twenty-game winner the season before and the best right-handed pitcher in the National League for at least the first half of the decade. Willie went 0-for-3, but took some consolation in having fouled off some pitches and worked Roberts for two walks. Anyway, the Giants won again. The next day, facing a career mediocrity, Russ Meyer, he went hitless in four at-bats, fanning twice, but again the Giants won and reached .500.

On May 28, Mays finally got a chance to bat as a Giant in the Polo Grounds. Many young hitters and outfielders were intimidated by the ballpark's weird horseshoe configuration — 475 feet from home plate to dead center field, 450 to right-center, and 425 to left-center — but the right-field foul pole was a mere 260 feet away, and a corner in left field had a sharp angle only 280 feet from home. The strange dimensions made the Polo Grounds a dream to both right- and left-handed pull hitters, but for most batters the fences were just too high and too far away.

The starting pitcher for the Boston Braves that day was Warren Spahn, who had led the National League in victories for the previous two years and would go on to win more games than any other pitcher in either league during the decade. Spahn, a sly left-hander, knew how to keep hitters, particularly young hitters, from reaching those shallow right- and left-field corners. In the bottom of the first, he got the first two Giant hitters on a pop-up and a dribbler back to the mound. Mays was still batting third — despite his 0-for-12 start, Durocher's faith in him had not wavered. In later years, Willie could not recall what pitch Spahn threw to him that he drove over the left-field roof for his first major league home run. All he could remember was that it was not a fastball. Spahn couldn't recall the pitch either. "I don't think it was a fastball," he quipped, "because I don't have one. I think it was a curveball. All I can really remember is that it was a damn good pitch. It looked great heading towards the plate and it looked great flying over the roof." For the first sixty feet, Spahn added, "it was a hell of a pitch."[6]

After the game, Willie's enthusiasm was tempered by the fact that Spahn and the Braves won, 4–1. He was relieved, though, to think that his slump was over. It was not. The next day, against the Braves' tough right-hander Lew Burdette, he went hitless and left four runners on base. It got worse. Over the next four games he didn't get a single hit; his batting average for his first 25 at-bats in the major leagues was .040. The word was out: the kid had trouble with curveballs (though he had hit that probably-a-curveball from Warren Spahn well over 400 feet).

Two days after losing to the Braves, 6–3, in the second game of a doubleheader, Durocher threw a tantrum in the clubhouse, knocking over a chair, after which he stormed up the stairs to his office and slammed the door. Willie, wondering if Leo's anger was directed at him, sat in front of his locker and cried while his teammates dressed. A few minutes later, Durocher reappeared in the clubhouse and, as he so often did, put his hand on Willie's shoulder. "What's the matter, son?" he asked. In a shrill voice that made him sound younger than his twenty years, the rookie told his manager between sobs that he couldn't hit big league pitching and he feared the Giants were going to send him back down to Minneapolis. Durocher became angry, but it was a righteous anger of precisely the kind that Willie needed to hear. Listen, he told his phenom, *he* was the manager and as long as he was, Willie would be *his* center fielder. In a loud voice, he told him that he had the potential to be the best ballplayer he had ever seen. Go get some sleep, Durocher told him, and start over tomorrow.

As he walked back up the stairs to his office, Durocher stopped, turned, and offered Willie some practical advice. Just stop trying to pull the ball so damn much, he said. Just meet it and hit it to right until you get your timing. Then, Leo promised, things would start to go his way. Oh — and hike your pants up a bit. Leo had long believed that umpires gave players with lower pants legs a larger strike zone. Or at least that was what he told Willie, to give him the illusion that he was getting an edge on the pitcher.

The next day Durocher implemented another shrewd tactic. Rather than simply drop Willie down in the batting order, he asked him if he would help the team by batting eighth. The tail end of the batting order, Leo told him, needed some punch. Willie, flattered that his manager would ask him to help out in any way, gushed, "Of course." That day against the Pittsburgh Pirates, Mays got two hits, including a triple to right-center field — where Durocher had told him to try to hit the ball — that would have cleared the fences in most big league parks by twenty or thirty feet, and he gunned down a Pirate runner at third base who dared to test his arm on a single to center field. He had also quickly learned not to be intimidated by the Polo Grounds' cavernous outfield, having discovered that balls hit at even a slight angle between the outfielders might go for singles in some parks but were easy doubles for him at home.

After he hit two two-baggers the next day, Willie and the Giants started on a roll. His teammates liked him, the fans adored him, and to the veteran New York sportswriters he was the black son they never had. But if Willie thought he was going to cruise through his rookie season, he soon discovered there were obstacles he hadn't yet considered. One of them was a pal from the Negro Leagues he had barnstormed with.

Frank Forbes was a successful black boxing promoter who had worked for and with most of the prominent black fighters of his era, including heavyweight champions Ezzard Charles and Jersey Joe Walcott, as well as the most popular and the greatest pound-for-pound fighter of his and perhaps any other time, Sugar Ray Robinson. Having staged bouts at the Polo Grounds, Forbes had built a good working relationship with Horace Stoneham and the New York Giants. It was no surprise, then, that the Giants turned over the care of their most valuable young property to Forbes. Forbes was offered a business relationship by the Giants: if he would find a safe place for Willie to live and keep a close eye on him, he would be allowed to share in promotions Mays did with the organization.

Through Forbes, Willie met the leading black celebrities of his day such as Robinson and Joe Louis, who had been heavyweight champion for all of Willie's formative years; he also met entertainers like Billy Eckstine and Dizzy Gillespie, who were as thrilled to be around the Giants' budding young superstar as he was to be in their presence. Monte Irvin recalled a breathless Willie phoning Cat Mays back in Alabama, saying, "Pop, you're not going to believe this, but *I just met Duke Ellington*. He came to the game last night."[7] In fact, Cat had met Duke Ellington when he played with a small combo at Bob's Little Savoy in Birmingham sometime in the mid-1930s.

Forbes told *Time* magazine in 1954, "When I first met Willie, I thought he was the most open, decent, down-to-earth guy I'd ever seen — completely unspoiled and completely natural. I was worried to death about the kind of people he might get mixed up with." It was assumed, of course, that Mays would be living in Harlem, a place Forbes found to be "full of people just wanting to part an innocent youngster from his money. Somebody had to see to it that Willie wasn't exploited, sift the chaff from the flour, figure out who was in a racket and who was in a legitimate organization."[8]

A cousin of Cat's who lived in Harlem offered Willie a room with his family, but it was crowded and noisy, with Willie's distant cousins going in and out at all hours. Willie, thought the Giants and Forbes, needed a "good home environment"—meaning not surrounded by family. Through his own contacts, Forbes found David and Ann Goosby on 155th Street and St. Nicholas Place — or about three good Willie Mays pegs from the Polo Grounds. Mrs. Goosby cooked regularly for Willie, did his laundry, and, with Forbes's help, looked after his every need as no one had done since Willie left Fairfield and Aunt Sarah.

"Willie's a good boy," Mrs. Goosby told a reporter from *Time*, "and all I have to lecture him on besides eating properly is his habit of reading comic books. That boy spends hours, I swear, with those comics."[9] If only Willie had been playing for the Yankees, he and Yogi Berra could have shared their stacks of comics.

Forbes, in turn, enlisted Monte Irvin's assistance when it came to outfitting Willie and showing him the best restaurants and places to go. Irvin not only was older than Willie but had grown up in a much more sophisticated environment. "He was such a countrified boy," Irvin told me, "that he had to be shown just about everything, but he learned very, very quickly."[10] Irvin was joking just a bit; Willie was not a country boy. He never rode a horse to school, as Mickey Mantle had. But nearly all young black ballplayers from the South received some ribbing from the older players, particularly those who had grown up north of the Mason-Dixon Line.

Forbes and Irvin felt they had to protect Willie from women. After each Giants home game, the players would find dozens of females waiting at the exit gate, supposedly looking for autographs but, according to Irvin, "really waiting to give Willie *their* autograph as well as their phone number." Sometimes, after a day game, Irvin would take Willie out to dinner, and Willie would empty his pockets of all the notes he had collected when leaving the ballpark. "I assumed that none of these girls was up to any good," said Irvin, "and in the course of our conversation, when Willie wasn't paying any attention, I'd crumple them up and throw them away." Sometimes Irvin would find notes from hustlers who wanted to act as Willie's agent "for commercial deals." Irvin tossed those messages away as well. Any legitimate businessman, he felt, would approach Willie through the ball club. Mickey could have used similar guidance from the New York Yankees.

Like all New Yorkers, Mickey had to learn to use the subway. On his first underground trip, he asked someone how to get to the ballpark. The fellow, who did not recognize Mantle, told him, No problem, just take the Lexington Avenue Express and get off at 161st Street. Mickey managed to end up on the wrong train and wound up instead at the Polo Grounds, where he heard clusters of happy Giants fans. He asked them what they were celebrating; they told him that the Giants had just beaten the Cincinnati Reds on a home run by their great new rookie, Willie Mays. Once he figured out what had happened, in a panic, he jogged over the Macombs Dam Bridge until he reached Yankee Stadium. After that, he mostly got around by cab.

Some nights were lonely. Mickey went to the movies as often as he could, catching noon shows when the Yankees had a night game or late shows after day games. "I usually sat in a last row balcony seat, alone, checking my watch because the rules were that you had to be suited up and ready for batting practice three hours ahead of time." His favorites, of course, were Westerns. Since they were also the favorites of Willie Mays, and since Willie's favorite spot was the balcony, and since many uptown New York movie theaters were integrated by the early 1950s, Mickey might well have been sitting close to Willie in the dark without knowing it. Or he may have passed Willie on the way in or out, as the Giants occasionally scheduled a day game in New York on days the Yankees were playing at night — and vice versa.

Some nights he was not alone. "Around that time," he would later say in a memoir, "a very pretty showgirl named Holly came into my life." Perhaps he met her in the balcony of a movie theater, or at the Stage Deli, eating a reuben sandwich. "Once in a while when the team was in New York and I had the evening free after a day game, we'd go out for dinner or Holly would hang out with me at the apartment on Seventh Avenue. I guess I developed my first taste for the high life then — meeting Holly's friends, getting stuck with the check at too many fancy restaurants, discovering Scotch at too many dull cocktail parties. It was a lot of fun — while it lasted."[11]

It didn't last too long, but it was long enough to get him into quite a bit of trouble. He would later claim to have met his first "agent" through a phone call — somehow the man got his phone number and woke him up early one morning to tell him of a "golden opportunity" he had for him. Before Mantle had finished brushing his teeth, a "short, chubby guy with a razor-thin mustache" was at his apartment with two contracts. One was for personal services, for which Mickey signed away 10 percent of all his earnings outside baseball for ten years; the second, for two years, gave the "agent" 50 percent of Mickey's endorsements, testimonials, and appearances.

"You don't have to sign till you see a lawyer," the agent reassured him, and of course, he had a lawyer to refer Mickey to. It strains credulity to think that Mantle signed the contracts. Where were Mickey's roommates to advise him on this? And why didn't Mickey, who consulted the Yankees and/or his father on nearly everything, ask someone else for advice? The answer is probably that Mickey trusted Holly. Shortly after meeting the shyster agent, Mickey found out that the man was "somehow" acquainted with her and had "sold" her 25 percent of his interest in Mickey's earnings.

In his various memoirs, Mickey never identified the man, but six years later, when Holly told her story to a scandal mag, his name was revealed as Alan Savitt. By all accounts, he seemed to be a road-show version of a Damon Runyon character. He promised to get Mickey endorsements, personal appearances, even movie deals: "The sky is the limit, trust me."

There was no Frank Forbes to handle Mickey's affairs or to protect him, as Willie was protected, but luckily Mantle had his own Monte Irvin in Hank Bauer. When Mantle told Bauer about his new arrangement with Savitt, the former Marine was appalled and acted quickly by introducing Mickey to Frank Scott, the Yankees' traveling secretary, who handled endorsement deals for other Yankee players. This time, Mickey checked him out, asking Bill "Moose" Skowron what commission Scott took from their deals. "The usual 10 percent," Moose told him. Mantle didn't have much schooling, but he knew the difference between 10 percent and 50. Bauer then hooked Mantle up with the Yankees' front office; it didn't take much muscle from a legitimate law firm to scare Mickey's "agent" away. Holly, though, would be a bit tougher to get rid of.

Just before the World Series started, Mickey met his father out in front of Yankee Stadium. Mutt was picking up tickets for himself and a friend, Trucky Compton, who had driven up from Commerce with him. Mickey showed up with . . . Holly. Smile on his face, Mick introduced her. "She's a very good friend," he told his father. Mutt tipped his hat and smiled. A little later he took his son aside and told him that he should "do the right thing and marry your own kind."

"It's not what you think, Dad," Mickey replied — a rather silly remark considering that it was of course exactly what Mutt thought. One wonders what Mickey had expected his father's reaction would be.

At the time, Mutt was sick — though Mickey did not yet know it. It was the Hodgkin's disease that ran through his family like a curse. He was about to see his life's dream fulfilled when Mickey stepped on the field for his first World Series game; he was desperate to make yet another dream come true before he died — that of seeing his son settled down and ready to raise a family. And a quick glance at Holly convinced him that Mickey was headed in the wrong direction. Merlyn was a sweet gal, he told Mick; she loved him and she was just what Mickey needed to keep his head straight. Mickey mumbled that he knew that. Well, then, Mutt told him, after the World Series was over, he had better get on back to Oklahoma and marry her.

Years later, in various accounts of Mickey's life, Mutt would come under some criticism for trying to keep too tight a rein on his son. Perhaps, but at least in this situation it's important to put everything in perspective. Mickey was nineteen, an unsophisticated hick with no one to look after him in the big city — as evidenced by the scrapes he managed to get himself into after being in New York for just a couple of months. Under the circumstances, it's hard to imagine that Mutt Mantle would have given his son any other advice.

Both Mantle and Mays spent the formative years of their careers under Hall of Fame managers. But while Willie could not have been luckier than to play for Leo Durocher, for Mickey, playing under Casey Stengel was a mixed blessing. Casey was a great manager, much better than Durocher, but personally he couldn't have been more wrong for Mickey.

Their managerial philosophies evolved out of their playing careers. Casey made his bones with the Giants; Leo made his with the Yankees. Durocher played more than two hundred games as an infielder with the Ruth-Gehrig Yankees, though he was better known as a shortstop for the Gashouse Gang Cardinals of the mid-1930s. He lasted seventeen years in the big leagues, hitting just .247 with only 24 home runs — Babe Ruth famously referred to him as "The All American Out" — and 31 stolen bases. His only genuine talent was his fielding — he led NL shortstops three times in fielding average — but if bench jockeying had resulted in the scoring or prevention of runs, Durocher would have been at the top of the league. The ultraconservative Branch Rickey thought that Durocher "had an infinite capacity for immediately making a bad thing worse." Still, when he needed a shortstop for the Cardinals in 1933, Rickey traded for Durocher. Because he learned to survive in the big leagues without being able to hit for power, Leo preferred teams that could get the ball in play.

Stengel was the better ballplayer, hitting .284 with 60 home runs and 131 stolen bases in fourteen years with the Dodgers, Pirates, Phillies, Giants, and Braves. Casey's greatest influence was Giants manager John McGraw, and his years under McGraw shaped him as a manager, particularly McGraw's tactic of "platooning" players to create favorable matchups.

Leo was a drinker, gambler, and shameless womanizer who cheated on one wife, actress Laraine Day, openly.* His approach to managing was notoriously old-school. When he began his first full season with the Giants in 1949, he immediately began striking from the roster the names who were better known for power hitting than speed and finesse. Casey, less of a tactician than Leo and more of a strategist, was more progressive and better understood the value of power in the new game. The Giants' loss was the Yankees' gain in August 1949 when Horace Stoneham, for $40,000 and in accordance with Durocher's wishes, sent slugging first baseman Johnny Mize to the Bronx, where he proved to be worth his considerable weight as a pinch-hitter and part-time player.

Sometime in the 1980s, about two decades after his managing career was over, references to Stengel as a "racist" began to pop up. This was in part the result of his famous comment when the Yankees finally signed a black player, Elston Howard: "I got one who can't run." For all his flaws, Durocher is seen as a pioneer in race relations, partly for a widely read statement he made to reporters in 1947 that he had seen "a million good colored players" and he would gladly have them on his team if blacks "weren't barred by the owners."†

Leo also stood up to Dixie Walker and several other Dodgers in 1947 when he heard about the rumor of a proposed strike if Branch Rickey signed black players. "I'm the manager of this ball club," he told them, "and I'm interested in one thing: Winning. I'll play an elephant if he can do the job. And to make room for him I'll send

---

* Roger Kahn recalls having a conversation with Durocher in a hotel lobby when a well-known Hungarian film actress walked by, tapped him on the arm, and called him "Dah-ling." "Fucked her last night," Durocher said to Kahn as the actress walked away (personal interview, January 2010).

† For his part, Commissioner Kenesaw Mountain Landis denied that the owners were prohibiting blacks from playing in the big leagues.

my own brother home. This fellow is a great ballplayer. He's going to win pennants for us. He's going to put money in your pockets and money in mine."[12] No doubt it took courage for any manager in the late 1940s to take such a stance. Ironically, "this fellow" proved to be Jackie Robinson, with whom Durocher did not get along. Durocher's preference was for black players who were not sharp-tongued with aggressive personalities. He got along splendidly with Willie Mays.

Most important, Durocher could see that all Willie needed was seasoning, while Stengel began, in the spring of 1951, a relentless campaign to mold Mickey — a campaign that would continue until Stengel was fired by the Yankees ten years later. Both managers wanted their star outfielders to cut down on strikeouts by learning to make contact with the ball. Mays, to a degree, was capable of this, while Mantle was not. But Durocher had a subtle way of getting Willie to do what he wanted him to do, such as when he suggested that Willie "just meet" the ball and hit it to right field. Casey never put it that way to Mickey; it was always "I think you should do it this way."

In the summer of 1951, Willie Mays resented no one, but he soon began to discover that at least a few players around the league harbored some resentment toward him. On June 26, Mays played his first game against the Dodgers and renewed his acquaintance with Roy Campanella, Brooklyn's genial but crafty Italian–African American catcher. Like Yogi Berra, his American League counterpart, Campanella's pleasant demeanor masked a fierce competitive spirit, but unlike Berra, he was not above using race to get an edge. "What do you think of him, Willie?" Campy asked Mays as he stepped into the batter's box against Preacher Roe. Mays blandly remarked that Roe was a pretty good pitcher. "You're lucky today," the catcher informed him. "Wait till you get Don Newcombe tomorrow. He hates colored rookies. He'll blow you down." Don Newcombe, a fearsome six-foot-four, 225-pound right-hander from Madison, New Jersey, was the major league's first great black ace. He had won nineteen games in 1950 and would win twenty-one in 1951. The sentiments attributed to him by his catcher regarding black rookies were false, but Campanella's baiting of Mays, according to his biographer, Neil Lanctot, was indicative of a feeling that "Willie hadn't yet paid his dues. Some players like Campanella had banged around the Negro Leagues for years and had left many of their prime seasons behind. Willie, a few of the older black veterans thought, had been coddled by the Giants and, compared to them, hadn't had a particularly rough time."[13]

Willie soon learned that Newcombe was not averse to brushing hitters of any color back off the plate. After facing him a couple of times, Mays learned that he was no more to be feared than Robin Roberts or Warren Spahn, but was to be no less respected. He also learned to not let himself be distracted by Roy Campanella. "Campy," he told him the next time the Giants played the Dodgers, "Mr. Leo says I'm not supposed to listen to you."

Mickey's struggles at the plate continued into July. Patience of the kind Durocher had shown with Willie might have paid big dividends for Stengel and the Yankees. But patience was not a cardinal virtue for the organization.

On the fifteenth, the Yankees were in Detroit for a series with the Tigers. Stengel had just checked into his hotel when he got a call from George Weiss. He then called Mickey into his room to give him the news: the front office had decided to send him down to Kansas City, where, Casey assured him, he would get his swing back. It would just be for a couple of weeks and he'd be back up in no time.

It wasn't just the strikeouts. Though they annoyed Casey no end, he didn't yet understand that the increase in power in big league ball meant an automatic increase in swings and misses. He had been spoiled by the performances of two extraordinary hitters, Joe DiMaggio, who struck out just 369 times in 1,736 games, and Yogi Berra, who ended his career with just 414 strikeouts in 2,120 games. Both these numbers were amazingly low for power hitters. Increasingly throughout the decade, sluggers would fan more and more often while reaching for the fences.

Mickey couldn't deny that his overall game was suffering; in a game against the White Sox, he had let a shallow pop fly to right drop at his feet. Ed Lopat, who did not suffer fools on days when he pitched, waited until they were in the dugout before grabbing the muscular teenager by the sleeve. "If you don't want to play," Lopat told him, just loud enough for others to hear, though they did not indicate that they did, "don't screw around with our money." Mantle later said that after that incident he could see the end coming; what he didn't know was that it was not the end, just an interlude. When he struck out five consecutive times in a doubleheader with the Red Sox, Stengel told reserve outfielder Cliff Mapes, "Get in there for Mantle. We need somebody who can hit the ball."[14] In a short time, Mickey would have both the position and Mapes's number 7. But right then it seemed like the end of the world.

Mickey would later recall that when Stengel told him of his demotion, the old manager had tears in his eyes and told him, on the way out of the hotel, "I'm counting on you." Had Mickey been able to put his situation in perspective, he would have seen there was nothing unusual about a nineteen-year-old being dropped to Triple-A to get his concentration back, but nothing could assuage the numbing sense of failure and the terrible knowledge that soon he would have to call Mutt and tell him what had happened.

The train that brought Mickey to join the Kansas City Blues took him to Minneapolis, where they were playing a series with the Millers. Once again, Mickey had missed playing against Willie, this time by less than three months.

In his first game, Mantle thought that bunting for a hit would be a smart way to show off his speed and let the team know he was hustling. After dragging the ball between the pitcher's mound and first base for a hit, he thought he'd be congratulated. Instead, manager George Selkirk (a former Yankee himself who just a few years before had managed Yogi Berra at Newark) rudely informed him that he had not been sent there to bunt. Get some hits, he told Mantle, and get your confidence back.

The Blues, like most minor league teams, were composed largely of players either trying to claw their way into the major leagues or fighting to keep from falling out of professional baseball altogether. Nerves were raw; drinking and fighting were common. Mickey, who was not drinking at the time, later said, "Pitchers carried pints of whiskey in their back pockets, right in the bullpen. It was like a comedy of errors."[15]

In such an atmosphere, Mantle could not get his game back. He wrote home to Merlyn to tell her how much he missed her, but did not dare write to his father. Among the Blues, he alone got fan letters, which caused resentment among the veterans. It irritated them even more when Mickey carelessly left the letters unopened. His teammates who took the time to look at them found out that nearly all were from angry fans accusing him of being a traitor and draft dodger—a few even contained death threats. One day a friend came to visit him from Oklahoma, and he and Mickey went out to dinner. As Mantle walked him back to the car, "a dried-up little old man tottered over, cigarette butt in mouth, looking like some kind of lunatic as he fumbled in his pants pocket for God knows what. Mantle froze; his nerves were almost on edge enough to believe that the old fellow was going to pull a gun on him. But it was just a scorecard. The man wanted it signed." Mickey snapped at him to get lost, but his friend grabbed him by the arm and reminded him that such fans paid his salary. Mickey apologized, signed the card, "then watched the old guy shuffle away, staring at him curiously, almost laughing because the whole thing was so pathetic."[16]

A few days later, Mickey worked up the courage to call Mutt at the Eagle Picher Mines. Mickey told him he was in Kansas City; Mutt quietly told him that he already knew, that he had been following him in the papers. With a catch in his voice, he told his father that he didn't think he could play anymore. Mutt asked where he was, and Mickey told him he was staying at the Aladdin Hotel.

Mickey told the story of what happened next many times. In his recountings, Mutt arrived just a few hours later—the drive took at least five — and sternly, though without anger, told Mickey that he hadn't raised any cowards. If he couldn't stick it out in Kansas City, he could come back and work in the mines with his dad. Mickey, stifling tears, told him that he would try again. Mutt, who was throwing clothes in his son's bag, stopped, smiled, and said, "What the hell, why not?" A little later, in the hotel coffee shop, Mutt reminded his son that "everybody has slumps — even DiMaggio. Take my word, it'll come together. You'll see."[17]

And of course it did. Two days later, against Toledo, he hit two home runs over a light tower in right field to go with a double and a triple. One of his teammates jokingly informed him that he should try for only a single in his last time up so he could "hit for the cycle." So, leading off the ninth, Mickey dragged a bunt down the first-base line and beat it out. Back in the dugout, a satisfied George Selkirk just smiled at him.

Mantle played in forty games for the Blues, batting .351 and driving in an amazing 50 runs. Near the end of August, he went to see a Western at a Kansas City movie house. He did not, like Willie a few months before, get a call from the ball club that interrupted the picture. It wasn't until he got back to the team motel that he found out that the Yankees wanted him back in New York.

Mickey first told the story of his minor league comeback to *Sport* magazine in 1956 and then repeated it over and over again through the years with little change. In each version, though, the only person he mentioned was Mutt. "Every time I heard someone in my family tell that story," Mantle's son Danny told me in 2010, "I'd hear someone say, 'Well, damn, Daddy wasn't the only one who went to see him. We *all* got in the car and drove over to Kansas City.' "

When Mickey returned to New York, he exchanged his first uniform number, 6, for the one he would always be remembered by — 7. It would become the most recognizable — and marketable — number of any baseball player ever. (Mickey was able to take the number because Cliff Mapes, who had worn number 7 since 1949, had been traded to the St. Louis Browns while Mantle was gone.)

On August 29, Mickey got his first look at the great Satchel Paige, who was by this time at least forty-five years old and was winding down his brief major league career with the Browns, for whom he would pitch his last two seasons in the major leagues.* Mantle's account of their meeting is an illustration of how self-deprecating Mickey could be. He recalled in *The Mick*:

> We had a runner in scoring position, bottom of the ninth, and I took two straight cuts, missing them both by a wide margin.
>
> Paige's next pitch was a fastball. I bunted and ran to first as fast as I could go. It was a foul ball, the last out of the game. Paige doffed his hat and flashed a big toothy smile. I was still running out the play, halfway up the foul line, as the Browns started back to their dugout.
>
> Moments later Casey was in front of my locker, arms crossed, his eyes burning into mine.
>
> "Nice going, son. You sure fooled us. Next time I want you to bunt, I'll give you the sign."
>
> He had every reason to ship me down to the minors.[18]

The story about bunting off Paige was a concoction on Mickey's part, apparently told because he didn't want to brag about his success off the legendary pitcher. In fact, Mickey hit a towering three-run homer off Satchel in the ninth inning, and the Yankees won, 15–2. Oddly enough, Mickey's home run off the man who might have been the greatest pitcher in baseball history has been lost to history — or at least part of baseball history: it is not recorded in the pitcher-versus-batter section of Baseball-reference.com, but is noted in the box score

---

*Not counting a one-inning stint with the Kansas City A's in 1965 in which owner Charlie Finley generously gave Paige an opportunity to qualify for an increased pension by playing in another decade.

of Retrosheet.com. Hank Bauer called it "the best wood I ever saw anyone get off Satch."[19]

Had Willie Mays not blossomed into one of the greatest players ever, it's doubtful that writers would have later made the case that he was the major spur to the Giants' incredible comeback during the last two months of the 1951 National League pennant drive. Most of the writers who made that case, most notably Charles Einstein and Arnold Hano, both of whom later wrote books on Mays, took their lead from Monte Irvin, the Alabama-born, New Jersey—raised star who became Willie's biggest booster on the Giants. "I believe to this day," Irvin told me in a 2009 interview, "that the main reason we made up those thirteen games [from the beginning of August] and caught up to the Dodgers and won that playoff was Willie. He just made everything seem better, more fun."

Like Crash Davis says in Ron Shelton's great baseball film *Bull Durham*, "The reason you *think* you're winning *is* the reason you're winning." But coming down the stretch in 1951, there were lots of reasons for the New York Giants to believe that they were winning, beginning with Monte Irvin himself. Irvin, who was elected to the Hall of Fame in 1973, did not make it to the major leagues until the end of the 1949 season, when he was already thirty years old, but in 1951 he hit .312 with 24 home runs and a league-leading 121 RBIs. According to Bill James's complex Win Shares method, which awards players points for every offensive and defensive contribution, Irvin was the Giants' most valuable player in 1951, followed closely by pitcher Sal Maglie, shortstop Alvin Dark, outfielder Bobby Thomson, pitcher Larry Jansen, shortstop Eddie Stanky, catcher Wes Westrum, and then Willie Mays.

Which is not to deny that Mays made contributions that could not be measured by cold statistics. His teammates, black and white, loved him; his joy in playing the game was contagious, a quality much appreciated during those tense late-summer weeks of the pennant race as the Giants fought furiously to overtake the hated

Dodgers. The press loved him too. As with Yogi Berra, they were amused by Willie's love of comic books and loved his famous habit of calling out "Say hey!" even if the phrase appeared in their stories much more often than Mays said it in real life.

It was during the heat of the pennant race that the myth of Willie Mays the innocent gained popularity as sportswriters referred to him as a "country boy" — though he had grown up in an industrial suburb and near the South's greatest industrial city. Mays's most recent biographer, James Hirsch, thinks that Willie, at least in this period, was "good-natured, shy, naive . . . untouched by cynicism. Mays all but shouted out his vulnerability." Hirsch also maintains that Willie was "unschooled in city life," but this is open to question. Willie knew Birmingham and its Fourth Avenue black culture fairly well, and by age nineteen he had not only barnstormed through many of the South's biggest cities but had been to New York and seen Harlem up close. Mickey Mantle at the same age was not half so schooled in city life, though he proved to be a quick study.[20]

Still, that's the way New York sportswriters wanted to see Willie, and that's the way the fans still remember him. Willie's popularity propelled him into his first award. Not that his contributions as a rookie didn't merit recognition. Roger Kahn admits, "We [the New York sportswriters] knew by the end of the season we were going to lobby for Willie as Rookie of the Year. He was just too damn popular not to win it. But looking back on it, I think we made the right decision." They did. Despite his lack of Triple-A experience, Mays hit, in his first 121 big league games, a respectable .270 with 20 home runs and 68 RBIs, and his hitting was arguably even more impressive than that: after getting just one hit in his first 25 times at-bat, he hit nearly .290 for the rest of the season. If he was not the primary cause of the Giants' incredible surge, he was certainly the embodiment of it.

Fate spared the twenty-year-old Willie Mays one huge test: in Game 3 of the National League Championship Series, when Bobby Thomson hit his immortal ninth-inning home run off Ralph Branca, Willie was kneeling in the on-deck circle. In the clubhouse after the game, Durocher walked over to Mays with a big smile on his face and told him he was surprised that, with the bases loaded, the Dodgers' manager, Charlie Dressen, hadn't had Branca walk Thomson and pitch to the rookie. "I'm glad he didn't," Mays replied. "I didn't want the pennant hanging on my shoulders."[21] In truth, Mays had a terrible playoff— 1-for-10 in the three games, striking out three times and making an error in the outfield. In the biggest game of the season, he was 0-for-3 at the plate.

Champagne corks went off in the Giants' clubhouse like firecrackers on the Fourth of July. Willie had his first taste of champagne — it was the first alcohol he had taken since Cat forced him to try some Jack Daniels back in Fairfield. He got sick and never drank champagne again. A few days earlier, when the Yankees had clinched the American League pennant, Mickey Mantle, not yet twenty, and egged on by his new pal, a utility infielder named Billy Martin, had drunk a bit too much champagne. He loved it.

The 1951 New York Yankees needed no ninth-inning playoff miracles to win their pennant, finishing five games ahead of the Cleveland Indians in the American League. Back from Kansas City, Mickey Mantle resumed his play in right field and did just fine the rest of the season. In 96 games, he hit .267 with 13 home runs and 65 RBIs, just three fewer than Mays, who had batted 123 more times.

The day after Thomson's home run, the emotionally exhausted Giants prepared to face the Yankees in the Bronx. Two baseball fathers, Mutt Mantle and Cat Mays, who would never know how much they had in common, were at Yankee Stadium to watch the first World Series game either had ever seen in person. (They had had the thrill of their lives the day before at the Giants-Dodgers playoff game at the Polo Grounds.) When an exuberant Willie emerged from the visitors' dugout, he was stunned. "I saw Joe DiMaggio for the first time. . . . I spotted him on the field surrounded by reporters, but I was too shy to go up and introduce myself. A photographer came over to me and asked if I would pose with Joe for a photo. 'Why would he want to take a picture with me?' I asked. The photographer brought me over and introduced us. I got the chance to talk with him for just a few minutes, a dream come true." Willie had no way of knowing it, but the couple of minutes he chatted with his idol was probably more time than Mickey had talked with Joe all season long. "That was the only time I got to see my boyhood hero play. And it was the only time when we posed for pictures when we were both playing.

"There was another ball player there, though, with whom I was destined to be compared over the years — Mickey Mantle . . . even though he was the rightfielder in 1951, he was going to be the center-fielder for many years to come. . . . He was the lead-off batter in the series. As luck would have it, I had an effect on his career."[22]

A good hour and a half before the first pitch, someone thought it would be a great idea to bring the two teams' celebrated rookie out-fielders together for a photo opportunity. And so Mickey Mantle and Willie Mays, the purest products ever produced by baseball, met for the first time and, bats on their shoulders, grinned like the schoolboys they practically were.

Mickey, a wad of bubblegum stuck in his apple cheek, grinned while Willie, still exuberant despite the apocalyptic playoff series with the Dodgers, joked with the photographers. They had, of course, heard of each other: Mays had been seeing Mantle's name in the sports pages since spring training, and Mantle had heard of Mays from Minneapolis Millers players and coaches during his brief visit to Minneapolis with the Kansas City Blues. "When I was up there," Mickey told Roger Kahn years later, "that's all I heard about. 'You should see Willie Mays field, you should see Willie Mays hit, you should see Willie Mays run the bases.' It was the first time I heard something that I was going to hear quite a bit over the next decade: 'Boy, I hope you turn out to be half the ballplayer Willie Mays is.' "[23]

Had they known each other a little better, or if Mickey had not been quite so shy, they would have had much to discuss: their love of Westerns, their enthusiasm for shooting pool, and having a father for a baseball coach. But the two rookies, both understandably awed by being at the World Series in New York, smiled, shuffled their cleats, and said little to each other.

Roger Kahn recalls his colleagues mumbling questions to each other such as "Is Mantle a little broader across the shoulders?" and "You think Mays's forearms are bigger?" and "Who's supposed to be the fastest?" (the consensus at the time was Mays) and "Who do you think would win a home run contest?" An unknown photographer snapped several shots of Mickey and Willie together, after which they laughed, shook hands, and went back to their locker rooms.

Having finally brought them together, the forces that had shaped their lives and careers seemed almost at once to erase the paths that had brought them there, as if to guarantee that their likes would never be seen again. The Negro League World Series that Willie had played in just three years before had ceased to exist; the Negro Leagues themselves were rapidly fading. So too was the highly competitive, finely tuned minor league farm system that Mantle had come up in; though it would produce many more fine players, Mickey would be the last superstar nurtured in the Yankees' minor league network. And within a few years, the world of industrial league baseball that had honed their skills at such an early age would all but disappear from the American landscape.

In Game 1 of the World Series, the rookies were a combined 0-for-8 as the Giants won, 5–1. The next day the Yankees came back to win, 3–1, though Willie was once again hitless while Mickey got his first World Series hit in two at-bats and scored a run. In the fifth inning, with the Yankees leading 2–0, Willie lofted a fly ball to right-center — not the pop-up it has often been described as but a fairly good shot that, had it gone perhaps another ten feet, might have been in the gap for an extra-base hit. Casey Stengel had told Mickey to run down fly balls hit in that area because "the Big Dago can't get there anymore." But DiMaggio did get to this one and called Mantle off. Mickey caught his cleat on an open drainpipe as he stopped, tearing up his knee and forever destroying the possibility that he would be the greatest player baseball had ever seen.

For many years Willie Mays made no mention that he had been the one who hit the fateful fly ball. Charles Einstein, who would come to know Willie better than any other writer, was of the opinion that Willie simply didn't know what he had brought about until another writer told him about it several years later. But by 1988, Willie — or at least his coauthor Einstein — seemed to have a complete memory of what had happened: "From that day on, Mickey seems to be marked with a sort of pity; people were forever saying 'Just think what he could have done if his knees weren't bad.' But Mickey had a great career anyway. Nonetheless, I felt bad about the accident."[24]

It's possible that an unknown Yankees groundskeeper, the man who left the drain uncovered, committed one of the most devastating errors in the annals of baseball. And Willie Mays was an unknowing assistant.

9

"Greetings"

The Yankees, even without Mantle in the lineup after his injury, won the World Series, as they always seemed to in those years. But nothing could dim Willie's enthusiasm. Two days after the World Series ended, Willie and his dad boarded a train at Grand Central Station bound for Birmingham's Terminal Station. Despite the Yankees' victory, the twenty-year-old had no regrets. In his coat pocket he carried a World Series check for the staggering sum of $5,000, the most money ever given to players on a losing team. He also left New York with assurances from Roger Kahn, Red Smith, and other prominent New York writers that he would soon be named National League Rookie of the Year. (They were right; Mays would become the third consecutive black player to win the NL's award, and the fourth in five years; it took sixteen years for a black player to win the honor in the American League.) What could possibly go wrong?

No sooner had he walked into Aunt Sarah's house in Fairfield than he found a letter that began with the word "Greetings."

Willie, like millions of American boys, wasn't sure exactly where Korea was. Now it looked like he might be going there. Willie shrugged and decided to have as good a time as possible while he waited to see what happened. He jumped into his friend Herman Boykin's car, and they drove to Big Tony's pool hall, where he got a hero's welcome from his boyhood pals. His friends slapped him on the back and told him that they'd get those Yankees in the World Series next year. The next day he bought furniture, appliances, and groceries for Aunt Sarah and for his mother, who had nine children and a husband out of work.

He also bought a new Mercury convertible in his favorite color, green; what had become of the green Mercury he bought with his signing bonus nearly two years earlier isn't known, but there were plenty of male relatives in the family who would have had good use for it.

No sooner had Willie unpacked than he prepared to cash in on his new fame. Ten days after the final game of the World Series, he was playing for Roy Campanella's Major League All-Stars in a barnstorming tour of black southern ballparks. Their opponents were the best players from the rapidly declining Negro Leagues; some of the best young players, such as Henry Aaron and Ernie Banks, would soon be joining Mays and Campanella in the big leagues, but for the rest — meaning just about anyone over the age of thirty, including some of Willie's old teammates with the Birmingham Black Barons — there was little hope of a career in professional baseball.

On Thursday, October 25, Willie and the rest of Campy's team headed back to Birmingham for a parade in Willie's honor. The city of Birmingham had announced that October 27 would be "Willie Mays Day," and Campanella's All-Stars would play the Black Barons at Rickwood Field following an afternoon parade. The game was played, and a grinning Roy Campanella, who had needled Willie unmercifully early in his rookie season, presented him with a trophy.

The parade, though, never came off. Police Commissioner Eugene "Bull" Connor canceled the parade permit — or at least several journalists, black and white, who showed up for the parade along with thousands of black and white baseball fans assumed that it was Connor's doing. Among them was *Birmingham News* columnist Alf Van Hoose, who for the next forty years was happy to tell anyone sitting next to him at the Alabama-Auburn game or any other sporting event how Connor had "embarrassed and humiliated Alabama's greatest athlete."* If Willie had thought for a moment that playing in a World Series for a major league team in New York had made him a privileged black man in Alabama, he was rudely awakened.

Before Thanksgiving, Willie reported to the Selective Service office and applied for a 3-A "hardship" exemption. He had, after all, eleven dependents, including a swarm of stepbrothers and stepsisters. The request was rejected. Willie didn't complain until thirty-seven years later in a memoir: "The Army claimed they weren't making a special case out of me, but I don't know of many people with eleven dependents who were being called up then."[1] His point was valid, but the Army stuck to its rules for hardship cases: it refused to exempt Willie because he didn't live in the home of the people being claimed as dependents. In Willie's case, the point made no sense, as he could hardly have been playing ball and earning the money to support his relatives had he been living at home. Unlike Mantle, Mays passed his physical with ease but failed the aptitude test[2] — he later claimed to have flunked it on purpose, which is almost certainly true. Because he was a high school graduate — in fact, one who had finished in the top half of his class — the draft board told him to take the test again, and the second time he passed.

The Giants had ended the 1951 season full of anticipation; after all, Willie Mays was poised to become the best young player in the National League. But as their 1952 spring training camp opened, spirits

---

*Van Hoose told me this on at least two different occasions. Alf was a longtime admirer of Mays, and the numerous columns he wrote about Willie were collected and reprinted by the University of Alabama Press in 2010. Not to take issue with his characterization of Willie as "Alabama's greatest athlete," but it should be noted that besides Mays, Joe Louis, Satchel Paige, and Henry Aaron — to name just three of the greatest — were all from Alabama.

were dampened at the knowledge that their budding star would soon be leaving for the Army. The mood went from gloom to doom when Monte Irvin suffered a nasty ankle break. Willie ran from the dugout, cradled Monte in his arms, and burst into tears. According to a writer named Carl Lundquist in *Baseball: The Fan's Magazine*, Leo Durocher was equally distraught, "as agonized as if the injury was to his own leg, loudly demanding of the fates, 'Why did it have to happen to him? Why couldn't it have been me? We don't need my ankle!' "[3]

The Giants might have survived the loss of either Irvin (who had batted .312 in 1951 and led the NL in RBIs with 121) or Mays, but not both. The 1952 season would become one of those bittersweet what-ifs for Giants fans as the team finished just four and a half games behind the Brooklyn Dodgers in the pennant race — the presence of either Irvin or Mays could well have closed that gap. In retrospect, of course, perhaps the larger what-if applies to Willie's legacy, specifically to the homers he didn't hit in 1952 — and in 1953, for that matter. It's entirely possible that those missed years stopped him from breaking Babe Ruth's career record of 714 home runs.

On the other hand, Willie could not know at the time just how lucky he would be to have been drafted. He would come no closer to combat than an occasional beanball while playing for Army teams, and more important, he would not be subjected to the kind of hatred and derision that tormented Mickey, who, wincing in pain from the osteomyelitis that had kept him out of the service, would hear accusations of "draft dodger" for the rest of the decade.

In the fall of 1951, as father and son headed back home to Commerce, Mickey realized for the first time how sick Mutt was; doctors in New York had made it clear to him. Mutt probably realized he hadn't long to live. In the words of one biographer, "Mickey returned to Oklahoma to get married. His father went home to die."[4] Mutt told Mickey he wanted him to marry Merlyn. There would be no more discussion on the subject.

Like Willie, Mickey went home with his World Series payday, in his case the even more mind-boggling sum of $7,500, a check larger than anyone in his hometown had ever seen. Like Willie, he was a hero, and like Willie, no sooner had he dumped his bags off at home and hugged his mother than he jumped into the car with his pals and headed for the local pool hall. He stayed out past midnight buying and drinking beer, listening to Hank Williams on the jukebox, and telling his pals tales of New York and the larger-than-life characters he had met — Casey Stengel, Joe DiMaggio, Yogi Berra, and Ted Williams. These were probably some of the last hours of pure relaxation that Mickey Mantle would know for the rest of his life.

On December 23, Mickey and Merlyn were married in a joyless ceremony at her parents' home in Picher. Only the immediate families and a best friend or two of Mutt's were in attendance. The bride and groom spent their first night together in what Mickey would later describe as "a dumpy little motel" a few miles from Picher. The honeymoon didn't last long. Mutt's deterioration could no longer be ignored. Mickey and Merlyn braved the treacherous winter highways of the Midwest to take Mutt to the Mayo Clinic in Rochester, Minnesota, where doctors confirmed what Mickey had been told in New York: his father's condition was terminal.

Unbeknownst to family, friends, the press, or anyone outside the Yankees' front office, Mickey had another reason for going to the Mayo Clinic. After an afternoon exhibition game during his first spring training in Fort Lauderdale the year before, Mickey had gone on a drunken tear with teammates who were never named; a Yankee club official, also never named, checked him into a hospital for treatment and dispensed enough cash to ensure that the incident never made it into the papers. In return, the Yankees insisted that Mickey seek treatment during the off-season. While Mutt was dying, Mickey, scarcely five months past his twentieth birthday, was fighting a drinking problem.

Early in April, mere weeks before Willie was due to report for military service, Leo Durocher brought the Giants from their Arizona training camp to his house in Santa Monica, California. Leo and his wife, actress Laraine Day, counted several Hollywood stars in their social circle, and at a party Leo threw a happy Willie shook hands with, among others, Ava Gardner, Frank Sinatra, Kirk Douglas, and Jack Benny. Humphrey Bogart, who was there with his wife, Lauren Bacall, kidded Mays for having overtaken his favorites, the Brooklyn Dodgers, in the previous year's playoff and told him he was glad for the Dodgers' sake that Willie was going to be away for a while. If you had to get ready for a stint in the Army, this was the way to do it in style.

On May 6, the defending NL champion New York Giants were at Sportsman's Park in St. Louis, where they lost to the Cardinals, 9–1. On that same day, the defending world champion New York Yankees played the Cleveland Indians at Yankee Stadium. They lost, 1–0, that afternoon, and Mantle was not in the lineup; Irv Noren played center field. Earlier in the afternoon, as he was dressing in his rooms at the Grand Concourse Hotel, where he now lived with Merlyn, Mickey picked up the phone. It was his manager. "Hi, Skip, what's up?" Casey took a deep breath and said, "Your mother called. She thought you were here at the Stadium." Mickey would later re- member that he looked out the window and stared out at the traffic along the Grand Concourse. Stengel began to stammer, and then told him the news that his father had died in a Denver hospital. Thirty-three years later, with unabashed emotion, Mantle recalled his reaction: "My father was dead. Why? What had happened to him in the thirty-nine years of his life, with all the scrambling and disappointments and frustrations? Where did it get him? He needed me and I wasn't there. I couldn't make it up to him. He died alone. I cried 'What kind of God is there anyway, to let him die like that!' " He slammed his big right fist into the wall and told Merlyn that he was going home for the services. Merlyn was taken aback; she told him she wanted to be there too. Mickey told her, "No, you don't need to," and walked out of the room.

Mantle made little mention of his reaction to his father's death in his earlier recollections, but in his 1985 memoirs, he claims he went to the Stadium and "when I got out to the ball park, Casey called me in his office. 'I'm really sorry, Mick, we all hate it. You can sit out the game tonight if you like, but I really think you should try to play.' I did play. I'm sure Dad would have wanted me to."[5] No doubt that's what Mutt would have wanted, but the box scores at Baseball-reference.com and Baseball Almanac do not list Mantle in the lineup that day.

Leaving Merlyn in New York, Mickey went home for the funeral. Mutt was buried in a miners' cemetery, the Grand Army of the Republic Cemetery in Ottawa County, alongside Uncle Tunney and Grandpa Charles; after the handful of mourners left, Mickey stayed alone by his father's grave. Lovell came over and tapped him gently on the shoulder, telling him the car was waiting. Mickey told her to go on ahead, he would catch up. Three days later, he returned to Merlyn at the Concourse Plaza Hotel. His misery was easy to put a face to; Merlyn's was not. The Concourse Plaza, as Mantle admitted, "wasn't the Ritz." Whenever Mickey was gone, Merlyn stayed alone. The room cost $100 a month (admittedly no small cost after Mickey peeled money from his paycheck to send back home), and it didn't have a stove, refrigerator, or television set. The walls were bare. When he was paid, Mickey would give her a $20 bill for food and tell her that if she ran short, "order in and charge it to the room."[6] Her only diversion was visiting other players' wives, hoping they had TVs.

The Giants beat the Dodgers, 6–2, on Wednesday, May 28. It would be Willie's last major league game for nearly two full seasons. Mays's performance in the game was unremarkable — he was hitless in four at-bats. (He would leave the Giants hitting just .236 in 127 at-bats with only four home runs, though no one thought that indicated what he would have done over the entire season.) What was memorable about the afternoon was the reaction of the Brooklyn crowd: when Mays's name was announced before the game, Dodger fans let out an earsplitting roar for the boy-man who had helped keep them out of the World Series the season before. "This was in Brooklyn, mind you," wrote Red Smith the next day in the *New York Herald-Tribune* in a tone of ashen awe, "where 'Giant' is the dirtiest word in the language. And the giant they were talking about and cheering is a baby only one year in the major leagues, a child who is only learning to play baseball."[7]

After the game, in words that sounded scripted but that Willie spoke sincerely, he told reporters, "It's undoubtedly for the best. I'm still young, and I might as well do my Army duties now. If everything goes well, I'll be only twenty-three when I get out. Many a fellow hasn't even reached the majors by then, so there will be plenty of time for me to play baseball. I'll probably be better off, stronger, more mature in every way."[8] No matter who helped him prepare his statement — and Monte Irvin is a likely candidate — that is exactly the way things turned out.

As Willie left Ebbets Field, Dodgers fans clamored for his autograph.

Two nights later, the Yankees lost to the Philadelphia Athletics, 2–1. Mickey Mantle had three hits and provided the Yankees' only run with a towering 450-plus-foot home run into the right-field upper deck. When he struck out to end the game, according to the *New York Daily News*, shouts of "Draft dodger!" and "Commie rat!" greeted him as he headed for the dugout.

On May 29, PFC Willie Howard Mays reported to Camp Kilmer, New Jersey (named for Joyce Kilmer, the soldier and poet who wrote "Trees") for induction, and the next day he traveled by train to Fort Eustis, Newport News, Virginia. There he went through eight listless weeks of basic training; at this point it was clear to just about everyone that Mays, who had been assigned to a transportation replacement unit, probably wasn't going to be seeing any combat. He promptly got into a near brawl with a white sergeant who thought his behavior at roll call insubordinate. (As a joke, Willie had his forage cap turned backward.) Or rather, his sergeant, who grabbed him and threw him to the ground, was brawling. Even though Willie could probably have overpowered his superior with ease, he knew enough not to fight with a white NCO.

No one, of course, could stay mad at Willie Mays for long, and within a short time he was practically the outfit's mascot. If Willie didn't understand what was expected of him when he was inducted, it didn't take him long to get the message: the Army wanted him to play baseball. He spent most of his time on tour with other major leaguers, including Johnny Antonelli (soon to be his teammate but in 1952 a pitcher for the Boston Braves), the Pirates' Vern Law, and the Yankees' Lou Skizas. "Of course," he recalled to Charles Einstein, "I enjoyed it. I was raised to say 'Yes, sir,' and I always respected authority, so the Army and I got along very well."[9]

In turn, authority loved Willie. Horace Stoneham used friends in the Army to keep track of Willie and see that he always felt cared for, and Leo Durocher sent him money for comic books and movies. Leo's attitude might be described as unabashedly paternalistic: once, he heard that Willie had taken a spill during a pickup basketball game and called him at the barracks to chew him out ("No more basketball, Willie!"). He also didn't want his prize stealing any bases in meaningless games. Mays quickly found that "Leo couldn't stand dumb plays, even if he was a few hundred miles away. When he got excited, he would scream and talk so fast he sounded like Donald Duck."[10]

Expectations for Mantle's 1952 season bordered on the ridiculous. Yankee pitching coach "Milkman Jim" Turner told sportswriters that he had never seen anyone who could excite other players the way Mickey could. (But then Turner had seen Willie Mays only in a couple of World Series games.) "When he gets up to hit," said Turner, "the guys get off the bench and elbow each other out of the way to get a better look. And take a look at the other bench sometimes. I saw Ralph Kiner's eyes pop when he first got a look at the kid. Luke Easter was studying him the other day, and so was Larry Doby." American

League umpire Charlie Berry thought that Mantle was so fast that bad calls had taken a couple of hits away from him. Mickey, said Berry, "was so fast that umpires first time they see him, don't believe him."[11] In other words, they sometimes called him out at first, not believing anyone could get down the line that fast.

Yet somehow the myth of Mantle's early career began to take hold — namely, that nothing he did before 1956 lived up to his potential, despite the amazing fact that he was the first player in team history to leap from a Class-C team to the Yankees' opening-day lineup. Milton Gross of the *New York Post* would write an article every season before 1956 suggesting that Mantle had actually been something of a disappointment.

Let's take a close look at 1952, the first year in which Mickey Mantle supposedly didn't live up to his potential. Mickey, age twenty, hit .311 with 23 home runs and 87 RBIs in 142 games. A pretty good year for anybody. But Mantle's year gets better and better the closer we look at it. With 75 walks and 171 hits, Mickey posted an on-base percentage of .394, and thanks largely to 37 doubles and 7 triples, his slugging percentage was .530. And so his OPS — on-base percentage plus slugging percentage — was .924, *the highest mark in the league.* But no one knew what OPS was at the time; most baseball writers scarcely knew enough to pay attention to on-base percentage. Most of them took note of his strikeout total of 111, shook their heads, and tsk-tsked about how much he still had to learn. Few noticed that he grounded into just five double plays all season long. According to Stats Inc., Mantle was 7.87 in its complex formula of Runs Created For 27 Outs — *the highest in the league.* Looking back on Mantle's 1952 season, Total Baseball, using a method devised by analysts John Thorn and Pete Palmer, concluded that Mantle had a Total Player Rating of 4.8 — second highest in the NL behind Larry Doby. All this from a player who didn't reach his twenty-first birthday until two weeks after the World Series.

Considering how much attention was paid to Mantle, it seems

amazing in retrospect that much of his true greatness was hidden from those who watched him most carefully.

Through most of 1952 the Yankees were locked in a furious pennant race with the Cleveland Indians; they wound up taking the pennant by two games. The big hitter down the stretch was Mantle, who hit .362 over the final three weeks — despite trouble from the knee he had injured in the previous year's World Series.

Even those who didn't appreciate him during the regular season found it impossible to ignore in the World Series. The Yankees beat the Brooklyn Dodgers in a tough seven-game Series. Mantle had 10 hits in 29 at-bats for a .345 batting average; the hits included a double, a triple, and two home runs. He had only three RBIs, but each came at just the right moment. In Game 6, with the Yankees down three games to two, Mickey hit a 430-foot home run into the Ebbets Field bleachers to give the Yankees a 3–1 lead; they hung on to win, 3–2. In the final game, batting from the left side against the Dodgers' fireballer Joe Black, Mickey broke a sixth-inning 2–2 tie with another towering shot into Ebbets's right-field seats. When he returned to the plate in the seventh inning, he slashed a single off Preacher Roe to give the Yankees a 4–2 lead. It proved to be the decisive run.

Mickey had so much ability that many sportswriters were reluctant to credit him with also being a smart player, especially in the field. Free, with DiMaggio's retirement, to grab anything in his range — on May 20 Stengel had given him the center-field job for good — he made sixteen put-outs in the Series and committed no errors — perhaps his best World Series play ever. In the eighth inning of Game 3, Jackie Robinson hit a sharp single, a low liner, to center field and made his usual daring swerve around first base. The move was obviously intended to test the nerve of the rookie center fielder. Mantle fielded the ball smoothly on one hop. Robinson jitterbugged about a third of the way down the line, trying to get Mickey to throw the ball behind him to first base, as many a National League outfielder had done. He would then break for second, which he often made standing up. In a story for *Sport* magazine, Milton Gross wrote that Robinson was trying to force "Mantle's arm against Jackie's speed, daring, and know-how on the bases. When it is you against Robinson, it is no simple decision to make.

> Mantle elected to hold his throw. Whether it was a deliberate or instinctive decision none can say, but Mantle watched Robinson, and Jackie, watching the fielder, came as much as 25 feet toward second. He slowed down, pretending to go back, and Mickey, meanwhile, came in several steps with the ball before cocking his arm as if to throw to first base. Suddenly, it seemed Jackie sensed he could not make the base. The Dodger stopped, stumbled, got to his feet again, and then scrambled back to first.
>
> It was a war of nerves on the bases, Robinson drawing on his years of experience and Mantle drawing from some inexplicable well of wisdom that seems to be his despite his youth, and it was a war Robinson lost.
>
> With that motion, Jackie went into high gear for second, yet Mantle still held his throw.[12]

He fired at precisely the right moment, and Jackie was out by perhaps six feet, the only embarrassing moment he suffered in World Series play. No one had ever seen Robinson the base runner shown up like that before.

Branch Rickey, who, according to legend, had tossed a checkbook at Yankees owner Dan Topping the year before and told him to fill in whatever he wanted for Mantle, saw the play. "Maturity," he told sportswriters afterward, "is something that cannot be measured in years. That young man's arms and legs and eyes and wind are young, but his head is old. Mantle has the chance to make us forget every ballplayer we ever saw."[13] Except perhaps one.

The following night, after the Yankees had clinched the Series, Jackie Robinson, with typical grace and style, told the press, "Mantle beat us. He was the difference between the two clubs. They didn't miss Joe DiMaggio. It was Mickey Mantle who killed us."[14] Robinson walked over to the Yankees' clubhouse to shake Mickey's hand. Mickey stared at the man whom he had driven from Oklahoma to St. Louis to watch at Sportsman's Park just a few short years earlier. He would later recall the moment as one of the proudest of his major league career.

A few days later, all of Commerce was abuzz with the news that Mickey and Merlyn, driving in from New York in Mick's brand-new Lincoln Mercury, would be in attendance at the high school football game between Commerce and Picher, where Mickey's sixteen-year-old brothers, twins Roy and Ray, would both be playing halfback. By six o'clock, he had not yet appeared. Down at the Black Cat Café, men interrupted their pool game to check their watches and make bets about whether Mickey would make the nearly 1,400-mile drive in time for the opening kickoff. One of the regulars pointed out that if Mick had been alone, he'd probably have made it, but Lovell, who was with him, wouldn't tolerate any speeding.

Those who bet on Mickey making it to the kickoff lost, but after a furious road trip Mickey, wearing a sport coat, slacks, and two-toned shirt, did get to the game in time to see almost all of the second half. He saw his brother Ray break ninety-six yards for a touchdown in a 13–0 whitewash of Picher.

One of the first things Mickey and Merlyn saw their first day back in Commerce was a proud notice painted on the window of Ott Chandler's drugstore: OUR MICK, OF THE NEW YORK YANKEES, IS THE MOST SENSATIONAL ROOKIE OF ALL TIME. Mickey grinned and graciously neglected to point out that he was actually in his second year in the big leagues.

In the Sunday paper, Mickey was no doubt pleased to see a syndicated story in which Hall of Fame second baseman Charlie Gehringer told a reporter that if he were choosing one player from any major league team to start a team with, he'd choose Mickey Mantle. Also, he might pick that kid from the Giants who was in the Army.

⊗ ⊗

"I have no pride in my Army career," Willie Mays confessed in his 1966 memoir, "but I have no apologies for it, either. I did what the man said. . . . So everybody came through just fine, and I played in something like 180 games in the service."[15]

Leo called him about every other day to see how he was faring. What Willie didn't tell him over the phone — perhaps he was laughing too hard at a sputtering Leo sounding like Donald Duck — was that

> I was working on something. They'd assigned me to the physical training department at Camp Eustis, and put me on instruction work. And there was this one boy there who taught the way to catch a fly ball was to hold his glove like he was taking out an old watch and looking at it.
>
> I said to him, "You gotta be crazy."
>
> "Why?" he said.
>
> "Because," I said, "only way to catch a routine fly ball is to hold the glove up in front of your eyes."
>
> "Why?"
>
> "Because," I said, "that way you never lose sight of the ball."[16]

The boy told Mays he would demonstrate his theory. After catching a fly ball Willie's way, he then allowed the ball to drop into his upturned glove, positioned right in front of his stomach. Mays told this story of learning his trademark basket catch numerous times; in none of them did he remember the name of the boy who showed it to him. Nor, to be honest, do any of Willie's explanations as to why the "basket catch" worked better than the traditional way make much sense:

> If I caught it out in front of my face, like I always had before, my body could be in any one of a number of positions — my feet, too.

But if I caught it down by my belt buckle, my body automatically took up what for me was the rightest, most comfortable stance. . . . I could never be off balance, catching a ball that way.[17]

Exactly how catching a ball above your head or at your waist would affect the position of your feet — assuming, of course, that you wouldn't use the basket catch while running hard for a ball hit either in front or in back of you — is simply not explained. Two things can be said about the basket catch: it worked for Willie and for Roberto Clemente (who later swore that he did not pick it up from Mays but developed the technique independently), and it didn't work for at least two generations of American boys who, trying to use the basket catch, turned their Little League coaches into basket cases.

In November 1952, Mays got a chance to perfect the basket catch during some on-the-job training. The Army gave him a furlough, and he rejoined Roy Campanella's barnstorming team. Monte Irvin, fully recovered from his broken ankle, marveled at how sharp Mays looked: "You'd never have thought Willie had ever been away. He looked as if he had been playing every day all season."[18] What Irvin didn't know was that Mays *had* been playing ball every day all season, sometimes against pitchers on the same talent level that Irvin was facing in the National League, including such major league GIs as the Dodgers' Joe Landrum and Don Newcombe and the Indians' Johnny Antonelli (who, to the shock of Mays, Irvin, and millions of New York Giants fans, would be traded at the end of the 1953 season for Bobby Thomson, the hero of the 1951 playoffs).

After the holidays, Willie once again petitioned the Army for a discharge, citing financial hardship as he now had twelve dependents and a pregnant mother with an out-of-work husband; his request certainly seemed reasonable. The Army felt otherwise. "I always have believed," he told Lou Sahadi thirty-five years later, "that if a lesser-known soldier had gone through that ordeal, he would have been free to leave. I don't know whether the Army was concerned because the public thought it would be playing favorites or whether there was just some technicality. All I knew then was that I was very sad . . . it didn't help my final months in the Army."[19]

What may well have been the cause of PFC Willie Howard Mays's inability to get a discharge was the public furor that surrounded Mickey Mantle's 4-F designation. In a time of war, the Army wasn't about to incur public wrath and face accusations of showing favoritism to *two* star young outfielders from New York baseball teams.

On April 15, 1953, Annie McMorris, Willie's mother, died while giving birth to her eleventh child. He learned the news while he was stationed at Fort Eustis. He cried unabashedly and was given leave to go home for her funeral. Annie had always told people that she was her son's biggest fan, reportedly hanging a Giants pennant on her wall and picking up their games on the radio whenever she could. But Willie never revealed whether he harbored any hurt or resentment for his mother having given him up to be raised by her sisters.

In 1954, on Mother's Day, he spoke briefly to a black newspaper, the *Chicago Defender*, and praised his mother as someone who had supported him through all his boyhood ambitions to become a ballplayer. "One of the things she told me constantly was how uncertain life was and how futile it was to grieve over the loss of someone you love. . . . Someone once asked me if I carry a picture of her. I don't. A picture might take me back to the past, might aggravate the hurt of knowing she is gone — physically. I'd rather carry her image in my heart, and that's the way she'd want it."[20] But this comment did not sound much like Willie. In fact, it didn't sound like anything else he ever said about his mother. In none of his numerous memoirs or interviews over the years did he elaborate on his feelings for the mother with whom he had spent relatively little time.

There's no doubt Willie loved his mother, but it's also true that the center of Willie's life was baseball, and Willie Mays's mother, like Mickey Mantle's, was never at the heart of that.

10

"Right Up There with the Babe"

A pril 1953 was a big month for Mickey. On April 12, two days before the start of the season, the Yankees were at Ebbets Field playing the Dodgers in an exhibition. When Mickey came up, there were the usual jeers, boos, and Brooklyn variations of the Bronx cheer plus the occasional cry of "Slacker!" or "Draft dodger!" Mickey tried to ignore them and chatted amiably with Roy Campanella, one of his favorite rivals. Suddenly the public-address system blared an announcement, "Ladies and gentlemen, now batting, number seven, Mickey Mantle." And then: "Mickey doesn't know it yet, but he just became the father of an eight-pound twelve-ounce baby boy!" To celebrate, Carl Erskine fed Mantle a fat fastball, which Mickey slammed on a line off the right-center field wall. As he pulled into second standing up, a smiling Jackie Robinson and Pee Wee Reese extended their hands while Mickey doffed his cap to the Dodger crowd, whose jeers had changed, suddenly, to resounding cheers.

As if to celebrate, five days later, on April 17, Mickey entered, if not baseball history, certainly the realm of folklore. Batting right-handed against the Senators' southpaw Chuck Stobbs — and with the wind in his face, everyone there that day swore — Mantle took a titanic swing and slammed the ball over the 55-foot left-field fence at the 391-foot mark, where it ricocheted off a 60-foot beer sign on the football score-board. That alone would have put the blast 460 feet from home plate. But the ball continued its flight until it landed in the yard of a house across the street.

In Griffith Stadium, Dick Schaap wrote, "4,206 spectators, 60 ballplayers, a dozen coaches and managers, a dozen sportswriters, and a few hundred assorted freeloaders went temporarily insane. They yelled, whistled, cheered, sighed, gaped, and, somewhat hol-lowly, laughed." One man went crazy like a fox. He was Arthur "Red" Patterson, the shrewd publicity director of the Yankees. Patterson bolted out of his seat as though he had been struck by Mantle's bat and disappeared in the same direction, though not quite so swiftly as the home run.

"On 5th Street, outside the ballpark, Patterson discovered a 10-year-old boy named Donald Dunaway clutching a baseball scuffed in two places — where it hit Mantle's bat and where it hit the score-board. The ball was still smoking."[1] The boy, Patterson later insisted, showed him the exact spot where he had found the ball, in the back-yard of a house at 434 Oakdale Street. Patterson quickly calculated the distance from the backyard to the bleacher wall, 106 feet, and came up with 563 feet from home plate.

No one is sure exactly what happened; the amount of money Pat-terson is said to have paid Dunaway has changed over the years, almost every time the story has been told. Patterson himself told reporters he gave the boy $5 for the ball; in May 1961, when Dick Schaap's paperback bio of Mantle (one of the volumes in the *Sport* magazine biography series) was published, the price was "$1 and the promise of three brand-new baseballs autographed by the entire Yankee team."[2]

The official distance — that is, the *first* official distance — was recorded as 563 feet. Before the home run even made it to the papers, it had grown two extra feet to 565.

Years later, Mantle liked to say that Patterson confessed to him that the ball had never even left the park. That story is unlikely, as many claimed to have seen it clear the left-field wall, and longtime Senators fans quickly noted that it was the first home run ever to do so. Researching the home run for the *Wall Street Journal* fifty years later, I consulted William J. Jenkinson, a historian for the Society of American Baseball Research (SABR). "There's no authenticity to the story," he told me. "Absolutely zero. We know the ball was a high fly hit into a strong head wind. Following its trajectory, there is simply no way the ball could have traveled 565 feet, even allowing for the roll when it hit the ground."

How far could it have gone? "I wouldn't argue with anyone who said it went 500 feet," Jenkinson said. "520 feet? Maybe. But 565 seems like something out of myth. My guess is that Patterson was trying to create a standard by which all future home runs would be measured."[3]

For what it's worth, years later Jenkinson succeeded in tracking down Patterson in the San Diego area, where he had retired after more than a decade of PR work for the Padres. "Red told me, 'Hey, come on. It was my job to make Mickey look good.' He didn't actually admit that he had added the distance, but he was clearly defensive about it." Patterson died in 1994.[4]

All that can be said with certainty about Mickey Mantle's most famous home run is that it was the longest anyone in the park that day had ever seen, and that everyone was pretty much in agreement that it went over 500 feet. Mantle later told me, "I kind of went along with what Red said, but to tell you the truth, I wondered what all the fuss was about. I had hit a few home runs before that were longer than the one in Washington — the one on the Southern Cal campus, for instance. And I hit a bunch a lot longer after that."[5] However far the ball went, on April 17, 1953, Chuck Stobbs,

Mickey Mantle, and Red Patterson combined to create the tape-measure home run.

What has long been forgotten about that game is how it high-lighted Mantle's extraordinary versatility. In the fifth inning, batting left-handed, he tried to drag a bunt to the right side of the field. He was moving so quickly out of the box that the ball shot off his bat and nearly reached second base while still in the air. This gave Mickey an opportunity to show off his incredible speed: he beat out the hit without a throw being made. In one game, Dick Schaap later wrote, "Mantle hit the longest home run and the longest bunt in history."[6]

There was yet another irony to Mantle's mythical 565-foot homer. Two days later in St. Louis, against the hapless Browns, Mickey hit another breathtaking shot in Sportsman's Park, where the left-field bleachers were about 380 feet from home plate. Several of his team-mates, including Gene Woodling, thought this one went farther than the one in Washington. "I was there when he hit it," Woodling recalled, "so I know how long the one in Washington went. He hit one out of there [in St. Louis] even better, but they publicized the one in Washington so much that they had to lay quiet on that one."[7]

Hank Bauer was even more emphatic: "He hit that ball [in St. Louis] even harder than the one in Washington. It may not have gone as far because it was on a little more of a line than the one off Stobbs, but I think it did go at least as far and probably further. I've seen some guys hit home runs almost as far as Mickey, but I've never seen like what he did in those two consecutive games against the Senators and Browns. It was awe inspiring."[8]

On June 15, Mickey got his first national magazine cover. *Time* pro-claimed him "Young Man on Olympus." The story, uncredited per the magazine's policy, called him a "corn-haired youngster out of an Oklahoma high school" and included a superb description of him at the plate as he batted against the White Sox left-hander Billy Pierce: "Bat cocked tight-handed, fingers flexing and caressing the handle, Mantle crouched at the plate and waited. . . . Mantle dug his spikes more firmly into the batter's box, hunching his fullback's body (5 ft.-11 in., 195 lbs.) into a deeper crouch. . . .

"Mickey Mantle set a muscular chain reaction in motion. Starting in the ankles, rippling through knees, hips, torso, broad shoulders, and 17-in. bull neck, he brought his bat around in a perfect arc to meet the ball with a sharp crack. High and deep it sailed." The story went on to say that Mickey was "that combination of color, speed and power at the plate that makes baseball turnstiles spin. Naturally, the Yankees are delighted" — though the story did not quote Mickey's own manager on the subject. "So, with duly diminished enthusiasm, are the other American League club owners. Mantle makes their turnstiles spin, too, and in a year when TV has all club owners worried." Actually, it was the flight of white middle-class families to the suburbs, away from urban ballparks, that had owners worried, but no one would say that at the time.

While the *Time* cover story was mostly laudatory, it did, at times, make Mickey seem like a bumpkin with a temper: " 'Standing around the outfield,' he was quoted as saying, 'I used to hope that they wouldn't hit to me. I was afraid I'd drop it. But now I just catch it and throw it in.' This kind of casual, frank statement given in an offhand manner, has raised some doubt among professional worriers about Mantle's competitive spark. Ordinarily phlegmatic, like DiMaggio . . . Mickey had been known to kick the water cooler or bruise his knuckles on the concrete walls in moments of angry frustration after striking out. Nowadays, reflecting the restrained professional pride of the Yankees, Mantle has learned to bottle up his anger over a strike-out or a miscue. 'I try not to let it bother me,' he says placidly.' "[9]

The story pointed out that Mantle was being paid $18,000 a year — a rather eye-opening salary for a twenty-one-year-old in the second year of the Eisenhower era — and also that he was making perhaps twice that again in endorsements. Indeed, Mickey's celebrity was well in place in the summer of 1953. After playing about two full seasons of major league baseball, he was the most sought-after endorser in American sports, with deals from Wheaties, Camel cigarettes, Gem razor blades, Esquire socks, Van Heusen shirts, Haggar slacks, and Louisville Slugger bats. He also would soon be endorsing, though not without some reservation, Beech-Nut chewing gum.

Just before his incredible home run in Washington, his first biography, *The Mickey Mantle Story*, by New York sportswriter Ben Epstein, was published. "One of the very few biographies," one writer commented, "ever written of someone barely old enough to vote."[10]

In May, the Duke of Windsor, on a goodwill trip to America, saw his first baseball game. He was, he told reporters at the game's end, "delighted." But he "particularly wanted to meet that switcher [switch-hitter] fellow." Red Patterson, a busy man that year, happily shuffled the Duke into the Yankees' locker room, where flash bulbs immediately began popping. "I've heard about you," said the smiling Duke, extending his hand. An embarrassed but grinning Mickey, in a line that could have come from Yogi Berra, replied, "I've heard about you too."[11]

Mays received the first and only injury of his Army stint on July 25: sliding into third base during a game at Fort Eustis, he chipped a bone in his left foot. Durocher, with Monte Irvin's injury fresh in his mind, nearly went into cardiac arrest. Willie recovered quickly. He would not be discharged until March 1 of the following year, but as the summer of 1953 came to a close, for all intents and purposes his uneventful military career was over.

While Mickey was being cursed and booed as a draft dodger by bleacher bums, Willie Mays, along with other major league ballplayers who had put in service time during the Korean War — including Billy Martin and Whitey Ford — were being investigated to see if they had been shown favoritism while in the military; "coddled" was the term that most often appeared in the papers. On July 22, a congressional report was released. Surprise! Several major league ballplayers in the armed forces *had* been coddled. (And for that matter, so was middleweight champion Sugar Ray Robinson, who was also investigated.)

The report, of course, was a waste of time. It didn't take a special committee to determine that a man playing baseball had an easier time than a man in a foxhole or a tank. And the players themselves had nothing to do with where they were assigned and what their duties were. Of course certain officers pulled strings to get the best athletes on their company baseball teams (just as the corrupt officer in *From Here to Eternity* wheels and deals to get Montgomery Clift's Robert E. Lee Pruitt on his boxing team). Mays was no more to blame for spending the Korean War playing Army baseball than Mantle was for receiving a 4-F from his draft board.

But the difference between them was this: Willie's service time was, if anything, a boost for his public image, while Mickey's rejection by the draft board would stain his reputation for a decade.

Mickey's titanic home run at Griffith Stadium had put him on the cover of *Time* magazine and helped him become a household name. But it didn't do much to enhance his stature with the New York press or Casey Stengel — "If he thinks he's got it made," Mantle's manager told Milton Gross, "I can show him where he's wrong"[12] — or for that matter, with the New York fans. The fans expected a spectacular home run every time they saw him play. Even the occasional short home run drew boos from some idiots in the stands.

As Mantle's maturity as a ballplayer grew, his immaturity as a man became more evident. Veteran sportswriter Maury Allen, my neighbor in nearby Montclair, New Jersey, recalled an incident that for him typified Mantle's childish attitude toward the press at the time. "It was in either May or June, I can't remember which," he told me, "but it wasn't too long after he hit that long home run off Stobbs. He was standing in the batting cage at Yankee Stadium, and I got up close to watch him take his cuts. He had been the subject of some uncomplimentary stories about how that long home run had caused some people to overrate him, that he still wasn't playing up to his potential. I wasn't one of them.

"I had written about how he was playing great ball for a twenty-two-year-old and everyone should be happy to watch him ease into

DiMaggio's role of leadership with the team. Anyway, he stepped back from the plate, looked at me, and said, 'Yer jus pissin' me off standin' there,' and stared at me until I moved away. I was appalled, but I almost burst out laughing. With Mickey, I soon found you had to get used to that kind of behavior."[13]

Just before the All-Star break, Mickey sprained his left knee while getting a quick jump on a liner nearly hit over his head by Cleveland's Al Rosen. Fluid accumulated under the kneecap. He played like he'd played most of the time: hurting. In August, setting up to make a throw from the outfield on a runner attempting to tag from third base, he tore ligaments in his right knee, the one he had twice had surgery on. Stengel wanted him out of the lineup; Mickey exasperated his manager by putting on a leg brace and staying on the roster.

His "off" season, as most writers called it, included a .295 batting average, 24 home runs, 105 runs scored, and 92 RBIs. Hardly anyone mentioned that the injuries kept him out of twenty-four games and limited his at-bats to 461, the lowest total he would have until 1962. In the World Series that year, against a superb Dodger team, he hit just .208 and struck out 8 times in 24 at-bats, but he made his contribution with two spectacular home runs. In Game 2 in New York, with the game tied at 2–2 in the eighth with two outs and a runner on first, Mantle hit a home run into the right-field seats. It was a "short-porch" job that didn't even rise to the second deck, but impressed everyone all the more because it was a line drive.

Then, in the third inning of Game 5 in Brooklyn, with the bases loaded and the Yanks leading 2–1, Mantle, batting against right-handed reliever Russ Meyer, stroked a long opposite-field home run into Ebbets Field's upper deck. He was just the fourth player in baseball history at that point to hit a grand slammer in the World Series. The shot scored what proved to be the winning runs in an 11–7 final.

It's a measure of how desperate Mantle still felt at this point in his life that he would later talk about the importance of that one swing. The grand slam meant so much to him, he later recalled, because "baseball wasn't a game to me as a spectator understands it. It was my job and my living and all I knew. Without it, I was going to be dragging fence posts back in Commerce or carrying a pick down to the zinc mines."[14]

In November 1953, Tom Greenwade, the scout who had bamboozled Mickey and his family out of thousands of dollars when he signed him, was assigned by the Yankees to take Mickey to visit Dr. Dan Yancey in Springfield, Missouri. The knee he had hurt before the All-Star break needed medical attention. Mickey swore at first that he would not have an operation under any circumstances; after looking at the X-rays, he relented. In February, Mickey was back in Springfield again; this time Yancey removed a fluid-filled cyst from the back of his right knee. Ordered to take it easy through all of spring training, Mantle complied.

To some sportswriters, Mickey seemed to be loafing, and several articles critical of him questioned his commitment. What made them worse was that several of these stories revived a photograph taken near the end of the 1953 season. In September, the Yankees were closing out the season against the White Sox; in the late innings of what would be a lopsided Yankees victory, Mickey began to blow a huge bubble from a wad of gum that seemed implanted in his cheek. An Associated Press photographer with a telescopic lens got the shot, and the next day Mickey's teammates, much to Stengel's irritation, were ribbing him about his bubble-blowing skills.

Something good did emerge from the incident: Frank Scott, who by now was handling Mickey's endorsement offers, called the Bowman bubblegum company and made a deal for Mickey to endorse its product. Bowman leapt at the chance, and soon Mickey had an extra $1,500 to split between Merlyn, for Mickey Jr.'s baby food and other household expenses, and Lovell back in Commerce. He didn't reveal until years later that on that afternoon against the White Sox he had actually been chewing Bazooka bubblegum.

Still, the bubblegum photo did little for Mickey's image with the press. In fact, some were questioning whether Mickey's bubble had indeed burst. "In the spring of 1954," Dick Schaap would later recall, "no booming fanfare surrounded Mantle. In fact, many of the men who had predicted greatness for him only one year earlier were forced to second-guess themselves."[15]

The bubblegum incident incensed Stengel, and he didn't mind letting the press know it: the phrases "juvenile silliness" and "kid stuff" began to appear in the sports pages when Stengel talked about his prize center fielder. Mickey sulked but kept his mouth shut. Some sportswriters, though they did not say it at the time, felt that Casey's punishment far outstripped Mantle's crime. "More important than Mantle's apologies," wrote Schaap, "was the way Stengel's voice thereafter took on an edgy tone when he referred to Mantle by his pet name of 'Ignatz.' " There was something almost derisive, he thought, in linking Mantle, a player who was supposed to be the successor to Ruth, Gehrig, and DiMaggio, with the name of a comic strip mouse (from *Krazy Kat*). "There is a hint here," he felt, "that in ambition Mickey falls short of his muscles."[16]

In 1954, Mickey Mantle was sensational, hitting an even .300 with 27 home runs, 102 RBIs, and a league-leading 129 runs scored. In the field, he led all American League outfielders — in fact, all major league outfielders, including Willie Mays — in assists with 20. (Mays had 7.) According to *Total Baseball*'s Total Player Rating, Mantle was the fourth-best player in the league, just behind Ted Williams and slightly ahead of his teammate Yogi Berra. Little of this, however, mattered to the average New York baseball fan, for two reasons. First, although the Yankees won 103 games, the most ever with Casey Stengel as manager, they failed to appear in the World Series for the first time in six years. The second reason was Willie Mays. The distance of Mantle's home run and his World Series heroics were yesterday's news. New York was about to be engulfed in a baseball tidal wave the likes of which it had not seen since Babe Ruth was at his peak. Willie Mays was back.

Willie came out of the Army bigger and stronger than when he had reported for duty. The scales showed a gain of only about three pounds, putting him up to 185—the weight Willie would carry for practically his entire major league career. But it was 185 pounds of awe-inspiring muscle. "All his baby fat was gone," recalled Monte Irvin. "Not that there was a lot of it to begin with."[17]

The Army's daily regimen of calisthenics, running, and baseball had kept Willie in superb condition. Longtime Dodgers broadcaster Vin Scully told Mays's second biographer, Arnold Hano, "When you first see him in uniform and read his physical statistics, he does not impress you as a terribly big man. But when you see him with his shirt off, he looks like the heavyweight champion of the world." Mays, wrote Hano, "has a magnificently muscled upper torso, upper arms, shoulders, and chest. He would undoubtedly have had such a torso even without Army exercises, but Fort Eustis hurried it along."[18]

Roger Kahn recalled seeing Mays in the Giants' locker room during 1954 spring training. "Mantle," he said, "had the most incredible upper body I had ever seen on a ballplayer, maybe anywhere. When I saw them both in the 1951 World Series, I thought Mickey was bigger and stronger. By 1954, Mickey was still a little bigger than Willie, particularly in the chest and arms, but it was closer."[19]

On a cold March 2, the Giants sent Frank Forbes to accompany Mays to spring training in Phoenix. Forbes met a grinning Willie at the Fort Eustis separation center, and the two immediately boarded a train headed to Washington, where they would be catching a second train for Phoenix. With four hours to kill between trains, Willie dragged Forbes to a theater within walking distance of Union Station to see *Shane*, which had premiered in September 1953 but, having proven to be hugely popular, had been re-released that spring.*

"We thought that, you know, this was Washington, so for once we didn't have to sit in the balcony. We could just sit in the middle of the theater with everyone else." Mays and Forbes watched the movie

---

* Or so, for some odd reason, Willie remembered when I interviewed him briefly in 1988 and talked about the strange events of the night of March 2.

without incident, but upon leaving the theater they were stopped and searched by two FBI agents. Mays recalled to me many years later: "They looked to me like they were after John Dillinger." Forbes was indignant; Mays was baffled and scared. At first he thought they had violated some sacred rule by sitting with white people in a movie theater.

It turned out that the agents had been tipped that two dark-skinned men they were looking for might be in that theater. After a few intense minutes, Forbes made it clear to them that they had nearly arrested the 1951 National League Rookie of the Year and that they would both be in hot water if the matter was pursued. It was never revealed who the agents were looking for or why they stopped two well-dressed black men coming out of the movies, but it almost certainly had something to do with an incident that had happened the previous day when four Puerto Rican nationalists who wanted separation from the United States had opened fire in the House of Representatives, wounding five congressmen. After some embarrassed apologies and handshakes, Forbes and Mays boarded their train to New Orleans, which would continue on to Phoenix.

Willie's troubles didn't end there. When the train stopped in the Crescent City, he jumped off to get a sandwich and soda, but by the time he got back the train had pulled off, with a frantic Forbes yelling to the conductors that he had "lost" Willie Mays. Willie quickly called Durocher in Phoenix and told him he was going to be five hours late. Leo, who had been counting the minutes until he saw Willie again, exploded. "Goddammit, didn't they teach you about trains in the Army?" he screamed into the phone.

When Willie finally arrived in Phoenix, the scene was eerie: there was no one there to greet him. In the clubhouse, the Giants' equipment manager, Eddie Logan, didn't even look at him. Just as Willie's feelings were on the verge of being hurt, the Giants' new pitcher Johnny Antonelli, recently acquired from the Braves, jumped out of the dugout and yelled, "Hey, Leo, here comes your pennant!"

The team had been giving Willie the silent treatment, but Durocher could contain himself no longer.

Willie recalled the scene to Lou Sahadi. "Leo turned around, and with a big grin he rushed at me and grabbed me in a bear hug that took the wind out of me. The last time I had seen him do that to someone was when Thomson's homer won the pennant for us against Brooklyn."[20]

Mays stepped into the batting cage as reporters marveled at his bigger biceps and the snap and power in his enormous wrists. On the first pitch, he stepped into the ball with his familiar lunge and swept the bat into it with his jackhammer swing, releasing his right hand from the bat handle about halfway through the motion. Since everyone there was quiet, watching and waiting to see what Willie would do, the crack of the bat resounded all the louder throughout the ballpark. Collective oohs and aahs and even one or two claps accompanied the ball over the left-field fences. Monte Irvin swore it was the longest shot he had ever seen, at least 430 feet. Antonelli laughed and said, "This kid hits 'em farther than Mickey Mantle." (He didn't, although he did hit them about as far as anyone in the National League.)

Durocher, basking in self-importance and reflected glory, told his audience of newsmen, "Willie must have been born under some kind of star. The stage always seems set for him to do something dramatic."

"Willie Mays," wrote Arnold Hano, echoing the famous promotion for the Clark Gable–Greer Garson movie, "was back, and Durocher had him."[21]

The Giants won their first spring training game with Willie Mays, 7–2. In what would prove to be an omen for the season, their opponent was the Cleveland Indians. Afterward, reporters ignored nearly all the other Giants and crowded around Mays's locker. "Willie answers all your questions breathlessly," wrote Bill Roeder of the *New York World-Telegram and Sun*. "He sounds like a guy who has just been told that his house is on fire."[22] The press couldn't get enough of him. One reporter shouted out, "How much money you going to ask for? Are you going to ask for $25,000?" Mays, who would sign for $13,000 that year, appeared to be stunned. "You crazy, man? If I ask for that kind of money, that man" — presumably Horace Stoneham — "take a gun and shoot me."[23]

The Giants beat Cleveland again the next day, with Mays hitting two doubles and making a sensational backhanded stab of a line drive that appeared to be in the gap. After the game, Cleveland manager Al Lopez, who had been watching Willie at batting and fielding practice as well as on the field, was asked to give his assessment of the twenty-three-year-old Giants outfielder. His answer stands as all-time proof that the most intelligent men can sometimes make the dumbest of statements: "Mays is a .270 hitter who might hit .300 if they teach him to bunt down the third base line."[*24]

He never did learn to bunt. Early in the season in a game against the Cardinals, Mays came up with runners on first and second and no outs. He attempted a bunt down the third-base line, but the pitch was up and in, and all he did was tap a dribbler to the pitcher, who fielded it and threw to third for the force-out. A visiting sportswriter cracked, "Ah-hah! They finally found Willie Mays's weakness — he can't bunt!"[25]

Sometime in 1954 — Arnold Hano reckoned that it happened in the spring before the start of the 1954 spring season, while Tris Speaker's biographer, Timothy Gay, places it in the fall, the day after Mays's catch off Vic Wertz in the World Series — two of the greatest center fielders of all time, many said *the* two greatest center fielders of all time, met in person.[†] Speaker was curious about the basket

---

* In 1979 I was living in Houston, Texas, and went to an autograph show that featured, among other baseball greats, Al Lopez. I asked Lopez if he had actually made the statement about Mays so often attributed to him. "Oh, my God, yes," he said with a big laugh. "I'd give anything to go back in time and erase that from people's memory."
† Either date would be possible. Speaker, who played from 1907 to 1928, including eleven seasons with Cleveland, was a big Indians fan and attended both regular and World Series games as well as spring training exhibitions. Actually, there's a very good chance that Speaker and Mays could have gotten together after both exhibition *and*

catch that Mays had perfected while in the Army. "See?" Mays lectured Speaker. "When I grab the ball that way with my right hand, I never get mixed up with the fingers of my left hand. They ain't there." Bill Rigney, who replaced Durocher as the Giants manager in 1956, related the story to a sportswriter. "He actually taught Speaker something," Rigney felt.

Whatever they talked about, Arnold Hano concluded, "it was apparently Mays who did the talking."[26]

On April 13, 1954, against the Dodgers, Willie Mays finally played his first opening day game with the Giants. It gave him a chance to face off with New York's other great National League center fielder, Duke Snider, who, at twenty-seven, was at the peak of a Hall of Fame career, having hit .336 with 42 home runs the previous season. As if intent on wasting no time catching up to Mickey Mantle, Mays, in the sixth inning of a 3–3 tie, lashed out at a Carl Erskine fastball and hit a line drive over the 414-foot marker of the Polo Grounds' left-field upper deck. Arnold Hano wrote at the time that the ball would have gone 600 feet had it not been stopped by the seats. (Hano confessed to me fifty-six years later that he was exaggerating, but insisted, "I think it might have gone at least 500."[27]) As if to toss his hat into the ring of the ongoing debate on who hit the ball harder, Branch Rickey began telling any sportswriter who would listen that Willie Mays swung with more power than any other player in the game — a statement that took in, of course, both Snider and Mantle.* For his part, Willie found the home run tremendously satisfying; the spotlight was back on him. "Now," he said in 1988 as he recalled that frame of mind, "it was my turn to show Mickey."[28]

World Series games. In 1954 the Giants and Indians faced each other several times during spring training.

* Rickey would later refine his statement in his 1965 book *The American Diamond*: "If there was a machine to measure each swing of a bat, it would be proven that Mays swings with more power and bat speed, pitch for pitch, than any other player" (p. 102). Rickey might be forgiven for his overstatement considering that, as a National Leaguer, he saw Mays play frequently and Mantle almost not at all.

The Giants' 4–3 victory ignited a Willie Mays frenzy that would not cool for the entire season. It might well have been that no baseball player, no athlete ever, fired up New York as Willie Mays did that season. The day after Willie's home run, the *New York Post's* Jimmy Cannon, one of the most widely read and certainly the most hyperbolic sports columnist of his time, wrote a piece titled "You're Willie Mays — A Young Legend." "You're Willie Mays of Fairfield, Ala., who is part of the small talk of New York. This shall be your city as long as your talent lasts." Mays, with only one rookie season and just 156 games of major league baseball under his belt, was already taking on the status of an icon: "Strangers, aching with loneliness, spoke to those who sat alongside of them [at the Polo Grounds] and they mentioned your name . . . you brought people together in the bantering arguments of sports. You made time pass for the bored with a bright brush. It is a fine accomplishment in a terrible age. . . . Your frantic image dashed across the screens of television sets. . . . You've become a metropolitan fable told in saloons and pool rooms and related on street corners, in home and playground."[29]

Cannon was a fast man with an adjective, but his column made a valid point: television, which was becoming increasingly important in American life and particularly in sports, had chosen Willie Mays as one of its darlings. And Willie's greatest TV performance was still several months away.

Despite the dramatic opening day home run, Willie began the season slowly, hitting around .250 for the first twenty games. Durocher then shifted him from the third spot in the order to fifth and asked him to stop pulling the ball and hit to right field. In most accounts, Durocher seemed to be asking his center fielder to try to hit with more consistency — for a higher average — and not so much power, but it may well have been that Leo wanted Willie to shoot for the short right-field porch in the Polo Grounds. Whatever his manager's purpose, Mays caught fire. In the next twenty games — of which the Giants won thirteen — he hit .450 and drove in 25 runs. By June,

Willie was hitting over .300, and on June 21 — as if to celebrate my birthday — he hit home run number twenty, which gave him as many home runs as he had hit as a rookie with more than three months left in the season.

So tuned in was all of New York to Willie Mays that on June 25, when Willie hit an inside-the-park home run against the Cubs, the Brooklyn Dodgers stopped their own game to announce the feat to their fans. And the Dodgers weren't the only hometown rivals to take notice of his performance. On July 7, *The Sporting News* noted, "Even the Yankees themselves spend half their time talking about Mays and what he does."[30]

The All-Star Game was played at Cleveland's Municipal Stadium on July 13. It was Willie's first All-Star appearance. The National League lost, 11–9, though Willie went 1-for-2 and scored a run. He played in every remaining All-Star Game for the rest of his career, and the NL won seventeen of the twenty-three. After the All-Star Game, the Giants went to St. Louis to play the Cardinals. It was there that Willie found he had lost perhaps the most important link to his past — Aunt Sarah had passed away. The team instructed Frank Forbes to travel back to Alabama with Willie for support. "The moment I walked into the house," Mays remembered, "I started to think about the years that Aunt Sarah had raised me, and I started to cry."[31] Nearly five hundred people attended Sarah's funeral; Willie was not one of them. Too upset to join the mourners, he stayed home, shut off in the bedroom he had slept in as a boy, a room so hot, he later said, that he almost fainted.

Here we must pause and consider that despite the small library of books and newspaper and magazine stories written about Willie Mays over the years, we really know very little about him. Mickey spoke of his inner feelings all through his career, but we don't know much about what Mays felt about the most significant moments and events in his life. As on the day of Aunt Sarah's funeral, there has always seemed to be a door closed between Willie and us. Why, for instance, did a twenty-three-year-old man — a professional ballplayer for nearly seven years, playing in America's largest city for two of them, and an Army veteran — need the Giants to send someone along with him just for support? Forbes, after all, had no connection at all to Willie's family. What did Frank Forbes do on the day of Aunt Sarah's funeral? Did he go to the church and the cemetery to represent Willie? Did he sit in the living room smoking cigarettes and reading the paper while Willie mourned in his bedroom?

On July 26, Willie caught up to Mickey as a cover boy for national magazines when *Time*, in anticipation of a big year for Mays and the Giants, devoted its first feature story to him. "A Boy in a Hurry" read the overwritten and generally condescending prose. "Willie Howard Mays, Jr., a cinnamon-tinted young man from Fairfield, Ala., on the edge of Birmingham, has fielded, batted and laughed the long-lackluster New York Giants into a state of combative enterprise. A husky, smooth-muscled athlete with a broad, guileless face, he plays baseball with a boy's glee, a pro's sureness, and a champion's flare.

"Though other centerfielders may have stood above him in statistics (Duke Snider, for instance), with his showman's manner and his in-the-clutch timing, Willie Mays is baseball's sensation of the season."

Above all, the story cemented Willie's image as a happy primitive in the minds of baseball fans everywhere: "Two or three nights a week, when the Giants are at home, the star centerfielder of the big leagues scoots down the block . . . to play a fast game of stickball with a band of ten- or twelve-year-old boys. Capering and joking with the kids, Mays catches their play, urges them in his high, giggle-edged voice: 'Throw harder! Harder!' "[32]

The newspaper and magazine photographs of Willie in the streets of Harlem playing stickball with kids touched a chord in America's subconscious that would never quite fade. Even today you can see the footage on numerous documentaries or websites and hear Mays reminisce about those times with analysts such as MLB.com's Harold Reynolds. Three years earlier, when Mickey Mantle had come to New York, he also played stickball in the streets with boys, less than two miles from where Willie joined the pickup games, but there were no photographers to record Mickey's stickball play.

There was only the slightest hint in the *Time* magazine cover story that there might be a deeper, more inaccessible Willie Mays who wasn't known to fans and sportswriters. "Willie," said Frank Forbes (identified by *Time* as "guardian Forbes"), "isn't loquacious."

Some Giants fans simply knew all along that their team was destined to win the pennant. "Do you want to know why the Giants are going to win the pennant?" wrote actress Tallulah Bankhead in the September 21 issue of *Look*. "Well, darlings, I can tell you in two words: Willie Mays.

"Not since John McGraw snatched Frank Frisch off the Fordham University campus to play second base have the Giants boasted so dazzling a star, such box office dynamite. I don't want to put the whammy on Willie, but it's my guess that before he shucks his Giants uniform in 1970 he'll be rated with Babe Ruth. But what am I talking about? Willie's right up there with the Babe now in my book. Let's not have any filibustering by Mickey Mantle and Duke Snider fans. They're both crack centerfielders and a credit to their parents, but they're not in Willie's class."

That a white woman — an actress and a celebrity from a prominent Alabama family yet — could write such glowing words about a black ballplayer made it clear that a new age was dawning in America. Willie Mays wasn't just the hero of black America — he was the greatest sports hero in all America. The popularity of boxing was in sharp decline, and football and basketball had not yet challenged baseball as America's national sport. Joe DiMaggio was retired; Ted

Williams and Stan Musial began the 1954 season as the best-known players in baseball, but they were grizzled veterans and Willie Mays was young and dynamic. He was the first great black *team* sports hero in American history and had now succeeded in winning over white fans in America's biggest city.

11

"In Here, It's 1954"

In 1954 the Giants, powered by Willie Mays, pitcher Johnny Antonelli (who won twenty-one games), and outfielder Don Mueller, finished five games ahead of the Dodgers. On the last day of the season, Willie beat out Mueller for the batting title, .345 to .342. The team had him skip the postgame press and jump on the next train to New York so he could appear on two different television shows in one night — *Ed Sullivan* and *The Colgate Comedy Hour*. Sullivan lobbed Willie a softball question: "What was it like to beat out a teammate for the batting title?" Willie smacked it over the wall: "If I hadn't won it, I would have wanted him to."

Despite the gesture, though, Mueller seemed to resent something about Mays — perhaps the way Leo favored him, or perhaps the fact that Willie took any ball he could get to, including, Mueller felt, some that he could have handled in right field. The next day, as the Giants suited up at the Polo Grounds for their championship team picture, Mueller walked past Mays's locker and said, "Hey, Willie, is it true that you're the best center fielder in baseball?" Mays knew he was being tweaked. He buttoned his shirt and said, without looking at Mueller, "The best right fielder too."[1] The two men did not speak again that day.

The Giants were big underdogs in the World Series against the Cleveland Indians, who won an amazing 111 games despite scoring 59 fewer runs than the Yankees. Pitching, of course, was Cleveland's strength: they led both leagues with a sensational 2.79 ERA — though the Giants had the best ERA, 3.10, in the National League.

In later years, the Giants and several writers who followed the team would argue that New York's four-game sweep of the Indians was not an upset, which is nonsense unless one simply believes that there can be no real upsets in baseball. If there have been upsets in the World Series, the Giants' victory in 1954 is probably the biggest ever. No team that had three Hall of Famers on its pitching staff — Bob Lemon (who won twenty-three games), Early Wynn (who also won twenty-three), and Bob Feller (near the end of a fabulous career but still capable of going 13–3) — should have been beaten in four straight games. And no team with a pitching staff that great should have given up twenty-one runs (while the Cleveland hitters scored just nine).

A theory would arise that the Indians became demoralized after Willie Mays's incredible catch in the first game; it was as unprovable as another notion, propagated by Mays himself as the years went by, that "The Catch," as it came to be known, wasn't the greatest play in baseball history.

One of the best accounts of The Catch can be found in Arnold Hano's *A Day at the Bleachers*, which also happens to be one of the greatest books ever written about baseball. "When the evening papers of September 28, 1954," reads the opening of Hano's book,

> reported that a dozen men and boys were already camp-
> ing across the street from the bleacher entrance outside

the Polo Grounds prior to the first World Series contest, I felt the urge.

I turned to my wife and said, "I think I'll go to the game tomorrow."

She said, "Don't you need a ticket?"

I said, "Only for the reserve seats. I'll sit in the bleachers."[2]

Nothing highlights the difference in professional sports then and now than the simple fact that in 1954 it was possible to simply show up at the stadium the day of a World Series game and buy a ticket. Hano's objective was to sit in the bleachers, watch a baseball game, and write about how he and the fans around him responded. No sportswriter ever had more spectacular luck than Hano on that day. No box seat near either team's dugout could have provided him with a better view of what happened on September 29, 1954.

Giants reliever Don Liddle was on the mound, "jerking into motion," Hano wrote, "as Wertz poised at the plate, and then the motion smoothed out and the ball came sweeping into Wertz, a shoulder-high pitch, a fast ball that probably would have been a fast curve, except that Wertz was coming around and hitting it, hitting it about as hard as I've ever seen a ball hit, on a high line to dead centerfield." Wertz was Vic Wertz, a powerful, pull-hitting first baseman who had come to Cleveland from Baltimore twenty-nine games into the season.

"For whatever it is worth," wrote Hano, "I have seen such hitters as Babe Ruth, Lou Gehrig, Ted Williams, Jimmy Foxx, Ralph Kiner, Hack Wilson, Johnny Mize, and lesser-known but equally long hitters as Wally Berger and Bob Seeds send the batted ball tremendous distances. None, that I recall, ever hit a ball any harder than this one by Wertz in my presence." *

---

* I called Mr. Hano and asked him if that was really true; had he, for instance, ever seen Mickey Mantle hit a ball harder than the hitters he named, including Wertz? "Well," he replied, "no, I didn't really see Mickey play that much in person. But I have

The ball would probably have landed in the seats in any stadium but the Polo Grounds, a ballpark that, as a friend of mine once said, "looked as if it was designed by M. C. Escher." I was there when I was a boy, and the oft-used term to describe the outfield, "cavernous," was immediately apparent. I thought it looked like the heart of a city. I'm told that in its last year, when I saw it, the center-field wall was only — that's the term they used, *only* — about 450 feet from home plate, much shorter than in earlier days.

In 1954 the official measurement was recorded at 483 feet, but both Roger Kahn and Arnold Hano have assured me that that was only part of the difficulty for a batter trying to reach the center-field seats. The wall in that part of center field reached up to — what height exactly? I don't know, and no history of the Giants or the Polo Grounds has ever been able to tell me. In the famous full-page picture of The Catch, which my father taped to my bedroom wall — a picture almost as dear to me as the photo of the rookies Mickey and Willie in 1951, which still gives me goose bumps — the section of wall Willie is racing toward looks to be at least three times, perhaps as much as four times, his height. To me, it looks to be 20 feet, perhaps 25.

And how far was Willie from the wall when he caught the ball? I'm judging a good 20 feet, which means that when Mays caught up with Wertz's drive, he was anywhere from 450 to possibly *460 feet* from home plate when he made The Catch.

But I've gotten ahead of the story. Back to Hano:

"And yet, I was not immediately perturbed. I have been a Giant fan for years, twenty-eight years to be exact, and I have seen balls hit with violence to extreme center field which were caught easily by Mays, or [Bobby] Thomson. . . .

"I did not — then — feel alarm, though the crack was loud and clear and the crowd's roar rumbled behind it like growing thunder. It may be that I did not believe the ball would carry as far as it did, hard

---

to admit, now that I think of it, that Mickey hit balls harder and longer than those guys."

hit as it was. I have seen hard-hit balls go one hundred feet into an infielder's waiting glove, and all that one remembers is crack, blur, spank. This ball did not alarm me because it was hit to dead center field — Mays territory — and not between the fielders. . . .

"And this was not a terribly high drive. It was a long, low fly or a high liner, whichever you wish. This ball was hit not nearly so high as the triple Wertz struck earlier in the day, so I may have assumed that it would soon start to break and dip and come down to Mays, not too far from his normal position.

"Then I looked at Willie, and alarm raced through me, peril flaring against my heart. To my utter astonishment, the young Giant center fielder — the inimitable Mays, most skilled of outfielders, unique for his ability to scent the length and direction of any drive and then turn and move to the final destination of the ball — Mays was turned full around, head down, running as hard as he could, straight toward the runway between the two bleacher sections.

"I knew then that I had underestimated — badly underestimated — the length of Wertz's blow."

Let's pause for a moment to admire Hano's writing. Thousands of words have been written about this single play, and none have approached his description. Here were a thousand words that were worth a picture. And yet he wrote that "no man can get the entire picture; I did what I could."

One of the things he saw while trying to keep his eye on the flight of the ball and Willie's pursuit was the runner at second base: "I saw [Larry] Doby, too, hesitating, the only man, I think, on the diamond who now conceded that Mays might catch the ball. Doby is a center fielder and a fine one and very fast himself, so he knows what a center fielder can do. He must have gone nearly halfway to third, now he was coming back to second base a bit. Of course, he may have known that he could jog home if the ball landed over Mays' head, so there was no need to get too far down the line."

As it turned out, Hano was right. In 1998 I asked Doby why he hadn't gone as far as third while the ball was in the air. "I really didn't think Willie had a chance to catch the ball," he said, "but then it jumped into my mind that if he did, what people would remember would be what a fool I had made of myself running nearly all the way home and getting nailed by fifty feet trying to scramble back to second base. It also occurred to me that if I was right, and the ball was over Willie's head, I could crawl home from second base on my hands and knees if I had to. You know what? If that ball had been over Willie's head, Vic [Wertz] would have had an inside-the-park home run."

Hano quickly calculated that Mays's catch, if he made it, "would not necessarily be in the realm of the improbable. Others had done feats that bore some resemblance to this.

"Yet, Mays' catch — if he was indeed to make it — would dwarf all the others for the simple reason that he too would have caught Lieber's" — that is, Hank Lieber's fly ball to Joe DiMaggio in the 1936 World Series — "or DiMaggio's fly" — in the 1937 Series — "whereas neither could have caught Wertz's. Those balls had been towering drives, hit so high the outfielder could run forever before the ball came down. Wertz had hit his ball harder and on a lower trajectory. Lieber — not a fast man — was nearing second base when DiMaggio caught his ball; Wertz, also not fast — was at first base when . . .

"Mays simply slowed down to avoid running into the wall, put his hands up in cup-like fashion over his left shoulder and caught the ball much like a football player catching leading passes into the end zone."[3]

The Catch transcended baseball. Over the years it has lived on. In football, whenever a receiver makes a long, over-the-shoulder catch, you hear the commentator say, "That was a Willie Mays catch," possibly to many young fans who aren't entirely sure what that means. Let me make one point. There is an enormous difference between any football catch of that sort, no matter how sensational, and the one Willie made in the 1954 World Series, and it is this: in football, the receiver always knows where the ball is supposed to be going.

Which makes so much of what has been written and said about this play over the years, much of it by Willie Mays himself, a lie. Somehow it has become acceptable for old-timer sportswriters and ballplayers to pop up every few years with a story about a play they saw Willie make that was somehow better than the Vic Wertz catch. This is a lie if they're talking about the entire play — Willie's astonishing stop, whirl, and throw, which kept Al Rosen, who was on first, from advancing to second and Doby, who was on second, from going to third and then home. (Against a center fielder with just an average good arm, Doby could have scored standing up, as shortstop Alvin Dark's throw would have been as far as the average center fielder's throw on a normal fly ball.)

But it is also a lie even if they're just talking about The Catch. I've seen a couple of these other great catches on tape, and they are indeed incredible. You can go online and listen to the great Ernie Harwell talk about a game at Pittsburgh when Rocky Nelson hit a screaming line drive between left and center and Willie, diving, knew he couldn't make the play with his glove and caught it with his bare hand. But I can't imagine where the ball could have been hit that Mays could not have backhanded it with his glove. The whole story sounds like one of those tales of Davy Crockett killing both a bear and a panther by shooting a lead ball into a rock between them, splitting the bullet — something like that. (Whatever really happened, the Rocky Nelson story has a great kicker. In the dugout, an excited Willie found his teammates giving him a cold shoulder, pretending not to have noticed his amazing play. Hurt, Willie walked over to Leo, who was standing at the end of the dugout, and said, "Here, Mr. Leo. Didn't you see? I just made a great play!" Durocher, in perfect deadpan, replied, "Sorry, Willie, I was in the can. I missed it. Could you do it again next inning?")

Then there was the spectacular catch on Cincinnati's Bobby Tolan in 1971, where Willie leapt several feet against a wire fence, crashing into teammate Bobby Bonds, to steal a home run from

Tolan. You can see this one online too, and it will take your breath away. You can also see the marker on the fence behind Mays and Bonds that says 380 feet.

The difference between The Catch and those — excluding the obvious fact that it was made in the World Series under tremendous pressure — is that Mays may have been 450 feet or more from home plate, and most important, *he had his back to home plate*. For the last twenty feet or so of his run, *he did not so much as glance back to see where the ball was.*

The Giants went on to sweep the Series in four games, and afterward, of course, some said they were the better team all along (if only because they had Willie Mays). The Giants, however, were *not* a better team than the Indians and had no business beating them. But then, the Indians, despite having won 111 games, were probably not better than the Yankee team they'd beaten for the AL pennant.

Willie won the National League's MVP Award, though his final statistics weren't that much better than Duke Snider's. Snider batted .341 with 40 home runs. Mays batted .345 (to lead the league) with 41 homers. Snider had an on-base percentage of .427 and a slugging percentage of .647; Willie's were, respectively, .415 and .667, the latter the best in the NL. But it was recognized that Snider played his home games in Ebbets Field, a much better hitter's park than the Polo Grounds, and besides, the Giants won the pennant. The next spring, according to Arnold Hano, to get one Willie Mays card "cost two Duke Sniders and three Mickey Mantles."[4] It would take nearly forty years for that ratio to reverse itself.

From the first game of 1954 through the final game of the World Series, New York had been on fire with Willie Mays love — though perhaps some parts of New York more than others. Expressions like "Safe as a Willie Mays triple" — Willie led the league that year in triples with 13 — were common. In the off-season and over the winter, fans continued to bask in the glow. Over the winter, a black vocal group, The Treniers, released a song they had recorded late in 1954, "Say Hey: The Willie Mays Song."

The Treniers' song was produced by a young arranger named Quincy Jones, who made the unmusical but commercially shrewd decision to use Willie himself as a backup vocalist. The lyrics, by Jane Douglass and Dick Kleiner, happily reviewed Willie's recent history:

> *When Willie served his Uncle Sam,*
> *He left the Giants in an awful jam;*
> *But now he's back, he's Leo's joy,*
> *And Willie's still a growing boy.*

The song was practically unheard by white listeners until it was used by Ken Burns in his 1994 documentary *Baseball*.

In the off-season, at his famous bar-restaurant, Toots Shor would tell anyone who listened, "I gotta start learnin' how to be a Giants fan."[5] But Toots was a Yankees fan at heart. Before Mickey and Merlyn went back to Oklahoma for the holiday, they stopped by Toot's for dinner. "Ya crumb bum," said a beaming Toots, patting a grinning Mickey on the cheek. "Ya lettin' that Giants kid steal all the thunder in this town. The Yankees gonna win the pennant next year? Ya gonna lead the league in home runs?"[6] The answer to the first question was yes, and the answer to the second question was yes — and also in triples, walks, and on-base and slugging percentage.

Bernard "Toots" Shor had come to New York in 1930 from the mean streets of South Philadelphia. The only one who called him Bernard was his mother, and only for a few years; she was killed when he was fifteen when a car jumped the curb and struck her as she sat on the stoop in front of their Wharton Street brownstone. His father never recovered and committed suicide a few years later. The nickname "Toots" was a present from his aunt — short for "Tootsie." Perhaps, like the father in the Johnny Cash song "A Boy Named Sue," she knew that with a name like that, Bernard would have to get tough or die.

He got tough. In the waning years of Prohibition, he hooked up with a well-known New York bootlegger named Billy LaHiff, who gave him his first job in New York as a bouncer. He was soon promoted to manager. If Shor seemed like a character out of a Damon Runyon story, he missed being one by only a few years. The middle-aged Runyon spent quite a bit of time in LaHiff's and introduced Toots to the stars of the New York demimonde, including such luminaries of the Italian, Jewish, and Irish underworld as, respectively, Lucky Luciano, Meyer Lansky, and Owney Madden.

In 1949 he opened his own place, Toots Shor — that was the club's name, just plain Toots Shor — at 51 West Fifty-First Street. For the next ten years, Toots Shor *was* New York. In 1957, when the greatest of all New York noir films, *Sweet Smell of Success,* was filmed, Tony Curtis's parasitic publicist, Sidney Falco, goes searching for Burt Lancaster's ruthless gossip columnist, J. J. Hunsecker, and finds him at Toots's saloon. That's what Toots preferred to call it — not a "restaurant" but a "saloon."

To paraphrase Claude Rains in *Casablanca,* everyone came to Toots Shor. Joe DiMaggio, of course, was a regular. So were Frank Sinatra and Jackie Gleason, both Shor cronies.* All were treated with rough good humor, but none were shown deference. When Louis B. Mayer flew in from Hollywood, he was miffed about having to wait for a table. "I trust the food will be worth all the waiting," he said indignantly to Shor. "It'll be better," Shor replied, "than some of your crummy pictures I stood in line to see." Mayer laughed, and the two became pals.

One remarkable evening Supreme Court justice Earl Warren, the country's highest-ranking judge, glanced across the room and saw

---

* In Don DeLillo's 1997 novel *Underworld,* Shor, Sinatra, and Gleason are at the Polo Grounds for the third game of the 1951 National League playoff. Gleason, having gorged on Jack Daniels and hot dogs, misses Bobby Thomson's home run when he's doubled up with the heaves.

Frank Costello, the most powerful figure of the New York mob, smiling and tipping his glass to him. Warren nodded and smiled back. On another memorable occasion, at least according to legend, two of America's greatest prose stylists were introduced when Toots said to Yogi Berra, "I want you to meet Ernest Hemingway, an important writer." Yogi, so the story goes, replied, "What paper you with, Ernie?"

Naturally, the New York Yankees, particularly Mickey Mantle, Whitey Ford, and Billy Martin, were among the "crumb bums" — Shor's term of endearment for his pals — who showed up almost nightly when the team was in town. Sometimes wives would be in attendance; a doelike Merlyn often smiled and gazed silently with amazement and admiration as America's greatest celebrities lionized her young husband. Sometimes the unholy trio would show up stag — though never, *never* with women not their wives, an indiscretion Shor frowned upon.

In one of the first episodes of *The Sopranos*, Tony's daughter, Meadow, chides him at the dinner table for being out of date. "Daddy," she says, "it's 1999." He tells her: "Out there, it's 1999. In *here*, it's 1954." In Toots's saloon, it was always 1954. In everyone's memory, the air was ripe with a complacent, confident America living the good life in the early Eisenhower era. Most of the clientele were men, everyone was well dressed, no one took himself too seriously, and no one would think of being crass enough to ask Mickey Mantle for an autograph.

In October 1954, Willie Mays, Monte Irvin, and several members of New York's first integrated championship sports team came to Toots Shor. Toots greeted them with enthusiasm. Though the saloon had few black customers, Toots Shor was one of the few nightspots in New York where there was no color line. Former heavyweight champion Joe Louis, the most famous black man in America, was a frequent guest, as was welter- and middleweight champion Sugar Ray Robinson. It was there that Mickey saw Willie for the first time since their meeting at the 1951 World Series. "I was happy for him," Mantle recalled for me in 1982. "He seemed just like a kid. He looked as happy as I felt in 1952 when we won. But I also felt a little strange. I couldn't get out of my head that, 'Damn, we won 103 games, they won, I think 95 or 96. [It was 96.] Maybe it should have been us playing them in the World Series that year. Anyway, it was the first year that we didn't win, and it just didn't feel right. It was really strange to be congratulating someone else."

Mickey remembered something else about Willie. "It seemed to me that he felt a little strange too. He didn't drink, which Toots had a lot of fun kidding him about. He stood around with a big glass of Coke and ice, smiling but not saying a whole lot." In fact, only a few days before, Willie had gotten sick in the visitors' clubhouse in Cleveland when the Giants had won the fourth game of the World Series. He had drunk just one glass of champagne, the first alcohol he had consumed since Cat had forced him to drink hard liquor back in Fairfield. In that one night at Shor's saloon, Mickey consumed more alcohol than Willie had up to that point in his life — possibly throughout his entire life.

During the 1950s and for at least a while into the next decade, black sports heroes relaxed in a world that Mickey and his Yankees teammates could not know. Birdland, at Broadway and Fifty-Second Street, a nightclub where Willie and his friends often went to hear musicians such as Charlie Parker, Dizzy Gillespie, and Bud Powell, was open to whites, but country boys from Oklahoma whose musical interests ranged from Bob Wills to Hank Williams didn't go there.

A spot more frequented by black celebrities was Harlem's Savoy Ballroom, located on Lenox Avenue between 140th and 141st Streets. Nearly a block long, the club was noted for its red-carpeted lounges and mirrored wall panels, and in the early fifties it became one of the first racially integrated clubs in New York. It called itself "The World's Finest Ballroom." Its nickname was "The Home of Happy Feet"; the dance floor took such a pounding from the hundreds of patrons every week that the club's owner, Mo Gale, who was Jewish, and manager,

Charles Buchanan, who was black, liked to tell first-time visitors that it had to be replaced at least every three years.

The Savoy Ballroom was the inspiration for numerous black clubs around the country, including one in Birmingham that Willie knew very well, the Little Savoy Café on Seventeenth Street in the Fourth Avenue district, the undisputed center of black cultural life in the city. Harlem's Savoy was probably the most popular nightspot for black luminaries of the sports and entertainment worlds, featuring not only great solo artists but entire big bands. On May 11, 1937, the famed Chick Webb vs. Benny Goodman Battle of the Bands — the first major performance by black and white bands — took place there before a crowd of four thousand.

It was a natural meeting place for black Alabamians when they came to the big city. Monte Irvin recalled that Willie's New York friends, most of them black players on the Giants and Dodgers, gave a party for him there after his return from the Army in 1954. Later that year, Irvin gave another party for Willie in one of the Savoy's private rooms, where he was presented with one of his many postseason awards. Guests included Frank Forbes, Sugar Ray Robinson, and singer Billy Eckstine.* All were eager to shake Willie's hand. It simply wasn't possible in 1954 America for a young black man to have climbed any higher on the social ladder than Willie Mays had.

The Giants' paternalistic attitude toward Mays intruded itself into every aspect of his life. Horace Stoneham thought that the postseason banquet circuit was one of the worst things for a player's waistline as well as his ego; someone suggested that to keep Willie sharp — he had, after all, played just two seasons of professional ball after losing nearly two seasons to the Army — they should have him play winter ball.

---

* Also that year, the Savoy had a visit from a soon-to-be-famous fictitious character, an Englishman named James Bond, who was taken there by his CIA liaison, Felix Leiter, in Ian Fleming's second 007 novel, *Live and Let Die*.

The Santurce, Puerto Rico, team Mays played for was managed by Herman Franks, who would someday manage Willie in San Francisco, and it was stocked with enough first-line talent to beat most major league squads. Prominent among them were a young outfielder from the Pirates organization named Roberto Clemente, who would make an inauspicious debut that season, batting just .255 in 154 games, and an overweight youngster named Orlando Cepeda, whose father had been a great Puerto Rican star. Also on the roster was a teammate of Willie's from the Giants, Ruben Gomez, who had won thirty games over the previous two seasons.

Mays dominated the league, hitting nearly .400, and was named the circuit's MVP. But a silly incident in January rubbed just a little gloss off Willie's halo. On January 11, Clemente, taking a break in batting practice, left the cage to get a new bat. Gomez, a fair hitting pitcher, jumped in and yelled to Milton Ralat, the batting practice pitcher, to toss him a few until Clemente got back. Willie was scheduled to hit next. Ralat, apparently not wanting to offend either Clemente or Mays, told Gomez that he wouldn't throw to him, and Ruben, either sulking or feigning offense, sat down on home plate. Mays stepped into the cage, moved over to the right side, and yelled for Ralat to pitch to him; Willie responded to his pitch with a hard one-hopper that struck Ralat in the shoulder. (Why there wasn't a screen to protect the BP pitchers wasn't explained.)

What happened next had to be pieced together from several accounts. Ralat apparently cursed Mays — why isn't clear, as Willie was simply doing what he was supposed to do when Ralat pitched to him — and Mays, reacting immaturely, made a move toward the mound. Ralat, who also should have known better, moved toward Mays. Meanwhile, Gomez, still holding his bat, jumped up from home plate and moved toward the team's star player. Gomez later said that he wanted to prevent a confrontation between Mays and Ralat and simply forgot to drop his bat. When Willie saw Gomez approaching, bat in hand, he turned and faced off, dropped his bat, and threw a punch, a short right-handed shot, at Gomez. If Willie had used his bat, or Gomez had used his, the story might have been tragic instead of farcical. When Herman Franks jumped in to separate them, Willie is supposed to have said, "Are you on the Puerto Ricans' side too?"

More than likely it was Gomez who passed Willie's remark on to the local reporters. The fans did not appreciate his comment, and the next day the man who had been the most popular visitor to Puerto Rican baseball since "the Great DiMaggio" was booed loudly when he came up to the plate. Three days later, Willie, telling reporters he had bruised his knee, went back to the States.

The participants played down the skirmish, and the pro-Mays New York press, anxious to preserve Mays's golden reputation, played along. Whatever really happened, Gomez pitched seven more seasons in the big leagues, and he and Mays got along just fine.

" I should have guessed that the 1955 season would have a tricky ending for us," Mickey Mantle told Mickey Herskowitz in *All My Octobers*. "It was the year *Damn Yankees* become one of the big hit musicals on Broadway."[7] The Yankees had come to look upon the World Series as their birthright; during salary negotiations, management practically argued that their World Series check was not a bonus the players earned but a part of their salary. Oddly enough, just about the only Yankee to see through this bit of sham was the squat catcher with the clownish public image, Yogi Berra, who proved to be a tough negotiator with general manager George Weiss. Early in his career, when Weiss argued that Yogi's $5,000-plus World Series share should be considered part of his compensation, Berra shrewdly replied, "I had something to do with that." (Yogi got most of the raise he asked for.)

It seems absurd in retrospect, but Mickey, by 1955, had not yet reached the level of the top salaried players. His salary for that year was just $17,000; Willie signed for $25,000 that year. With Patterson handling his deals, however, Mickey brought in a steady stream of cash endorsements. There's no way of knowing the total precisely, but his endorsement deals surely exceeded his salary, and because he was white, they were worth several times what Mays could get. Neverthe-less, money was still tight for Mickey. Back in Commerce, he built a fine house for his young family at the cost of nearly $16,000 and also bought a brand-new Lincoln, but he might not have been able to afford both purchases if Merlyn's father hadn't owned a lumberyard and given him a break on building materials.

Like most ballplayers, Mickey gave little thought to the future. Before he left Commerce for spring training, he had given away what would one day prove to be a small fortune in jerseys, bats, and home run balls. He also gave a friend his 1953 World Series ring. Who knew that in thirty years' time those items would have such value? After all, Mickey Mantle had not yet invented nostalgia.

Most preseason prognosticators assumed that the retooled Yankees, even without their veteran starters Allie Reynolds, Ed Lopat, and Vic Raschi, would bounce back and overtake the Indians for the pen-nant. Their likely opponent, most thought, would be the New York Giants, who had, after all, won the World Series in dazzling fashion. They had Willie Mays at his peak, and so far Mays had yet to play on a Giants team that failed to win the NL pennant. In the Bronx, the addition of new pitchers Bob Turley and Don Larsen, along with veteran pitcher Jim Konstanty (the former "Philly Whiz Kid" the Yankees had faced in 1950), held up nicely. Two new players, a power-hitting former college football player named Bill "Moose" Skowron and a catcher-outfielder, Elston Howard, the Yankees' first black player, helped the team maintain a small lead over the Indians for most of the season. They ended up beating them to the flag by just three games.

The biggest addition to the roster was Howard, a superb catcher — from the start some thought he was even the equal of the Yankees' three-time MVP catcher, Yogi Berra. Howard was also a capable out-fielder. And he could hit. Howard didn't simply endure the pressure of being the first black Yankee — he thrived. On May 14, against the Detroit Tigers, he hit a dramatic two-out game-winning triple that brought the normally reserved Yankees out of their dugout. Mantle asked Billy Martin and Hank Bauer to stall Howard on the field while he ran ahead into the clubhouse. When Elston entered, he found a row of his teammates, all grinning, and a trail of white towels — in some stories they are red — from his locker to the showers. It was a tradition for new Yankees who had won their spurs.

Sometime during the 1955 season, Mickey began needling his beloved teammate Yogi Berra about how overrated the catcher's job was. How tough could it be, Mickey asked Yogi, to call pitches with someone like Whitey Ford on the mound? After all, it was always the pitcher who had the final say. Before a game against the Red Sox at Fenway, Mantle laid it on. Finally, Yogi threw up his hands — Okay, he told Mantle, *you* go ahead. *You* call the pitches for Whitey. They agreed on a signal: when Mickey stood straight up in center field, he wanted Ford to throw a fastball; if he bent over with his hands on his knees, he was calling for a curve. This may sound a bit frivolous for professional ballplayers, especially Yankees, who were locked in a pennant race, but there was really no risk involved. If Berra disapproved of Mantle's call, he'd change it. (And of course Whitey, who knew of the arrangement, had final approval of the pitches.)

As it turned out, Mickey did a pretty good job. Ford shook him off only four or five times, and the Yankees were leading 2–0 after seven innings. But even though Mantle did not have to spend hours squatting behind the plate, he found calling the pitches mentally exhausting. When the Yankees piled into the visitors' dugout before the start of the eighth inning, Mickey walked over to Yogi, slapped him on the shoulder, and told him, "Okay, I got you this far. Take it the rest of the way."[8]

The first season in which Mickey and Willie were regarded as equals — or at least near equals — was 1955. In 1954 Mantle had been perceived by most sportswriters as one of the four or five best players in the American League, but Mays was clearly the best player in baseball. Many thought Mickey, from 1952 through 1954, might have been the most overrated player in baseball; in truth, he might have been the most underrated. In 1955, though, there was no doubt in anyone's mind: Mantle batted .306 and led the AL in home runs (37), walks (113), triples (11), and both on-base and slugging percentage. By *Total Baseball*'s ranking, he was clearly the best player in the AL.

Willie Mays was even better in 1955 than he had been the previous season, batting .319 and leading the NL in home runs (51) and slugging percentage (.659), with an on-base percentage of .400. He also, like Mantle, led the league in triples (13). His power might have been even more impressive than that. There were few statisticians in the 1950s who bothered to notice such things, but in 1955 Mays had not entirely mastered the art of hitting home runs at the Polo Grounds—that is, he had not yet learned how to hit the ball with power to the opposite field. (Mantle, who switch-hit, never had to.) Mays hit 29 of his 51 home runs in the seven other NL ballparks; if he had done as well playing in New York, he would have been a couple of hanging curveballs away from tying Babe Ruth's single-season home run record of 60. No doubt the frenzy that would have accompanied such an achievement would have lit up New York all summer and even into a fall in which the Giants were never in the pennant race. Despite finishing third behind the Dodgers and Braves, they trailed eighteen and a half games behind Brooklyn and were never in the race all season. The 1955 season, said one writer, finally disproved two things: "that Willie Mays could not play on a team that did not win a pennant" and that "every team that Willie Mays played on had to win the pennant."9

In 1955 Willie added a new dimension to his game: he used his great base-running skills to begin *stealing* bases, a rare talent in the 1950s, when most batters simply reached base and stayed there until someone slugged them in. In 1954 he stole 8 bases in 13 attempts; in 1955 he stole 24 in just 28 tries. In the field he led all outfielders with an eye-popping 23 assists and 8 double plays, and his range factor per nine innings was just a hair under three putouts per game, a healthy 0.6 above the rest of the league's center fielders.

Mantle was very nearly as good, averaging 2.76 putouts per nine innings, and he stole 8 bases in 9 attempts. (The Yankees were not a base-stealing team, relying mostly on power, and Mantle attempted steals only late in the game when the score was close.) It was not noticed at the time that he grounded into just four double plays, while Mays grounded into twelve. It was noted, however, by analysts of the next generation. Bill James, in his 2002 book *Win Shares*, taking into account all the contributions Mickey and Willie made at bat, in the field, and on the bases, calculated that Mantle in 1955 was exactly as good as Mays — despite the fact that Mickey finished the season limping. On September 16, in a 5–4 victory over the Red Sox, he suffered a severe muscle tear in the back of his right thigh as he tore down to first base to beat out a bunt. He played in only two more games the rest of the season, both times as a pinch-hitter.

The missed at-bats might have cost Mickey the MVP award (which was won by his teammate Yogi Berra). Indeed, the voting showed an odd prejudice against Mickey, who finished fifth behind Berra, the Detroit Tigers' twenty-year-old outfielder Al Kaline (who led the league in batting at .340), Cleveland's Al Smith, and Ted Williams. By most objective ratings, Mantle was the best player in the league that season, so it's curious that he was never a serious contender for MVP. It was almost as if the voters were saying, "Unless you live up to what we think is your potential, we're not going to vote for you." Not wanting to diminish Yogi's achievement, Mantle never complained publicly, but privately he told a couple of writers that he was puzzled that he wasn't at least a serious MVP candidate.

Just as strange was that Mays finished fourth in the voting for the NL MVP; another catcher, Roy Campanella, took the award. Duke Snider and Ernie Banks also finished ahead of Willie. (Snider was named top player by *The Sporting News*.) Like Mickey, Willie was by all objective yardsticks the best player in the league — in fact, he was *by far* the best player in the league. Why was he not named MVP for the second year in a row? There is no clear answer to that question. It's easy enough to say that Snider's team won the pennant that season, but Ernie Banks would win MVPs in 1958 (a year in which Mays was a substantially better all-around player) and in 1959; Ernie's team, the Chicago Cubs, finished sixth both years. It was almost as if the voters were saying, "C'mon, Willie, you're so good and you've got so many years to win this thing, let's give someone else a chance."

Mickey limped, literally, into the World Series, where, for the third time in four years, the Yankees played the Dodgers. Mantle missed the first two games, both of which the Yankees lost. They would win three of the last five, but it was not enough as the Dodgers won their first and only World Series. It's difficult to believe that a full-strength Mantle would not have made the difference in at least one of those four losses, particularly the first three games, which the Yankees lost by a total of three runs. In the first inning of Game 3 — the first time Mantle stepped onto the field — he pulled the thigh muscle again chasing down a ball hit by Carl Furillo. He had just two hits in ten at-bats for the entire series.

So the 1955 season ended in disappointment for both Mickey and Willie. Up to that point in their professional careers, both of them, from the minor and Negro leagues on up, had scarcely known anything but winning. For Willie, years of frustration with the Giants had just begun. He would first lose his beloved manager, then his beloved city. At least, as the year ended, he had the distinction of being recognized as easily the best player in baseball. That was about to change.

12

"A Whole Different Ball Game"

"Bliss was it in that dawn to be alive," wrote Wordsworth. "But to be young was very heaven." It was also great in 1955 to be young and a Yankee.

In October, a grinning Mickey Mantle and Billy Martin hopped on a bus to make a train connection out to Ebbets Field for the World Series with the Brooklyn Dodgers. It took the other passengers a good thirty seconds or so to realize who they were riding with. There were some shouts, whistles, and encouragements from their fellow riders. No one, apparently, said anything to Mantle about his 4-F draft status; no one asked for an autograph. These were, after all, just two happy young men on the way to work, both of them working for good money, perhaps not much more than some of the men riding with them. Within a year, Mickey Mantle would no longer be able to take public transportation anywhere.

Scarcely anyone who saw Mickey Mantle or Willie Mays in public during that time knew anything about their off-the-field anxieties. The men who wrote about New York's two young center fielders told only of their childlike antics: Willie playing stickball in the streets of Harlem, Mickey in the dugout wearing a cowboy holster, aiming a cap gun at a photographer — probably a cap gun but in the photograph it certainly looks real — and Mickey and Billy going at each other with water pistols or cans of shaving cream.

When the Yankees were on the road, writers knew that the after-hours escapades often went well beyond boys being boys. If, in the fall of 1955, Mickey Mantle was not yet an alcoholic, he was well on the way. According to one anonymous Yankee, after a night game in Detroit both Mantle and Martin, thoroughly drunk, crawled out on the ledge outside their hotel room window on their hands and knees — twenty-two stories up. Unable to crawl backward to their room, they were forced to circle the building looking for an open window.

David Falkner, one of Mantle's biographers, wrote that one night Mickey and Billy took him to dinner at the posh and pricey Harwyn Club, where they gawked at, among other celebrities, Grace Kelly and Prince Rainier. "We had dinner with Rocky Marciano. Can you believe that?" Actually, Rocky was seated at the next table. In such elegant surroundings, Mickey showed up with a whoopee cushion and slipped it onto a friend's seat before he sat down. Hilarity ensued — at least at the Mantle-Martin table. Princess Grace's response was not recorded.

After dinner, the merry pranksters went to a cocktail party. In the words of one of the party, "this real fancy place, like on the twentieth floor . . . and here's Teresa Brewer sitting there." Billy whispered in his ear that Brewer, one of the most popular female singers of the decade, "kind of liked Mickey a little bit."[1]

There was one piece of very good news to begin the 1956 season with: both Mickey and Willie would be making a lot more money.

Frank Scott, who had been handling endorsements for six Yankee players, including Mickey, began taking on new clients. According to Scott, it was Mickey who suggested to him that a popular black player such as Mays might be ready to cross over into the mainstream; Mays apparently had said as much to Mantle when they met at the All-Star Game and he asked Mickey to drop a word to Scott.

Scott, the Yankees' traveling secretary for years, was fired by George Weiss when he refused to spy on the players' late-night activities for the Yankees general manager.* He recounted their conversation years later for Dick Young: "Mr. Weiss, if you were to ask me whether such-and-such a ballplayer was out late, I would have to tell you and I will. But I can't go running to the front office, voluntarily, with stories about the ballplayers."[2]

Scott got the idea of handling endorsements when he visited the Berra family in New Jersey. Yogi, grateful for some arrangement Scott had made for him, opened a drawer full of new watches and told Scott to choose one. "Where'd you get those?" asked an astonished Scott. Yogi told him they had been given to him for doing pregame and postgame radio and TV shows as well as an occasional personal appearance. Scott shook his head; he knew that companies could afford to pay the players more than a watch for their time and trouble — which, he understood, they had bought in bulk.

Scott talked Yogi and then several other Yankees into letting him represent them for radio and TV appearances, personal appearances, and endorsements, both individually and in groups. At first some producers balked, saying that if he wanted, say, $500 for Yogi Berra or Mickey Mantle to do a personal appearance, they could get someone else cheaper. Scott called their bluff and put the biggest names in baseball under his wing. Soon producers began to meet Scott's terms.

---

* Or that, at least, was the way Scott told the story. He told the players that he quit because he refused to spy on them, a decision that earned him a loyal following. Scott, who was my neighbor in nearby Maplewood, New Jersey, until his death in 1998, always insisted that he quit. He once told me, "The Yankees have my letter of resignation. You can find it in their files." I never went to look for it, but I have no doubt it was there.

Before Willie joined Scott's roster, Frank Forbes had been handling his endorsements, but they were usually smaller deals. The advertising departments for most products plugged by athletes assumed that black players didn't have PR clout. Thanks to Scott, Mays's endorsement income did go up — but the sad truth was that in 1955 Mays was the only black athlete to make substantial money off the field, and even with Scott on board, his endorsement fees never came close to Mantle's. In 1956 Mays made perhaps $8,500 in appearance and endorsement fees, while Mantle pulled in over $70,000 — but then, in 1956 Mantle's career was off into the stratosphere.

When asked if Mays resented Mickey's superior commercial pull, Monte Irvin responded, "Yeah, kind of. I think it always bothered him. Willie didn't have an ounce of racism in him, and he really didn't believe that most people responded to him with any kind of racial prejudice. I think he was really frustrated by his inability to make more money."[3]

Charles Einstein was even more blunt: "Oh, I can tell you it bugged the hell out of him. And I'll tell you something else: though he never said it publicly, Mickey was always resentful that his salary was never as big as Willie's."[4]

By 1962, Scott would have more than one hundred top athletes, most of them baseball players, in his talent pool. Dick Young wrote that Frank Scott represented more talent than any other man in sports. "Do you want Mickey Mantle for a hair goo commercial? Call Frank Scott. Do you want Warren Spahn for the Ed Sullivan show? Call Frank Scott. Do you want Don Drysdale to play the part of a lanky, two-gun villain on The Rifleman? Call Frank Scott."[5]

In February 1956, Willie Mays got married. The news stunned even some of the writers who knew him best. The Giants' paternalistic treatment of Willie had been so effective that no photograph of him with a woman had ever been published. Willie's bride was Marghuerite Wendell. The two had been introduced in the spring of the previous year by Oscar Hammerstein at the Red Rooster, a popular Harlem restaurant where Willie had been known to hand out monogrammed sports shirts.

It would have been impossible to find two black people born in America in the 1930s who seemed more different than Willie and Marghuerite. No one knew exactly how old she was. She told some reporters that she was two years Willie's senior, but one journalist claimed that she was at least six years older than the twenty-four-year-old Mays, and possibly more than that. She was stunning. Apparently she had come to New York from St. Louis when she was nineteen and somehow met Bill Kenny of the Ink Spots. A little more than a year later, she gave birth to a baby girl and told Kenny that he was the father; later she told him he was not. The child was taken in by Marghuerite's family and dropped out of her narrative as soon as she married Mays; there is no mention of her in any subsequent stories regarding the couple.

Marghuerite later told reporters that she and Kenny had divorced in 1949, though there was no hard evidence they were ever married. She was married, legally, in 1954 to a Detroit doctor named Roland Chapman. The marriage lasted less than a year, but through Chapman she met former heavyweight champion Joe Louis, a native of Detroit, and was seen with him at nightspots in New York. (Some reports had it the other way around, that Louis had introduced her to Chapman.)

"Margie," as her friends called her, knew virtually everyone who was anyone in black New York nightlife, from musicians like Dizzy Gillespie and Duke Ellington to boxers such as Sugar Ray Robinson. Interestingly, she knew nothing about baseball, though she called herself a Joe DiMaggio fan. At least she and Willie had that in common.

Though Willie had been seeing her for some time by the time the marriage was announced, only a couple of black papers had bothered to report on the relationship. According to Charles Einstein (who hadn't known about the impending marriage even though he had just finished working with Willie on his first book, *Born to Play Ball*, published in 1955), Horace Stoneham tried to prevent the marriage.

"We all heard that he [Stoneham] had talked to Roy Campanella and asked him to talk to Willie," Einstein said. "At any rate, that's what Roy later told me and others."[6]

Stoneham was most displeased that Frank Forbes could not talk what he believed was sense into Willie. In fact, Willie was so incensed by Forbes's attempts that it ended their relationship as well as the Giants' association with Forbes. After the wedding, Roger Kahn — one of the few writers Mays trusted to do an interview — visited the newlyweds at their home in Queens, which was "more luxurious than anything I could imagine Willie being able to afford," Kahn discovered.

"They had a huge television, I mean huge for the time. A screen maybe twenty inches, and two big closets just packed with clothes. If Willie had less than two dozen suits, I'd have been surprised." On the wall were reproductions of paintings by the great masters in gilt-edged frames. "I'm guessing that Willie had not selected those for his living room," said Kahn.

"All the time," Kahn recalled, "I kept staring at the furniture, the carpets, the satin bedspreads, and asking myself how all of this could have been covered by his salary. I don't think he could have paid for it all even if he had been making the money Mickey Mantle was making on endorsements."

Another thing that puzzled Kahn was "the lack of almost any family or close friends around Willie. Monte Irvin was a good friend, but they had had some kind of falling-out over a business affair — a liquor store, I think — and weren't quite as close for a while as they had been. And one thing you never heard Willie talk about was Cat." Mays had moved his father to New York in 1954 and rented him an apartment in Harlem. Willie took care of his father, but, said Kahn, who saw Cat on rare occasions at the ballpark, "Cat seemed increasingly pathetic. He told me once that he missed all his old friends back in Fairfield and Birmingham" — presumably the crowd that hung out at Bob's Little Savoy — "and didn't see or hear from Willie all that often."[7] No one had any way of knowing it at the time, but within a couple of short years Cat would be isolated from his son completely when the Giants left New York forever.

As he began the 1956 season, Mickey Mantle's relationship with the press was no better than it had been five years before. Almost all the New York press corps liked him, or at least wanted to like him, but as Whitey Ford succinctly phrased it, "Mickey would always let a reporter know that he had asked his last question."[8] He could have been thankful, however, for at least one thing: in those days the press did not follow up on embarrassing rumors regarding ballplayers.

Either in the winter of 1954–55 or 1955–56 — Mickey could never remember exactly which year this happened and gave three different accounts in his later life — Mantle came close to a good stiff jail sentence.

It happened when Mickey was in Oklahoma, bored, nursing an injury he'd sustained playing basketball.* The young man who just a few years before had been homesick for Commerce was now itching to get back to the Copa, Toots Shors's place, and the rest of the New York nightlife. He fought off the ennui of a bleak Oklahoma winter by hanging with out-of-work pals, shooting pool, and drinking. One Friday night he took off to join his buddies at the 400 Club, a rowdy bar he had often heard about while in high school but didn't see the inside of until he was twenty-four. Merlyn, calling to him from the front porch, asked him how long he'd be gone. Just a couple of hours, he replied.

---

* Just after the World Series, Mickey had put together an amateur basketball team, the Mickey Mantle–Southwest All-Stars, consisting of players from his friend Harold Youngman's construction business (industrial leagues back then often had basketball as well as baseball teams) and some friends and family, such as his brothers Roy and Ray. They were good, and in two real games against the visiting Harlem Globetrotters they proved indeed that white men could jump. Mickey coached and played — foolishly, as it turned out. On a fast break, he twisted his bad knee and was taken the next day to a Springfield, Missouri, hospital. His old friend Dr. Yancey removed a piece of torn cartilage. He would have a slight limp right into spring training.

Mickey went from boilermakers to scotch-and-soda to vodka to wine and finally to bourbon. Around five in the morning, thoroughly inebriated, he started home. On the way back, he saw some pals packing their car for a fishing trip. What the hell, he said, I'll go with you. He did not, of course, bother to inform Merlyn or anyone else in his family. Falling asleep in the backseat, he did not wake up until the car pulled up at Lead Hill, Arkansas. Two days later, he finally arrived back home, thinking that somehow his wife would be placated by the tub full of bass he had caught. But even the thought of fresh fish for dinner did not improve Merlyn's mood.

A few days later, he went out with his friends again; they dropped him off shortly before sunrise. He found his front door locked. After some futile pounding, he went to the garage and found that locked too. He then risked his million-dollar right hand by smashing the glass on the window panels, cutting himself on the shards. Upon lifting the garage door, he was startled to find the car gone, and then dumbfounded when he entered the house to find Merlyn and Mickey Jr. gone as well.

A neighbor who had been out with him heard the noise, got dressed, and walked over to find the American League's All-Star center fielder bleeding profusely. His friend had the good sense to wrap up Mickey's hand and drive him to the nearest hospital at Cardin. The doctor who gave him thirty stitches might have saved his career. The friend then drove him to his in-laws' house, where Mickey's outrageous behavior continued. He demanded the car keys from his father-in-law, who wisely refused after getting a good look at the dried blood on Mickey's clothes and his bandaged hand. Mantle charged into the house, grabbed the keys off the kitchen table, went to the car, and, in front of his astonished father-in-law, threw Merlyn's clothes (and several bags of groceries) all over the car. Then, jumping into the car, he backed up at full speed into a telephone pole.

He jumped out of the car and started running down the road toward town. Mr. Johnson got into his own car, picked up his son-in-law, and drove him home. The next day Merlyn and Mickey Jr.

came back, and everything was okay again. For a while. Whispers of the incident made it back to New York, but nothing appeared in print. No sportswriter dared to risk his livelihood by alienating the New York Yankees' front office.

Willie Mays also had some friends in the New York press. In the fall of either 1954 or 1955 — Arnold Hano recalls it as '55, but James Hirsch in his long biography of Mays places it in 1954 — a pregnant woman claimed that Mays was the father of her child. Frank Forbes and Monte Irvin had worked hard to screen Willie from the legions of young females waiting around after Giants games, but they apparently could not watch him twenty-four hours a day. Mays flat out denied even knowing the woman, who hired a lawyer and demanded child support.

Forbes worked a small miracle to keep the incident out of the press. A couple of months later, a blood test was conducted, and the results indicated that Mays was not the father. The woman was not placated and claimed the test was phony. Roger Kahn always believed that she was bought off to keep her from going public, which would have been a huge embarrassment to Mays and the Giants. What was the truth? "I think the test was legitimate," said Kahn, "and I don't think Willie was the father. But I also think that the woman thought Willie really was the father, and that he could have been."

"I also think," said Kahn with a shrug, "that none of us tried very hard to find out the truth."9

It's a shame Willie Mays did not pick 1956 to have his best year. The season began with all kinds of undercurrents. Already, back in the spring of 1955, there had been rumors that despite the Giants' World Series victory, the obnoxious Leo Durocher had had a falling-out with Horace Stoneham. One much-publicized cause was a testimonial dinner at a Los Angeles country club where Leo's Hollywood friends, including Frank Sinatra, Bob Hope, Kirk Douglas, and Danny Kaye, had all appeared. Kaye brought the house down by walking out with his shirt hanging out and his fly open. After crashing into a table, he asked the crowd, "Where can a guy take a piss?" It was understood that Kaye, a devout Dodgers fan, was mocking Stoneham, who was known to have a drinking problem. Durocher, so the gossip columnists reported, had almost fallen out of his seat laughing; an item in *The Sporting News* related that "they'll be talking about it [Kaye's performance] from Toots Shor's to the Stork Club for weeks."*[10] And they did. It was assumed by writers who followed the Giants that nothing short of a pennant, and perhaps not even that, could save Durocher's job. They were right.

With just a few games left in the 1955 season, Durocher asked Mays to step into the tunnel behind the dugout, where he quietly told Mays that he would not be back as manager the next season. Willie was, Leo told him, the greatest ballplayer he had ever seen and he had already spoken to the new manager, Bill Rigney, about how to treat him. Then he leaned over and kissed Willie on the cheek. It was perhaps Durocher's most gracious moment in a big league uniform. It would be Willie Mays, after all, who was responsible for Leo getting into the Hall of Fame, though Leo would not live to see the honor. Mays's most comprehensive biographer, James Hirsch, said it this way: "Whatever his shortcomings as a person, Durocher's development of Mays stands as a monumental contribution to baseball. Mays believes that in 1951, every other manager in the big leagues would have sent him back to the minors. That's what any responsible manager would do with any young player in the throes of despair. Mickey Mantle, to take one example, was sent down as a rookie. . . . Had Mays returned to Minneapolis, his self-image shattered, his vulnerabilities exposed, the arc of his career would have been quite different."[11]

Actually, Willie's performance in 1956 was a great deal better than most people thought. Distracted, sometimes suffering from nervous exhaustion, and desperately missing Leo, he had his worst season —

---

* In case there were any doubts about how Leo felt about Stoneham, it should be remembered that he included the incident in all its gross detail in his 1976 autobiography, *Nice Guys Finish Last*.

Mickey shot a mean game of pool. Here he's back at Commerce's Black Cat Café, where he learned the game while in high school, with a boyhood pal looking on. In the first few years when he came home from the baseball season, "They could not get my Yankee cap away from me." NATIONAL BASEBALL HALL OF FAME, COOPERSTOWN, N.Y.

Like Mickey, Willie learned to shoot pool as a teenager; here he lines up a shot at his boyhood haunt, Big Tony's. Big Tony lectured the schoolboys about the importance of education but let them play for free "over one of the old, torn tables in the back of the room." According to Richie Ashburn, on their barnstorming trip to Syracuse, Willie thought he could take Mickey but got taken instead. SPORT MEDIA GROUP

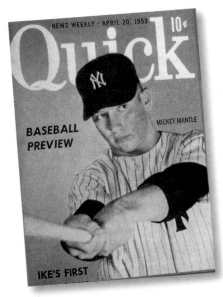

The Quick and the Deadly. A grim-faced Mickey, not yet twenty-one, aims his bat with mean intent for the cover of the popular newsweekly *Quick* at the start of the 1953 season.

Willie making "The Catch" off Vic Wertz, in Game 1 of the 1954 World Series. In recent years it has become popular to disparage the play as not being among Willie's best. This is nonsense, as a simple study of the play will confirm. Mays's speed in reaching the ball — which could have been *more than 450 feet from home plate* — was amazing in and of itself. On top of that, he caught the ball with his *back to home plate.* For the last twenty feet or so of his run, he didn't so much as glance back to see where the ball was. SPORT MEDIA GROUP

Willie Mays Day at the Polo Grounds in August 1954. Behind Willie and to his left is Frank Forbes, the boxing promoter and all-around sporting man whom the Giants hired to watch over Willie. The Yankees never thought to hire someone to watch over Mickey.

The sign on the right reads, "Hip, Hip Hooray for the Birmingham Belter," a nickname that did not stick. SPORT MEDIA GROUP

The Remarkable Mickey Mantle. Mickey got his first *Life* magazine cover on June 25, 1956, as he pursued the Triple Crown. It was *Life*'s biggest-selling sports-themed issue until Mantle and Maris shared the cover while in pursuit of Babe Ruth's home run record in 1961.

GETTY IMAGES

"Willie Mays Leads Giants into San Francisco," April 28, 1958. The issue sold poorly; readers in the New York area didn't want to be reminded.

GETTY IMAGES

The Perfect Catch. Don Larsen's perfect game, October 3, 1956, at Yankee Stadium. In the top of the fifth inning, Gil Hodges came to bat for the Dodgers and hit the longest shot any Brooklyn player had in the entire game, a low-lying drive hit deep into center field. Off Hodges's bat, it looked like a triple. Mantle, running at full speed, backhanded the ball, preserving the only perfect game in World Series history.
SPORT MEDIA GROUP

Late in 1954 Willie was backup vocalist for the Treniers on "Say Hey: The Willie Mays Song," arranged by the young Quincy Jones. Most white listeners didn't get to hear it until it was included on the soundtrack of Ken Burns's PBS documentary *Baseball*.
SPORT MEDIA GROUP

"I Love Mickey." Teresa Brewer cowrote the words and music to this 1956 record. According to Mantle's friends, Brewer was a big fan of Mickey's. But Mickey's foray into popular music was no more successful than Willie's.

Not So "Confidential." Mickey thought his 1951 "relationship" with showgirl Holly Brooke was long forgotten by 1957, when Holly peddled her story to *Confidential* magazine. Mickey tried to buy up all the copies of the magazine at an airport newsstand to keep Merlyn from finding out. No such luck—a stack of them mysteriously appeared on their front porch.

... **I OWN 25% OF MICKEY MANTLE**
... and there were times when he was mine—**100%**

by HOLLY BROOKE

Left, above: The perfect subject for the perfect author. Willie and Charles Einstein, 1957. Einstein collaborated with Mays on three books, most notably *Willie's Time: A Memoir* (1979), the only ballplayer biography to be named a finalist for the Pulitzer Prize. Einstein followed Willie and the Giants to the Bay Area in 1958. In 1980 he moved back east to a New Jersey town called—really—Mays Landing. This book could not have been written without him.
SPORT MEDIA GROUP

Left, below: October 11, 1958. Mickey and Willie sign barnstorming contracts for "Mickey Mantle's All-Stars vs. Willie Mays's All-Stars." The man looking over their shoulders is unidentified.
PHOTOGRAPHER UNKNOWN

Left: "And out there's where you hit that fly ball in the 1951 World Series where I stepped on the drain and twisted my knee . . ." A helpful Mickey refreshes Willie's memory before their 1958 barnstorming game. George Plimpton was scheduled to pitch to both lineups before the game and actually got Willie to pop out. But Plimpton took so long that he never got a chance to pitch to Mickey. (He described the experience in his book *Out of My League*.) CORBIS

Right: If you were in Syracuse on October 11, 1959, you could have bought a grandstand ticket for $2.50 to watch Mickey's All-Stars vs. Willie's All-Stars with former middleweight champion Carmen Basilio as umpire. There was a home run hitting contest, too. COURTESY OF THE SYRACUSE POST-STANDARD

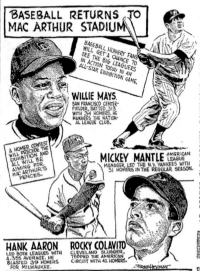

Top Diamond Stars of Nation At MacArthur Stadium Today

Imagine being able to see all these players on one field for $2.50. Mays, Mantle, Henry Aaron, and Rocky Colavito were the big attractions at Syracuse's MacArthur Stadium. Drawing by Fred Heyman for the *Syracuse Herald-American*. COURTESY OF THE SYRACUSE POST-STANDARD

The cards that inspired this book. The way I remember it, I got both of these cards in the same pack when I was ten years old — that's my story and I'm sticking to it.

SPORT MAGAZINE '60 ALL-STAR SELECTION

MICKEY MANTLE Outfield/American League

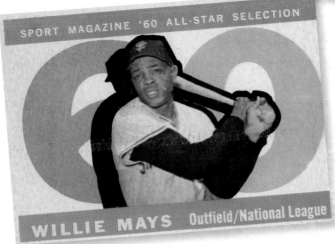

SPORT MAGAZINE '60 ALL-STAR SELECTION

WILLIE MAYS Outfield/National League

The Fans' Favorite! In 1961 Bill Hoebler, a young fan from Pittsburgh, suggested to *Sport* that the magazine sponsor a nationwide contest to determine "The Fans' Favorite." Hoebler volunteered to count the votes and received a pile of cards and letters weighing over 17 pounds from all fifty states. Mickey won, though one wonders what the count might have been had Willie still been playing in New York. SPORT MEDIA GROUP

Roger Maris, Willie, and Mickey at the 1961 All-Star Game in San Francisco. Willie had no idea that in a couple of hours he would be the victim of a Mickey–Whitey Ford prank involving a bet with Giants owner Horace Stoneham. NATIONAL BASEBALL HALL OF FAME, COOPERSTOWN, N.Y.

In January 1962, *Sport* magazine published a special edition devoted entirely to Mickey and Willie. In the magazine's two national polls, Mickey was voted the best player by the fans, Willie by players, managers, and sportswriters.

SPORT MEDIA GROUP

and his worst season, according to *Total Baseball*, was as good as any other player in the NL. (For that season *Total Baseball* ranks him in a virtual tie for best player with Milwaukee's Hank Aaron, who led the Braves to a second-place finish, just one game behind the Brooklyn Dodgers.)

For the first and only time between his rookie season and 1964, Mays hit under .300 — his final average was .296. He had 36 home runs, but only 84 RBIs. But the low RBI total was in large part because the Giants' team batting average was just .244, tied with the Cubs for lowest in the NL. They were simply not getting runners on base, so there were relatively few for Willie to drive in. As if to compensate, he led the NL — in fact, both leagues — in stolen bases for the first time with the then-breathtaking total of 40 and also led NL outfielders in double plays with 6. Even though it didn't look like it, Willie Mays was still the best all-around player in the National League.

But Mickey Mantle . . . as Yankees announcer Mel Allen put it, "The way he was in 1956, and in 1957, too, there was nothing like him in baseball history."

If titles like "The Dean of American Sportswriters" were given solely on merit and not merely on readership, the *Washington Post*'s Shirley Povich would have been ranked up there with Red Smith in New York. Povich, one of the few progressive-minded writers in his profession, had championed Jackie Robinson, Larry Doby, and other black players before it was fashionable. Perhaps because he was an out-of-town writer — in New York anyone who wasn't a New York writer was an out-of-town writer — he also worked hard at developing a working relationship with Mickey Mantle. In Florida, he wrote on April 4, "one feeling has been inescapable for the past month. This is Mickey Mantle's year. This is the one when he'll burst into full magnificence, hit more and longer home runs than anybody else, lead the league in batting, perhaps, and certainly get more extra base hits than anyone else."[12]

Mickey Mantle won the Triple Crown in 1956, just the fourth

time in baseball history that a player had accomplished that feat —
the first three winners were Rogers Hornsby, Lou Gehrig, and Ted
Williams. Mantle led the league in home runs (52), home runs at
home (27) and on the road (25), total bases (376), runs scored (132),
runs batted in (130), batting average (.353), and slugging percentage
(.705) — the last an almost unbelievable one hundred points higher
than second-place Ted Williams. There was only one important category Mickey did not lead in — on-base percentage, where he finished
at .464, fifteen points behind Ted Williams. He stole 10 bases in 11
tries, and in the outfield he averaged 2.80 putouts per nine innings,
0.46 higher than the league average. (Mays that season averaged 2.44,
0.41 higher than the NL average.) And Mickey did it all wearing a
brace on his right knee for most of the year.* Years later, statisticians
would rank Mantle's 1956 season as at least the best season of the
decade — with the possible exception of his 1957 season.

On opening day at Griffith Stadium in Washington, the park
where he had hit his titanic home run in 1953, Mickey hit two towering home runs over the center-field wall, both estimated at well over
500 feet. (Red Patterson must have taken the day off.) With Mantle
leading the way, Yogi Berra, batting in front of him, also caught fire
and finished the season with 105 RBIs. The Yankees quickly built up
a big lead over the Cleveland Indians. After beating them on May 16,
they never relinquished the top spot again and won the AL pennant
by nine games.

The entire 1956 season was one of milestones for Mickey. On
May 18, he hit a home run batting right-handed and then, later in the
game, one from the left side; on Memorial Day, May 30, against the
Senators, batting left-handed, he ripped a ball so high and hard that
it appeared to the awestruck crowd that it was going to be the first ball
ever hit out of Yankee Stadium. (The stadium roof was exactly 120
feet from the ground; the ball struck the grandstand's facade a foot,
maybe a foot and a half, from its very top.) And on June 18, against

---

* Courtesy, lest we forget, of the Harlem Globetrotters.

the Tigers in Detroit, he became just the second player after Ted Williams to hit a ball over the roof of Briggs Stadium. Peter Golenbock, the Yankee historian, estimated that "the ball was going so fast when it struck the facade that it still had enough momentum to rebound more than 100 feet back onto the playing field. Had the facade not stopped it, the ball would have traveled more than 600 feet. It just didn't seem possible that a baseball could be hit that hard."[13]

Before the season ended, perhaps even halfway through, while he was pursuing Babe Ruth's single-season record of 60 home runs, Mickey Mantle became perhaps the most famous ballplayer since Joe DiMaggio had burst onto the national scene during his 56-game hitting streak in 1941. In fact, some thought he had become more famous than DiMaggio — more famous than even Babe Ruth himself at his peak. *Newsweek* and *Time* featured him on their covers in the same week; after the Memorial Day home run, *Life* magazine did the same; and pop songs and a biography followed in the tail of his comet. Duke Snider, already a national celebrity before Mantle played a game in the big leagues, would later comment on his own fame in comparison with that of Mays and Mantle: "At the height of my fame . . . in 1955 after we won the World Series, and [at the height of] Willie's . . . in 1954 after they won or in 1955, he and I could still go out in public without being mobbed. It was nothing like the way it was for Mickey in 1956 and 1957. That was a whole different ball game."[14]

Mickey's dream season got off to a rocky start. In the spring of 1956, Casey Stengel had lost patience with Mickey for what he regarded as overswinging. Like Leo Durocher, Casey was convinced that strikeouts were bad — or at least worse than other kinds of outs — and that cutting down on them was good, even if it resulted in fewer home runs. (No one was yet paying attention to the fact that since 1951 Mantle had hit into fewer double plays than any regular player on the team except Phil Rizzuto, who had appeared in fewer games.) After Mantle struck out for the third time in an exhibition game with the Giants — a game in which Willie Mays hit two doubles — Stengel lost his temper and actually told several reporters that Mickey was "stupid." It was understood that this quote would not appear in print, but Joe Trimble of the *Daily News* did write a piece for *Look* magazine that asked the question "Is He a Rockhead as Some Claim?"

As the 1956 season progressed, Stengel found it more difficult to criticize his young phenom. In the middle of one of the greatest seasons of any ballplayer ever, he gave an interview that appeared in whole or in part in numerous papers in the New York area.

> Sure the feller is not a finished center fielder. Mays and Snider could have an edge, but the feller is getting so he can catch them as good as anybody with his tremendous arm, although he still throws to the wrong base now and then. But it takes time for a feller to learn how to play the outfield if he never played it before he got into the big leagues. . . . Never put his foot into the outfield until I told Mr. Hendrix [presumably Casey meant Tommy Henrich] to see how he looks in right field. So now he's my center fielder but he didn't become my center fielder, that is, when he wasn't crippled, until 1952 after DiMaggio quit.
>
> You might say his shifting from right to center forced him to start all over again and learn how to execute. I know because I played in all the fields. And he's catching on as a center fielder just as he is at the plate, waiting for the good pitch. All he's got to do is meet the ball and it will leave any park. If you cut most of his drives in two, they'd still be homers. But, unfortunately, they only count as one.[15]

Not even in a season when Mickey was leading the major leagues in both batting *and* home runs could he entirely please his manager.

Around this time a reporter is alleged to have asked Mantle, "Mickey, if you could hit .400 or 60 home runs, which would you choose?" Mickey is reported to have replied, with a smile, "I'd choose the .400." Then, pausing a moment for the surprised reporter, who naturally thought Mantle would choose the home run record, he continued: "Because if I hit .400, the way I swing, I'd get the 60 home runs." As it turned out, he got neither. He had to settle for what was merely the greatest season since the heyday of Babe Ruth — superior to any season by Joe DiMaggio, Ted Williams, Stan Musial, Duke Snider, or Willie Mays.

"The Remarkable Mickey Mantle" read the caption of Mickey's first *Life* magazine cover. It pictures a grinning Mickey, batting from the left side of the plate as he looks into the camera. That put him two years up on Willie, who may have had a pop record but would have to wait until 1958 for *Life* to make him a cover boy. Shortly after, Mickey finally got *his* pop record. Unlike "Say Hey: The Willie Mays Song," it made the mainstream airwaves and was played all over the country. "I Love Mickey" was a cheerful but innocuous ditty with lyrics penned by the enormously popular singer and Mickey fan Teresa Brewer. Like Willie, Mickey made a contribution to his own record. At the end of each chorus, after Ms. Brewer chirped, "I love Mickeeeeeey," Mantle piped in, "Mickey who?" And at the end, "Not Yogi Berra?" Like Willie, Mickey was not invited back to a recording studio. Mantle and Brewer made the rounds of some talk and variety shows to plug the record,* which led to rumors among Mickey's friends of a romantic involvement.

Whatever the truth, it's clear that Mantle was living two separate

---

* At an Atlantic City autograph show in the spring of 1982 featuring Mantle and Mays, I purchased a button slightly bigger than a fifty-cent piece with a photo of Brewer in a Yankees uniform with a bat on her shoulder and a smiling Mick, wearing a polo shirt and also holding a bat, with the caption "I Love Mickey." It cost me $10. I would happily have paid three times as much.

lives: the devoted father and happy husband, as photographed in magazines and for advertisements, and the hard-drinking libertine. The sports press was well aware of the second, but by the unspoken gentlemen's agreement of the period, kept it from the public.

In the fall of 1956, Mantle made an appearance on *The Ed Sullivan Show*. On the same bill was a blond actress who was Hollywood's most popular leading lady. Roger Kahn recalls discussing rumors about her with Mickey. "I hear she's frigid," said Kahn. "Not with me," Mickey shot back.[16]

Had the Yankees lost the 1956 World Series, our perspective on their dominance of the decade would be very different. The Yanks hadn't been world champions since 1953, and with Mantle having an MVP/Triple Crown season, a failure to beat the Dodgers for the second consecutive year might have knocked the Yankee world off its axis. The pivotal game of the Series was Game 5, perhaps the most famous nine innings in baseball history. It was, of course, the day Don Larsen picked to pitch his perfect game, and Mickey Mantle not only preserved Larsen's gem but provided all the offense his team needed.

In the fourth inning, the Dodgers' Sal Maglie made a mistake, hanging a curveball over Mickey's power zone; Mantle deposited the ball in the right-field seats, a few feet to the left of the foul pole. In the booth, Yankees announcer Mel Allen recited his famous "It's going, going, GONE!" Then, "How about that!" The Yankees would score again later, but with the Dodgers held scoreless, Mickey's home run was all the Yanks needed to prevail.

Two innings later, Mickey made the most important play of his career. Larsen fired a hard slider to Gil Hodges, who hit it deep into the vast territory of Yankee Stadium's left-center field. Right fielder Hank Bauer recalled that his immediate thought was *Damn, that ball is maybe a triple, or even an inside-the-park home run!* With just about any other outfielder in baseball, it might have been. The ball rode a wind that was blowing out toward the left side of the field;

Mantle, who began his pursuit with a fast backpedal, turned quickly and began a furious chase on a hard angle toward the wall. In the Dodgers' home park, Ebbets Field, the ball would have been a home run, but this was Yankee Stadium, and as the ball began its descent, everyone realized it would not reach the fence and just *might* be caught . . . if Mickey could run it down.

And that's what he did. He simply ran the ball down. In full stride he extended his glove and, backhanded, speared it in the web. On the radio, listeners heard Allen say, "Hodges hits it to deep left field, Mantle is digging hard, Still going . . . *how about that catch?!*" Mickey later said, "I just put my head down and took off as fast as I could. I caught up with the ball as it was dropping, more than 400 feet from home plate. I had to reach across my body to make the catch, and luckily the ball dropped into my glove. . . . It was the best catch I ever made. Some people might question that, but there's certainly no question it was the most important catch I ever made."[17] Larsen got his perfect game, of course, and the Yankees went on to win the World Series. The world was back on its axis.

Mantle's catch in the 1956 Series was not so spectacular as the one Willie Mays made in the 1954 World Series. But in retrospect, two questions should be asked. First, wasn't there as much at stake for Mickey in 1956 as there was for Willie in 1954? Was there perhaps more pressure on Mantle since he was running a ball down to try to preserve a perfect game? And here's something else to ponder: if Mickey Mantle was the fastest player in the game in 1956, as many believe, who else could have made that play? Willie Mays perhaps, if only because he might have gotten the jump half a step sooner.

Willie Mays was fantastic that season and clearly once again the National League's best player. He batted .333 with 35 home runs, led the league in slugging percentage at .626, and also led in stolen bases, for the second straight year, with 38. He hit 20 triples to lead the league for the third time in his career. But the Giants were dismal, finishing twenty-six games behind the league-leading Milwaukee Braves. The Yankees won the AL pennant again, but would lose a tough seven-game series to the Braves.

Meanwhile, going into the 1957 season, Mickey Mantle's star power was unchallenged by any other athlete. It would not be approached in American sports until Michael Jordan in the 1990s. But in Jordan's time, the other major professional sports also commanded attention. In 1957 baseball was without question the national pastime, and Mickey Mantle its brightest star.

Mantle was perhaps better in 1957 than in 1956, although it wasn't readily apparent on paper. He hit for his highest batting average, .365, but his home run total dropped from 52 to 34 and his RBIs from 130 to 94. Whenever possible, American League pitchers that year simply would not give Mantle the chance to hit home runs off them. They walked him 146 times — an average slightly lower than *one walk per game*, 34 more walks than he drew the previous year.

Some old-time sportswriters thought that Ted Williams deserved to be MVP that year after hitting an incredible .388 to lead the majors. Williams also led both leagues in on-base percentage (.526) and slugging percentage (.731) and hit more home runs (38) than Mantle. But by *Total Baseball*'s system as well as Bill James's Win Shares — which both take into account the significant advantage Williams had playing in the league's best hitting park, Fenway, and Mantle's all-around contributions (for instance, he stole 16 bases in 19 tries) — Mickey was not only better, but better by a significant margin.

And yet, the public's adoration of Mickey was still mixed with currents of anger and resentment. "Even that year," Hank Bauer would recall, "you'd still hear some of the vilest stuff directed at Mickey because of the draft board thing. In one home game where Mickey hit a three-run homer to put us up big, there were some Marines sitting in a box seat fairly close to our dugout. They were yelling at Mickey some of the worst slurs I've ever heard in a ballpark. I mean, in New York you'd have some guys who would get drunk and call you a bum and worse, but I never heard anything like what they called Mickey. One game it was so bad, you could hear it from the dugout. Mickey was clearly shaken up, though he kept staring straight ahead and pretending he didn't hear them. I wasn't in the game, so I thought I'd do something to calm things down. Between innings, I walked over and leaned into their box, and said, 'Hey, fellas, c'mon. Why don't you calm it down a bit? The guy's playing hard, he's in pain — why don't you cut him a break?' I guess they knew I had been in the Marines, so they just kind of nodded and said nothing. But I could never figure it out, why Mickey, by doing nothing at all, could bring out the worst in some people."[18]

There were worse incidents that never made the papers. The writer Gay Talese remembers that in 1957, before a game with the Senators, "a young girl — she couldn't have been more than fourteen and was probably even younger — went under the rope that kept the fans away from the players as they got out of their cabs at the stadium. She ran up to Mickey and punched him — I swear to God, she punched him on the side of his head, right above his ear. Then she tried to pull his hair and claw his face. Mickey was startled — who wouldn't be? — and a cop ran up to pull the girl away. She was slapping at him and shouting something, and Mantle, his hands over his face, put his head down and ran into the players' entrance. What provoked her? No one had any idea. I asked Mickey later, and he just stared at me with a bewildered look on his face and shook his head. But one thing stuck with me: when Mickey ran into the entrance, some of the fans who had been watching were booing him. By the way, as I recall, he was hitting about .370 at the time."[19]

The undercurrent that drove this intense dislike of Mantle in some fans has never been explained. In 1957, perhaps a few were put off by Mickey's salary haggles with the Yankees. Until then, unlike Yogi Berra, Mantle had never argued over his salary. But after making $32,500 in 1956 — an absurdly low figure, even for that time — Mickey got it into his head that he should be paid as if he were one of the best players in the game. We don't know exactly what Mays was paid for the 1957 season, though writers who knew both ballplayers insisted that Willie was paid more. Mickey told George Weiss that he wanted $65,000, a salary, he pointed out, that would put him on a par with Ted Williams, Stan Musial, and, according to the rumors, Willie Mays.

Weiss countered with the ridiculous argument that he couldn't afford to double Mickey's salary every year — as if that had anything to do with what Mantle deserved for the 1957 season. Neither man budged. And then, Mantle later revealed, Weiss took out a manila folder and showed it to him, sitting back in his chair and twiddling his thumbs while Mickey flipped through reports from private detectives on Mantle's private after-hours life and on several of his exploits in the company of Billy Martin. Weiss hinted that Mickey certainly wouldn't want any of these reports to get back to Merlyn.

It was, of course, blackmail, though no one would call it that at the time. Finally, Yankees owner Del Webb, who thought Mantle should be paid a salary at least close to what Willie Mays was getting, intervened. The following year, though, when Mickey hit a career-high .365 and won his second straight MVP Award, Weiss tried to cut his salary again. Mickey went to Webb, who told his GM that Mantle should get at least a token raise. Weiss finally gave in: for winning his second straight MVP Award, Mantle was given a raise of $500 to $65,500.

A month or so later, some fans found yet another reason to be miffed at Mickey. Holly Brooke — or at least that's the last name she was using in the spring of 1957 — was back in Mickey's story. It was the same Holly whom Mickey had introduced to Mutt back in 1951 and who had gotten Mickey tangled up with the sleazy agent Alan Savitt. Mickey and Merlyn were on a trip to Havana when all of a sudden stacks of the March issue of *Confidential* magazine were piled up at airport newsstands. The cover promised a story on "The Doll Who Owns 25% of Mickey Mantle." Inside, Holly bragged, "I own 25% of Mickey Mantle . . . and there were times when he was mine 100%!"

If Holly was telling the truth — and some of the details dropped in the story indicate that she was — then there had been more to the relationship than Mickey had let on. For instance, when he was sent back to the minors, she claimed to have spent three days with him in Columbus, Ohio, and when the Yankees brought him back up, she said she had stayed with him in Washington, which was in fact where the Yankees were at the time. At every airport stop, Mickey and his friend Harold Youngman bought up every copy of Confidential they could find to keep Merlyn from seeing it. Their efforts were in vain. When they returned home, there was a bundle of several copies waiting for them; no one knew who put them there.

For the most part, the press was obliging in not mentioning the story or simply dismissing it as fiction. Looking back, it appears that a great deal of it was not fiction. Holly insisted that she had loaned Savitt $1,500 in cash in 1951 with the promise that if he didn't pay it back by early 1952, she would own 25 percent of Mickey's burgeoning endorsements empire. Of course, when she had first met Mickey, he was not married, but, she said in the story, they had continued to see each other over the years, including in the late summer of 1956. Apparently, she felt she was still entitled to the 25 percent, even though the Yankees' lawyers had long since voided the contract Mickey had so foolishly signed. The Confidential story, then, was her way of collecting what she thought was her due.

One detail she revealed was that she had met Mickey at a small club called Danny's Hideaway, which over the years would prove to be a fateful venue for Mickey and the Yankees. It was one of Mickey's favorite nightspots, and in May 1957, Mickey, Billy Martin, Whitey Ford, Hank Bauer, Yogi Berra, Johnny Kucks, and their wives gathered there to celebrate Billy Martin's birthday. According to Mickey, "We had dinner at Danny's Hideaway and then someone said we had time to catch Sammy Davis, Jr. at the Copa."[20] Every Yankee fan knows what happened next. Or rather, no one really knows what happened.

The legend is that some members of a bowling team at a nearby table got rowdy and rude and shouted some insults at Davis — Mantle would later recall he heard the slur "Little Black Sambo." A while later, the chief instigator of the group, a man named Edwin Jones, was laid out on the floor near the men's room by either Billy Martin or Hank Bauer (who, despite his Marine Corps background, was never known to have engaged in a public brawl) or, perhaps more likely, one of the Copa's bouncers. Yogi Berra, whom everyone trusted, famously insisted that "nobody done nothin' to nobody."

But for solidarity's sake and to appease the daily papers, which had a field day with the incident, the Yankees' front office fined everyone. Mantle, Berra, Ford, Bauer, and Martin were fined a stiff $1,000; Kucks, who made a great deal less than the better-known players, was fined only $500. So was Gil McDougald, who never even made it to the Copa. Clearly, the fines were intended as a message to the public that the Yankees intended to keep their house in order: they were announced before the group even appeared in court. Gil McDougald was perhaps the most furious. At the end of the season, though, when the players picked up their World Series checks, they found that the amount of their fine had been added to the total.

During the court hearing, the district attorney took less than an hour to determine that there was insufficient evidence to convict Bauer or any other Yankee; Jones subsequently dropped his case against Bauer as well. George Weiss, however, did not drop his case against Billy Martin, whom he had long since decided was a bad influence on Mantle. Someone had to go, and it was certainly not going to be the most valuable property in the major leagues. But Weiss did not make a move right away.

Almost a month later, on June 13, during a game with the White Sox, the Yankees' Art Ditmar knocked Larry Doby down, part of an ongoing brushback war between the two teams. Doby, who had been sensitive to knockdowns since becoming the American League's first black player with Cleveland in 1947, was furious and, according to Ditmar, said that if he threw that close to him again, he'd stick a knife in his back — although Doby always denied having said this. Ditmar responded by suggesting that Doby have sexual relations with himself. Doby rushed the mound, threw a punch, missed, and both benches emptied. Just when it looked as if order had been restored, Martin asked Ditmar what Doby had said to him, and Ditmar foolishly mentioned the knife comment. Martin went ballistic and attacked Doby and nearly started the brawl all over again. Or at any rate, he would have if the two sides hadn't been stunned by Martin's behavior. The Yankees' Tommy Byrne thought that Billy had "lost his nut."

Martin's hysterical attack on Doby gave Weiss as much of an excuse to get rid of him as anything that did or didn't happen at the Copa. Two days later, the word came down that Billy had been traded to the American League's version of limbo, the Kansas City Athletics. Petulant and hopelessly irresponsible, he blamed Casey Stengel for not standing up for him and held a grudge against the old man for years.

The New York Giants used Frank Forbes and Monte Irvin as Willie's surrogate big brothers to screen him from what they regarded as the wrong kind of females and other kinds of trouble. On the other side of town, the Yankees left Mickey Mantle unprotected, and the result was Holly Brooke, a disreputable agent, and incidents of public drunkenness with Billy Martin. Both ballplayers, however, grew into manhood without maturing into men.

Bill Rigney, who at first had a rough time communicating with Mays, finally made a breakthrough. "Willie does not need a manager," he told reporters, "so much as a father figure."[21] Of Mickey Mantle, precisely the opposite could have been said.

The Christmas of 1957 was the last one Mickey and Merlyn would spend in Commerce. Mickey's old town no longer provided relief from the pressures of New York. With family, old friends, and former schoolmates showing up at the door at all hours, many asking for autographs, favors, or handouts, life at home was no longer relaxing. Mickey would slip out at nights for drinking binges with a few of his closest friends, with many of whom he had played sandlot ball. That was it. The next year he insisted that they not go back to Oklahoma for the holidays. Merlyn would miss her own family and friends, but went along with Mickey's wishes.

There were compensations. No matter how much he drank, Merlyn later wrote in her own memoir, "Mick never slapped me or hit me or tried to hurt me. . . . I could push the bad times aside because it is very easy to get caught up in the American way of fame. I was bored, and when I did get to be a part of it, I enjoyed the life style."[22] Both Merlyn Mantle and Marghuerite Mays were unhappy in many ways, but they both enjoyed the lifestyle.

13

"Exactly the Same Ballplayer"

On September 29, 1957, an overcast Sunday, at approximately 4:20 PM, Willie Mays came to bat as a New York Giant for the last time. The Giants were down, 9–1, in the ninth as the Pirates' Bob Friend nearly shut them out with only six hits, two of them by Mays. Arnold Hano described it this way: "There was a sizeable round of applause as he took his last stance. He shifted his feet around, his head down. A pitch came in and another, and the count was one-and-one, and all the time the applause was building, over 11,000 fans rising out of their seats. Pretty soon the applause was so loud that Mays had to acknowledge it. He stepped out of the box and touched his hand to his cap. It was, to me, another first.

"I do not recall hearing another ovation given a man after the pitcher has started to work on him. The whole business was unsettling to Mays. 'I never felt so nervous,' he has since said. 'My hands were shaking. It was worse than any World Series game. I tried to hit a home run. I tried very hard to show them how I felt. I wanted to do something for the fans.'

"He tried too hard, the way a man will, and hit a ground ball to short. He was out at first, and when he trotted back to the Giant dugout, the applause followed him. Dusty Rhodes hit another ground ball to short; the Giants had lost their fourth ballgame in a row, and the Giants' tenancy at the Polo Grounds was over. The fans poured onto the field, running past and over the stadium guards. They tore up the bases and uprooted home plate, ripped the fences and the bullpen benches and chased the players all the way to the dressing room stairs."

The guests of honor, among whom were numerous old Giants greats, including Sal Maglie and Carl Hubbell, and John McGraw's widow, Blanche, filed quietly out of the Polo Grounds. Ray Robinson, who edited the paperback series "Baseball Stars of the 1950s," recalls that "it was not exactly the kind of occasion you remember with fondness. It was an ugly day, and Willie Mays was leaving forever."[1] (Robinson had no way of knowing that little more than a year later he would see Willie playing in New York again, at least for one game.)

Two fans out in left field mournfully waved signs. The first read, GO, TEAM, GO, while the second one read, STAY, WILLIE, STAY. Almost as if in response, Willie popped out of the dugout and waved to the remaining fans. No one ever asked him whether he was saying good-bye to the fans or grabbing one last look at the Polo Grounds.

It was the last game in New York for several writers, who would be shifted to other assignments. One of them, Charles Einstein, would follow Mays and the Giants to San Francisco to cover baseball for the *San Francisco Examiner*. (The year before, he had relocated from New York to Arizona, where he followed the team through spring training.) Some who had at least a passing acquaintance with professional football, which had been rapidly gaining in popularity thanks to increased television exposure, were shifted to that beat. Still others gathered up their things — a coffee cup, an ashtray, a scorecard, a souvenir that had no value except to them — and looked around at the press box they would never see again.*

A lucky few got the plum assignment of covering the Yankees, who would be, starting in 1958, the only game in town. "In the press box at the Stadium," Hano wrote, perhaps unfairly but with the conviction of a true believer, "after a ball has been hit to deep center, where it falls behind Mickey Mantle or whoever, there is a delighted laugh and someone will say, 'Willie Mays would have had it.' Nobody argues."[2]

The beginning of the end had come on August 19, 1957, when Horace Stoneham held a press conference to announce what everybody feared was true: "We're going to San Francisco in 1958." A reporter asked Stoneham, "How do you feel about the kids in New York from whom you are taking the Giants?" "I feel bad about the kids," Stoneham replied. "I've seen lots of them at the Polo Grounds, but I haven't seen many of their fathers lately."

It was true. Attendance in the old ballpark had been dwindling over the previous two seasons. In 1957 fewer than 656,000 had turned out. In fact, it was true for most of the teams in the so-called golden age of baseball. Three of the big leagues' original sixteen teams had already moved — the St. Louis Browns back east to the baseball-rich city of Baltimore, and the Philadelphia A's and Boston Braves out west to, respectively, Kansas City and Milwaukee. The old urban ballparks were harder and harder for whites who had moved to the suburbs to travel to, and many of the ballparks were crumbling and poorly serviced. New York, in its arrogance, had ignored all the warning signs.

There had been all kinds of negotiations going on behind the scenes for months. One story had Stoneham trying to make a deal for the team to move to St. Louis; yet another had the Giants moving

---

* Or thought they would never see again. Who, at the end of the 1958 baseball season, could have foreseen the rise of the New York Mets in this very same Polo Grounds five years later?

to fresh territory for major league baseball in Minnesota. For years afterward, baseball writers would argue whether Dodgers owner Walter O'Malley — who was moving his team from Brooklyn to Los Angeles — had talked Stoneham into the move, but in retrospect, it was inevitable. The Giants were leaving, and the city that gave them by far the best deal was San Francisco.

In San Francisco, after all, Stoneham's Giants could continue their long, bitter rivalry with O'Malley's Dodgers, and California already had a long and storied history in professional baseball. The Pacific Coast League's San Francisco Seals (who would move to Phoenix, Arizona, as part of the Giants organization) and Oakland Oaks had a well-established rivalry, as did both of the Wrigley family's teams, the Los Angeles Angels and San Diego Padres, down south.

No big league fan had to be told that Ted Williams (formerly of the Padres) and Joe DiMaggio (of the Seals) were products of the PCL. Over the years the Yankees in particular had mined the Bay Area, not only for DiMaggio but for Tony Lazzeri, Lefty Gomez, and Billy Martin, while the Brooklyn Dodgers had taken first baseman Dolph Camilli (the NL's 1941 MVP), the Cincinnati Reds catcher Ernie Lombardi, and the Washington Senators shortstop Joe Cronin, who played for twenty years, mostly for the Red Sox and Senators. And of course, there were DiMaggio's two brothers — Dom, who played his entire career for the Red Sox, and Vince, who played for five different teams over a ten-year career.

Though Mays did not know it, there was a great deal of resentment waiting for him in his new city. For the first time in his professional baseball career, Willie Mays would experience booing, and the reason was one Mickey Mantle could have warned him about: he wasn't Joe DiMaggio.

In January, the Giants held a press conference at Seals Stadium, where they would be playing their home games, to publicize the signing of Willie's 1958 contract for $67,500; only Ted Williams, at about $100,000, and Stan Musial, at an estimated $80,000, were paid more. (This was only a few months after the American League's two-time MVP, Mickey Mantle, was trying and failing to get $65,000.) Willie chatted with reporters while Marghuerite, wearing a full-length mink coat, vogued in the background with her poodle Pepy on a leash.

Few of the writers present had actually seen Mays play. In November of the previous year, after the season had ended, Mays had barnstormed into the Bay Area, leading a team of black major leaguers such as former Negro League stars Henry Aaron, who had won the MVP Award in 1957, and Ernie Banks, who would win it in 1958 and 1959, to play two games against some local minor leaguers, mostly Pacific Coast League veterans. Jim Hamilton, later a journalist and scriptwriter for Sam Peckinpah, recalled going to one of the games with his family. Hamilton noted that the crowd was composed mostly of blacks and Latinos. "We were surprised because all of the big leaguers were great players, and, of course, we all knew that Willie Mays would be coming here in just a few months. Most local fans knew the PCL players too."

The pitcher for the minor leaguers — Hamilton did not recall his name — was supposed to have been a former Negro Leagues player who had known Willie back when he was a teenager with the Birmingham Barons. Perhaps miffed because he had never gotten his big league shot, the pitcher threw a pretty good fastball right in the direction of Mays's head, which was covered by nothing more than a New York Giants cap.*

Willie got up and glared at the mound, meeting the pitcher's cold stare in a blaze of indignation. On the next pitch, said Hamilton, "Willie lunged with that huge, sweeping swing and pulled a slightly outside pitch over a clock in deep left-center field." How far was the shot? "I'm not sure," Hamilton said. "The fence to dead center was about 430, and this ball was at least twenty feet past that, probably

---

*For a nominal fee, many major league teams let barnstormers wear their team uniforms, regarding it as good promotion.

more. Since the ball was hit over the clock, I'd have to say it was 460 to 470 feet." A stringer from the *San Francisco Chronicle* remarked, "I think that's farther than any home run Mickey Mantle has ever hit." Only two writers, both stringers from the Bay Area papers, had shown up to cover the game.

San Francisco prided itself on its sophistication, and certainly in relation to most of the country at the time, the city possessed a liberal attitude about race. But a short time after Willie and Marghuerite rented an apartment, a brick crashed through their window. Neither had ever experienced anything like it in their lives. For his part, Willie had never crossed any racial barriers in Alabama that would have provoked such a hostile act. Charles Einstein, who was there, saw it this way: "For the fact that they could now call themselves big-league, San Franciscans welcomed the Giants with open arms. The greeting for Willie Mays superstar was somewhat more restrained. To chauvinistic residents of the Bay Area, Mays was the hated embodiment of New York. Also he had the temerity to play center field at Seals Stadium where the native-born DiMaggio had played in his minor-league days. Also Mays was black. The brick that crashed through his apartment window almost as soon as he moved in had to reflect at least one of those viewpoints, if not all three." *[3]

Willie and Marghuerite had left New York in debt, largely because of her extravagance. According to one source, Willie had borrowed as much as $65,000 against his salary. They did not yet know where they would be living in the San Francisco area or how much a home would cost them. All they had been told was that good houses there did not come cheap. As it turned out, good houses for blacks, even in one of the most progressive-minded cities in the country, scarcely came at all. In November, the *San Francisco Chronicle* shocked not only Bay Area readers but fans all over the country with an article

---

* In a 1999 letter to me, Charlie Einstein suggested yet a fourth possibility: "A Dodger fan."

that related the Mayses' problems in closing a deal on a house. One man, Walter Gnesdiloff, had turned down the couple even when they met the asking price for his house. His sentiments echoed those of many white Americans of the time: "I'm just a union working man," he said. "I'd never get another job if I sold this house to that baseball player. I feel sorry for him, and if the neighbors said it was okay, I would do it."[4]

The story created such an uproar, though, that Gnesdiloff finally gave in, and by February Willie and Marghuerite, emotionally exhausted, moved into their new house. An ABC commentator, Edward P. Morgan, made a concise assessment of their situation: "It seems that some of the citizens of San Francisco, often called the country's most sophisticated city, dwell behind picture windows which do not conceal their prejudices."[5]

On April 21, the city of San Francisco gave the Giants a welcoming parade, and a week later Willie and the Giants appeared on the cover of *Life* magazine. The cover photo showed him leaning out of a convertible, talking to fans on Market Street; in the background was a long line of Chinese revelers in full parade costume. The caption read "Willie Mays leads Giants into San Francisco."

There was little text on the inside, just six pages of photographs of fans in Los Angeles and San Francisco acting crazier than college football fans at the arrival of the Dodgers and Giants. One photo was captioned "Uncomfortable hero Willie Mays, who ducked out on official welcome, performs first duty in San Francisco airport: walking his wife's poodle Pepy." Indeed, Willie was uncomfortable, but nothing *Life* had to say indicated why.

The expectations put on Willie in San Francisco were unfair and unrealistic from the start. In February, *Parade* magazine ran a story supposedly written by Rigney — ghosted by Charlie Einstein — that quoted the Giants manager as saying, "Mays will hit 61 homers." He went on to reason that the Polo Grounds power alleys were 450 feet in left-center field and 480 in dead center; in 1957 alone, Willie had hit at least ten balls that traveled more than 460 feet — take that, Mickey Mantle! — and went for outs.

This was a continuation of a myth that followed Willie around his entire big league career: that he was burdened by his own home park. In fact, he had hit 94 home runs in his time at the Polo Grounds, one more than he had hit in road games. It's true that it had taken some adjustment for Willie to hit those home runs — he had to pull the ball sharply down the left-field corner or, on outside pitches, hit it to the opposite field — but there were adjustments to make in other league parks as well, and Mays was ultimately the same hitter at home and on the road.

In contrast, it was always assumed that Mantle had a big home run advantage playing his home games in Yankee Stadium, with its short right-field porch. (After all, most pitchers were right-handed, and Mickey would be batting left-handed most of the time.) In fact, Yankee Stadium had some pretty deep power alleys as well in those years, and from 1951 to 1957, Mickey actually lost a few home runs there, hitting 100 at home and 107 on the road.

"Willie," Rigney said in the *Parade* article, "stands 5'11", weighs 185 pounds, and there isn't an ounce of fat on him. He has tremendous stamina, and he's not injury-prone." In addition to the 61 home runs, Rigney thought Seals Stadium "will also help him hit .380 and drive in 150 runs."[6]

Bill Rigney probably thought he was doing his star player a good turn by telling everyone how spectacular Mays was going to be, but by those standards — and *only* by those standards — 1958 was a big disappointment for Willie. Mays batted .347 and led the league in stolen bases and runs scored, but lost the batting title to the Phillies' Richie Ashburn, by just three points. Nevertheless, his batting average was still a good thirty points lower than Rigney had predicted, and he drove in 50 fewer RBIs than his manager had expected. His home run total, 29, was less than half of Rigney's anticipated 61.

It wasn't just Seals Stadium that let him down. Willie hit 16 home runs there, but only 13 in all other parks. Clearly, as he had done in the second half of 1954, Mays was trying to stir things up by getting on base and hitting the ball in the gaps. By any reasonable yardstick, it was an outstanding season. San Francisco fans did not always think so. For the first time in his professional baseball career, Willie Mays was booed. New York sportswriters were outraged. Their anger fueled their San Francisco counterparts to write rejoinders, and the fans picked it up from there.

In a 1985 dual profile of Mantle and Mays in *Sports Illustrated*, Ron Frimrite wrote that "in '58, the team moved to San Francisco and Mays lost his adoring New York press as well. Much had been made, most of it nonsense, about San Francisco's rejection of Mays, the myth, largely of New York contrivance, having it that the fans there were so locked into the memory of Joe DiMaggio, a local boy, that they could not accept this newcomer from the East. So prejudiced were the fans against the transplanted New Yorker, the story goes, that they adopted a near rookie, Orlando Cepeda, as their own favorite. After Nikita Khrushchev's visit to San Francisco in 1959, Frank Conniff, then the national editor of the Hearst newspapers, was moved to comment, 'What a city. They cheer Khrushchev and boo Willie Mays.' The reality of the situation was much simpler. His new fans in the West simply required that Mays prove to them he was as good as people in the East said he was. He did, and they gave him his due."[7]

Frimrite could not have been more wrong. He shouldn't have found it so far-fetched that Giants fans rejected Mays because he wasn't DiMaggio; such a thing had already happened in the case of DiMaggio and Mantle. Second, the notion that San Francisco fans adopted Orlando Cepeda as their favorite was not a concoction of East Coast sportswriters; at the end of the season, the fans voted him the Giants MVP, ahead of Willie even though Mays out-hit Cepeda by thirty-five points, had four more home runs and twelve more stolen bases, scored thirty-three more runs, and had an on-base percentage seventy-seven points higher and a slugging percentage seventy-one points higher. Not to mention playing a far more demanding defensive position than Cepeda did at first base.

Finally, the idea that Willie Mays had to prove to San Francisco fans that "he was as good as people in the East said he was" is lunacy. Willie Mays had been the best player in the National League and possibly in all of baseball for four years, and even those who hadn't seen him play on national TV were capable of reading statistics. He had averaged over .320 with better than 40 home runs for the previous four years, led the National League in stolen bases for three consecutive seasons, and was the best outfielder in baseball. What exactly was it that Willie Mays had to prove to San Francisco?

Whatever the reasons, in 1958 and for much of the next three seasons San Francisco fans went out of their way to show Willie Mays how little he was appreciated. And they wouldn't completely warm up to him until he helped San Francisco humble hated Los Angeles in the most exciting pennant race major league baseball had seen since Willie Mays was a rookie.

In 1956 some fans had booed Mickey Mantle as a draft dodger, or for not being Joe DiMaggio, or for not being Babe Ruth, or for coming so close to being Babe Ruth. In 1957 many had booed him for not having been the Mickey Mantle of 1956. In 1958 they booed him for not being the Mickey Mantle of 1956 and 1957.

Out-of-town fans may have booed him for being a Yankee, but what excuse was there for the fans in New York? The Yankees won eight pennants and six World Series during the decade, and Mickey constantly played in pain. There were some injuries the fans weren't even aware of. For instance, in 1958 Mickey played through the season on a bad shoulder that had been injured in Game 3 of the '57 Series by Red Schoendienst. When Milwaukee's pitcher, Bob Buhl, tried a pickoff throw with Mantle at second, the ball sailed into center field. Red went up in the air for the ball and came down on a diving Mickey's right shoulder "like a sack of cement."

"I got through the game okay," Mickey recalled to Mickey

Herskowitz years later, "and played in the next two, but I couldn't swing the bat freely and the shoulder nagged at me for years. I hit my homer batting left-handed [in the fourth inning] into the right-center field bull pen against Gene Conley, but I would never again hit with that same power from that side."[8]

Mantle spent his winter as usual — undergoing surgery, but this time on his shoulder instead of his knee. Literally adding insult to injury, George Weiss tried to cut the salary of America's home run king by $5,000. By the time he reached spring training in 1958, Mickey's shoulder was a little better, but the ache in his right knee had grown worse: he had developed shin splits. The Yankees compounded the problem by playing Mantle in nearly every spring training game when a little rest might have helped his shoulder and knee mend more completely. After all, there was plenty to be made in the Grapefruit League as well, and fans who heard that Mickey Mantle wasn't playing sometimes asked for their money back or didn't come out at all.

In 1958, for the first time in their careers, Mickey Mantle and Willie Mays were just about exactly the same ballplayer. Despite his injured shoulder, Mantle hit .304, led the AL in home runs (42), total bases (307), walks (129), and strikeouts (120). He stole 18 of 23 bases. He was the best player in his league by a wide margin, though many baseball writers thought he had slipped considerably from his MVP years of 1956 and 1957. They gave him no support at all in the MVP voting, in which he finished a distant fifth behind former Yankee Jackie Jensen, now with the Boston Red Sox. Jensen probably wasn't even one of the five or six best players in the AL that season. Mantle out-hit Jensen that year by eighteen points, had a .443 on-base percentage and a .592 slugging percentage to Jensen's .396/.535, and hit seven more home runs. Jackie, though, led the league in RBIs with 122, while Mickey, who played on a team where most of the batting order contributed to driving in runs, had "only" 97.

The Yankees once again won the AL pennant and, for the

second time in four years, avenged a World Series loss to an NL team, this time coming back to beat the Milwaukee Braves after being down three games to one.

In the National League, the Chicago Cubs' fine shortstop Ernie Banks was voted MVP, but Willie Mays, who finished second in the voting, was the better player.

Who was better that season? When Bill James added it all up for his 2002 book *Win Shares*, he rated them in almost a dead heat — Mays with 40 shares for the season and Mantle with 39. But they accomplished their feats in home ballparks 3,000 miles apart.

Mantle's aching body was beginning to make baseball unpleasant for him — the grind of day-to-day play with night games, double-headers, and constant traveling was wearing him out. The traveling, in particular, was tough. Willie Mays enjoyed traveling — there were new sights to see and the possibility of an adventure in every city. To Mickey, "there were too many nights on the road, too many lonely hotels and bars."[9] By the end of the decade, he would have four sons, whom he scarcely knew.

Having won consecutive Most Valuable Player Awards and earned four World Series rings did nothing to improve Mickey's relationship with reporters. "It was getting harder and harder for me to deal with the press," he admitted years later. "Especially the New York writers. They'd come in and there'd always be somebody trying for the jugular. Leonard Schecter of the New York Post was one of them. He'd ask his questions and the next day I'd read things that didn't sound like me. If I told him he had twisted my words around, Schecter would say, 'Oh, no, you really said that.' It was a no win situation."[10] Mickey finally decided to stop talking to Schecter and confined nearly all his remarks to sportswriters he trusted, especially Dick Young of the *New York Daily News* and Shirley Povich of the *Washington Post*. In the 1960s, as Mantle's career began to wind down, he became very friendly with a rising young sportswriter named Dick Schaap, who, in 1961, would write the lively little paperback in the *Sport* magazine biography series, *Mickey Mantle: The Indispensable Yankee*, which was one of this author's inspirations. I've always wondered how different Mickey's career might have been if, like Willie, he had had a friendly press — or at least a couple of supportive writers like Arnold Hano and Charlie Einstein — from his first season as a Yankee.

Fans, who could not begin to understand Mickey's shyness, were a plague. In the twenty-first century, the bane of the professional athlete is paparazzi and bloggers; in the 1950s, an unspoken agreement kept the press at a comfortable distance from athletes, but fans felt no such compunction. "I was a walking billboard," Mickey said. "I make no bones of the fact that I've always had a private corner, an innate shyness that prevents me from feeling comfortable when talking to strangers. As for my kids, I didn't want them subjected to the kind of attention I was getting, so they were shielded."

After the 1958 World Series, the Yankees' front office gave the players tickets to the Ringling Brothers Barnum & Bailey circus. The Mantles — Mickey, Merlyn, Mickey Jr., and David — drove from their rented home in River Edge, New Jersey, to Madison Square Garden for the show. For a while, everyone had a great time. "We got to see almost the whole show, the clowns, the lions and tigers, and the ringmaster cracking his whip. But finally the fans spotted us." Swarms of autograph seekers disrupted the crowd and threatened to interrupt the show. A sullen Mantle moved his family out of their seats; Mickey Jr. and David cried, and clusters of fans, bitter that they were denied autographs, hissed, booed, and cursed.

"The autograph problem," he said in 1985, "is still with me. Ever since the mid-'50s I haven't been able to take my family to attend a circus or ball games or any other big public events."[11] Even some old off-season pleasures were souring for him. Mickey, along with Billy Martin and sometimes Whitey Ford, enjoyed bird hunting — mostly ducks and quail — in Oklahoma and Texas. In 1959, though, at Billy's insistence, they went deer hunting. Mickey shot his first and last deer. When they tracked the animal down, it was still alive and, Mantle recalled, "looking at me with those big brown eyes, as if he was saying

'Why in hell did you shoot me?' And I was trying to figure out the same thing."[12] He never went deer hunting again.

By the end of the 1958 season, Mickey was happy that the Yankees' prestige had been restored in the World Series. He was also hurting from shoulder to knee and badly in need of some off-season relaxation, but he had more pressing concerns. His third son, Billy, named for the now-departed Martin, had been born the previous year, and despite the hefty World Series check, Mickey was desperately in need of some off-season income to support his growing family. When he asked Frank Scott if he had any ideas, Scott replied that he could think of only one: barnstorming.

The term was almost as old as baseball itself. According to Thomas Barthel in his 2007 book *Baseball Barnstorming and Exhibition Games, 1901–1962,* "The 'barn' part of the word was used to emphasize the rural aspect of the games. The 'storm' was used to describe the speed of the movement from city to city. . . . The Negro Leagues barnstormed all the time; the majority of those games were played *during* the regular season, though some were played afterwards."[13] For the most part, the owners "hated barnstorming and tried repeatedly to have the touring delayed, or banned, or restricted. Battles between commissioner and player would go on and on over the matter of barnstorming."[14] By 1963, this conflict had become irrelevant: barnstorming had died a natural death from a combination of major league expansion and televised baseball, which made Willie Mays the last great attraction of the barnstorming era.*

Mantle had played in a few off-season exhibition games, but barn-

---

* There may have been one more reason. Frank Robinson, who barnstormed from his first postseason in 1956, once told me that he thought one of the biggest reasons for the demise of barnstorming was professional football: "Things changed very quickly after 1958, when the Baltimore Colts and New York Giants played that great championship game. I remember in 1956 and '57 we really didn't have much competition for Sunday barnstorming games, but by 1959, and then for the next three years, you could see interest declining quickly. It seemed like everyone wanted to stay home on a Sunday in October and watch football."

storming wasn't a way of life for him as it was for Willie Mays and other black players of his time. For them, the money from barnstorming made up in large part for the money they didn't get for endorsements. White players, at least some of them, could afford to be more selective. But in the fall of 1958, the greatest of them, Mickey Mantle, who had three children and numerous family members back in Oklahoma, including his mother, depending on him, couldn't afford to be picky. Willie Mays needed the cash too. He had a swarm of dependents in Alabama, his father Cat, whom he was moving into an apartment in Oakland, and, perhaps more pressing, an extravagant wife who had run up enormous bills for personal expenses and home furnishings on both coasts.

Neither player much wanted to spend the off-season playing. Mickey was hurting; Willie finished the season physically drained and suffering from nervous exhaustion. But the best way they could supplement their income, as Frank Scott pointed out, was to play baseball against each other.

Years later, baseball writers would claim either the 1960 American League–National League All-Star Game at Yankee Stadium or the 1961 exhibition game between the Giants and Yankees at Yankee Stadium as Willie Mays's return to New York. Actually, it was a now almost forgotten barnstorming game on October 12, 1958. "Both of them got a huge kick out of the game," recalled Scott. "They both selected the players they wanted" — actually, Frank Scott did most of the selection, as he represented all of them in endorsement deals. Mickey's All-Stars included his teammates Whitey Ford and Elston Howard; White Sox second baseman Nellie Fox, who would win the league's MVP Award the following year; Detroit outfielder Harvey Kuenn and Cleveland outfielder Rocky Colavito*; and though he scarcely qualified as an All-Star by any definition, Mickey's best friend, Billy Martin, then with the Detroit Tigers. At the very bottom

---

*In a bizarre trade just a couple of months later, Colavito and Kuenn would be swapped for each other. Kuenn went on to win the league's batting title, while Colavito led the AL in home runs.

of the roster was the Yankees' third-string catcher, Ralph Houk, who was enormously grateful for the chance to earn a few extra dollars.

Willie's team was even more formidable, composed of future Hall of Famers Richie Ashburn of the Phillies, the only outfielder in baseball, many felt, with as much range as Mays; the Cubs' Ernie Banks, NL MVP for 1958 and 1959; Frank Robinson, who would later win the MVP in both the National and American Leagues; and the Pittsburgh Pirates' second-base fielding wizard, the Ozzie Smith of his day, Bill Mazeroski. The Dodgers' Johnny Podres and Gil Hodges, who were winding down their careers, were also on the roster; Scott knew they would draw some fans from Brooklyn.

Nothing indicates the state of baseball in 1958 more clearly than the notice at the bottom of the promotional posters for the game: "No Television — No Radio." Even Scott, who was years ahead of his time as a savvy promoter, felt that TV and radio exposure would hurt sales rather than promote interest. Today, of course, such an event would probably be on ESPN TV and radio, not to mention streamed live on the Internet.

The game drew 21,129 fans, which was regarded as a huge success since the attendance was considerably more than the Yankees, Giants, or Dodgers had averaged per game in 1957. The next day the *New York Times* headline read, "Mays' Team Wins Exhibition, 6–2." Willie Mays "had the hitting and the pitching on his side yesterday as his National League All-Stars whipped Mickey Mantle's American League All-Stars 6–2 at Yankee Stadium."[15] Willie went 4-for-5, including three hits off Whitey Ford, beginning a long domination of the AL's best pitcher that would continue throughout their careers. Ray Robinson, who was at the game, recalls that Mickey and Willie "were both grinning when they brought their score cards up to home plate and shook hands. But the crowd was clearly on Willie's side."

The *Times* account supports Robinson's memory: "The Giants' Mays, roundly applauded each time he stepped to the plate, and the Phillies' Richie Ashburn got seven hits between them. . . . The

21,129 spectators cheered Willie Mays' every move. Willie provided an exciting note with his daring base running."[16] Mickey — who went 1-for-2 before taking himself out of the game — got a few boos when he came to bat.

The 1958 Mickey-Willie All-Star game had an odd side story. George Plimpton, the intrepid sports journalist who would later write about his experience playing for the Detroit Lions in *Paper Lion* and on the professional golf tour in *Bogey Man*, wanted to use the event to write about what it was like to pitch to a batting order of major leaguers. He first approached Frank Scott, "the players' agent — a powerful figure in the world of professional athletics. He is often described as the October Santa — parlaying World Series heroics into lucrative engagements of the banquet circuit for the outstanding players. He's such a success at making money for athletes off the playing field that almost any day on television you can see his clients selling things, showering, shaving. . . . He was closely identified with a group promoting the game, and he and I had a number of conversations over the phone — always pleasant, but he was skeptical. Most of the time he wanted to know who was to be held responsible. Suppose I got killed. All sorts of things happen on the pitcher's mound. Did I remember Herb Score [hit by the Yankees' Gil McDougald] and the terrible line drive that nearly blinded him? Or suppose I beaned somebody? Did I want to have a Ray Chapman on my conscience — the fellow Carl Mays killed with a submarine ball?" A Carl Mays hitting a Willie Mays? Only imagine.

Finally, Plimpton sought the advice of Toots Shor, pater familias of sports in New York City. Shor advised him, "What you need is cash. That's all. Cash. Get your editor to put up cash." Toots told him to tell Frank Scott that he had, say, $2,000 for the players to divide up, in which case the players would be so anxious to have Plimpton pitch that "they'll carry you out to the pitcher's mound on a goddam divan." Finally, *Sports Illustrated*, which had Plimpton on assignment, managed to scratch up $1,000 for whichever team got the most hits off Plimpton, and as Shor had predicted, the captains of both squads agreed to let him pitch.

Plimpton had no idea that he was about to step into a nightmare. He was delighted to meet Mays, who came into the locker room "with a rush, shouting greetings in his high, rather squeaky voice, an arm upraised, waving — smaller, much smaller in stature than I'd imagined, and yet so ebullient the locker room came alive the moment the door swung shut behind him." Moments later, Plimpton spoke to Mantle, who immediately asked him about the money. After much whispering between Mantle and Scott, it was agreed that Plimpton would get his chance a half hour before the game. Both sides would send up eight batters — pitchers would not bat — and the team with the most bases would divvy up the prize money.

What Plimpton had not counted on was that big league players simply wouldn't swing at pitches they did not like. The National Leaguers were up first, and Mays became so impatient with Plimpton's off-target tosses that he swung on an outside pitch and hit a towering pop to second base. As Plimpton stood on the mound at Yankee Stadium, he did get a sense of what it was like to pitch to professionals. Behind him were Billy Martin, taking a turn at short, and Nellie Fox at second "with a chaw of tobacco" tucked in his cheek. In center field was Mickey Mantle: "Of all of them standing there, Mantle's was the power you sensed — seeing it in the heavy shoulders and arms sloping from a neck as thick as a water main. His large boyish face has gone heavy; he turns his head slowly, his eyes pale and impassive, so that there is something in his manner of the cat family: imperturbable, arch, and yet because the boyishness is still there, he wears a faint expression of suspicious stubbornness, of petulance."[17]

Having used up all his time throwing failed curves in the dirt to the National League, Plimpton never got to pitch to Mantle. Instead, the players were told there would be a $2,000 prize, $1,000 for each team. Plimpton paid the extra money out of his own pocket. "A small price to pay for the opportunity," he told me many years later.

Ⓓ Ⓓ

In Plimpton's opinion, Mickey played listlessly that day "compared to Mays," who seemed to be enjoying himself immensely. Mantle, he felt, "seemed stolid, almost indifferent . . . during his early years as a Yankee, he had kept a cap pistol in his locker, and for a couple of seasons around the major league circuit, he and Billy Martin used to bang away at each other while Yogi Berra and some of the others would join in with water pistols. But the Mantle I was introduced to by Frank Scott seemed long past the cap pistol stage. His jaw moved slowly and barely perceptively on gum."[18]

I interviewed Richie Ashburn, who played in all the Mickey-Willie exhibitions, for *Philadelphia* magazine in 1993. Rich, as he preferred to be called, thought that Mantle was miffed at the cool reception he got from the fans at Yankee Stadium. "Of course, there were a lot of old Giants fans there, but I don't think he expected the boos. I don't believe that he resented the way they felt about Willie, but I think he had some kind of mistaken attitude that after winning back-to-back MVPs everyone in New York was ready to see them as equals. It just wasn't that way."

Ashburn was surprised to find that Mantle was eager to barnstorm again the next year. "He was different," he recalled. "A lot more light-hearted. If I had to guess, I'd say it was because he was playing outside of New York."

The first game of the 1959 tour was played in Philadelphia, where the man who put Mickey and Willie together on the same baseball field was known as "Mr. Basketball." Eddie Gottlieb, the owner and first coach of the Philadelphia Warriors (the NBA's Rookie of the Year Award is named for him), was born Isadore Gottlieb in the Ukraine in 1898. Like Abe Saperstein of Harlem Globetrotter fame, Eddie loved both basketball and baseball and was a big promoter of Negro League ball in the Philadelphia area. He contributed some crowd-pleasing ideas to the occasion, such as a home run contest before the game that was won by Gil Hodges, who received a plaque from the South

Philadelphia Optimists Club. Mays won the game with a grand slam-mer, though Mickey had two doubles and a single.

The next day the players and coaches piled their equipment onto two buses and headed up to Syracuse, where former welter- and middleweight boxing champion Carmen Basilio was promoting the game. On the drive upstate, Ashburn recalled, Willie and Mickey engaged in a poor-mouthing contest that had the rest of the players laughing out loud. "It was hilarious. Willie would say, 'Man, my dad didn't have enough money to buy me a bicycle. I had to share one with the kids in my family.' Then Mickey would say, 'Oh, man, you had bicycles? We had an old horse that we used to haul stuff around with, and I had to ride him to school.' Then Willie would say, 'Oh, man, you got to ride to school on a *horse*? I always wanted to ride on a horse.' This went on for about an hour, and finally even the two of them were cracking up."

The game itself, finally won by Mickey's team, was a lark. Basilio, a huge baseball fan, wanted to play his favorite position, shortstop, for a couple of innings. Mickey told him, "Hell, yes. What am I gonna do? Tell the guy who whipped Sugar Ray Robinson that he can't play baseball with me?" Carmen did just fine, handling two chances cleanly.

Mantle, Ashburn noted, did not bat left-handed in either game. "I didn't realize it till the games were over, but Mickey never batted left-handed, even against right-handed pitching. Later I found he was still nursing his right shoulder, but he did fine in that Syracuse game. Willie hit a ball out to the flagpole in center, about twenty feet over the fence. I'd say it went about 420. About two innings later, Mickey got up with a grin and did a Babe Ruth thing of pointing out towards the flagpole, like that's where he was going to hit it. He popped the ball up, and the players on both teams got a good laugh out of it. He came off the field with a shrug and a smile. But two innings later, he did hit one out there, probably about twenty feet farther than Willie's. From his dugout, Willie feigned indignation as Mickey rounded third. 'Hey, man, what you doin' stealin' my thunder?' Mickey just laughed and said, 'Hey, man, I told you that's where I was going to hit it.' They were just a couple of big kids."

In the final inning, Mantle pulled a stunt he would have never tried in a big league game. "Willie was leading farther and farther off second base, daring the pitcher to try and pick him off. He didn't know that Mickey had ordered the shortstop and second baseman — Nellie Fox was at second and I forget who was at short — to stay away from the bag. Mickey gave a signal and came charging in from center field, the pitcher wheeled and threw, and they picked Willie off second. Mickey laughed and jumped around like a kid while Willie shook his head in disbelief. The whole thing was so silly. It was like something you would see in a company softball game." The crowd of nearly eight thousand, who had paid a total of $20,000 to watch, were delighted. The final score was 4–2, American League All-Stars.

After the game, there was a dinner at the local Knights of Columbus, to which Basilio belonged. "They had a pool room there," Ashburn told me, "and Willie said to me, 'Watch this. I'm gonna get some back from Mickey for that game today.' " But after an hour of pool shooting that had everyone enthralled, the ace of Big Tony's in Fairfield had to give way to the hustler from the Black Cat in Commerce — "and I think about $50 went with that. Mickey was proud as a peacock, you could see that he really loved Willie and that there was a bond there as well as a real rivalry. Willie shook his hand and smiled, and then in a fake tough guy voice said, 'Man, I'm gonna give up this table to someone else now. But I'm gonna get you back someday.' "[19]

It's true that both men probably should have been home taking hot baths and watching football on television. But even if it was work, the off-season baseball was therapeutic. Baseball historian Thomas Barthel relates a story about Mickey told to him by Ted Kubiak, a former major league infielder and son-in-law of Irv Noren, Mickey's onetime roommate. Noren's job, Kubiak said, was "to get him safely back to his room many a night after their nights on the town; Irv did not drink, so he was the designated chauffeur."

Sometime in either 1955 or 1956, Irv and Mickey decided to drive together to California. "Pretty soon they went through a small town and saw a group of young boys playing baseball behind a school. They thought it would be a good idea to have some fun, so they stopped to watch. Irv asked the boys if he could pitch to his buddy because his buddy said he could not strike him out. The boys did not want these 'old guys' to take up their time, so they said no. After bribing the boys with some new baseballs they had in the car, Irv began throwing to Mickey, who hit everything and, of course, was hitting the balls over the school much to the surprise of the boys. Finishing up, Irv asked them if they knew who Mickey Mantle was, and they did. 'Well, this is Mickey Mantle!'

" 'No way,' they said. Mickey had to show them his driver's license. They left the boys the new balls and got on their way. What a story for those kids to tell their kids!"[20]

After the first barnstorming tour in 1958 came one of the strangest chapters in Willie Mays's young life. He and Marghuerite adopted a baby and named him Michael. According to James Hirsch's biography, Willie now had extra time to spend with the baby and "enjoyed his duties. When Michael couldn't fall asleep, Willie would put him in his car and drive him around the block until he nodded off. He even learned how to change diapers."[21] But Michael Mays would remain, until this day, a shadow in his adopted father's life. He was scarcely mentioned in interviews, and the two were almost never seen in public together. It has never been clear what role, if any, Michael played in Willie's life. Nor did any of Mays's biographers ever delve too deeply into the relationship between Willie Mays and his adopted son.

By the end of the 1958 season, both Willie and Mickey were living outside New York. The Mantles had bought a four-bedroom house that cost nearly $60,000 in the tony Preston Hollow section of Dallas. Merlyn had long since decided that life in the New York area, even in the suburbs, was fraught with distractions, at least for Mickey. The trouble was that life back in Commerce had been no better. "People were knocking at their door all hours of the night," recalled one of Mickey's friends, "wanting to borrow money. They'd come over and use their bathroom. Can you believe that? People just wouldn't leave them alone."[22]

Mickey had fled from their Commerce home whenever possible. When Merlyn was nine months pregnant with Billy, Mickey, Whitey Ford, Billy Martin, and another friend, Harold Youngman, left on their annual Thanksgiving hunting trip on a ranch outside Kerrville, Texas, owned by another of Mickey's friends, a man named Hamilton Wilson. Merlyn thought Mickey might delay his trip a few days in anticipation of the arrival of the baby; he did not. On the day the pals left for their hunting trip, Merlyn, already feeling labor pains, checked herself into a hospital in Joplin, Missouri. On hearing of the birth of a boy, Youngman flew Mickey to Joplin on his private plane. When he saw Merlyn in the hospital room, she burst out crying and said, "You could have waited a few more days before taking off like that!"[23]

But if Merlyn thought that moving Mickey to a house near Dallas was going to improve his instincts as a husband and father, she would be sadly mistaken.

14

"Neither One of Us Was Joe DiMaggio"

For Mickey and Willie, the 1959 season was one of discontent. It was, oddly enough, the only season until the Yankees' collapse in 1965 in which a Willie Mays–led Giants team won more games than a Mickey Mantle–led Yankees team. San Francisco finished in third place, 83–71, just four games out of first. That was the good news; the bad news was that the hated Dodgers finished first. Giants fans smarted at the thought that somehow Willie Mays had not done quite enough to make up the difference. For the first time in six seasons, Willie was probably not the league's best player that year; that unofficial title should probably have gone to the Braves' Henry Aaron, who did not win the MVP that year, or to the Cubs' Ernie Banks, who did. But Willie had still done plenty for his team, batting .313 with 34 home runs and 113 RBIs. He led the NL in stolen bases for an amazing fourth consecutive season.

Plagued with age and injuries, the Yankees had their only bad season under Stengel. Like the Giants, they finished third, but at 79–75, finished a full fifteen games behind the pennant-winning White Sox. Mickey, now twenty-seven, had a miserable year — at least that's what many said. Playing in pain all season, he batted just .285, his worst average since his rookie season, with 31 home runs and 75 RBIs. He failed to lead the league in runs scored for the first time in four years. And yet, in hindsight, he was probably the best player in the American League — or at any rate, at least as good as the White Sox's Nellie Fox, who finished first in the MVP voting. Bill James would give Fox 30 Win Shares for 1959, the same as Mantle. *Total Baseball* would rank Mickey number one in its Total Player Rating, with the Tigers' Al Kaline second; Fox wasn't in the top five.

Mickey Mantle and Willie Mays ended 1959 in bad shape, both physically and psychologically. Their teams had been disappointing, and both were booed by the hometown fans. They were hurting — Mantle from old injuries, Mays from stomach distress and dizziness. Their marriages were not happy, and they were both badly in need of money. Mays probably summed it up best ten years later in *Esquire*: "Mickey used to get booed a lot at Yankee Stadium. I didn't have any problem like that until later, when the Giants moved to San Francisco. Then I got booed. It wasn't so much what we were. It was more what we weren't. Neither one of us was Joe DiMaggio."[1]

During 1960's preseason, Mickey and Willie again found relief from the pressures of life by playing baseball — against each other. This time it was in an episode of *Home Run Derby*, the seminal TV sports reality show that presaged the annual Home Run Derby festivities that now take place before the All-Star Game. In early February, Mickey and Willie flew to Los Angeles, where the contest was held in Wrigley Field — the *other* Wrigley Field, which the family had built for their Pacific Coast team, the Los Angeles Angels.

The rules were simple: anything a batter swung at and did not hit over the fences between the fair poles was an out. One significant difference between home run derbies then and now was that this one had an umpire calling balls and strikes. Another was that it was played over nine "innings." Wrigley Field was chosen not only for its warm-weather location but for the fairness of its outfield — the distances were 340 feet to both the right- and left-field walls.

The prize money was by no means negligible. The winner received a check for $2,000 and was invited back to compete the next week, and the runner-up got $1,000. There was a $500 bonus if a batter hit three home runs in a row, with another $500 for a fourth consecutive home run and $1,000 each for any more consecutive homers. The right-handed pitcher was a strong-armed outfielder named Tom Saffell, who had played for four seasons in the big leagues and, in 1960, was playing left field and pitching for the Hollywood All-Stars. His job was to groove batting practice fastballs down the middle.

Charlie Einstein, who flew into Los Angeles with Willie to write a story about the home run duel, later sent me a scratchy VHS tape of the derby with a letter. "Mickey," wrote Einstein, "took these one-on-one confrontations more seriously than Willie, and he wasn't above using some gamesmanship to get an edge. On the tape you can hear him say to Willie and Mike Scott, the announcer, 'I'm gonna bat right-handed.' He sounds like he doesn't want to put Willie at a disadvantage by batting from the left side of the plate. He was faking a little bit. He didn't *want* to bat from the left side of the plate."

What Willie didn't know — what a lot of people didn't know at the time — was that Mickey was still hurting a lot from his injury in the 1958 World Series, and that it hurt every time he batted from the left side. He actually had an advantage batting from the right, even if there wasn't a left-handed pitcher on the mound. Before the contest began, Einstein told me, "I heard Mickey mumble to Willie, 'You wanna put a little money on the side?' Willie's eyes narrowed — he thought he had Mickey because Mickey had volunteered not to bat left-handed. Willie later told me they had put down a side bet of $500. Now, you have to remember that was a lot of money back then when these guys weren't getting multimillion-dollar paychecks. Both of them could have used that money."

Willie was the "visiting team" — he wore a Giants gray road

uniform. In the first inning, he hit four home runs. "Watch carefully," Einstein noted. "He allows himself a little grin after the fourth one. Mickey came up and hit a terrific shot that looks as if it traveled over 450 feet. When he walked up to the press box after the inning, he passed Willie and said with a grin, 'Can I get two for that one?' Willie laughed at that, but it always bugged him a little that Mickey got so much attention for his tape measure home runs." In fact, anyone viewing the tape can see that, in his half of the inning, Willie hit a shot almost as far as Mickey's; it looks as if it sailed into the backyard of a house out past the left-field area of the ballpark. "Willie thought he could hit them as far as Mickey. He couldn't, but he could hit them pretty far. He once said to me, 'Maybe I don't always hit 'em as far as Mickey, but I hit 'em far enough.' He was right about that. It's a silly thing, but I think it unnerved Willie just a bit to find out once and for all that he just couldn't hit a ball as far as Mickey."[2]

Going into the fifth inning. Willie was leading 7–2. When Mickey flopped down in the press box chair, he said, "This is getting embarrassing." He said it with a grin in that aw-shucks country boy manner. Scott responded, "Well, you just didn't bring your home run swing with you."

But Mickey was working on Willie. In the seventh, with Willie up 8–3, Mickey passed him while going to bat and said, "Willie, man, we ought to add up the length on all these. I think my three went as far as all yours." Willie tried to laugh it off, but he was a little indignant. "Man, what you been lookin' at? Did you see the one I hit by that pole in center field? I got you today, man." Mickey just grinned and made a gesture like *Hey, what do you want from me?* He then went out and hit three towering homers.

Willie was now concerned not so much with winning but with matching Mickey distance for distance, and he started overswinging. When they switched places for Mickey's half of the inning, Mickey said, "You want to double that bet?" Willie just looked at him and said, "You on, man." But he didn't get good wood on a pitch for the rest of the contest, and Mickey got three more in the final inning to win, 9–8. If you watch the recording, you can see Willie in the press box, the smile gone.

So Mickey not only got his $2,000 prize money, he got Willie's $1,000 for finishing in second place. Willie pointed a finger at him and said, "I'm gonna get you on the golf course." Actually, he got him at the All-Star Game.

The 1960 *Home Run Derby* episodes have since aired on ESPN Classic and are now available, impeccably restored, on DVD.* There's no better visual record of Mickey Mantle and Willie Mays at bat. Mickey stands in the box with his feet close together, then spreads them as he snaps his brutally powerful shoulders and forearms, bat gripped throughout the follow-through, the barrel slamming into his back. Willie looks remarkably similar to Mickey in chest, shoulders, and forearms; his feet are spread apart wide in imitation of Joe DiMaggio as he shifts his weight forward off his front foot, lunges at the ball, and releases his right hand from the bat about two-thirds through his wide, sweeping swing. The whole contest is a magnificent display of power and hand-eye coordination.

The Giants began their new season in Candlestick Park, which was supposed to improve Willie's home run total. Instead, vicious gusts of wind off the ocean knocked power drives down into left field. (Baseballs weren't the only thing affected; early in the season, Orlando Cepeda took a called strike three and turned to flip his batting helmet toward the team dugout in disgust. His teammates watched in wonder as the wind picked up the helmet and carried it ten rows deep into the stands.) Mays had not yet mastered the art of hitting with power to Candlestick's right field, and so for the first time in five seasons his power numbers suffered: he hit just 12 home runs at home and 17 in

---

*Henry Aaron went on to win the overall competition, taking six of seven derbies. Mickey was second, winning four of five.

the rest of the league's ballparks. There was no question, though, that Willie Mays was still the best player in the National League — or at least one of the top two or three.

But the Giants were mediocre at best, finishing fifth at 79–75, sixteen full games behind the surprising Pittsburgh Pirates, who, though they were sixth in an eight-team league in home runs, nonetheless led the league in both batting and runs scored. The NL's best players that year were (and probably in this order) Mays, Ernie Banks, and Henry Aaron, but Pittsburgh shortstop Dick Groat was named MVP by virtue of winning the NL batting title — and for being the captain of the pennant winner.

Mays finished third in one of several baffling MVP votes he was to endure during his prime years. Yes, Groat's Pirates did win the pennant, but there surely was not a single player, coach, manager, or sportswriter, even in Pittsburgh, who truly thought that Dick Groat was a better or more valuable player than Mays. Groat out-hit Willie by six points, but that's where the comparison ended. Mays's OBP was 10 points higher, .381 to .371, his slugging percentage of .555 was 161 points higher, and he out-stole Groat, 25 bases to zero. He drove in 103 runs to Groat's 50 and outscored him 107 runs to 85. Mays also edged out Groat in hits, 190 to 186. And none of this took into account the fact that Willie was hurt by his own home ballpark, where he was just .299, versus .338 on the road.

In several seasons in Mays's career, one cannot help looking at the MVP voting and saying, "What were they thinking?" The only explanation that makes any sense is one Charlie Einstein offered: "There was just a feeling back then that Willie was so much better than most National League players that he was going to win four or five MVPs before it was over. So every year they seemed to look for other players to give it to."[3]

One could make the same case for Mantle in that period, except that Mickey's numbers were harder to appreciate because the importance of on-base percentage wasn't understood and strikeouts were still regarded with too much importance.

Early in 1960, Mantle's biggest MVP competitor was on his own team. Early that year, the Yankees had traded with Kansas City and acquired Roger Maris, who ended up winning the AL MVP. Maris missed tying Mantle for the AL home run title by one, 39 to 40; he led the league in RBIs with 112 to Mantle's 94. He also out-hit him .283 to .275 and led the league in slugging percentage with a .581 mark to Mantle's .558. Yet Mickey was the better player: he stole 14 of 17 bases (to Roger's two steals on two attempts), and his slugging percentage was higher by twenty-eight points, .399 to .371. Though Maris had 18 more RBIs, Mantle scored 21 more runs, 119 to 98. By both *Total Baseball*'s ratings and Bill James's Win Shares method, Mantle had the edge.

But no one in 1960 was ready to make that argument for Mickey. For one thing, he had been in Casey Stengel's doghouse earlier in the season when it looked like he wasn't hustling (though in fact Mantle was playing in terrible pain at the time). For another, most writers simply looked at his .275 batting average and 94 RBIs. Few considered that Maris had more RBIs than Mantle because he was lucky enough to hit for most of the season in the cleanup spot in back of Mickey, or that Mickey, despite his comparatively low batting average, was on base so often. He walked 111 times, 40 more than Maris.

Thanks to the two of them — the "M&M Boys," as they came to be called — and Bill Skowron, who hit .309 with 28 home runs, the Yankees, after trailing the Baltimore Orioles for part of the season, wound up winning the pennant by eight games. But for the Giants, the season was, in the words of Arnold Hano, "a memory of dropped pop flies, stupid base running, futile hitting, ineffective spot pitching, and incomprehensible, reprehensible managing, buried beneath jeers and laughter, all on display in a beautiful new ballpark."[4]

⊕ ⊕

"I don't want to talk about 1960," Willie told San Francisco reporters after the last game. "A bad year. I don't like to dig up the past. Let it rest."[5]

Willie at least had a great year on the field, and there were compensations. One came after the season when the Giants toured Japan; the fans there were fascinated by Willie and cheered wildly at everything he did, from the hotel to the ballparks. He was sick on much of the Japanese tour with swollen gums and his usual stomach distress. But he hit nearly .400 with eight home runs in nine exhibition games, and on being unanimously voted the tour's MVP by the Japanese sportswriters, he was awarded a brand-new Datsun Bluebird.

After a victory over the Tokyo Giants, Willie caught the final fly ball, then wheeled and fired it into the stands; the Japanese fans, new to the gesture, nearly went berserk. It was front-page news in several Japanese papers.

There was another, even more satisfying moment for Willie that year. It came during the All-Star Game. Mickey had always been indifferent toward All-Star Games, partly because he'd played in so many World Series that All-Star Games seemed anticlimactic, and partly, perhaps, because of the pregame parties and his drinking bouts with pals from both leagues. It was no secret that on the day of the game Mantle was invariably hungover and sleep-deprived, often having come back to his hotel room just before daylight.

Willie, of course, was Mr. All-Star, eventual holder of nearly every All-Star Game record. Mantle was proud that in 1956, at Washington's Griffith Stadium, he and Willie had both hit home runs off the other league's left-hander, Mickey off Warren Spahn and Willie off, of course, Whitey Ford. Outside of that, Mickey had little to show for his yearly trips to the midseason classic.

On July 11, 1960, in Kansas City, in the first of two All-Star Games,* Mays went 3-for-4 with a triple in the first inning, a single in

---

* From 1959 to 1962, to raise money for the players' pension fund, two All-Star Games were played.

the second, and a double in the fourth. In the sixth inning, he missed by inches pulling off the most spectacular feat in All-Star Game history when he hit a long drive to center field that Harvey Kuenn leapt to the top of the wall to haul in.

Two days later, back in New York at Yankee Stadium for the second All-Star Game, Willie Mays took the field to an adoring crowd: "Every time Willie came up to bat," one writer phrased it, "the place went wild as if the 38,362 spectators were all former Giants and Dodgers fans."[6] Mantle, by his own admission, came hungover, sore-kneed, and thinking about the iced beer waiting in the locker room. Dodgers manager Walter Alston had Willie lead off; he blooped a single to center field that Mantle fielded lazily, on one hop — Mickey was not about to make a diving attempt at a ball in a game that did not count in the standings. After rounding first and faking a stop, Mays shifted into the next gear and slid into second without a play, well ahead of the throw from the embarrassed Mickey. It provided just one more reason for New York fans to cheer Mays and boo Mantle.

In the third inning, with nobody on, Ford tried to snap a curveball over the outside corner. Willie sent it into the left-field bleachers. In the sixth, Willie singled and stole second. When the day was over, Willie had three hits, Mickey had none, and the NL had breezed to an easy 6–0 win.

Willie, though, had no thought of showing Mickey up; clearly his focus, revealed in his postgame comments, was on the New York fans. He always wanted to do well in New York, he told reporters, since "this is where I started to play ball, and I have friends here. The fans here understand the game, and when you're in a slump they go along with you. This is the best place to play ball."[7] There was no other way to read what he said: he had friends in New York, not in San Francisco; the fans out west did not understand the game so well as those in New York and were too willing to get on him when he was in a slump. New York, not San Francisco, was the best place to play ball. Mays's remarks, of course, were picked up in the Bay Area papers.

Two days later, the season resumed at Candlestick Park against the defending champion Dodgers. When Mays came to bat in the first inning, he was roundly booed by the home crowd.

In October 1983, *Us* magazine sent me to Buffalo, New York, to interview O. J. Simpson, who was then sharing the broadcast booth for *Monday Night Football* with another former Southern Cal running back, Frank Gifford.* After a Jets victory over the Bills, I got together with Simpson at a nearby hotel. He was in good spirits, getting good money and great exposure from the *Monday Night* gig, and he had also recently become engaged to model Nicole Brown.

He told me about his years as a juvenile delinquent growing up in San Francisco. He was a member of a youth gang, the Persian Warriors, and when he was fourteen spent a weekend in juvenile hall for being involved in a liquor store robbery. After he got home, he told me, "I was in my room, staring at the ceiling, when I heard some people talking downstairs. I first thought my father was going to show up and whup me — that's about the only time I saw him, when I got into trouble."

Simpson's mother called for him to come downstairs, and who should he find in his living room but — Willie Mays. Willie was friendly with a man named Lefty Gordon, a youth counselor at the Booker T. Washington Community Service Center in western San Francisco. He was happy to give some time helping a youth whom Gordon regarded as both troubled and promising. Mays put in more than a few minutes.

"I was expecting a lecture," Simpson said, "but instead he asked me if I wanted to spend the day with him. So we drove around." The two got into Willie's car and ran some errands. Together for about two hours, they "just talked about things like baseball, football, what kind of car he owned. Stuff like that." Simpson, a freshman, had just begun playing high school football, and he told Mays he was thinking about going to college in Utah. Willie advised him to go to Los Angeles —

---

* My profile of Simpson ran in the magazine's February 1984 issue.

UCLA or Southern Cal — where he'd be closer to his mother and get more media exposure.

"Man," I said, "that must have been exciting. Were you thinking back then that someday you could be as famous as Willie?"

"Naw, mostly, when we were sitting in the car, I was thinking, 'Man, this is really Willie Mays. I bet I could take him.' "

It was Willie Mays's destiny to dominate All-Star Games, but Mickey Mantle's to star in the World Series. The 1960 Series with the Pittsburgh Pirates was Mantle's greatest, although it would end with Mickey weeping in the visitors' locker room at Forbes Field only twenty minutes after Bill Mazeroski's home run sailed over the ivy-covered left-field wall.

Mickey's most memorable moments of the series came in Game 2. He had gone 0-for-3 in the opener in Pittsburgh, striking out his last two at-bats as the Yankees dropped Game 1. He then struck out in his first time at the plate in Game 2 — three consecutive whiffs in the World Series. It was not a good omen, but as the Pirates' left-hander Fred Green discovered in the fifth inning, an omen was only as good as the next pitch. Green threw Mantle a sharp breaking ball — a good pitch, as both men later acknowledged — and Mickey slammed it about 420 feet to the opposite field. In the sixth, he struck out again. Then, against reliever Joe Gibbon, Mantle hit a fastball over the center-field fence, where the ball landed at a spot that had never been reached by a right-handed hitter, 440 feet from home plate. He would finish the Series hitting .400 with 10 hits, 11 RBIs, and 8 runs scored.

The 1960 World Series is inevitably recalled by Yankee fans and former players as one they should have won. In truth, there wasn't that much difference between the two teams: the Yankees had won 97 games during the regular season, the Pirates 95. It's true that the Yankees led both leagues, easily, in home runs, with 193, 70 more than the Pirates. (With 170, the Milwaukee Braves, with Henry Aaron and Eddie Mathews leading the way, was the only other team in the big leagues with more than 150.) But New York and Pittsburgh had remarkably similar numbers in other areas. The Yankees led the AL with 746 runs, just 12 more than the Pirates, and posted a 3.52 ERA to the Pirates' 3.50. The truth is that Pittsburgh had no reason to fear New York: from 1959 through the end of the 1960 regular season, the Pirates had won just three fewer games.

Casey Stengel, after winning seven World Series with the Yankees, would be forever blamed by the New York press and Yankee fans for losing his last one. He had held Whitey Ford back from the first game at Forbes Field to pitch the third game at Yankee Stadium, which gave Ford just two starts in the seven games instead of three — if he had started Game 1, he would also have started Game 7. It is often forgotten that Stengel's most trusted coaches — Ed Lopat, Frank Crosetti, and Ralph Houk — also thought that starting a left-hander at Yankee Stadium instead of Forbes Field was a sound strategy.

It's also forgotten that up to then, good as Whitey had been in World Series play, he was just 5–4 in nine World Series decisions and had not won a World Series game in three years. His reputation for invincibility was to come in the 1960 and 1961 Series, in which he pitched thirty-two consecutive scoreless innings to break Babe Ruth's record of twenty-nine and two-thirds. Casey's choice of Art Ditmar to start the Series, in the hindsight of history, seems ridiculous. But in 1960 Ditmar had finished 15–9 with an ERA of 3.06 to Ford's 12–9, 3.08. (Ditmar had also topped Ford the previous year with a 2.90 ERA to Ford's 3.04.)

The Yankees out-hit Pittsburgh in the seven games by a whopping 82 points and outscored them by a ridiculous 55–27. But as any real baseball fan knows — and New York fans certainly should have known, as they saw the most World Series — how many runs a team wins by means nothing in baseball. The three games the Yankees won — Games 2, 3, and 6 — they won by a total of 38 runs. But that was in large part because Pittsburgh manager Danny Murtaugh quickly conceded the contests once the Yankees pulled ahead, refusing to commit his best relief pitchers. Yogi Berra, who had never been known to publicly denigrate an opponent, was the most openly bitter.

"We were the better team. That dirty, lousy infield beat us," he said, referring to a would-be double-play ball that took a terrible hop and struck shortstop Tony Kubek in the throat in the seventh game. Yogi went on: "What an excuse for a major league ballpark. We didn't lose this one, it was taken away from us."

But the truth is that the only real point of superiority for the Yankees was Mickey Mantle. Mays, who was at the second game in New York as a spectator, would recall Mickey's performance with awe eight years later in *Esquire:* "He didn't just beat pitchers, he broke their hearts. He hit two home runs off Fred Green in the 1960 World Series" — actually, the second home run was hit off Joe Gibbon — "and somehow Green was never that good a pitcher again."[8] Nor Gibbon.

Both Willie and Mickey went into the 1961 season with new managers. The Giants finally replaced the ineffectual Bill Rigney with Alvin Dark, who had been the shortstop and team captain on the 1951 National League and 1954 World Series–winning Giants teams. (Dark had been born in Comanche, Oklahoma, about 290 miles from Commerce; Mickey played a couple of games there in his teens.) From 1961 through the rest of Willie's career, his managers would pretty much be defined by one characteristic: their ability to get along with Willie Mays. Good or bad, all of Mays's managers after Durocher had, as far as Mays was concerned, one drawback — they weren't Leo.

Mickey, too, caught a break. His relationship with Casey Stengel had never quite lost its abrasive edge. Mantle never complained about it publicly, partly because he knew Stengel, however wrongheaded he was, wanted Mickey to be a winner, and also in large part because Stengel helped Mantle *be* a winner: their ten-year collaboration had produced seven pennants and five World Series rings. But the new manager, Ralph Houk, had no intention of molding Mickey into anything and saw him, at age twenty-nine, as the de facto team captain.

ⓓ ⓓ

In 1961 Mays mastered the capricious winds of Candlestick Park, wowing the fans with terrific catches on bloop flies that would have been routine in other ballparks but were adventures in San Francisco. He also hit 21 of his 40 home runs there. According to *Total Baseball*, he was the second-best all-around player in the National League, slightly behind Henry Aaron; Bill James's Win Shares also has Aaron as the best by a slight margin.

Nineteen days into the 1961 season, on April 30, Mays did something that Babe Ruth, Ted Williams, Joe DiMaggio, and Mickey Mantle never did. Not only did he hit four home runs in one game — two off the Braves' ace right-hander Lew Burdette — but he hit four home runs, *all of which traveled more than 400 feet.*

All season long, Willie would be locked in a home run race with his teammate Orlando Cepeda, who would end up leading the league in both home runs (46) and RBIs (142). But in 1961 they were not the home run hitters the country was fixated on.

Orlando Cepeda and Roger Maris took some of the spotlight off Mays and Mantle. In both cases, it's difficult for a fan looking back in time to understand how this was possible, since clearly Mickey and Willie were the superior ballplayers. For Mays, the feeling was particularly strange, as he had never in his professional career, beginning with the Birmingham Black Barons, been the subject of anything but the whole spotlight and total adoration. Nor, in truth, had he ever been worthy of anything less. His performance hadn't slacked off when the Giants moved west; on the contrary, he had averaged over .325 for the three seasons he had played in San Francisco, slightly better than he had averaged over his four full seasons in New York. There was no answer as to why he was booed except that the fans resented him, either because New York still clung to him or because, as he said, he wasn't Joe DiMaggio. Or maybe it was both.

For Willie, 1961 seemed to mark a turning point. The Giants still were not pennant contenders — finishing third, eight games in back of the Cincinnati Reds — but the boos slackened considerably after his four-home-run game against Milwaukee. Many even began to cheer him as loudly as they cheered Cepeda.

Roger Maris's impact on Mantle's image was different. At first Maris was seen as a savior, which, in a way, he was, having appeared at precisely the right time, 1960, when it looked as if the Yankees were falling from power. Things quickly changed. Though Maris had a reputation for being polite and cooperative with writers in Cleveland and Kansas City, he became sullen and uncommunicative as he and Mantle began their race for Ruth's home run record. Like many players before and after him who were thrust into the spotlight, he did not enjoy the experience and failed to express joy at the adulation Yankee fans were heaping on him. The sports press in New York tried to manufacture first a rivalry, then animosity between Maris and Mantle, when in fact Mickey not only liked and admired Roger but was grateful that someone had stepped up and taken some of the attention off him. They even shared an apartment, along with reserve outfielder Bob Cerv, in Queens, close to Kennedy Airport. "Between games," Mickey told Herb Gluck, "we'd hang around and read, relax, listen to country music. Sometimes we'd go out to eat in a nearby restaurant, and we talked about the home run duel quite often."[9]

Outside of the record's symbolic value as a measure of excellence, Mantle had no particular ambition to surpass the Babe, and Maris even less so. But as the season went on and the pair appeared together in *Life* magazine and on every TV variety show from *Ed Sullivan* to *Perry Como*, the record was all anyone wanted to talk about. Many Yankee fans who had booed Mickey for years forgot why and wanted a longtime Yankee to break the record; they redirected their hostility toward Maris.

By no means, though, did all of them forget to boo Mantle. Twenty-one years later, a tired, haggard Mickey sat in the Echelon Mall in southern New Jersey and told me, "I can still remember some of them sons-of-bitches — please don't repeat that when you write this — who booed me. I can still remember where they sat and what they looked like. I swear to God, it was ten or eleven years since that draft board thing and some of them were still screaming 'Draft dodger!' at me."[10]

Willie's memories of this time are a little less reliable. He told this story to Bob Costas in 2010:

"Before the first game of the 1962 World Series, Mickey [Mantle] and Whitey [Ford] came out early to San Francisco to play some golf. They played at the Tony Olympic Country Club and ran up a tab of about $5,000. They didn't have the cash, so they signed Horace Stoneham's name. When Mr. Stoneham found out, he told Whitey he'd forgive the debt if Ford could strike me out just once. You have to remember, I did pretty good off Whitey. I hit a home run off him in the 1956 All-Star Game. I used to kill Whitey all the time.

"I got three more hits off Whitey in my first three times at-bat. The fourth time, I got behind on the count. Ford threw a nasty spitter that dropped like a stone, and I struck out. I looked out to center field and saw Mickey jumping up and down and clapping. I turned to Elston Howard behind the plate and asked, 'Elston, what is wrong with that fool out there?' Elston just shrugged and said, 'I can't tell you now, but I'll tell you later.' "[11]

Something very much like this did happen, but it wasn't 1962, it was 1961, and it was the All-Star Game, not the World Series. It was also during Willie's first at-bat, not the fourth. It also didn't involve a sum anywhere near $5,000.

In Mantle and Ford's 1977 book with Joe Durso, *Mickey and Whitey: An Autobiography of the Yankee Years*, Whitey Ford recalled the real story. "They played the [All-Star] game on Tuesdays," Ford told Durso, "and we got there on Monday, so Mickey and I headed right for the golf course. It was the place where the owner of the San Francisco Giants, Horace Stoneham, was a member, and we played with his son, Peter. But we didn't have any equipment with us, no golf shoes or sweaters or anything. So Pete Stoneham said: 'Just sign my father's name . . . ' and so we signed."

At a party that night given by Toots Shor, Ford went over to Horace Stoneham to pay back the $200 tab that he and Mantle had run up. Stoneham had another idea. According to Ford, he said, " 'Look, I'll make a deal with you. If you happen to get into the game tomorrow and you get to pitch to Willie Mays, and you get him out, we'll call it even. But if he gets a hit off you, we'll double it. You owe me $400 — okay?'

"So I went over to Mickey and told him what Horace said, but Mickey wouldn't go for it. No way. He knew that Mays was like 9 for 12 off me lifetime, and he didn't have any reason to think I was going to start getting Willie out now, especially in his own ball park. But I talked Mickey into it, since we had a chance to get out of it without paying Horace anything. Now all I had to do was get Willie out."

As it turned out, Ford was scheduled to start for the American League. Ford got the first two hitters and then Roberto Clemente doubled. Mays, in the cleanup spot, came to bat.

"Well, I got two strikes on him somehow, and now the money's on the line because I might not get to throw to him again.

"So I did the only smart thing possible under the circumstances: I loaded up the ball real good. I threw Willie the biggest spitball you ever saw . . . so I struck out Willie Mays. It was a money pitch, and we just saved ourselves four hundred dollars."

Mays was quoted in Ford's book: "At the time, I didn't know what was happening out there. I knew about Whitey's curve ball and his slider, but I didn't know he had a drop, too. I saw Mantle come in clapping his hands and acting sort of strange, and I couldn't believe it was only because they got me out in an All-Star Game.

"Later, Mickey and Whitey told me about it and why they loaded one up on me. Did they apologize for it? You must be kidding."[12]

It didn't occur to Mickey until he got back to the dugout that he might have offended Willie. "It didn't dawn on me right away," he recalled in one of his several memoirs, *All My Octobers*, "how it must have looked to Willie and the crowd. It looked as if I was all tickled about Mays striking out because of our big rivalry, and in the dugout, when Whitey mentioned my reaction, I slapped my forehead and sputtered, 'Aw, no . . . I didn't. How could I . . . What a dumb thing. Anyway, we kept our money and later Whitey told Mays why I was acting like an idiot and he just laughed."[13]

As every Yankee fan knows, Mickey Mantle finished the 1961 season in a hospital bed, cheering for Roger Maris when he finally hit the monumental 61st home run in the last game of the season. Mickey made it to the World Series, but just barely.*

Jim Murray, the great Los Angeles–based sportswriter, would write a couple of years later, "I remember Mantle clearest in the World Series of 1961. He could barely stand. A strange infection in his hip had not responded to penicillin and had been cut out. He had a silver dollar hole in his hip. In batting practice he hit five balls out of the lot, two off the scoreboard and one off the left fielder's belt buckle, and the man, presumably a National League rooter, climbed up the Crosley Field tower and got ready to jump."[14]

The next day, wrote Murray, "he hit one off the centerfield fence but barely made first base, like a guy crawling with an arrow in his back. 'Look at his pants!' someone cried. They were covered with blood. He was hemorrhaging."[15]

Mickey enjoyed the season, especially the change in attitude from Stengel to Houk. "I was the designated team leader," he would later tell Mickey Herskowitz, "and he showed his confidence in me by telling not only the players, but the writers. He wanted people to know that this wasn't some kind of symbolic role, where I would take the lineup card to the umpires . . . he made me a better player and

---

* Mantle, like many celebrities of the time, including Marilyn Monroe, John F. Kennedy, and even the Yankees announcer, Mel Allen, was a victim of the crank physician Max Jacobson, aka Dr. X, aka Dr. Feelgood. After the Series, Mantle told Herb Gluck, "Dr. Max sent me a bill. I never paid it. I wanted to see him, [but] a few years later he stopped practicing" (Mantle and Gluck, *The Mick*, p. 196).

perhaps a better person. When I was bothered by an injury or playing poorly, I tended to be withdrawn. Some of this was just self-protection. But you can't lead a team by sulking."[16] He led his team in the World Series with simple inspiration. The Yanks crushed the NL champion Cincinnati Reds (with their MVP Frank Robinson) in five games, even though Mickey was able to bat just six times and got just one hit.

The 1961 season was Mickey Mantle's third best in the major leagues, behind 1956 and 1957. He hit a career-high 54 home runs in just 514 at-bats, *30 of them on the road.* He batted .317, drove in 128 runs, and led the major leagues in slugging percentage at .687. His secondary statistics were also amazing. He stole 12 of 13 bases and hit into just two double plays all season. Maris was again named MVP, but for the second straight season there was no doubt even in the minds of many who voted for Roger that Mickey was by far the superior ballplayer. As Dick Schaap later said, "When a guy breaks a major record like that, as Maris did in 1961, it's a major snub if you don't give him the MVP award. It just wasn't done back then." Mays would find that out the next season when he lost the MVP vote to Maury Wills. But in 1961 Mickey Mantle was better than Roger Maris, Willie Mays, or any other player in baseball by a wide margin.*

Charlie Einstein would later recall that in the winter of 1962, "we were all waiting for the bad news about Willie's marriage."[17] Mays had left Marghuerite in San Francisco and was temporarily unavailable to the press; back in the Bay Area, she guardedly told reporters that there were "frictions" between them. She would not say if they were planning to legally separate. She also claimed, "I don't know where Willie is."

Though the press didn't know it, Willie was home with friends

---

*There will always be some debate as to how much Maris and Mantle's home run race in 1961 had to do with expansion and so-called watered-down pitching. But it should be noted that the AL's batting average in 1961 was .256, exactly what it had been the previous year, and that the league ERA of 4.03 was up only a fraction from the 3.88 of the season before.

and family in Birmingham, which was where Willie went over the winter to wait for spring training. He did not bother to inform Cat, who was living alone back in the Bay Area, and in fact Willie was out of touch with nearly everyone but a few old friends in Alabama. In 1962 the mainstream press still had a great deal of difficulty tracking down a black celebrity, who could easily withdraw into his own culture and almost disappear from public view. At least for a while.

Sometime before he reported to the Giants camp in Phoenix, Willie was back in touch with Marghuerite, who traveled to Arizona to meet him, bringing their adopted son Michael with her. Before he left Birmingham, Willie gave an interview to *The Sporting News* and was asked if he thought the "frictions" Marghuerite spoke of might have been caused by her extravagant spending. Willie replied that all wives overspent, "but in my case it's been my own fault. I would say I'm just growing up.

"I've always been the type of guy who would say fine whenever she said she wanted something, I was making money. It would come easy and go easy." On arriving in Phoenix, Willie uncharacteristically lambasted the press for fostering rumors of an impending divorce and insisted he had left San Francisco only because members of Marghuerite's family were living at his house. (There may have been some truth to this, as Marghuerite's sister had been living with them for a while.)

Little more was said about the matter until July 10, when Marghuerite filed suit for a separation in Superior Court in San Francisco. She wanted a hefty $3,500 a month to support herself — which did include support for their adopted son — and nearly $19,000 in lawyer's fees and other expenses. The suit specified that Mays "ignored her presence in the home and has spent almost all his evenings away from home." In that, at least, Marghuerite Mays and Merlyn Mantle had similar complaints.

From the early 1950s through the early 1970s, *Sport* magazine set a new standard for sports journalism that hasn't been approached since, My father started buying me the monthly magazine when I was ten, and for the next six or seven years *Sport* and Norman Mailer formed the bulk of my serious reading. *Sports Illustrated* was great, but *SI*, in an era when you couldn't see all the highlights every night, was read for news; *Sport* was for reflection. The writers and editors included Dick Schaap, Roger Kahn, W. C. Heinz, Ed Linn, Charles Einstein, Dick Young, Ed Fitzgerald, Frank Graham Jr., Arnold Hano, Ray Robinson, Al Silverman, Paul Hemphill, and even, in the early '70s, a dynamic young writer named James Toback, who would make his mark within a few years as a screenwriter and film director. *Sport* was more than just great writing: the color covers and portraits by the great Ozzie Sweet were the most beautiful ever to appear in a national magazine.

From 1951 through Mays's retirement in 1973, Mantle and Mays appeared on the cover of *Sport* twenty-six times, more than any other athletes. For nearly fifteen years, it just didn't seem to be spring unless Mickey and Willie were on the cover of *Sport*. In 1962, *Sport* did something unprecedented: it devoted an entire issue to just two play-ers. Looking back on it today, that special issue still provides a cutaway view of Mantle and Mays and their impact on baseball and American culture early in 1962.

One article, "The Fans' Favorite," attempted to settle the issue of who was better, Mantle or Mays, through "a worldwide election." The article had been inspired by a young fan and reader of *Sport* from Pittsburgh named Bill Hoebler who wrote to editor Al Silverman and asked, "Why not put an end to the Mantle-Mays feud once and for all with a nationwide election? It is only right that the fans should determine who is the best player — Mays or Mantle." The voting ended on June 20, 1961, with Hoebler receiving seventeen pounds of postcards from all fifty states, the Caribbean, the Bahamas, Ger-many (presumably from U.S. servicemen stationed there), Canada, and South America.

To my shock at the time, Mickey won by more than 500 votes. I realize now that that point in 1961, with Mantle and Maris pursuing

Ruth's home run record and Willie still playing second fiddle in the hearts of Giants fans to Orlando Cepeda, was probably the only time in their careers when Mickey could have won a popularity contest with Willie.

More important from a historian's point of view was the article accompanying the results of the contest, which asked and attempted to answer the question: "Who's the Best?" Though there was no author attribution, the text on Mays was written by Arnold Hano and the Mickey chapters by Dick Schaap, whose Mays and Mantle biographies in the *Sport* library were excerpted elsewhere in the magazine. Editor Al Silverman wrote the introduction to the "Who's the Best?" article: "The baseball skills of Mickey and Willie are well-rounded and superlative. Each can hit for power and for average. Each fields with game-saving skill. Each can inspire a team. Each can beat you on the bases. Each, since coming to the big leagues in 1951, has been called the best ballplayer in the game.

"Who's better? Since 1951 the question has been argued long and loud in dugouts, clubhouses, newspapers, and magazines. Since 1951 the winner most often has been . . .

"Willie Mays.

"Mays remains the choice today. For the same reason he has been picked so often through the years. He can do more things better. It is possible, some people say, that no player in baseball has ever been able to do so many things, so well."

The article cited a study that the Los Angeles Dodgers commissioned in 1960 to determine the worth of ballplayers. Al Campanis, then the Dodgers' chief scout (here called "Alex"), told *Sport*, "Of all the players we rated, Mays is the only one judged to have a perfect score on every count. I know this. The Dodgers would be willing to pay $1,000,000 for Mays right now." The issue of whether Mays should have been paid a chunk of that million dollars was not raised; this was sixteen years before free agency came to baseball.

The article was quick to add that "from the point of view of a team, a reason, a major reason, for not considering Mantle worth

$1,000,000 is his history of injury. Mickey's physical future is insecure. Mays, off his past, looms as a good risk physically."

The story quoted everyone from Mickey's and Willie's managers — Casey for once put in a rare plug for Mickey ("Mickey Mantle's the fastest-running home run hitter I ever saw") — to players and former players (Hank Greenberg thought that "on sheer ability, it has to be Mickey," but to Braves catcher Del Crandall, "if there's anything like a complete ballplayer, Willie is it").

The piece concluded that Willie was "the best ballplayer in the game," with Mickey close behind. For nearly forty years I accepted that verdict as gospel.

"Mays and I were friends," Mantle recalled to Mickey Herskowitz, "from our New York days in spite of all the talk of a heated rivalry. Our rivalry was on the golf course, where we hustled each other whenever we got the chance. I wanted to beat Willie, but I would never embarrass him, and I didn't like it when someone else did."[18] Mantle, like others observing the San Francisco situation from a distance, could not understand the refusal of Bay Area fans to embrace Willie Mays.

But in 1962 something magical happened. For the first time, both Mickey Mantle and Willie Mays were cheered almost without reservation by their hometown crowds. By their managers too: both Alvin Dark and Ralph Honk made Willie and Mickey de facto team captains, though they didn't put it in those words.

The pennant races fired fan loyalty and enthusiasm. The Yankees had a terrific team and finally, with their typical late-season surge, pulled away from the Minnesota Twins, winning 96 games and taking the pennant by five games. There was no mystery to the Yankees' success: though this wasn't the '61 team, which won 109 games, they still led the AL in runs scored — with 10 fewer than the '61 team, which they would have made up easily had Mantle not missed so many games — and finished second in ERA at 3.70, just a tiny fraction behind the Baltimore Orioles.

The Giants had even more power than the Yankees: they also led their league in runs scored and scored 61 more runs than the Bronx Bombers. The pitching wasn't overwhelming — the team ERA of 3.80 was good for sixth best in the league. But the rotation had some terrific starters, most notably Jack Sanford (24–7), Billy Pierce (16–6), and a flamboyant, high-kicking young right-hander who had burst into stardom that season with an 18–11 record, Juan Marichal. Perhaps what won San Francisco fans over was the thrill of their first real pennant race, and it was a classic. The Giants had to pick up four games with only seven remaining just to tie the Dodgers — an even tighter squeeze than in 1951, when the New York Giants had tied the Brooklyn Dodgers on the final day of the season.

In the final game, the Giants, facing the expansion Houston Colts, were tied in the eighth inning. Houston's best pitcher, fast-baller Dick Farrell, tried to blaze one by Mays, who rocketed the ball fifteen rows back into the left-field seats. The Giants won, 2–1. A delirious crowd in Candlestick Park remained in the stands until they found out that the Cardinals had beaten the Dodgers down the road in Chavez Ravine, resulting in a tie for the pennant. Just as in 1951, there would be a best-of-three playoff to determine who moved on to the World Series.

The dirty secret of the Giants' season, one seldom mentioned to this day, was that, as good as they were — and they won 103 games, seven more than the Yankees — they probably won the pennant because of Sandy Koufax's middle finger. The Dodgers' Koufax was 14–5 before being afflicted by a blood clot, and though he tried to pitch again, it was a disaster. In the first game of the playoff, Mays smashed a two-run homer off him in the first inning, and the Giants were off to a rout.

Los Angeles overcame a big Giant lead to take Game 2. During the third, which will forever be emblazoned in the memory of every Giants fan, the Dodgers went into the ninth inning with a 4–2 lead. With the bases loaded and one out, Willie came to bat against Ed Roebuck, who had won ten of eleven games that season. "I wanted to be up," Willie would remember. "This is something I had been waiting for . . . how long? . . . eleven years. I wanted it to be on my shoulders. No scared rookie now."[19] Mays was referring to being in the on-deck circle when Bobby Thomson hit his "shot heard round the world" in 1951.

Mays slashed Roebuck's first pitch back near the pitcher's ankles; the ball was hit so hard that it tore Roebuck's glove off. That made it 4–3, bases still loaded. The Giants went on to score three more runs. Al Dark called on Billy Pierce to pitch the ninth inning. With two outs and no one on, pinch-hitter Lee Walls hit a soft fly to Mays. Willie had started the inning thinking that if he made the final out, he would hand the ball to Billy as a memento. In the excitement of the moment, he forgot his promise and turned, wheeled, and fired the ball into the right-field seats. Later he went into the Dodgers' locker room to seek out one of their coaches, Leo Durocher. After a hug, he noticed that Leo had on the T-shirt he had worn on the day eleven years earlier when Bobby Thomson hit his home run. Leo, smiling, told him, "I guess the magic didn't work this time." "Yeah, it did," said Willie. "The Giants won again."

San Francisco was in a daze at the prospect of the World Series, and all the nation's press could focus on was the prospect of seeing the two best players in the game, Mantle and Mays, on the same ball field. In fact, the Series featured two of the finest and deepest rosters ever to face each other. Besides Mantle, the Yankees had future Hall of Famers Whitey Ford and Yogi Berra, who was nearing the end of a fabulous career; they also had two players who would be touted for the next few decades by many as Hall of Famers — Roger Maris (whose 33 home runs in 1962 would have been more than satisfactory for any player who hadn't hit 61 the year before) and catcher Elston Howard (the AL's MVP that year). In addition to Mays, the Giants had Orlando Cepeda, Willie McCovey, and Juan Marichal, who would all be voted into Cooperstown. They also had another future Hall of Famer in pitcher Gaylord Perry, but he figured in only four decisions in 1962. (Unfortunately, they lost Marichal in Game 4 when, after giving up just two hits in four innings, he caught a Whitey Ford fastball on his finger as he tried to hit a sacrifice bunt with two strikes. Had Marichal been available to pitch relief in Game 7, things might have turned out differently.)

The 1962 World Series was still in doubt in Game 7, in the bottom of the ninth with two outs and the winning runs on base. The inning began with the Giants down, 1–0, and Matty Alou beating out a bunt; Yankees starter Ralph Terry then fanned Felipe Alou and Chuck Hiller, both trying desperately and failing to bunt Matty to second. The game — and the World Series — came down to Ralph Terry versus Willie Mays. Terry — perhaps surprised that he was still in the game at that point, as he was the pitcher who had surrendered Bill Mazeroski's Series-ending home run just two years before — was not about to give Willie a pitch he could pull. He might have been better off challenging Mays and inviting him to hit a ball into the strong wind in left field. Instead, Terry missed with two outside pitches, and with a 2–0 count, Mays knew he would now get something to hit. Terry threw a third straight breaking ball, but this one was on the outside corner of the strike zone and Willie lashed it to right field, over the head of first baseman Bill Skowron and into the right-field corner of Candlestick.

Everyone in the ballpark, including players in both dugouts, immediately thought that the game would be tied. They hadn't counted on two things — first, that the rain-soaked grass would slow the ball down before it hit the corner, and second, the speed and efficiency with which Roger Maris would field the ball and fire it back to cutoff man Bobby Richardson. The speedy Alou had a more than decent chance to score, but Giants third-base coach Whitey Lockman held him up.

For the next fifty years, Giants fans would argue about whether Lockman should have let Alou try to score. Mays, who once proudly remarked, "I never had a third-base coach," thought that sending a fast runner in a situation like that forced the team on the field to make *two* good plays — first the throw from the outfield to the cutoff man, then the throw from the cutoff man to home plate. Sending the runner, Mays thought, gave you better odds than betting on the next batter to get a hit — even the most efficient hitters seldom had more than a one-in-three chance of getting a hit in *any* situation, and Alou's chances of scoring, he thought, were better than one-in-three.

At any rate, that left the Giants with Alou the tying run at third and Mays the winning run at second. The tall, powerful, and talented rookie Willie McCovey was up next. Yankees manager Ralph Houk astonished all observers by making two decisions. First, he left Terry in to pitch. Second, he chose not to walk McCovey and pitch to the right-handed Cepeda, who was on deck. Whatever Houk was thinking, on the first pitch McCovey smashed a hard liner about knee-high off the ground. In a split second, every Giant fan envisioned the World Series coming down to Roger Maris trying to throw out Willie Mays, the potential winning run, at home plate. But Bobby Richardson, who scarcely had to move on the play, leaned to his right and speared the ball for the out. Richardson's was not a great play — the ball was practically hit to him — but it was certainly a timely one.

In the clubhouse, a weary Mickey forced a smile. After so many spectacular World Series, he had now earned a ring despite seven games in which he hadn't hit "a damned thing except maybe some rented golf balls."[20] Willie, showered and dressed, made his way into the visitors' clubhouse. Mantle, soaked in champagne and clad only in shorts and a T-shirt, was unwrapping the rolls of tape that had been wound around his legs. Mickey rose as he approached. Willie, unconcerned about what the champagne might do to his suit, accepted Mickey's embrace. "Mickey looked so tired," Charlie Einstein recalled, "that you would have thought that he was in the loser's locker room." Before he left, Willie leaned over and whispered something in Mickey's ear. Mantle guffawed, pointed at Mays, and said, "We gon' see 'bout that." According to Einstein, Willie had told Mickey, "I'll see you on Mr. Stoneham's golf course [that is, Horace Stoneham's country club's course] tomorrow. By this time tomorrow afternoon all that nice World Series money is gonna be in my pocket." Thirty-five years later, I asked Einstein who won their grudge golf match. "Oh, I don't know," he replied. "They were both pretty bad. That is, they both had the talent to be great golfers, but they didn't really give a damn about the game. All they did was bet the same $10 over and over to see who could hit the ball farther."

The Series had not been a showcase for either Mantle or Mays. In May, Mickey, furiously trying to beat out a soft infield grounder, had put on a burst of speed and pulled a right hamstring. He then proceeded to tear two ligaments and some cartilage in his *left* leg. He didn't show up in the lineup again until June, and for a week or so he could do nothing but pinch-hit. He played in terrible pain through the rest of the season and in the World Series was practically useless. Willie, too, seemed flustered; after stroking his usual three hits off Whitey Ford in the opening loss, he simply could not get his rhythm at bat. Until, that is, the ninth inning of the seventh game.

"During the final game, Mickey heard a fan yelling at him from the bleachers, 'I came out here to see which one of you guys was the better centerfielder. But it looks like I have to decide which one is worse.' There was a momentary pause, and then his foghorn voice echoed: 'Hey, Mantle, you win.' "[21] The story gained wide circulation, but it was almost certainly apocryphal, invented by Mickey.

Despite the fact that he, like Mickey, hit no home runs, Willie took a different memory with him from the 1962 World Series: the San Francisco fans had finally warmed up to him. "It only took them five years," he would put it a quarter of a century later.[22] He also had a dream that haunted him for years: "I could still see myself running to third on a triple as the tying run scored, instead of being stuck at second base because the watered-down outfield grass held my hit to a double."[23]

Charlie Einstein had a favorite moment from the 1962 Series that had nothing to do with success or failure. "I have a memory," he wrote in the greatest of all books written about Willie Mays, *Willie's Time*, "of the afternoon of October 5, 1962" — after the Giants' Jack

Sanford had shut out the Yankees, 2–0, in Game 2 — "when I was standing in the hallway that separates the home and visiting teams' dressing rooms at Candlestick Park. . . . That day's game had just ended, and as the players came in from the field, my eye fell on Mays and Mantle as they entered together, immersed in private conversation of the sort two consummate, tired professionals will have at the end of a day's work. There was no sensation that one was black, the other white. The only visible difference between them lay in the tools of their trade: Mays having been in the field when the game ended, had what Mantle did not have — a pair of flip-up sunglasses dipping like a lower lip from the visor of his cap."[24]

Willie was thirty-one. Mickey would be thirty-one in fifteen days. As they walked off the field that day, neither could have had an inkling that an era had ended in more ways than one. Neither man would ever win a championship again; in fact, Mantle would play only one more great season. It would be three more years before Willie finally passed up Mickey in career home runs, but for all intents and purposes, their rivalry was over.

There were other changes in the wind. In 1962 the National League had expanded for the first time, and so Major League Baseball was on the move and would grow until it had teams in every part of the country. In two months, Vince Lombardi's Green Bay Packers would play Allie Sherman's New York Giants for the second consecutive year in the National Football League's championship game; the ratings would supply grist for those who argued that professional football, at least as a TV attraction, was going to bypass baseball. And the next year would bring social and political change with such a violent jolt that it would call into question baseball's — and therefore Mickey's and Willie's — relevance to American culture.

15

"Flash, Dash, and . . . a Nervous Rash"

T he American League and National League Most Valuable Player votes for the 1962 season were among the strangest the game has ever seen. Mickey Mantle, who probably should have won the award for eight straight seasons from 1954 through 1961 if any kind of objective analysis had been used, finished number one, despite having missed thirty-nine games because of injury. Per game and per inning, there was no one in the AL who could begin to challenge him that year. He batted .321, hitting 30 home runs in just 123 games, and led the league in walks with an amazing total of 122 — almost exactly one per game. With 96 runs scored, he just missed notching at least 100 runs for a tenth consecutive season.

He also grounded into only four double plays. As an illustration of how amazing a statistic that is, consider that Willie Mays, who at this point in their careers surely was running faster than Mickey, grounded into nineteen. Mickey led the league with an on-base percentage of .488, second in his career only to the .515 he posted in

1957. He also led the league in slugging percentage at .605. When combined in OPS+ (on-base percentage plus slugging percentage), a favorite stat of twenty-first-century analysts, his average was 1.093, the third highest of his career.

The only argument against Mantle's MVP candidacy was that he hadn't played enough games, but absolutely no one could argue that he wasn't the best when he did play. In any event, many writers now understood that they had shafted Mickey in previous seasons and that given his history of injury, 1962 was probably going to be his last shot at an MVP Award.

Mickey was on the golf course when informed of the MVP vote. If he won one more time, one of the sportswriters told him, his four awards would set a major league record. In that case, he said, he was going to win it in 1963. He was deluding himself.

Over in the National League, Willie Mays's situation was, from a modern analyst's perspective, bizarre. Dodgers' shortstop Maury Wills won the award that year by seven votes, 209–202. Wills's successful pursuit of Ty Cobb's single-season stolen base record, 96, was seen by writers in NL cities as, roughly, the 1962 equivalent of the Maris-Mantle assault on Ruth's home run record the previous year (though, of course, it didn't capture quite so much of the public's imagination).

To understand the logic of many sportswriters of the time, I turned to *Inside Baseball* (a magazine produced by the editors of *Sport*) and the cover story of the April 1963 issue, "Is Wills Really More Valuable Than Mays?" In it, Fred Katz, a *Sport* associate editor, gives weight to "the psychological ways each helped his team." Here Wills pulls in front: "By inspiring his teammates and intimidating the other team, Maury constantly gave the Dodgers the psychological edge when he was on base." Such an argument cannot be disputed, since it is based on nothing but speculation.

Also contributing to psychological impact, Katz continues, is "the nature and effect of slumps. Every power hitter has hit bad days, and Mays was no exception in '62. And when he wasn't hitting, his value to the Giants decreased. Other players either played over their heads or the team suffered. A player like Wills has few slumps because he'll take his hits any way he can get them. And if he can't get them, a walk to a player like Wills is still as good as a hit. . . .

"The battle for the MVP award," Katz concludes, "was to prove as tight as the pennant race. But when the selectors kept in mind the original concept for the award — giving it to the man who contributed the most to his team's overall success — the logical choice had to be Wills. Maury's value to the Dodgers was based on flash, dash and giving opponents a nervous rash, which even Willie didn't do in '62." If this had been a debate, I'd have quickly pointed out that a walk to *any* player, at least in many situations, is "as good as a hit." I'd also have pointed out that slumps or no slumps, Mays not only had the higher batting average, .304 to .299, but considerably more walks than Wills, 78 to 51.

And did Katz and others who voted for Wills really think that opposing pitchers didn't get "a nervous rash" when Willie Mays came up to bat against them? Is that even a valid question to ask when it comes to MVP voting? Such measures are far too subjective to be of any real use. How, in fact, is one to determine how much a player contributes to his team's success except by objective stats? Of course, no one ever doubted that Willie Mays contributed as much as any player in the game to the "intangibles" that helped his team win, and on that basis there is no doubt that Mays's overwhelming edge in statistics should have put him not only ahead of Maury Wills for the 1962 season, but *way* ahead.

No matter how many bases Maury Wills stole, no matter how much of a "psychological edge" someone may have thought he gave his team, in 1962 Willie Mays was by far a greater and more valuable player. Both men scored 130 runs, but Mays drove in 141 to Wills's 48. Willie had 49 home runs to Maury's 6. For all of Wills's considerable skill at stealing bases, his ability to *reach* base was not especially impressive — his on-base percentage was .349 to Mays's .384, and Mays's slugging percentage of .615 was 222 *points higher.*

If Mays hadn't been able to contribute on the bases or in the field, there might have been some room for a Wills partisan to sneak an argument in the side door, but in fact Willie was acknowledged by many to be one of the best base runners in the game, if not the best (and had in fact stolen 18 bases of his own that year), and was a better fielder in center than Wills was at shortstop, leading NL outfielders with 2.80 chances per nine innings, 0.73 above the league average.

Total Baseball's player rankings for the season don't place Wills in the top ten that year. Its Total Player Rating shows that Frank Robinson, not Wills, was right behind Willie as the best player in the league. According to Bill James's Win Shares, Wills was not even the most valuable player *on his own team*; that was Tommy Davis, who hit .346 with 27 home runs.

Whatever their reasons, the baseball writers of Willie Mays's time once again found a reason not to name the best player in the National League the Most Valuable Player. And if I sound a little angry about this, it's because I am. The first year I started to pay attention to baseball in any depth and detail was 1962, and after working through all the numbers with my father, I was shocked — we were both shocked — to pick up the paper a couple of weeks after the season and find out that Willie Mays had been cheated out of the MVP Award he so richly deserved.

Somewhere it ought to be recorded that Willie Mays should have been the NL MVP that year, so I'm making this the place.*

Of all the strange baseball facts one could dig up from 1954 through 1964, this may be the strangest: Willie Mays, who was regarded by nearly everyone as the best all-around player in the game and who was undoubtedly one of the most popular players in the game, was in fact the best player in the game for nine and possibly ten

---

* In the little-seen but amusing 1971 film *The Steagle*, directed by Paul Sylbert, Richard Benjamin plays a New York college professor unnerved by the Cuban Missile Crisis. He delivers a nonsense rant to his class in which he argues the irrationality of Maury Wills winning the 1962 MVP over Willie Mays and then gives a hilarious lecture on the subject in pig Latin. Even in pig Latin, the case for Mays made more sense than the vote for Wills.

of eleven seasons. Yet the baseball writers named him the MVP only once in that span. In contrast, Giants fans in the late 1990s and early 2000s were awed by Barry Bonds's total of seven MVP Awards. But if those who voted for the award had understood the value of statistics in the 1950s and 1960s as they did half a century later, Willie Mays would have won at least *nine*.

W ho was the best in 1962? Mays, no question, if one goes by quantity. He played in every game, battling nervous exhaustion by the end of the season to put the Giants into the World Series, and had a fantastic season. It was probably Mantle, though, if one judged by quality. Willie's combined OPS+ was .999, and Mickey's was 1.093. On the bases, I would give Mickey the slight edge. Even with his bad legs, he stole 9 bases without being thrown out, while Willie was thrown out 4 times stealing 18 bases. And again, there are those double plays—Mickey hitting into only 4 to Willie's 19. But in the field, it was evident that Willie was now covering more ground than Mickey, who was slower than he had been a couple of years before.

Who was the best in 1962? Adding it all up, I'd say it was too close to call.

O ver the winter of 1963, Mickey Mantle had a brainstorm: why not market a product for black and white baseball fans alike? He mentioned the idea to Frank Scott. Scott, at first, was skeptical. As far as he knew, no one had attempted to cross racial lines to plug sport products—or, really, any kind of products. But when he gave it some thought, it occurred to Scott that sports would be the most likely area for a breakthrough. He soon figured: What the hell? Why not give it a try?

And so from a modest beginning, a great tradition was born. In the spring of 1963, a plastic Wiffle ball with both Mantle's and Mays's faces on the package made its appearance in toy stores. It sold so briskly that the manufacturers, Zippee, quickly issued two more related products: a set that included a plastic bat and a Mickey

Mantle–Willie Mays "home run trainer," which consisted of a ball, a bat, and an ingenious device that sent the ball up into striking range. I honed my own deadly long-ball stroke through fantasy competitions between Willie (me batting right-handed) and Mickey (me batting from the other side).

Who was the ultimate victor? Too close to call.

Over the winter, the New York Yankees finally made Mickey Mantle the highest-paid player in baseball. The man who had been the league's best player since 1954 got a salary that put him on a scale with the game's elder statesmen, Ted Williams and Stan Musial: $100,000. But Mickey stayed the highest-paid player in baseball about as long as it took for him to complete a home run trot. Almost before the ink on his contract had dried, Horace Stoneham saw the Yankees' $100,000 and raised it $5,000, making Willie Mays the new highest-paid player in baseball.

Willie would be needing every bit of that raise, and a lot more. Before the season ended, Marghuerite and Willie had told friends they were divorcing. Who initiated the proceedings is unknown and probably irrelevant, since both were in agreement to end the marriage. The proceedings, however, proved to be prolonged, bitter, and costly. "I was lonely too," he would recall, "during those long dreary winter months." For one of the few times in any of his memoirs, he mentioned his adopted son. "Michael was now living in New York with his mother. I could see him only a few times a year. I wanted to have someone with me all the time. I had the sense I was peaking as a player, and now it was time to look for something more out of life. This was the thought always lurking in the back of my mind — the back, but hardly ever in the front." Maybe, he thought, he should have listened to friends who had told him not to marry an older woman.

All these thoughts came to him while he was recuperating in Mount Zion Hospital in San Francisco from nerve and stomach trouble. "I realized I had wasted a lot in the course of my career. I had given away time — maybe by not always being with people I should have been with. And I had also given away too much money. Everything had come quick and easy for me. I had spent money foolishly. I had lent it to people I thought were friends. I had spent too much money on trivial things and never thought about the future."[1]

In Dallas, where Mickey and Merlyn had finally settled their family, Mickey was far from lonely, but in his own way he was as depressed and desperate as Willie. For years now he had been tortured by thoughts of how bad a father and husband he was; he was caught in a spiral of drinking and debauchery that was building a wall between him and his family.

He had come to hate the traveling and regretted the time away from his four boys.

"I missed them," he would recall nearly twenty years after his retirement, "and I'd remember certain days, like the time I took them to the Stadium. They had good seats behind first base and really seemed to be enjoying themselves. Between innings I came back to the clubhouse for one reason or another, just to see how they were doing. During one of the visits, big Pete Sheehy, the equipment manager, drew me aside. He put a finger to his lips. 'Shhh . . . you gotta see this.' We went into the players' lounge. The kids were curled up on a divan, sound asleep. Mickey, Jr., with a ring of strawberry soda pop around his mouth, David holding a half-eaten hot dog, little Danny nestled against Billy's shoulder — just the four of them, sleeping, mustard smeared all over their faces. I'd give anything to have a picture of that day.

"I found it hard to keep such moments in focus."[2]

By 1963, his drinking and nightlife had made it difficult for him to keep almost anything in focus. Early in June, against the Orioles in Baltimore, he leapt up a chain-link fence trying to catch a ball that he probably should have given up on. He fractured his left foot, and at the time it appeared as if he might be finished for the remainder of the season. It can't be proven that Mick's consumption of alcohol or lack of sleep had caused the injury, but at the very least both could have affected his judgment in trying to make the play in the first place. At any rate, the doctors thought he was making progress by late summer and gave him the okay to play.

During another road trip to Baltimore, Mickey and Whitey Ford went on a tear the night before a game. The next day, out at the ballpark, Hank Bauer, retired as a player but coaching for the Orioles, came over to say hello. A moment later, he rushed into the clubhouse and ran back to Mickey on the field. He shoved a bottle of mouthwash into his friend's pocket and told him to use it quickly or it would be obvious to everyone what he had been doing the previous night. Mantle and Ford, who was not scheduled to start that day, sat on the extreme left of the visitors' dugout and tried to sleep it off. In the seventh inning, though, Ralph Houk needed a pinch-hitter and told Mickey to get a bat. Mantle protested that he was still on the DL; Houk informed him that he had been activated that morning. Wearily, Mickey hobbled up to the plate. Ford had some good advice for him: swing at the first pitch. Mantle later said he saw three balls coming at him and decided to swing at the one in the middle. He hit it long and far into the left-field seats. As he rounded third, he saw the Orioles' All-Star third baseman, Brooks Robinson, standing near the bag, hands on his hips, shaking his head and grinning.

Increasingly, though, Mantle's misadventures could not be dismissed with a smile. Soon after Mickey came off the DL, he and Merlyn were having dinner with Yogi Berra and his wife, Carmen. Berra drank, always vodka and always with a built-in limit of three; for Mickey, three was just a warm-up. After dinner, when the Mantles were climbing into their car, Yogi hollered to Merlyn that Mickey should not be driving. Mickey either did not hear what Yogi said or was perhaps a bit indignant at Yogi's paternalism. At any rate, he began to drive faster and faster until Merlyn started screaming for her husband to slow down. Distracted, Mickey took his eyes off the road and then suddenly looked back "to see a telephone pole coming straight at us. We hit it head on; Merlyn went through the windshield; the rear view mirror just creased the top of her skull."[3] They were taken to a nearby hospital, where Merlyn received multiple stitches across her scalp. The Yankees managed to keep news of the incident from reaching the local media.

Mickey and Merlyn's marriage at this point had become like the couple played by Jack Lemmon and Lee Remick in *Days of Wine and Roses*, the Oscar-nominated film released the year before. Both were alcoholics. As one of Mickey's biographers, David Falkner, put it, "The most serious injury Mantle played through during his career was the one he inflicted on himself and others by consuming prodigious amounts of alcohol. No single injury by itself did more to compromise the people he loved, his overall health, his physical condition, and his ability to play the game he cared so much about at the level he expected of himself than his chronic drinking."[4]

So strong was the Yankees' 1963 roster — which included Elston Howard at catcher, a brash, young, high-kicking right-hander, Jim Bouton (who finished 21–7), and an even brasher first baseman from Brooklyn, Joe Pepitone (who hit 27 home runs) — that they survived the loss of Roger Maris for more than 70 games and Mantle for nearly 100 and still walked off with the AL pennant, winning 104 games. Maris hit 23 home runs despite his injuries, while Mickey was probably, judging from the numbers he posted up until his injury at Baltimore, headed for a sensational season before being relegated to the DL.

It might have been an MVP-worthy season. In the 65 games he played, he batted .314 and his on-base percentage of .443 and slugging percentage of .622 gave him an OPS of 1.065, higher than all but 1961, when he hit 54 home runs, and his MVP season of 1957. He had 15 home runs, one for every 11.2 at-bats. Projected over, say, 500 to 540 at-bats, he would have had around 45 home runs, at the least tying Harmon Killebrew for the AL home run title.

In the NL, Willie Mays had exactly the same batting average as Mickey, .314, and played the season without injury or a recurrence of his stomach problems. He finished with 38 home runs, 103 RBIs, a

.384 on-base percentage, and a slugging percentage of .582. The last two marks were considerably lower than Mantle's, but Mays was able to post them over a season in which he played 157 games. Willie, though, was also slowing down a little. He stole just 8 bases that year, his lowest total since 1954. He was still the game's best player, which would be confirmed many years later when *Total Baseball* ranked him ahead of Henry Aaron by a solid margin. And according to Bill James's Win Shares, Willie was once again the most valuable player in his league, well ahead of the eventual winner in the MVP voting, the Dodgers' Sandy Koufax.

But only one Giant improved from 1962 to 1963, Juan Marichal, who blossomed into a superstar, winning twenty-five games. Despite Marichal's great pitching and another stellar season from Willie, the Giants were never really in the race and finished eleven full games behind the Dodgers.

Much of the blame fell on their manager, Alvin Dark, an intense, intelligent, and well-intentioned man who just couldn't seem to overcome the complexities of managing one of the first big league teams to be composed of blocks of black, white, and Latin talent. The press reported all season about divisions in the Giants' clubhouse, and neither Dark nor Mays, for that matter, quite knew what to do about it. "With things going badly," Willie would recall nearly a quarter of a century later, "Dark tried a number of tactics, including clubhouse talks. A lot of them left us shaking our heads. He brought in stuff that just didn't belong in the clubhouse. Who cared if he supported Barry Goldwater? He used to bring religion in, too. One time he said that Jesus was the only man in the history of the world who was perfect. Maybe Dark was searching, reaching out to us, but he didn't convert anyone to his politics or his religion, and, actually, no one took him seriously when he started that kind of talk."

Dark came down particularly hard on one of the team's most popular stars, Orlando Cepeda. During one game he benched Cepeda for what he perceived as lack of hustle and then, in the late innings, called on him to pinch-hit. Chico, as his teammates called him, had been waiting the whole game to vindicate himself and, overanxious, swung at the first pitch and hit the ball back to the pitcher to start a double play. Disgusted at himself, he flung the bat and loped to first base. "That set off Alvin," said Mays. "In the clubhouse after the game, he screamed at Cepeda in front of everybody. I was watching Orlando. I knew that with his temper he might just explode and haul off at Dark." Despite the rivalry that the San Francisco press and fans had constructed between Mays and Cepeda, Willie genuinely liked Orlando and had kept a close watch on him for years. Mays had even headed off a nasty brawl once by tackling Cepeda in a 1958 game against Pittsburgh to prevent him from going after another player. (Onlookers said it was a sensational tackle too, a play in which Mays gave up at least twenty-five pounds to his teammate.)

The 1963 World Series was the fifth time in twelve seasons that the Yankees and Dodgers had faced each other in October. The result was a shocker, with the Yankees swept in four games. In fact, the Series was closer than a sweep would indicate. Game 1 featured the sensational Sandy Koufax, 25–5 with a 1.88 ERA that year, against Whitey Ford, who had perhaps his greatest season at 24–7 with a 2.74 ERA. The match was, in the words of Dodgers announcer Vin Scully, between "a pitcher who *can't* be beaten and a pitcher who *won't* be beaten."

Ford had just one bad inning, the second, in which he gave up four runs. That was all Koufax needed for a 5–2 win. I was there, my heart pounding with every pitch Koufax threw.* Mickey, after all, had won so many World Series rings that I thought it was okay for him to lose just one, and Sandy had fired my imagination. Plus, getting out of school for the day to see the most publicized baseball game of the

---

* My heart beat fast again in 1975 when I saw *One Flew Over the Cuckoo's Nest* and heard Jack Nicholson's R. P. McMurphy doing his fake television commentary — Nurse Ratched wouldn't let the patients watch the game — for a room full of mental patients: "Koufax's curveball is breaking like a fucking firecracker!" he told them. I was there, and he was right.

year was nearly too much to absorb. Koufax struck out fifteen that day, including the first five Yankees, and was everything he had been built up to be.

But it took some luck to ensure the sweep. The Dodgers took Game 2 with relative ease; in Game 3, Don Drysdale outpitched Jim Bouton, just barely, winning 1–0. And in Game 4, the gritty Ford rebounded to outpitch Koufax, giving up just two hits but losing 2–1 when Joe Pepitone lost a throw to first base in a sea of white shirts down the left-field line.

Mickey had a terrible Series, just 2-for-15, though in the seventh inning of the final game he finally caught up to Koufax's fastball and hit a rocket into the left-field seats for the Yankees' only run. It was no consolation.

In 1963 the rules — the size of the strike zone, the height of the mound — all favored pitchers. And Koufax — tall, handsome, and glamorous with a fluid and graceful motion, a Jewish boy from Brooklyn who put movie stars in the premium boxes for Dodgers home games — was the premier figure in baseball, with 11 shutouts, and a no-hitter against the Giants on May 11 (after taking a perfect game into the eighth inning) to add to the one he had thrown the previous season against the Mets. Practically for the first time in ten seasons, Mickey and Willie surrendered headlines and magazine covers to another player.

But it wasn't just another ballplayer that Mickey and Willie were losing headlines to. For the first time another sport was challenging baseball's hegemony as America's national pastime. In 1961, Roger Kahn had prophetically written about the growing popularity of professional football: "There's still plenty of cheering coming from baseball parks all across America, but the big noise is now coming from pro football stadiums. It may be the noise of the future."[5]

In a way, Kahn's point was exaggerated: big league baseball and professional football were never really rivals, as their seasons scarcely overlapped. Compared to baseball, few fans ever went out to the stadium to see their favorite team play in person; enthusiasm for pro football was almost exclusively a relationship between the fans and their TV sets. There was little cultural significance attached to, say, the pursuit of specific records or to the game's history, the way there was with baseball. And in any event, there was no clear division between fans of one sport and the other. In most of the northeastern and midwestern cities, where the NFL first took hold, fans followed the fortunes of their local major league baseball or pro football team seamlessly without bothering to make distinctions about which one they liked best.

But as the fifties came to a close, it became obvious that the names of some pro football stars were becoming common currency in American households the way only baseball players had been before. The most prominent was Baltimore Colts quarterback Johnny Unitas, who led his team to a sudden-death victory over the New York Giants on December 28, 1958, in the first game that captured a massive national TV audience. By 1963, most casual sports fans across the country also recognized Cleveland running back Jim Brown, Green Bay Packers runners Paul Hornung and Jim Taylor, and linebacker Ray Nitschke. Head coach Vince Lombardi had become a more familiar face to most Americans than any major league baseball manager.

There was something else too, something more difficult to pin down. Beginning with the shock of JFK's assassination in November 1963, events in the outside world began to intrude into the lives of Americans in a way that simply could not be assuaged by sports and recreation. In particular, the civil rights movement, which had been smoldering throughout the South during the previous decade and receiving a relative modicum of press coverage, now began to dominate the media. In May 1963, Jackie Robinson and former heavyweight champion Floyd Patterson traveled to Birmingham, Alabama, to support the Rev. Martin Luther King Jr.'s nonviolent protest. Willie Mays, who was in a better position to know Birmingham's history of segregation than any other black athlete, was nowhere to be seen. Of course, the baseball season had begun and Mays was playing every day, but there wasn't even a public statement of solidarity from Willie for what was happening in his own hometown. It would later be argued by his apologists that Mays, who had not had much formal education, felt inadequate beside Robinson, but Mays had considerably more education than former heavyweight boxing champion Floyd Patterson, who had been in and out of reform schools as a boy.

Birmingham commissioner of public safety Eugene "Bull" Connor, who had once called Barons and Black Barons games on the radio when Willie was growing up, turned fire hoses on those who were marching against segregation, and Willie Mays, by now a hero in relatively liberal San Francisco, still had nothing to say. And I, still well into an intense phase of hero worship, had nothing to say about his silence.

Though it wasn't obvious at the time, the process by which Willie Mays would become marginalized, first in black culture and then in American culture as a whole, was now beginning. Mays was still the most famous black athlete in America, the most famous since Joe Louis was at his peak, and Mays was the first great black team sports star. But within a couple of short years, that would come to be seen by many as not enough, as stars like the Boston Celtics' Bill Russell and the Cleveland Browns' Jim Brown began speaking out openly against injustices within their own sports. Then, like a cultural hurricane, Cassius Clay won the heavyweight championship, became Muhammad Ali, and captured the imagination of a whole new generation.

Just how different Willie was from the new breed of black sports hero and how insulated he was from the events that produced them became obvious in 1962, when a young St. Louis Cardinals outfielder named Curt Flood, born in Houston but raised in Oakland, took a deep breath and joined Martin Luther King and Jackie Robinson at the tenth annual meeting of the NAACP in Jackson, Mississippi. Flood had no idea what he was getting himself into, but he had a very good idea of what he wanted to get himself and his children out of. And he refused to live in a world of segregation without protest.

In 1964, after Flood's team had won the World Series and six years after Mays had discovered racism when he tested the Bay Area housing market, Flood tried to buy a house for his family — which included four children and one on the way — in the small town of Alamo, about twenty-eight miles east of San Francisco. When the owner, after accepting Flood's offer, gave in to pressure and tried to back out of the deal, Flood faced a situation almost precisely the same as the one Mays had encountered. But Flood stood his ground, took the man to court, and won. Though he received anonymous death threats, Flood also found unexpectedly strong support from white residents of his new town. He did not receive support from Willie Mays, who knew exactly what Flood had been going through.

By 1964, Stan Musial was retired and Ted Williams had been gone for four years, and so Willie Mays and Mickey Mantle found themselves the elder statesmen of baseball. Mays had been settling into the role for a couple of years. For Mickey, who had always tried to avoid responsibility, it was a new experience.

Young players from every team in the league were fond of passing on stories to reporters about how Mantle would pat them on the shoulder after a game or wander over to the cage during batting practice to offer some words of advice or encouragement. Phil Linz recalled being a rookie with the Yankees in 1962. He hadn't dared to speak a word to his idol, much the way Mickey had been terrified of approaching Joe DiMaggio in 1951. One day after a Yankees victory, he was astonished to turn around and find both Mantle and Whitey Ford asking him out to dinner. "I didn't yet have the courage to even fantasize about something like that," Linz told *Sport*.[6]

In a story that echoed Elston Howard's from nearly a decade before, Jim Bouton recalled breaking in with the Yankees in 1962: "The game I started in the Stadium, I shut out the Senators. After the game, I went on Red Barber's TV show. It lasted about 15 minutes, and then I walked to the clubhouse, opened the door, and there was a row of towels — a white carpet, you know, stretching from the door to my locker. Later I heard the idea was Mickey's. It really made me feel like part of the ball club."⁷ For every story like that, though, there was one about Mantle giving a sportswriter the cold shoulder or ignoring a fan's request for an autograph.

The Yankees began spring training with a burning desire to avenge their humiliating sweep at the hands of the Los Angeles Dodgers, and the players were confident that they'd have the opportunity. Though many did not say so outright, privately, as Clete Boyer would later admit, "we figured we had a better chance to make it back to the Series than the Dodgers did."⁸ Still, there was no denying that the team was getting old — or at least, with Mickey Mantle and Roger Maris constantly hobbled from injuries, the team was *looking* old.

Other Yankees were getting creaky too. Elston Howard had won the MVP Award the year before, but was now thirty-five years old. He had given up what was almost certainly a Hall of Fame career by sticking with the Yankees when he might have demanded a trade to another team, and he lost years of his prime playing backup to Yogi Berra. An exception would seem to have been the team's ace, Whitey Ford, who had flourished under the managing of Ralph Houk. While Stengel had restricted Ford's starts, often using him as a spot starter and occasional reliever, Houk had made him a regular part of the rotation, and Ford had responded by posting a remarkable 66–19 record from 1961 through 1963 and finishing 17–6 in 1964. What wasn't apparent was the strain the regular work had put on Ford's slender frame at that relatively late point in his career.

There was one thing the Yankees definitely did not have going for them in 1964: for the first time since 1947, they would not have Yogi Berra on the roster. To everyone's surprise — including Berra's — the Yankees' owners had bumped Houk up to the front office and given Yogi a shot at managing the team he had helped win fourteen pennants. When asked if he wanted to manage, Yogi's reply was classic: "Manage who?" But Berra had his own unique way of being serious, and if he could get someone to listen, he had an incredible store of baseball knowledge to draw on. Not for nothing had Casey Stengel called him "*Mister* Berra, my *assistant* manager."

For Mickey's part, "I was happy for Yogi, if you think managing a baseball team is a good thing to have happen to you. I don't think you heard the word 'communication' so much in 1963, but some people wondered if Yogi could give orders, if he would be taken seriously. I wasn't worried about his doing the job. He knew the game. He had been calling pitches all his life."[9]

The season would prove to be full of rough patches for both the Yankees and the Giants. Things started promisingly when Dark made Willie Mays the team captain — the first black team captain in baseball. Willie tried hard to cooperate with his manager. Despite the many clumsy remarks Dark had made on the subject of integration, Mays felt a personal loyalty to him for the way Dark had helped him as a fellow player when Mays was a rookie in 1951. Although they had subsequently clashed over the years, Willie felt that "it took a lot of guts on Dark's part to name me captain. I admired his courage for doing it."[10]

Actually, the Giants didn't play all that poorly except near the end, but they just couldn't seem to catch the young and powerful Philadelphia Phillies, who had a sensational rookie, Dick Allen. They had their best chance in the last couple of weeks when the Phillies collapsed, but the Giants faded too, and it was the Cardinals who took over the league lead. The Giants not only didn't finish second, they didn't even finish third — that was the Cincinnati Reds, who, like Philadelphia, won 92 games, just one fewer than St. Louis. The Giants finished a frustrating fourth, the more so because a solid surge at almost any point in the season could have given them the pennant. Incredibly, despite the presence of *five* future Hall of Famers — Mays, Cepeda, McCovey, Marichal (21–8 that season), and Gaylord Perry (who was only 12–11 but had an ERA of 2.73) — the Giants never seemed to be clicking on all cylinders.

When the Giants stumbled near midseason, Dark's treatment of Mays baffled not only sportswriters but Willie himself. During a series against the Mets, he benched Willie for two games. Perhaps Dark had Willie's collapse from exhaustion the previous season in mind and felt that, after all, the Mets were the one team the Giants could beat without him. Willie, thinking about the easy pickings he always got against Mets pitching, was incensed. Nonetheless, he went out of his way to make Dark understand that he was still with him.

In late July, Dark gave a hugely controversial interview to Stan Isaacs of *Newsday*. He would later claim his comments were not reported accurately, but what appeared in print was toxic: "We [the Giants] have trouble because we have so many Spanish-speaking and Negro players on the team. They are just not able to perform up to the white ballplayer when it comes to mental alertness. You can't make most Negro and Spanish players have the pride in their team that you can get from white players. And they just aren't as sharp mentally."[11]

No matter what Dark actually said — though Isaacs was adamant that he had quoted the manager accurately — there was simply no way the comments as they appeared in print could have done anything but anger and divide his players.

After surgery on both knees over the winter, Mantle had one goal for 1964: "I wanted to be healthy for him." That is, for Yogi. "I wanted to have a good year for him. We had been friends and teammates since the first day I met him, in spring training in 1951.* I had a fear that the season might be a rough one and that managing might change him, so I tried not to dwell on such things. What I didn't expect was what a terrific year it would turn out to be, how he would pull the club together and lead us into the World Series, and then get fired."[12]

---

*Actually, Mickey had met Yogi in September 1950 when the Yankees brought him to St. Louis before a game with the Browns to acquaint him with the organization and introduce him to some of the team's officials and players.

There was something else Mickey didn't expect: that this would be his and the Yankees' last hurrah. The Yankees started the season slowly, and injuries did not help. At one point in late spring, the whole starting outfield was on the bench. Roger Maris helped out by playing center field when Mantle could not, which turned out to be frequently. For the first time since his rookie season, Mickey spent extensive time in right field.

No matter how Yogi shuffled the lineup, nothing quite worked. By June, the mayors of Baltimore and Chicago, whose teams were battling for the AL lead, were making public bets of dinners: Baltimore's Theodore McKeldin would get a steak dinner if the Orioles won, and Richard Daley would get a plate of softshell crabs if the White Sox took the flag.

What Mickey did not mention in his memoirs, and possibly did not know, was that in the Yankees' front office Ralph Houk was undermining Berra's authority by letting players come directly to him and air their grievances, no matter how petty. Many of the players thought Yogi had been set up for failure. As Jim Bouton put it, "Why the hell did Ralph Houk leave his door open for people who wanted to complain about Yogi? What kind of GM encourages complaints about his own manager?" Yogi, said Bouton, was a good manager, "but Houk was a bad GM. He made bad baseball decisions, and then he undermined Yogi." Bouton thought Houk's behavior was "indefensible."[13]

Clete Boyer was even more adamant when I interviewed him in 2007 for my biography of Yogi: "That stuff he [Houk] said about Yogi having communication problems with the players was bullshit, and everyone knew it. Who did Yogi have trouble communicating with? Not with me. Not with Ellie Howard . . . not with Mickey or Whitey, who played their hearts out for him. Did Mantle and Ford stay out a few nights when Yogi was manager? Hell, yes, and they did it when Casey was manager, and you know what? They even did it when Houk was manager. . . .

"The truth was that Houk was jealous of Yogi. Houk had been

nothing but a scrub, a backup, for years, and he resented the fact that Yogi was a much greater player and much more popular. And in my opinion, just as good a manager."

Mickey played hard for Yogi, but he could have done a little more — as could have Yogi's longtime battery mate, Whitey Ford. "That club," Mantle would later recall, "would have been a test for anybody. It had such free spirits as [Phil] Linz, [Joe] Pepitone, and Jim Bouton — not to mention Whitey and me. Yogi had named Ford his pitching coach, and we were the team's senior citizens, but what the heck, we still broke a few curfews." Mickey actually took credit for helping Yogi in what seems, in retrospect, to have been an incident that clearly reflected a lack of maturity.

"I'm not trying to brag," he told Mickey Herskowitz in 1994, "but in a way, unintentionally, I might have turned the team around for Yogi." In late August, with the Yankees still trying to gain traction, the team suffered a near-disastrous four consecutive losses to the White Sox, including two in a doubleheader. On the bus ride from Comiskey Park to O'Hare Airport, Phil Linz broke a complete silence by playing "Mary Had a Little Lamb" on a harmonica he had bought the day before. Berra turned and shouted toward the back of the bus for Linz to stop. Linz either didn't hear what Yogi said or pretended not to and turned to Mantle to ask him to repeat it. Mickey, picking the wrong time to be mischievous, told him Yogi said, "If you're gonna play that thing, play it faster." When Linz proceeded to do exactly that, Berra sprinted to the back of the bus and knocked the harmonica out of his hands; it nicked Joe Pepitone on the knee, and Pepitone let out a mock scream of pain. Mantle related, "Soon everybody but Yogi was laughing."

The silliest two minutes in Yankee history dominated the sports pages for days, with the dominant theme being that the players were taking advantage of Yogi. For once, the writers were probably right: the players *had* been taking advantage of their manager, and it was, in no small part, because Mantle and Ford, who knew as much about the Yankee tradition of silent dignity in defeat as anyone, let them do it. They should have been watching Yogi's back instead of acting like schoolboys.

It's true that the team did start to turn around at that point and went on to edge out the Chicago White Sox for the pennant. That they did so was due largely to Berra's refusal to panic, and also to two additions to the pitching staff—a hard-throwing right-hander called up from Richmond in August, Mel Stottlemyre, and Pedro Ramos, a terrific relief pitcher acquired from Cleveland. Ramos was particularly glad to join the Yankees, not just because of the World Series shot the trade brought to him but because he'd been the victim of some of Mantle's most awesome upper-deck home runs.

The 1964 World Series against the St. Louis Cardinals was a classic, featuring the two players who would probably have the most influence on the game for the rest of the century—Jim Bouton, whose 1970 memoir *Ball Four* forever destroyed the last vestiges of innocence that surrounded Mickey Mantle and every other major league ballplayer, and the Cardinals' Curt Flood, who would sue baseball in 1970 for the right to become a free agent. (He would lose the case in the Supreme Court, but his suit paved the way for the binding arbitration that would win free agency for the players by 1976.) It was also a Series that pitted sibling third basemen against each other: the Yankees' Clete Boyer and the Cardinals' Ken, who would be named the NL's MVP that season. It was the first World Series for St. Louis since 1946—the one Mickey had listened to on the radio while lying in a hospital bed in Oklahoma City as doctors worked frantically to save his leg from osteomyelitis.

The Series went the distance. In the seventh game, two exhausted starters, Mel Stottlemyre and Bob Gibson, both faltered. But Gibson held on for a 7–5 victory despite being tagged for three home runs. The third was hit by Mantle, a booming, opposite-field, three-run shot in the sixth inning.

Mickey finished the Series with a .333 average, an OBP of .467, and 3 home runs. His 8 RBIs led both teams. He also had one of his most dramatic World Series moments ever in Game 3 when he hit a home run in the ninth inning to win the game, 2–1. He had had a terrible day in the field, mishandling a hit by Tim McCarver in the fifth inning that led to the Cardinals' only run and nearly misjudging a liner by Curt Flood in the Cardinals' half of the ninth inning, stumbling but recovering just in time to make the out. When he walked up to the plate in the ninth, he passed Elston Howard in the on-deck circle and told him, "You might as well go on in. I'm gonna hit the first pitch I see out of the park." Sure enough, Barney Schultz floated a knuckler at him, and Mickey slammed it into the right-field third deck; a few more feet and it might have cleared Yankee Stadium. "I acted out of frustration," Mantle said later, "not showmanship."

The year 1964 marked the end of Mickey's amazing record of league dominance. He hit .303 with 35 home runs and 111 RBIs and led the American League in OBP at .426, but he was no longer a threat to steal. He was a far cry from the six-season stretch in his prime in which he'd recorded 10 or more steals, 100 in all, and was caught stealing just 14 times, figures remarkable not only for the shape his legs were in but also in light of how seldom the Yankees really needed for him to steal. He had also been reduced to a merely adequate outfielder. For the first time in ten full seasons, dating back to 1954 (and not counting 1963, when he missed nearly a hundred games), Mickey did not finish in the top five in *Total Baseball*'s Total Player Rating. It was also the first time since 1955 (again, not counting 1963) that he failed to finish first. But he led all American League players in Bill James's Win Shares for the ninth time since 1955 (excepting '63). By James's calculations, no player in baseball history — not Honus Wagner or Ty Cobb or Babe Ruth — had tallied such a record in Win Shares.

Mays, like Mantle, drove in 111 runs and led the National League with 47 home runs. He did not regard his season as a particularly good one and was not shy about saying so publicly, because he had failed for the first time in eight years to hit .300, finishing at .296, though he did lead the NL in slugging percentage (.607). He tied with the Cubs'

Ron Santo for first place in Total Player Rating, his ninth time in first in eleven years. Only Honus Wagner, who finished first ten times in eleven years, had a better record in Total Player Rating than Willie.

Two weeks after the season's end, Willie appeared, in full Giants uniform, on the television show *The Hollywood Palace* with host Buddy Ebsen, star of *The Beverly Hillbillies*:

"You look a little glum, Willie," Buddy said.

"Yeah," Willie shrugged. "I didn't hit .300 this year."

"Well," Ebsen said consolingly, "you hit 47 home runs. That ain't hay" (a reference, probably, to Willie's nickname, the Say Hey Kid).

Willie shrugged sheepishly and then proceeded to whack Wiffle balls thrown to him by comedian Jack Carter.

The show's producers had asked Mantle to appear with Mays, but he declined the offer. "He was his league's home run leader this year," said Mickey. "I didn't lead my league." (Harmon Killebrew led the AL with 49.)

"Yeah," Willie said when he heard of Mantle's reply through Frank Scott, "but he's still got more home runs than me for our careers." Mays was correct. Mickey finished the 1964 season with 454, and Willie was one behind at 453. That Willie knew this proved how carefully he had been following Mantle's performance. What Willie did not know, and what Mickey was only beginning to admit to himself, was that Mickey's era was over.

Finally, the friction in the Giants' clubhouse reached Willie himself. In a game against the Cubs at Wrigley Field, the Giants had a six-run lead in the eighth inning. Chicago's slugging third baseman, Ron Santo, slammed a ball into center field that, well, Mays may have given up on. "Who knows?" he would later say. "If the game had been closer I might have chased against the wall, taken a chance. Maybe in the back of my mind I thought about the big lead we had and said to myself, 'Take it easy. Don't get hurt on a ball that can't hurt your team.' And maybe I just didn't hustle after it the way I should have."[14]

And maybe Willie was being too hard on himself: underneath the ivy at Wrigley Field was a brick wall that had shortened and even ended the careers of some fine outfielders.

Anyway, what had been brewing all season finally boiled over: the Cubs went on to tie the game and win in extra innings, and Dark snapped at Willie in the clubhouse — as if his play on the fly ball was the only one that mattered — and Willie, though he thought he should have tried harder for the ball, snapped back. It was the first time in years he had had an open confrontation with his manager.

In a bleak and hopeless September, Willie, playing harder than ever, in a game at Candlestick, came to bat against the Cubs with the bases loaded. He swung viciously at the first pitch and missed, and then dropped to one knee with his head spinning. The game was stopped while Doc Bowman, the Giants' trainer, ran out on the field with smelling salts and then walked him off the field. At the hospital, they told him he was again suffering from exhaustion.

16

The Boys of Summer
in Their Ruin

On April 14, 1965, in the third game of the season at Connie Mack Stadium, Willie Mays lashed into a curveball from future Hall of Famer and senator from Kentucky Jim Bunning and drove it over the center-field wall. The two-run shot, besides helping the Giants beat the Phillies, had a significance that no one appreciated at the time: it was home run number 455 for Mays's career, and it finally put him ahead of Mickey Mantle. It was a lead he would never relinquish.

In fact, though Mays had missed nearly two full seasons in the Army, Mickey had missed so many games through injury that through 1964 he had actually played only 32 more games than Willie. But Willie had, up to that point, 499 more at-bats. Mantle had given up hundreds of plate appearances to bases on balls, leading the American League in walks five times. Mays always had a healthy proportion of walks, but never led the National League. Anyway, Willie still had some superstar left in him, but Mickey, though he had four seasons left to play, was running on empty.

Both Mickey and Willie started the 1965 season under new managers. Herman Franks, who had been a Giants coach and, for a couple of years, Durocher's right-hand man, was given the job. Immediately, he did what all Giants managers of the era were supposed to do: he proclaimed his admiration for Willie Mays.

For Mantle, the loss of Yogi Berra as his manager was near-apocalyptic. In perhaps the most disgraceful episode in Yankees history, his longtime friend and teammate had been undermined throughout the season by GM Ralph Houk — and then, to add insult to injury, he was fired despite successfully guiding the team to Game 7 of the World Series.

The circumstances were similar to what happened to Casey Stengel after the Yankees lost the seventh game of the 1960 World Series: How could the Yankees have gotten rid of Casey if he had won another championship? What, everyone wondered, would the Yankees have done if Whitey Ford's arm had not gone bad, if Jim Bouton had been available to pitch an extra game, if Bobby Richardson hadn't booted a couple of routine chances in the field? With Stengel, of course, there was one other crucial factor — his age. "I made the mistake of turning seventy," he said in his last classic remark before leaving the team. "I'll never make that mistake again."

Yogi, though, was just thirty-nine, and despite the Phil Linz–harmonica silliness — or perhaps, if you believed Mantle and a couple of the other veterans, because of it — he had pulled the team together, won the pennant, and, if not for an extraordinary string of unfortunate incidents, would have won the World Series. To compound the treachery, the Yankees, in a spectacular act of duplicity, offered the job to the manager Yogi had faced in the World Series, Johnny Keane, who had his own problems with the St. Louis front office. As it turned out, Yogi Berra had no idea how lucky he was to be fired by the Yankees at precisely that time.

Mickey, caught in the middle, made no public statements on the matter. It was a situation he could have never envisioned. Yogi had been his pal since he had been a raw rookie, one of the first players on the team to make him feel at home. Essentially he had been the friend and mentor Mickey so much wanted Joe DiMaggio to be. Still, it must have occurred to Mickey around that time that if he had shown a greater quality of leadership, there might never have been the perception that Berra had let the team get out of control. Had Mickey Mantle showed the maturity on the Yankees that Willie Mays had on the Giants, Yogi might have kept his job.

But Mantle's loyalties were divided. Houk had been Mickey's friend too, the man who had publicly announced that Mickey was now the leader of the team. It was Houk who had released him from the pressure of "living up to his potential" that Casey always placed on him, and thanks in part to Houk, Mickey had blossomed, winning two MVP Awards and two more World Series rings.

As the 1965 season started, Mickey Mantle had a great many other things to think about as well. Shortly after the 1964 World Series, the Columbia Broadcasting System purchased 80 percent of the Yankees for the astonishing sum of $11.2 million. No one knows precisely how the deal originated (though William S. Paley, president of CBS, and Yankees owner Dan Topping were old country club pals). Topping and the other previous owner, Del Webb, each retained a 10 percent share in the team. Webb would sell his share in 1965, just before the franchise began its nosedive; Topping divested his soon after in 1966, presumably for less money than Webb got. An unnamed writer in the August 21, 1964, issue of *Time* magazine wrote, "Topping and Webb had already taken tremendous profits since purchasing the club with Larry MacPhail in 1945 for $2.8 million. Two years later, they bought out MacPhail for two million, got that back and more when they sold Yankee Stadium and the land under it for $6.5 million in 1953. All the rest was gravy."

Why did they sell the team to CBS? One reason might have been declining attendance, which in the early 1960s was still the primary source of income for a baseball team. Attendance in 1963, even with the Yankees winning the pennant, was just under 1,309,000, the lowest since World War II. The drop in numbers might have been due in part to the frequent injuries to Mantle and Maris, the star players who most fans wanted to see, but a far bigger reason was the flight of white middle-class fans to the suburbs and the increased time and effort it took to get to the Bronx.

Whatever the reasons, the sale signaled the beginning of the end of baseball's flagship franchise. It was hoped in 1965 that Whitey Ford, at age thirty-six, would anchor the rotation for a few more seasons while the talented young trio of starting pitchers — Jim Bouton, who had won 39 games in the previous two seasons, Mel Stottlemyre, and Al Downing — would give the team the kind of starting pitching that "the Big Three" — Allie Reynolds, Vic Raschi, and Ed Lopat — had given Casey Stengel's early seasons.

It was not to be. The irreverent Bouton hurt his arm and lost his fastball forever; he won only four games in 1965, and at the end of 1968 he would be sold to the Seattle Pilots in the Pacific Coast League, although he would rejoin the AL the next year when the Pilots became an expansion team. Stottlemyre was terrific in 1965 at 20-9; for the next nine seasons, he waged a heroic battle, maintaining himself as the Yankees' number-one starter as he tried to lift a bad-to-mediocre team into the first division, winning 21 games in 1968 and 20 in 1969. Al Downing, who was 13-8 in 1964, pitched well for the next three seasons, but with little support. In 1968 he hurt his arm, and after two indifferent years was traded to Oakland.*

Ford, gritting his teeth and trying to work his way back from arm trouble, managed to win 16 games in 1965. He would win just four more games before calling it quits in 1967, twenty years after the Yankees signed him as an amateur. His career was fabulous: he won 236 games against 106 losses, giving him the best won-lost percentage of any twentieth-century pitcher in the Hall of Fame. His career ERA

---

*In 1971 Downing made a comeback with the Dodgers, winning 20 games; he pitched through six more seasons and is unfairly remembered mostly as the man who gave up Hank Aaron's record-breaking 715th home run.

was 2.75, a little better than that of the best left-hander in the NL over the same period, Warren Spahn (3.09). But that didn't begin to tell all of Whitey's story. His career ERA was 0.89 runs per nine innings better than the AL average over the span in which he pitched. The truly intriguing question is whether he would have had greater numbers if Ralph Houk had been his manager instead of Casey Stengel. Casey often held Whitey out of the rotation to pitch against the league's toughest contenders. He never got a chance to pitch in a regular four-man rotation until Houk became manager in 1961, and he responded over the next four seasons with an 83-25 record for a mind-blowing .769 win-loss percentage. That his relatively slight frame could have taken such a heavy load for several more seasons is open to debate, but it's likely that those long nights out with Mickey took a lot of innings out of Whitey's left arm.

The real decline of the Yankees came because the stars aged and there was no new talent to replace them. The old farm system had dried up from neglect and budget cuts; the last significant product of the Newark Bears for the Yankees was Yogi Berra back in 1946, and the last superstar produced by the scouting system was Mickey Mantle (though the Kansas City minor league team did give them Bill Skowron in 1953). In truth, without the trade pipeline from Philadelphia and then the Kansas City A's in the 1950s — of which Roger Maris was the crowning achievement — the Yankees dynasty might not have made it out of the decade. Yet another blow to Yankee supremacy was the new draft rule, first implemented in 1965, which limited teams to signing one prospect per round and kept the Yankees from stockpiling talent, as they once had done.

Maris missed nearly three-quarters of the 1965 season and hit only 8 home runs; in 1967 he was traded to St. Louis, where, as a platoon player, he helped the Cardinals win two pennants. Elston Howard, often playing hurt in 1965, caught just 95 games and batted .233. Joe Pepitone, who was supposed to be the next Yankees superstar, did attain genuine stardom in 1966, hitting 31 home runs and winning a Gold Glove at first base (where he replaced Skowron). After that, nightlife, gambling, and a general inattention to the game eroded his skills. He occasionally missed games, claiming he was being pursued by bookies; he may have been telling the truth. Shortstop Tony Kubek never recovered from a back injury and retired after the 1965 season.

But perhaps the saddest case of all was that of Tom Tresh, the talented switch-hitting youngster who was cursed with the label of "the next Mickey Mantle" when he was called up in 1962. He was in double digits in home runs every season, and four times had 20 or more, including a high of 27 in 1966. He was also a Gold Glove–caliber outfielder. In 1967 Tresh hurt his knee badly in an exhibition game and underwent surgery. Though he had some sporadic success afterward, he never really achieved what everyone thought was his real potential. Neither did any of the subsequent "next Mickey Mantles." Tresh was traded to Detroit in 1969 and then retired.

Mantle played in agony the entire season, batting just 361 times in 122 games, but for all that he did not play poorly, hitting 19 home runs with 6 stolen bases in 8 tries. (Why he tried at all to steal a base is baffling.) He batted just .255, but his on-base percentage was a more than respectable .379 — just 19 points fewer than Willie Mays, who led the NL that season. In fact, Mickey's OBP was higher than that of Tony Oliva, who won the AL batting title at .321. The Yankees finished in sixth place, 77-85.

On September 18, 1965, the day Mantle played in his 2,000th game, he was honored at Yankee Stadium. (For all his injuries, Mickey played in more games than any other Yankee until Derek Jeter surpassed his total in the next century.) The Yankees lost the game to Denny McLain and the Tigers, 4–3; Mickey went 0-for-3 with a walk.

Though it was supposed to be a day of celebration, there was a hint of sadness in the fall air. Not only was it the end of a dismal season, but some of the guests symbolized a time that would not come again. Mel Allen, for instance, the longtime Yankees announcer with the Alabama twang, whose "How about *that?*" and "Going, going, *gone!*" signature home run calls were dear not just to Yankee fans but to baseball fans all over the country, was in attendance. Toots Shor, the famous saloon owner who had relocated his famous nightspot but could never quite recapture its place as the center of New York night-life, was also there.

All through the late summer of 1965 there had been rumors that Mantle was thinking of retirement, and now, with the downfall of the Yankees empire a reality, he was caught in a deluge of sentimentality for a lost era, one in which, just a few short years before, many fans had booed him unmercifully. A sellout crowd — the first and last of the 1965 season for the Yankees — sported bedsheet signs that declared, DON'T QUIT, MICK! and similar sentiments. Mickey was given a new car, two quarter horses, a Winchester rifle, and a six-foot, 100-pound Hebrew National salami. As the salami presented an enormous logis-tical problem — it would have cost far more to transport it back to Dallas than it was worth — Mickey gave it to New York archbishop Francis Cardinal Spellman, who sent it on to several Catholic chari-ties, where it was carved up and enjoyed at several church events. A smiling Merlyn received a mink coat, and the family was given vaca-tion trips to Rome and Puerto Rico.

Joe DiMaggio flew in from the West Coast for the ceremony. Though it went largely unnoticed by most writers, who had written so much about DiMaggio's aloofness to nineteen-year-old Mickey in 1951, the two had developed an interesting professional relationship over the years. Whether DiMaggio was ever truly jealous of Mantle will always be a subject for speculation, but by the 1960s the now silver-haired Yankee Clipper was always happy to shake Mickey's hand and talk a little shop with him around the batting cage, usually during spring training. This was quite possibly the extent to which DiMag-gio could relate to most of his former teammates and acquaintances. (Oddly enough, Mickey's great pal Billy Martin was an exception, one of the few people who could make the Great DiMaggio laugh.) For his part, Mickey had long since lost most of his shyness around Joe and was happy to have him in New York for his special day.

After reading his introductory appreciation of Mickey, Joe waved and stepped away from the mike. Then, alone among the Yankee players, former players, officials, and guests, he noticed one person standing at the back of the on-field crowd, looking alone and uncomfortable. DiMaggio walked over to Lovell Mantle, took her by the arm, and brought her over to her son and daughter-in-law.

Mickey would have three more such days, and he remains the only player ever to be so honored. One of these events came in 1997 — two years after his death.

Willie Mays had his days, but not enough of them. There was a day for him at the Polo Grounds in 1954. "A bunch of Trenton fans," he recalled to Charles Einstein, "came in and gave me some things — a picture and a watch, things like that.* I had a 'day' at the Polo Grounds in '63, too, after the Giants moved to San Francisco and the Mets were playing there.

"In San Francisco, they don't go in for things like that so much. They gave me a banquet, for charity, at the Fairmont Hotel in 1964, but on the field the only 'day' I can remember was for Stu Miller, back in 1962, and the papers, or at least one or two of the writers, got on them for it — you know, the old story of why donate something to a baseball player who earns more than you do to begin with. . . . I still feel funny about having my biggest 'day' in New York when I was with the visiting team, but that's how it happened."†1

Probably Mays thought that after the excitement of the 1962 pen-

---

* Willie's memory on this, as on many incidents during his career, was faulty. Charles Einstein recalled dozens of guests and "a mountain of presents" on this Willie Mays Day. A photo of the occasion shows Willie surrounded by ballpark beauties, one holding a banner calling him THE BIRMINGHAM BELTER.

† In a 1998 letter to me, Charlie Einstein told me, "Willie was always very bitter about the fact that the San Francisco Giants were so reluctant to give him a day. He brought up the Stu Miller thing over and over — he would remind me of it years later, long after most people remembered who Stu Miller was. Stu Miller was a pretty good relief pitcher for a couple of years with the Giants, but the thing he was best known for was getting caught in a stiff wind on the mound in Candlestick Park and getting blown off. That was one of Stu Miller's two great distinctions. The other was being the answer to the question 'What San Francisco Giant who was not Willie Mays got a day in his honor in the 1960s?' "

nant run there would be a major thaw in the attitude of San Francisco fans toward him. If it happened, he never quite perceived it that way and could never help but contrast the difference between New York and California fans — the latter always, to his mind, withholding some affection from him.

In 1965 the San Francisco Giants were locked in a tense and bitter pennant race with the Los Angeles Dodgers that looked to be a repeat of the 1962 season. For some odd reason, the two archrivals did not play each other until April 29 in Los Angeles, where Don Drysdale defeated Juan Marichal, 2–1. The rules were different then and slanted toward pitchers, who were allowed to throw inside about as often as they wanted. In this game, Drysdale knocked down *five* Giants batters — that is, four different hitters, with Felipe Alou going down twice. Marichal was angry and told reporters that if Drysdale tried it again, he would retaliate. Drysdale, in turn, shot back that if Marichal did throw near the heads of Dodger batters, he would personally take out four Giants — "and I don't mean the .220 hitters."

In practical terms, of course, Drysdale meant he would be throwing at Willie Mays. He could have been threatening to throw at Willie McCovey, but this was unlikely since McCovey, a left-handed batter, was far less susceptible to Drysdale's sweeping, right-handed, near-sidearm fastballs. In fact, McCovey had hit several of his longest home runs off Drysdale. Also, McCovey, at around six-four, was nearly as big as Drysdale and was happy to let reporters know that he would not hesitate to charge the mound.

As the heat of summer came on and the pennant race heated up with it, the tension between the two teams grew. On August 19, they began a four-game series at Candlestick Park that looked very much as if it would settle the issue of who would win the pennant — and presumably, with the swift and shocking decline of the New York Yankees, the World Series as well.

The Giants lost the first game in fifteen innings despite a colossal two-run homer from Willie; they won the second on another Mays home run, and in the third game — again despite a clutch home run from Willie that tied the game — the Dodgers won in eleven innings. The fourth and final game on Sunday, August 22, was televised across much of the nation on NBC. It would become one of the most famous games in baseball history, not because it was a pitching duel between the two best starters in baseball, the Dodgers' Sandy Koufax and the Giants' Juan Marichal, and not because Mays won the game with a dramatic home run — his fourth in four games. The victory, as it turned out, would be the most bitter of Willie's career and would cost the Giants the 1965 National League pennant and, realistically, Willie Mays's last chance in his prime to get back to the World Series.

I've studied the incidents surrounding this game many times, but was never quite satisfied that the story I heard from interviewing the primary players was corroborated by my research. This is how I put it together for a story for the *New York Times* in 2000.

What most people remember is the shock of the violence and the blood, which somehow seemed even more horrific on a black-and-white TV. They did not know then, and they probably do not know now, that the racial tensions and tumultuous politics of the mid-sixties were boiling over on that Sunday afternoon.

Neither ace was at his best that day, and by the third inning it was 2–1, Los Angeles — a typical score for a nine-inning Marichal-Koufax match. Juan, who was not averse to throwing inside, knocked down Ron Fairly and Maury Wills. Koufax was averse to brushback pitches; with his speed, he was afraid he might kill someone. Still, he was pressured by his catcher, John Roseboro, to retaliate with a high-and-inside fastball when Marichal came to bat. On the next pitch, low and inside, Roseboro dropped the ball and picked it up behind Marichal. He then threw it back to Koufax, barely missing Marichal's head. Marichal thought it was closer than that; he would forever claim that the ball nicked his ear.

"Roseboro was sending him a message," says Charles Einstein in *Willie's Time*. Marichal didn't like the message. He spun around, bat in hand, and began screaming: "Why you do that? Why you do that?" Einstein said some choice Spanish terms were sprinkled in as well.

Roseboro's chin music has somehow been excised from everyone's memory of the incident. What is also forgotten is that it was Roseboro who moved toward Marichal, not the other way around. For most of the 42,000-plus crowd, the first indication that something was wrong came when they saw Marichal smashing Roseboro's head with his bat. Blood immediately began to flow from a deep scalp wound; to many stunned onlookers, it appeared as if Roseboro's eye had been knocked out. Players and coaches on both teams rushed toward home plate. Mays, a friend of Roseboro's, got there first. He immediately grabbed the Dodger catcher, partly to protect him and partly, as he later revealed, to keep him from attacking Marichal. As Mays led Roseboro off the field, he cradled his bleeding head and moaned, "Johnny, Johnny, I'm so sorry."

When order was finally restored, a shaken Koufax walked the next two hitters and then gave up a three-run homer to Mays, giving the Giants a 4–2 victory. They may not have realized it that night, but the Giants' season was over. Marichal, 19–9 before the game, lost three of his last four decisions after coming back from an eight-day suspension, which was seen by many as remarkably light. He was also fined $1,750 by the league, a bigger bite, it's true, in a time when top stars made $90,000 to $100,000 a year, but almost nothing compared to what fans and much of the press were screaming for. The Giants lost the pennant to the Dodgers by two games.

The Marichal-Roseboro clash haunted Mays for years. Years later he told Charlie Einstein: "Thinking back on it, I really don't think Juan should have been playing at all. He was pretty strung out, full of fear and anger, and holding it inside. How can you tell a city and a team that they have to lose a pennant because of problems they don't know about happening thousands of miles away?" (Mays was referring to the bloody civil war going on in the Dominican Republic, which had Marichal rushing to the phone every day to check on the fortunes of friends and family—particularly another man named Juan Marichal, his cousin, a politician who would become the country's vice president.) If anything good came out of the incident, it was Mays's enhanced reputation. After the game, talking to reporters, Dodgers manager Walter Alston said, "Mays was the only player on either club who showed any sense." If there was any doubt in anyone's mind that Willie Mays was now the elder statesman of baseball, this game removed it.

But not even Mays's reputation could save the coming seasons for his team. The Giants would finish second every year from 1965 through 1968; not until 1971, when the league was split into two divisions, would they earn a first-place finish, winning the Western Division before losing to the Pittsburgh Pirates in the 1971 playoffs. If there was one baseball regret Willie would take with him into retirement it was his failure, except for a brief flash in 1973, to star in another World Series. Except for The Catch in the 1954 Series and the double in the ninth inning of the seventh game in 1962, he scarcely had a significant moment in seventeen World Series games and never hit a home run.

There were consolations. Willie Mays may very well have had his best year in 1965. He led both leagues with his all-time season high of 52 home runs, the third time in four seasons he won the home run title. He batted .317 and led the NL in both on-base percentage (.400) and slugging percentage (.645). He was clearly the best player in his league and finally walked off with his second MVP Award—the bitter irony being that he'd had to wait eleven years after the first one to get it. No other player in baseball history went so long between MVP Awards.

By the end of the 1965 season, Mays was, with Mantle's decline, the most revered and the best-known professional athlete in America. He was also suffering from dizziness, stomach pains, and chronic loneliness. He scarcely saw his son Michael except when the Giants traveled to New York to play the Mets. For that matter, he scarcely saw

Cat, who had found his own niche in the black bars, pool halls, and nightspots of the Bay Area.

On the other side of the country, Mickey slogged through a miserable, grueling season, most of it spent alone except for his nighttime binges with Ford and a few old fringe New York buddies from the golden days. Sometime in the early 1960s, on a night when Mickey was playing out of town, Merlyn thought she heard an intruder in their house, pulled out a gun, walked downstairs, and fired in the dark. It was never determined if someone was actually trying to break in, but the incident showed how frayed her nerves were. Soon after, she packed up the boys and went back to Oklahoma. For her too, alcohol had become impossible to control. "Every day was a cocktail party," she would later recall. "That was our lifestyle. We were just country people when we first came to New York. We didn't have anything, and suddenly Mick was the toast of New York. It scared us both to death." Both she and Mickey were very shy people, and alcohol was "our way to cope with it."[2]

In 1966 the inevitable collapse came. For the first time since 1912, when they were the New York Highlanders,* the Yankees finished last. Even worse, because of the addition of two clubs, they were the first Yankee team ever to finish lower than eighth. Mickey was practically regarded as washed-up. In fact, he was simply injured a lot and playing in terrible pain when he wasn't. Though hardly anyone realized it, his performance on the field was outstanding. In just 108 games, he batted .288 with 23 home runs. He worked pitchers for so many walks that his OBP was a commendable .392, with a more than respectable .538 slugging percentage.

No one who saw Willie Mays play in 1966 thought his skills were greatly diminished. He didn't steal bases as he once did, and he didn't quite get a jump on the ball in center field as he had five years earlier,

---

* Or the "Lowlanders," as some wag in a New York paper called them in 1966; I'll never know who because I clipped only the headline and taped it to my bedroom door.

but he was still regarded as one of the best players in the game — if not the best — and he was certainly still considered one of the most dangerous hitters. At the end of the season, he had accumulated 542 home runs, eight more than Jimmie Foxx, at that point baseball's all-time right-handed home run champion, and number two behind Babe Ruth's all-time 714. Probably the number-one question for most observers going into the 1967 season was this: could Willie Mays catch Babe Ruth?

Willie Mays, as Bill James wrote in *The New Bill James Historical Baseball Abstract*, "was considered to be slipping; he hit 'only' .288 with 'only' 37 home runs and 'only' 103 RBI. He was still the best player in the league; he just didn't look so good if you compared him to what he had done the previous five years."[3] *Total Baseball*'s Total Player Rating placed Willie only fourth (number one was Cubs first baseman Ron Santo). Bill James ranked him number one in Win Shares for the season, a good indication that he should have been named MVP. Mays, though, finished third in the voting, behind Roberto Clemente and Sandy Koufax. The Giants once again came agonizingly close to the NL pennant, finishing just one and a half games behind the Dodgers.

But what, then, of Mickey Mantle, who had the same batting average as Willie and, amazingly, a slightly higher OPS — .930 to .924?

Mantle's last few years are generally considered by analysts to be a dreary and depressing time, better left unexamined, but they deserve a second look. In 1967 he hit just .245, but managed 22 home runs and 17 doubles in 144 games, 131 of them while playing at first base. Though he could scarcely follow through when batting from the left side, he managed to work AL pitchers for an impressive 107 walks, the first time he had passed the 100 mark in that category since 1962. His on-base percentage was .391, with a .434 slugging percentage. He actually had a better season than Willie, who played in 141 games and also had 22 home runs, but batted only .263 with a .334 on-base percentage, the lowest of his major league career, and a .453 slugging percentage. Mickey's OPS that season was .825, compared to Willie's .787.

Nonetheless, it was brutally obvious to everyone who saw him play that Mickey was a shell of the player he had been just a few years before. As early as the 1966 season, when Mickey was still just thirty-four, George Strickland, a scout for the Cleveland Indians, filed a report to his front office in which he refrained from putting the customary grade on Mantle's entry. "This guy," he wrote, "is ageing and he's showing it and I really don't feel he should be playing right field now. The injuries are just too much for this guy to overcome. If he comes back, it won't be for any length of time, because there is just too much chance for him to re-hurt himself, and he's just got too much going against him with the bad arm and the bad legs. He can't throw at all right now and it is just tough to see a great player get old and lose it so quick."[4]

I n the spring of 1966, George Carlin, appearing on *Perry Como's Kraft Music Hall*, did one of his most popular routines. Carlin's sportscaster, Biff Burns — "In the Sport Light Spotlight, spotlighting sports in the [pause] Sport Light Spotlight" — announced a trade: "The San Francisco Giants have traded outfielder Willie Mays to the New York Mets in exchange for the entire Mets team. The Giants will also receive $500,000, two Eskimos, and a kangaroo." Years later, when I was writing for the *Village Voice*, Carlin sent me a note commenting on a column I'd quoted him in. This led to an exchange of letters. I mentioned his bit on the Willie Mays "trade" and asked whether he'd ever heard from Mays about it.

"Willie sent me a letter," said Carlin, saying what a big kick he had gotten out of it. "I would have sent him a tape, but we didn't have tapes back then, so I sent him a printed copy of the routine.

"I grew up and went to school in that area they call White Harlem. There was just a handful of old Catholic families left, mostly Irish like mine, some Poles. When we played stickball, all the kids I knew wanted to be Mickey Mantle. I guess they felt they were guarding some last bastion of racial integrity. But I was a Willie Mays man. I couldn't make a basket catch to save my life, and at bat I'd lunge at the ball like Willie and miss it by a mile. But if being Willie Mays is your dream, who cares how well you actually played? If you fantasize about being Willie Mays, you fantasize about winning."[5]

Jim Bouton, trying to pitch with a bad arm, appeared in only seventeen games in 1967 and remembered having little contact with Mantle, who seemed to be in another world. He recalled a spring training game between the Giants and the Yankees in which Mickey and Willie "seemed so tired that you wondered how they made it onto the field. When they saw each other, they didn't even come over and shake hands, they just nodded and went about their business."

At the end of spring training in 1967, Mantle and the Yankees stopped off in Birmingham for an exhibition game with Carl Yastrzemski and the Boston Red Sox. My mother and I were there with a few thousand enthusiastic fans. In his first at-bat, on the first pitch, Mickey slammed a wicked line drive over the corner of the right-field fence — in fact, just about where you would hit it to get a cheap-shot home run at Yankee Stadium. According to *Birmingham News* sportswriter Alf Van Hoose, Mickey's shot landed just a few feet from Willie's only home run at Rickwood Field, in 1948. Neither Mickey nor Willie ever knew that they would be forever tied in home runs hit at Rickwood.

"I felt relieved," Willie remembered years later, "with the coming of the 1967 season. The pressure of hitting number 512" — of passing Mel Ott's career total and becoming the NL's all-time home run leader — "was gone. But even though I had a good spring, I was beginning to wonder about the reliability of my skills when the regular season began."

Early in the season, in a game at Crosley Field, Gary Nolan, a nineteen-year-old fireballer for the Cincinnati Reds, fanned Willie

Mays *four times* — all of them swinging. In four trips, the man who had passed up Mel Ott on the all-time NL home run list managed only two weak foul balls without putting a single ball in play. "Okay," said Willie, "the kid was good. But he was only 19. And I had never struck out four times in a game before."[6]

The entire season was depressing. For the first time, sportswriters in some National League cities began to tell their readers that the Willie Mays they saw off the field was not the ebullient "Say Hey Kid" they had been reading about for so many years. One Philadelphia writer approached Willie for an interview before the second game of a doubleheader in which an exhausted Mays would not play. "Why aren't you playing?" he asked. Mays did not answer. "I'm keeping my thoughts to myself" was all he would reply. "You want a story, you write what you want." And so he did: "Everybody thinks Willie Mays is nice, friendly, warm, sociable, fun-loving . . . a joy to be around. It will come as a shock to those out there in fantasyland that Willie Mays is cold, surly, suspicious, uncooperative. He is not an easy guy to talk to."[7] There was no indication from the writer that just maybe he had just caught Willie Mays on a bad day.

Mickey was now playing first base, but it quickly became obvious to most American Leaguers that he could no longer move with major league–quality agility, even at his new position. Dave Nelson, a rookie for the Cleveland Indians that year, had grown up idolizing Mantle. In May, he saw Mantle in the flesh for the first time and recalled how strange it was to see the smiling hero from his baseball cards standing near first base with a blank look on his face. Major league baseball, however, was played to be won, and Nelson was determined to do what he had to do. In his first at-bat, he slapped a bunt down the first-base line that Mickey simply could not get to on time. "I had no idea at the time," Nelson said later, "that other clubs had decided some things for themselves out of reverence for him. I had great speed, so [my bunt] was a base hit. I turn around half-way down the right field line and there's our first base coach walking towards me, and he stops me and tells me, 'Hey, Dave, we don't bunt on Mickey out of respect for him.' I go to myself, 'Oh-kayyyy.' So then I walked back to first base, and I'm standing next to Mickey Mantle. I'm looking at this guy's arms, and they look like tree trunks, and I'm saying: 'Man, he's gonna punch my head off.' And then he pats me on the butt and he says, 'Nice bunt, rook.' And I look at him and say, 'Thanks, Mr. Mantle.' "⁸

For Mickey, the 1967 season consisted of a few short ups and a lot of long downs. In July, he was hitting just above .230 but was given the honor of being named captain of the AL All-Star team. But unlike Willie, who took the midseason classic as seriously as regular-season games — if not more so — All-Star Games for Mickey were "like a cocktail party to me and Whitey."⁹ In 1967, in Anaheim, he showed up, chatted with reporters, shook hands with former teammates and longtime friends, and hugged his old manager, Casey Stengel, who told anyone who would listen that Mantle was the greatest ballplayer he had ever managed — something he had somehow neglected to say during all the years he had actually managed Mickey. Mantle was also asked to do a ceremonial handshake with Willie.

He arrived late, missed the team photo, struck out in a first-inning at-bat, showered and dressed in the locker room, and caught a cab to the airport to fly back to Dallas and get out to the golf course in time to see Cincinnati's Tony Perez win the game for the NL with a home run in the fifteenth inning. Or at least that's how Mickey remembered it. Since the game started at 4:15 PM in Anaheim, or 6:15 PM Dallas time, it's unlikely he would have been out playing golf that night.

Willie played the whole game and went 0-for-4.

For the first time since he had wept in the Giants' locker room sixteen seasons before, Willie Mays began to doubt himself. In a July game at Candlestick against the Braves, Mays began to shake. He thought it was a fever, but could not rule out an anxiety attack of the kind that had sent him to Mount Sinai Hospital on more than one occasion. Herman Franks asked him to stay in uniform long enough to deliver the lineup card to the home plate umpire, a shrewd move, as the other team would then think Mays, if he wasn't starting, was at least available for reserve hitting. Reserve outfielder Ty Cline started in the outfield. It was a bad night for Giants center fielders: trying to beat out an infield chopper, Cline pulled a muscle and had to come out of the game. Jesus Alou was the only other outfield sub available, and he had injured his leg just two days before. Willie quickly pulled off his jacket, reached for his glove, and trotted out to center field. His legs felt like lead, and he could scarcely swing the bat when his turn came in the order. The next day he checked into a hospital for five days. Whatever the problem, he already felt exhausted this early in the season.

When he finally got back into the lineup, Willie found that he simply did not feel strong. In fact, he would admit, "I never felt strong again for the rest of the season."[10] He would also admit to Bob Costas in a 2009 interview that he was taking amphetamines — "reds" — at the time, though he explained, "The trainer would give us this stuff and we didn't always know what it was." In a game at Atlanta, with the Giants leading 1–0 in the third, San Francisco had runners on second and third with slugging third baseman Jim Ray Hart due at bat. Billy Hitchcock, Atlanta's manager, startled everyone from the fans to both dugouts by signaling to his pitcher to intentionally walk Hart — to get to Mays. Willie was dumbfounded: "They were loading the bases to pitch to me! That had never happened to me before. I was furious and embarrassed, but raring to go. . . . Maybe I couldn't blame Hitchcock, but I also couldn't wait to get up to bat with the bases loaded. Did I concentrate! Make me look bad, huh? I smacked a single past first base and the runs were enough for a victory."[11]

August saw the first depressing story on Willie Mays to appear in a national sports magazine. The first sentence of "Say Hey No More," written by Mark Mulvoy for the August 7 issue of Sports Illustrated, seared the eyes of a high school student who had worshiped Willie since his first pack of baseball cards: "Sitting there in the Giants' clubhouse in Candlestick Park, Willie Mays looked old and sick." It didn't get much better after that: "His eyes were like road maps — Route 1 from San Francisco to Santa Cruz — and the circles beneath them said that Willie Mays does not sleep too well at night any more. His voice was somewhat muffled and restrained — the vigorous 'Say hey' is only a memory." (Actually, no sportswriter I ever knew remembered Mays using the phrase "Say hey" since 1954.)

Mulvoy portrayed a Willie Mays for whom the joy of playing base-ball was gone, a man approaching middle age for whom the game had become a chore, a job — an increasingly difficult job. "Despite all this," Mulvoy wrote, "Willie has not even thought about retirement. 'I'd like to play for a long time more,' he said, 'but I'll stay around only if I do a good job. I'd have to make some adjustments, maybe bat second and hit more to right field. Maybe I'd have to play left or right so I won't have to run so much. But I won't play first base like Mickey — not for the Giants. If I played first and [Willie] McCovey went to the outfield, we'd weaken ourselves at two places.' " But before it was all over, Willie would be at first base — just like Mickey.

The Giants were bad in 1967, winning ninety-one games and fin-ishing second in the league but a full ten and a half games behind the eventual World Series winner, the St. Louis Cardinals. They were never in the pennant race, despite a red-hot 20-7 record during September. The Yankees were much worse, winning just seventy-two games and ending up ninth in their division, twenty games behind the Red Sox.

Mickey and Whitey Ford began the 1967 season as the last of the old guard from the Yankees' glory years. Like Mantle, Ford had been struggling valiantly against the odds. In 1965 he had won sixteen games for a terrible team, but in 1966 his arm could no longer take the strain. He started just nine games, and though his ERA, 2.47, was excellent, he was able to win just two of seven decisions. In 1967 he lasted into the second month of the season before calling it quits.

For the first time since they had broken into the major leagues, both Mickey Mantle and Willie Mays were, from a baseball perspective, irrelevant. Both had 22 home runs. Mickey, sore and limping through every game, actually played more games than Willie, 144 to 141, though 131 of them were at first base. Willie, exhausted for much of the season and needing constant rest, hit just .263, eighteen points higher than Mickey, though Mantle, able as usual to work an at-bat for a base on balls, had finished with a .391 on-base percentage — fifty-six points higher than Mays.

By the winter of 1967, his skills greatly eroded and his future in baseball very much in doubt, Mickey was desperate to cash in on his celebrity. Frank Scott was constantly bringing in small endorsements, but the best offer came from a dynamic advertising executive named George Lois. Lois had practically created the sports celebrity TV commercial back in 1960 when he struck a gold mine for Puss and Boots cat food by having Yogi Berra talk to a cat, who told him how much he enjoyed the company's product.*

Lois, perhaps the most important figure in the American advertising industry, would become famous in the late 1960s for his *Esquire* covers. In the early 1980s, his "I Want My MTV!" slogan would become an American catchphrase, as would his "In Your Face!" campaign for ESPN a few years later. When it came to sports stars, Lois broke the rules. For instance, instead of using Berra as a pitchman, he brought out Yogi's sweeter qualities by having him engage in an intimate conversation with a cat; the commercial not only got men to laugh, it had enormous appeal to women, who, after all, bought the vast majority of cat food.

In 1967 Lois was working on the sales of the maple-flavored oatmeal cereal Maypo. As usual, he decided not to do things the usual

---

* Legend has it that Yogi did not know that the voice of the cat was his longtime battery mate, Whitey Ford. When told that it was "the Chairman of the Board," Berra supposedly asked, "That was Frank Sinatra?"

way. "Instead of a kid wailing at his mom for Maypo," he wrote in his 2003 memoir, $ellebrity, "I made a 180 degree turn away from the obvious. Instead of *kids* crying *I want my Maypo!* I used the greatest superstars of professional sports to sell Maypo to small fry, five to twelve years old. Maypo had always been considered a baby cereal, and to really hit one out of the park, I had to appeal to the pre-teenagers. I showed Mickey Mantle, Johnny Unitas, Wilt Chamberlain, Ray Nitschke, Oscar Robertson and Don Meredith, all in one television spot crying for their Maypo and shedding lifelike tears, here was the ultimate sissyfication of the American macho sports hero, a twisteroo on the unconscionable hustles by jocks who manipulated kids through hero worship. Instead, the sports greats in our spot sold obliquely, displaying self-mocking wit."[12]

Despite the rise of football by 1967, and despite his own decline, Mickey's spot was still the most popular. Frank Scott, who was still handling occasional endorsement deals for both Mantle and Mays, mentioned to Lois that a spot with America's two greatest sports icons might be a big hit. Lois thought it was a natural and invited Mickey and Willie to his studio. Mantle quickly did his "I want my Maypo!" face and, with a little artificial help from Lois's assistant, burst into tears. When Mays's turn came, however, there was a problem. He did take after take, staring into the camera impassive as a TV newscaster. No matter how Lois implored him, Willie refused to feign sorrow over being denied his cereal. "Willie don't cry," he said, staring straight ahead. "Willie don't cry."

In desperation, George whispered to Mickey that they were in danger of losing the commercial. Mantle suggested that he take Willie for a brief walk to see what he could do. A few minutes later, they returned, a smiling Mickey with his arm around a stern-faced Willie. Mays sat down, recited his lines, and practically burst into tears without any help. Afterward, Lois thanked Mickey for saving the spot and asked what he had said to Willie. "Aw," said Mantle, "I just had a little talk with him. He knows I love him."

⚾   ⚾

On January 7, 1968, Mickey and Willie put in an appearance at a sporting goods fair at the New Yorker Hotel. By that time, they had become relaxed enough with each other to exchange a few good-natured barbs. "You sure you know how to use one of these things?" Willie quipped as Mickey held up a glove. "Man," Mickey said in reply, as he tried on Willie's mitt, "some people said I couldn't carry your glove. Now I see why. It's so damn *big*."[13]

The fair was also an opportunity for *Esquire* magazine to put together a photo shoot and dual interview, which appeared in the August issue: "Mantle Fans Mays/Mays Fans Mantle — Willie and Mickey Appraise Each Other in Relation." Mickey's text (written, as he revealed to me at a 1985 party for *The Mick*, by Dick Schaap, who had written Mantle's paperback biography in the *Sport* magazine biography series) contained some genuine appreciation and insight: "Outside of Joe DiMaggio, Willie Mays is the greatest all-around baseball player of my time. Certainly he's been the most daring. Mays would steal home, a tough play and one in which you've got a great chance to look bad. Willie didn't even think of that, he'd just go. Nine times out of ten, he'd make it." (Mickey was almost right — Mays stole home eight times in ten tries in his career.)

"He was always a better glove man than I was because he had that same confidence. I'd run up to a single to center, say, squat down and block it in case I missed it. I always had that little doubt in the back of my mind that I might not catch it. But Willie would come charging in, scoop up the ball on the dead run, and fire. The basket catch is easy for him, so he has fun with it. He makes it so easy that sometime people think he's showboating. I think *some* of his style is for the fans, but I don't see anything wrong with that.

"I used to feel I was as good as he was, but now Willie has finally gotten out a little ahead of me. He's kept his health better than I have. He seems to run as well as he used to, although not quite so much.

He's a leader, too, and I'm not. He'll go to the young players and try to help them. [Note: As *Sport* magazine revealed several times, so did Mantle.] He talks it up on the bench. He *wants* to be a leader. I just want to be one of the players."

Mantle was surprisingly candid about another matter that was increasingly close to Willie: "People keep asking him if he thinks he can break Babe Ruth's lifetime home-run record. What do they expect him to say? I'll tell you that I don't think he can do it. He came into this season 150 home runs behind Ruth. He's 37 now. Say he plays three or more years. Even if he plays four more, he must average more than 35 home runs a year, and that's a lot. But I hope he does it."

Toward the end of the piece Mantle grew reflective. "I suppose the toughest thing for both of us is the thought of quitting. Baseball's our business, our life. But if we have a couple of days in a row where we strike out three times and don't get a hit, people say, 'Maybe he's had it.' You don't want to reach a point where people just think you're hanging on."

Clearly the subject was very much on Mickey's mind.

Mays's essay — actually written by Charles Einstein — started with the Mantle performance that had most impressed him: his two home runs in the 1960 World Series. "I would rather be compared to Mantle than pitch to him. He didn't just beat pitchers, he broke their hearts."

"It's difficult to imagine a successor to Mantle; no one is likely to combine the speed and power and be able to hit so well both right-handed and left.

"Mickey used to get booed a lot at Yankee Stadium. I didn't have any problems like that until later when the Giants moved to San Francisco. Then I got booed. It wasn't so much what we were, it was more what we weren't. Neither of us was Joe DiMaggio.

"I've seen ballplayers do the job on just guts, but I've never known a guy do it over so long a time. Mantle can still swing, but when he does, his legs almost seem to collapse. The man is in pain and hitting is tough enough when you're feeling good. They tell me he bandages his legs from top to bottom before every game and that he's been doing it for a long time. Everybody's got an idea on how to help him. Even I've made a suggestion; I've got a machine that I think helped me, and I sent one to Mickey." (According to Charlie Einstein, this was a kind of small whirlpool for the feet and knees. Mantle was hugely appreciative and sent Mays a case of wine in return — when Roger Kahn reminded Mickey that Willie didn't drink, Mickey sent him a note of apology and a basket with some fine Russian caviar.[14])

"Two years ago, the Yankees decided to play him at first-base. Some guys wouldn't have moved after all those years, but Mickey went to spring training and made himself learn the job. I watched him on television the other day. He's never going to be a Gil Hodges, but he won't embarrass himself, either. I don't know when he's going to quit, and I don't think he does." (Willie did not know it, but Mickey had already made his decision.)

" . . . Nothing's worse than being the big man on a losing ballclub. They lose, and I know he's thinking to himself, 'They were expecting me to do something.' "

In perhaps his most perceptive insight, Willie said, "I'd have to guess that he was always the biggest guy in his crowd." And who would have known better than the biggest guy in *his* crowd?

"More was always expected of him. A lot of the men in Mickey's family, it seems, died at an early age. A man can't help feeling some pressure from a thing like that."

According to Einstein, Mickey and Willie had a good time cutting up at the photo shoot. Willie made rabbit ears behind Mantle's head; Mickey reciprocated with his middle finger. "Hey, man," Mays said when they arrived at the studio, "I want to see what you wrote about me. What did you write about me?"

Mickey replied, "I bet it's better than what you wrote about me."

"Fact is," Mantle admitted in one of his memoirs, "it's hard for me to sit and listen to anything concerning money and finances. Today when my lawyer, Roy True, starts talking about a $100,000 contract, he'd better get it told in twenty minutes — thirty tops — or I'm out of his office and on my way to the golf course."[15]

And so, as Mickey Mantle approached his late thirties, his financial situation became desperate; he had learned nothing in all those years. Yogi Berra, despite his public image, was a shrewd, tough negotiator who could have given Mickey a great deal of advice in the subtle art of negotiation. In the same 1985 memoir, Mickey said, "The only regret I have is that in my day we were so dumb we didn't know how to handle our financial dealings with the front office. They told me $32,500 was a lot of money, and I thought it was. When you go from making $35 a week in the mines to playing for the Yankees and within five years you've signed a $32,500 contract, it's pretty hard to believe you're worth more than that."[16]

Yes, but Mickey should have known better. The years should have taught him something. In some ways he had matured: he was no longer curmudgeonly to sportswriters, he did his best to accommodate autograph-seeking fans, and he went out of his way to offer advice and assurance to both teammates and young players on other teams. In June 1967, a story in Sport declared, "Willie Mays still is something special, still is one of the two most popular players in the game — Mickey Mantle is the other."[17] It was true. Willie and Mickey were baseball's elder statesmen by that time. But in many ways — in their relations with women and with their children, in financial matters — they never grew up.

As Mickey entered the 1968 season, it became apparent that after several years of unrelenting pain when batting from the left, he was now practically useless from that side of the plate, partially owing to the right shoulder injury he had sustained in the 1957 World Series, which had never quite healed. For his career, in fact, he batted nearly fifty points higher — .330 to .281 — from the right side.* In addition

---

* In 1982, working on a story for Inside Sports, I interviewed Mantle at the Echelon Mall in Voorhees, New Jersey. One question I asked him was: "Why didn't you consider batting right-handed all the time? It would have been less painful, and I'll bet it would have added several points to your batting average."

to the chronic shoulder pain, nearly all the cartilage in both of his knees was gone; when he tried to run, he could feel the scraping of bone on bone.

The 1968 All-Star Game marked the last time Mantle and Mays would shake hands in uniform. Forty-two years later, Hall of Famer Harmon Killebrew recalled that looking at Mickey and Willie that day was "heartbreaking. It seemed that just a few years before these guys were, for me, a symbol of eternal youth — always smiling. Now they looked as if it took a big effort of energy just to crack a smile."[18] Mantle, a reserve on the AL roster, struck out in his only at-bat; Willie singled in the first inning off Luis Tiant, went to second on an errant pickoff throw, scooted to third on a wild pitch, and came home on a ground-ball double play by McCovey. It wasn't much, but in a 1–0 victory it was enough to earn Mays his second All-Star MVP Award. (But that total is deceiving: the award wasn't presented until 1962, by which time Mays by rights should have already had three All-Star MVP plaques.)

By July 27, Mickey had dipped below his career batting average, .300, never to rise above it again. On July 29, he struck out four times in one game; on the way back to the dugout, teammates heard him mutter, "This is my last year."

On August 4, the Yankees, hoping to boost declining attendance, held yet another Mickey Mantle Day — officially, Mickey Mantle Banner Day. Mickey grinned wearily as a long procession of fans filed by with hand-painted Mantle appreciation banners, trying to win a handshake and season tickets. Five days later, Mickey lost his cool and cursed the home plate umpire for a strikeout call. It was just the seventh time since 1951 that he was thrown out of a game.

The home runs were now few and far between. On September 19,

"I just don't know the answer to that," he said. "We just didn't think that way back then, though oddly enough, I did a couple of times when batting against Hoyt Wilhelm and that damned knuckleball of his. I don't know why, but I could just see the break on that pitch better from the right side." He also said "If I'da played for the Boston Red Sox at that point in my career, with that wall in Fenway, I think I woulda batted right-handed all the time."

two days after a powerful Detroit Tigers team clinched the AL pennant, Mickey hit a memorable home run — memorable because it enabled him to pass up Jimmie Foxx for third place on the all-time home run list and because it proved to be the most controversial of his career.*

Denny McLain was the last pitcher in baseball to win thirty or more games — he would win thirty-one in 1968 — as well as the only ballplayer to be convicted of extortion, racketeering, and drug possession.† He was also one pitch shy of being the last man to give up a home run to Mickey Mantle.

In the eighth inning, when Mantle walked into the batter's box, Detroit fans, realizing that this was probably their final chance to see Mickey, gave him a standing ovation. McLain stepped off the mound in a show of respect, giving Mickey the crowd's full attention. Well on the way to winning his thirty-first victory, McLain decided to be gracious: stepping back onto the mound, he grooved Mantle a batting practice fastball. The astonished Mickey watched it go by, looked down at Tigers catcher Jim Price, and said, "What the fuck was that?" Price, knowing very well what McLain was trying to do, shrugged and said, "I dunno." "Is he gonna do it again?" Mantle asked. Again Price shrugged. "I dunno."

Price started to walk out to the mound, but McLain waved him off and said, loud enough for both dugouts and many fans and Mantle himself to hear, "Just tell him to be ready." But all Mickey could manage was a foul on the next one, and the count went 0-2. McLain gave him one more, same location, same speed, and Mickey drilled it on a line into the right-field seats. First baseman Norm Cash slapped him on the butt with his glove as he rounded first; as Mantle rounded second, characteristically with his head down, he yelled out to McLain, "Thank you thank you thank you!" All McLain could think was *Jesus Christ, I'm going to get a letter from the commissioner.*

---

*Willie had by this time moved up to second place on the home run list, second only to Babe Ruth.

†In 1985, just three years after Denny McLain Day at Tiger Stadium.

Just so he would not be misunderstood, on the next pitch McLain threw a ninety-mile-per-hour fastball that put Joe Pepitone in the dirt.

Sure enough, Commissioner William Eckert sent McLain a letter criticizing him for assaulting the integrity of the game and suggesting that an investigation would be forthcoming. However, no investigation took place. Apparently someone in Eckert's office reminded him that the home run was hit by Mickey Mantle, the best-loved player in the league, and that any investigation would surely end in a popular denunciation of the commissioner. Two days later, Red Smith, writing in *Women's Wear Daily*, summed up the entire affair: "When a guy has bought 534 drinks in the same saloon, he's entitled to one on the house."[19] And on September 20, Mickey deprived McLain of the distinction of being the last pitcher to give up a Mantle home run when he laced number 536 off the Red Sox's "Diamond Jim" Lonborg.

In his final season, 1968, the thirty-six-year-old Mantle had his worst batting average ever, .237, but still hit 18 home runs and walked 106 times to finish with an OBP of .385. These numbers have to be considered against the backdrop of one of the worst periods for batters that baseball had ever seen. Carl Yastrzemski, at .301, was the American League's only .300 hitter that year.

Meanwhile, Mickey's marriage had become a sham; he seldom saw Merlyn and spent even less time with their sons. Mickey Jr., who was fifteen the year Mickey retired and would one day schedule his dad's business appointments and personal appearances, played Little League ball in the hope of getting his father's attention. (After high school, he made a halfhearted attempt at playing minor league ball.) In his teenage years, he scarcely knew Mickey Sr. at all. "My dad helped me some," he told *Sports Illustrated* in 1985, "but you gotta remember he wasn't around all that much when I was growing up."[20]

There was, however, one mitigating factor, and it was by no means a small one: a new generation had come of age in the wake of the Mickey Mantle legend, and these fans saw him in an entirely uncritical light.

In 1968 they also began to see him in a nostalgic light. Crowds in other American League cities had once flocked to see their hometown heroes take a shot at bringing down the mighty Yankees; now, in their ruin, the Yankees remained gate attractions, almost entirely because of Mantle. Clearly, fans knew that the second half of the 1968 season was Mickey Mantle's farewell tour.

This time the crowds turned out to cheer him. The booing, the insults, the hazing over his draft status controversy were long forgotten.

Though he had decided to retire, Mantle had several reasons for not yet making the announcement. For one, there was always the lingering hope that some miracle of medical science could restore a modicum of his former speed and take away the pain. Another was a reason that could not have been anticipated: Mickey Mantle made a gesture to help the players' union.

In his memoir *A Whole Different Ball Game: The Inside Story of Baseball's New Deal,* Marvin Miller, the founder and first executive director of the Players Association, recalled: "After a discouraging discussion of the total lack of progress in the pension negotiations, they [members of the Players Association's board of directors] decided to go ahead with the previously discussed policy of recommending that no player sign his 1969 contract until a benefit plan agreement had been reached. This was a strong move." The board recessed so the player reps could contact their teammates for their approval.

The Yankees' player rep, pitcher Steve Hamilton, told Miller that "the most interesting conversation he had was with Mickey Mantle, who, although never hostile to the Players Association [which had been established in 1967], had always seemed somewhat aloof. Steve thought of this when he called. Mickey's response was that it really didn't affect him because he had finally made his decision not to play in 1969." Had Mickey, Hamilton asked, told anyone of his decision to retire? Mantle said he had not. Hamilton made a request: would Mickey delay announcing his retirement and give the union permission to include his name with all the players not to sign contracts? "Mantle had only one question: 'Would it help the players?' 'Yes,' Steve replied, 'it would.' 'Then hell yes,' Mick replied. 'Use my name.' "[21]

For one bright shining moment at least, just before it was all over, Mantle supported his fellow players and the union. Willie Mays would never have such a moment.

The year 1968 was a bad one for hitters, as indicated by Bob Gibson's microscopic 1.12 ERA. The National League's ERA was just 2.99, and the American League's was a fraction lower at 2.98. Just two seasons earlier, the NL had posted a 3.61 mark to the AL's 3.44. But in 1968 the strike zone, the height of pitching mounds, and the tolerance of the umpires on inside pitching took a toll on hitters. Considering that environment — and his thirty-seven years — Willie didn't do badly with 23 home runs, 79 RBIs, a .289 batting average, and 12 stolen bases. But it could no longer be denied: he wasn't the best center fielder in baseball anymore. It became official on August 19 when the cover of *Sports Illustrated* featured the Cardinals' Curt Flood making a circus catch against Wrigley Field's ivy-covered wall and proclaimed him baseball's best center fielder.

The announcement affected at least one reader in Alabama so much that, the day after the issue hit the stands, he went to high school football practice early, smarted off to the coach, and got kicked off the team. So much for my football career.

Near the end of the season, Roger Kahn saw Mantle at Yankee Stadium during a game in which Mickey did not play. Two days later, Kahn saw Willie at Shea in a series against the Mets in which "I wish Willie hadn't played." Willie struck out three times against Tom Seaver and misplayed a fly ball in center field. "I thought of the second part of the line from the Dylan Thomas poem, which I had not used for my book about the Jackie Robinson Dodgers: 'I have seen the boys of summer *in their ruin.*' "

17

Say Good-bye to America

On March 1, 1969, at a press conference at the Yankee Clipper Hotel, Mantle surprised teammates, front-office people, and reporters when he announced his retirement in a calm, composed statement. "I just can't play anymore," he said. "I don't hit the ball when I need to. I can't score from second when I need to. I can't steal when I need to."[1] His teammates were shocked but not surprised. Mickey was numb; for him, the rest of the press conference passed in a blur. He would later tell Dick Young that he had no memory of what he did for the next few months.

"Baseball was all I'd ever known," he later recalled. "I wasn't in much of a mood for a celebration."[2] For the first time since he was nineteen years old, he was no longer a professional baseball player. In fact, he wasn't a professional anything. All his recent business interests, including a bowling alley in Dallas, had gone under. He now found himself thirty-seven years old, walking on bad legs, with no marketable skills. He had a wife and four children to support and a gaggle of relatives back in Oklahoma to help out.

It had been eighteen spring trainings since he had made his first appearance with the Yankees. Reflecting back on his thoughts at that press conference, Mantle said, "It seemed like so much longer. It felt like it had been fifty years since I first played for the Yankees."[3]

The Yankees invited him back on June 8 for a "day." It was the first sellout at Yankee Stadium since the World Series back in 1964. His uniform was folded and presented to him; his number 7 was retired. Yankees announcer Frank Messer told the crowd that Mickey had "worn it with pride his entire Yankee career." (No one remembered that the first number he had worn as a Yankee was 6.) After the ceremony, he posed for pictures in the pressroom. Someone pushed a television camera in his face, and a reporter asked him, "Who do you think was the better ballplayer, you or Willie Mays?" Without even hesitating, Mickey replied, "Willie Mays is better. I don't mind being second. If I'm second, I'm pretty good."

Willie Mays *did* mind being second. After Mays passed up Jimmie Foxx in 1966 for second place on the all-time home run list, the primary question among baseball fans was: Could Willie do it? Could he pass up the Babe? But 1967 through 1969 weren't good slugging years for Mays or almost anyone else; in those three seasons combined, he hit just 58 home runs, six more than he had in 1965 alone. As the 1960s wound down, another challenger to Ruth's record emerged, and Willie, for the first time in his career, had to take a backseat to another player in his own league.

Henry Louis Aaron, three years younger than Mays, was born in Mobile, Alabama, in 1934 and, as a shortstop for the Indianapolis Clowns, played in many of the old southern ballparks that Willie had played in. "Hank," as he was identified on his Topps baseball cards and as he came to be known, had had none of the breaks that Willie had benefited from: he had no mentors like Piper Davis to guide him through professional black baseball, and instead of liberal New York, with its comparatively progressive front office (remember that the Giants roomed Willie with a black veteran, Monte Irvin), Aaron broke into the majors in white-bread Milwaukee, a town with a relatively small black population. When Mays had the misfortune of leaving New York, his team went to San Francisco, which, as it turned out, was by no definition a bastion of racial understanding, but it was light-years from the city that Aaron's team moved to in 1966 — Atlanta.

In 1967, as Mays's home run production began to drop off, Aaron began to pick up speed. From 1967 to 1971, Willie hit 104 home runs, while Henry smashed 197. Aaron also, early in the 1972 season, surpassed Willie as the highest-paid player in baseball — in fact, Aaron's three-year, $600,000 contract made him the highest-paid player of all time. Aaron never saw himself as a hero and gave little thought to catching Babe Ruth. By the end of the 1971 season, Aaron trailed Mays by just seven home runs, 639 to 646. But he still didn't believe he would beat the Babe's 714. "Hey, Wayne," he asked Wayne Minshew of the *Atlanta Journal-Constitution*, "do you think I have a chance at it?"[4]

Mays apparently resented Aaron for supplanting his supremacy in home runs and in salary. In fact, if the information in Howard Bryant's 2010 biography of Aaron is correct, Mays had been harboring a strange resentment toward Aaron for many years. "For his generation, Mays exemplified the rare combination of physical, athletic genius, and a showman's gift for timing. What went less reported and, as the years passed, became an uncomfortable, common lament was just how cruel and self-absorbed Mays could be."[5] In 1957 Reese Schonfeld, a young reporter for a Boston television station, was at the Polo Grounds for a charity game between the Giants and Braves; while his cameraman was changing film for an interview with Aaron, Mays trotted in from center field and started ragging on Aaron: "How much they paying you, Hank? They ain't paying you at all, Hank? Don't you know we all get paid for this? You ruin it for the rest of us, Hank! You just fall off the turnip truck?" Mays, who grew up in the big city of Birmingham, was fond of deriding Aaron as "country."

According to Bryant, Willie began to lay it on thicker, finally calling Aaron "one dumb nigger!" Aaron was so shaken that manager Fred Haney decided to take him out of the game. Willie, Bryant wrote, "committed one of the great offenses against a person as proud as Henry: he insulted him, embarrassed him in front of other people, and did not treat him with respect." The closer Aaron got to the magic number 714, the more apparent it became that "Willie would never surrender the stage easily to the man who had always played in his shadow." When the press began to treat Aaron's breaking the record as inevitable, Willie told a reporter that "yes, Henry would break Ruth's record," but he added, "Maybe I will, too."[6] Even though Willie rebounded to hit 28 home runs in 1970, no one believed he could do it.

Mays and Aaron "were not friends . . . there was something about Willie that wouldn't allow a real friendship with Henry. Willie wouldn't, or couldn't, ever give Henry his due as a great player, and that inability on Mays's part to acknowledge Henry as an equal was what really burned Henry."[7]

On April 8, 1974, Mickey's old teammate Al Downing tried to slip a pitch by Henry Aaron, who slammed it over the fence for his 715th career home run. Mickey Mantle remembered, "I watched him on television that night and saw the ball go over the left centerfield fence in Atlanta Stadium. I can imagine how he felt circling the bases and listening to the gigantic roar. I know the pressure that built up before he hit it. I know what the feeling is. I wish everybody in America could have that feeling just once, to hear all those people cheering and knowing it was for them."[8]

One truly wonders what Mays's feelings were at that moment. One also wonders what America's reaction would have been if Willie Mays instead of Hank Aaron had broken Ruth's record. Aaron received hate mail and death threats, and there were even reports of his children being harassed at school. There is no way of knowing how much of this was due to the most fabled record in American sports being shattered by a black man playing in the Deep South just a few years after the height of the civil rights movement. The accomplishment would likely have gone much more smoothly for Willie, whose home base was San Francisco and who had the kind of media support in New York that Aaron could only yearn for.

As the sixties came to an end, New York had a new sports hero. Joe Namath, quarterback for the New York Jets, had put the American Football League on the map with a sensational upset of the old NFL establishment Baltimore Colts. In the flush of victory, Joe opened an Upper East Side bar called Bachelors III, and Mantle began to hang out there, often in the company of Whitey Ford and Billy Martin. Though there was a twelve-year age difference, he and Namath hit it off immediately. Dick Schaap, who knew both Mantle and Namath as well as any writer, quipped that if not for Mickey's wife and family back in Dallas, "Joe might have thought about changing the name of the bar to Bachelors IV."⁹ The two men became close, and Mantle confided in Namath. Joe told one beat writer, "Mick's the only male in his family to make it past age forty-one. We talk about that now and then — jokingly, but with some seriousness — that if he had known he was going to live that long, he'da taken better care of himself."¹⁰ Despite the warning, Namath did not take Mantle's story to heart and began his own serious problem with alcohol.

In the winter of 1969, it appeared as if Mantle had finally found a business interest outside baseball. The year before, advertising guru George Lois had put Mickey's and Joe's faces on a new business venture, an employment agency called Mantle Men & Namath Girls. The catchphrase was "Our people are pros, just like us." The two seemed to be having a great deal of fun in their TV commercials for the company, one of which showed Joe typing away, and they made personal appearances together. The company seemed to be booming, but the spring and summer of 1969 brought the first big recession the United States had seen since the Korean War, and as Lois put it, "suddenly there were fewer jobs to fill, and our dream concept fell on rough days."[11] Mantle Men & Namath Girls was sold to another agency.

The friendship between Mantle and Namath, though, continued on without missing a beat. In 1969, Joe hosted an hour-long program, *The Joe Namath Show*, rife with adolescent male horsing around. The December 22 episode featured Mickey Mantle, Willie Mays, and the Baltimore Colts' Willie Richardson, whom Namath had played against earlier in the year in the Super Bowl. Bets were placed as each man tried to tap a golf ball into a cup placed at the end of a long strip of artificial turf. Mickey did well, but Willie's putts spun inexplicably to the right and left within inches of their target. A baffled Mays asked in a high-pitched whine, "Hey, man, what's the matter with this thing?" Mantle, sitting in a guest chair, broke up with laughter. The setup was rigged to keep Willie's putts from going in. Mickey had bet Willie $100 a stroke before the show, but in his glee at Willie's frustration broke down and admitted the fix. After the show, Mantle, a grin on his face, approached Mays and asked him to pay up. Willie told him they'd play for double or nothing at Horace Stoneham's country club the next time Mickey was in the Bay Area.

Even in the twilight of Willie's career, most baseball fans — particularly this fan — knew virtually nothing of his character flaws. In fact, we knew nothing about the dark side of any of our sports heroes. In a way, the fans of my generation didn't care to know. In 1969 our lives had moved on to more important subjects, to the Vietnam War and domestic antiwar demonstrations and bombings. Culturally, sports had been displaced by Woodstock and Altamont. Even within the world of sports, Willie Mays began to seem almost antiquated, a hero from an age whose ideals had already passed.

I witnessed this for myself at the University of Alabama, which became integrated in the midsixties. By the end of the decade, I found myself surrounded by black kids my age whose interest in sports was as strong as my own. Even though Willie Mays had grown up and learned baseball just a few miles from where we were going to school, he was not one of their idols. Jim Brown, the most outspoken black football player of his era, and Bill Russell, who was playing the final season of a career that saw him win eleven championships with the Boston Celtics, had both supplanted Willie among black youth — white youth too, for that matter. Muhammad Ali, of course, transcended sport in a way that did not seem possible in those safe and comfortable 1950s and early 1960s. Brown, Russell, and Ali were my heroes too. But increasingly I found that the esteem in which I had held Willie Mays was not shared by my black friends; on more than one occasion the term "Uncle Tom" even crept into our conversations.

One terrible day in the early fall of 1969, my father and I stopped by Willie Mays Fried Chicken and Hamburgers, which was on Birmingham's north side, close to where the Civil Rights Institute stands now. To our delight, Willie was seated a few tables away, talking to a man I recognized as Jesse Lewis, owner and publisher of Birmingham's most successful black-owned newspaper, the *Birmingham Times*. (I had interviewed Lewis about the civil rights movement for my high school paper the year before.) I thought about walking over to their table and introducing my father to Lewis, and thus allowing my father to shake hands with Willie Mays for the first time in his life. Before I could make my move, we realized they were in the midst of an argument, one that could be heard throughout the restaurant. Mays was hotly defending his lack of participation in the civil rights struggles in Birmingham, a city he had once called "the most racist in America."

Lewis seemed calm and, as I saw it, nonconfrontational, but Mays was loud, aggressive, and clearly heated. We never discussed it, but I could tell that my father, who had been a staunch supporter of civil rights, had been shaken in his hero worship. For my part, I was surprised at how much overhearing the conversation between Lewis and Mays upset me, and I thought back to that moment in 1963 when

Mays had conspicuously failed to join Jackie Robinson and Floyd Patterson in supporting Martin Luther King Jr.'s Birmingham rally.

When I became a man, I thought I had put away childish things, but it never occurred to me that my love for Willie Mays was one of those. Or at least it had not occurred to me that I had been foolish ever to see Willie Mays as a hero. I had been wrong to assume that Willie had been part of the civil rights struggle simply because he was black and from Birmingham. It was difficult to reconcile my admiration for Mays with the fact that he had done nothing off the field to merit my worship.

A couple of weeks after seeing Mays at his chicken restaurant, my father and I drove across town to have some fried chicken at Mickey Mantle's Country Cookin'.* On that day in 1969, he had just turned thirty-eight and somehow managed to look both younger and older than his age. He smiled and autographed a *Sport* magazine that contained Dick Young's story "Farewell to Mickey Mantle." I told him that he had hit a home run the first time I saw him play at an exhibition at Yankee Stadium against the San Francisco Giants in 1961. He smiled and said, "Yeah, but that was Willie's day." (I remember Mickey's chicken as being fully the equal of Willie's. Mantle later told me, "You know, I never got a chance to tell Willie, but I was going to give him a slogan they wouldn't let me use: 'To get a better piece of chicken you'd have to be a rooster.' ")

As we left, my father turned to me and said, "My God, he looks tired." A few days later, at the *Birmingham News*, where I was putting in time as a go-fer, I mentioned to Howell Raines, one of the editors,

---

*The name of Mantle's short-lived chain of restaurants has been incorrectly identified by biographers. Mantle and his backer chose "Country Kitchen," but a Wisconsin-based company informed Mick's lawyers that they already owned that title. So shortly before the restaurants opened, everything was hastily changed to "Mickey Mantle's Country Cookin'." That was the name of the one in Birmingham.

Mickey's restaurants have also been incorrectly identified as "fast food." Actually, they were cafeteria-style restaurants of a sort popular in the South and parts of the Midwest where customers had their choice of chicken, fish, ham, or beef and three vegetables with biscuits or cornbread — "meat and three," as they still say in Alabama.

that I had been to the opening of Mantle's restaurant and that he appeared bleary-eyed and looked as if he was in need of a good sleep. "Well," Raines confided to me, "nobody at this paper is going to write it, but I have it on good authority that Mickey and Bear Bryant got together and went on a legendary binge the night before. It's amazing he made it to the restaurant opening at all."*

Early in January 1970, Curt Flood filed a $1 million lawsuit against Commissioner Bowie Kuhn and Major League Baseball. The previous October, Flood had been traded by the St. Louis Cardinals to the Philadelphia Phillies, a team Flood did not wish to play for in a city he did not wish to play in. What he wanted was nothing less than the overthrow of the long-standing "reserve clause," a part of every player's contract that bound him to his team, making him, in Flood's phrase, "a well-paid slave [but] a slave nonetheless."

Willie appeared on *The Tonight Show* and was asked by host Johnny Carson what he thought of Flood's suit. Mays's reply was vague; he told Carson that he hadn't studied the case "too much. I don't know all the arguments. . . . I'm not going to get involved." Despite the urging of players' union head Marvin Miller, no active major league player came out for Flood, even though overturning the reserve clause would have made all of them free agents and increased their salaries many times over. Most of the players later confessed to being afraid of retribution from management. Only Jackie Robinson, who had been retired for more than a decade, showed up to support Flood.

In his autobiography *The Way It Is*, which was published a few months after the suit was filed, Flood wrote: "All but a very few major

---

* Mickey's restaurant chain went public in June 1969. Mantle thought "we served the best chicken you ever ate, not to mention the beans and ham hocks, chicken-fried steak, creamed gravy, beef stew, and ice tea in Mason jars." He was right; the food was great. But the venture made Mantle a millionaire only on paper. The financial end of the business was grossly mishandled; after the majority stock changed hands several times, the chain was bankrupt the following year (Dick Young, "Farewell to Mickey Mantle," *Sport*, April 1969).

leaguers share my view of baseball reality. Among those who do not, the most prominent is the great Willie Mays, who reports from the privileged isolation of his huge success that he has absolutely nothing to complain about."[12] Mays's attitude toward free agency in baseball never really changed. James Hirsch argues that there was a consensus among his contemporaries in favor of free agency, but that "Mays believes something important was lost with free agency. Mays wants to see players make as much money as possible, and while he has always felt aligned with the owners, he's never had any stake in their profits. Free agency, to Mays, was not simply about the dollars. It was about values. Mays prizes stability, order, and loyalty, and the reserve clause ensured that rosters were family stable and that teams could be kept together. Free agency, however, invited disruption for management while obliterating any pretense that the players were loyal to their teammates, their organizations, or to their cities." Further, Hirsch writes, "Mays' central point — that the demise of the reserve clause contributed to a free-wheeling money culture, which has diminished the players' devotion to the game, fed their conceit about their self-worth, and raised self-aggrandizement to an art form — stands as a reasonable critique of the modern game."[13]

Many sports fans would agree that the modern athlete's "self-aggrandizement" occasionally reaches distasteful heights — although to what extent that is a result of free agency is anyone's guess. Beyond that point, though, Willie's position defies logic. Since when did being paid more money ever diminish a player's devotion to the game? Did having economic control of the players diminish the *owners'* devotion to the game? And where was Horace Stoneham's and Walter O'Malley's and other owners' loyalty to their fans and cities when they packed up their teams and moved them to new cities that promised higher profits?

Where, in fact, was the concept of loyalty at all when players had no choice as to where they played? How can one truly say that any ballplayer, up to and including Willie Mays, was being loyal to his teammates, organization, or city when he had no choice as to where he played? And if Mays truly "wanted to see players make as much money as possible," how exactly did he think that would happen when the players had no power to negotiate?

Of course, the irony—which must surely have occurred to Willie Mays over the years, and especially late in his career when he was plagued with financial difficulties—is that no player who ever stepped onto a baseball field would have been a more prized free agent than Willie Mays in his prime.

On July 18, 1970, in the second inning of a game against the Montreal Expos, Willie, in front of a hometown crowd, stroked an 0-2 pitch that one-hopped between shortstop and third base for his 3,000th major league hit. At the time, he was just the ninth player in baseball history to reach that milestone. In a cover story for *Sports Illustrated*, Roy Blount Jr. asked rhetorically, "Who else is still flashing a verve that dates back to the Korean War? 'The only difference between the young Mays and the old Mays,' says Montreal manager Gene Mauch, 'is that it's hard for a 39-year old man to feel up to playing like Willie Mays every day. But when he feels like it—when I see him up at the plate with the lineup card and he has that look, I say, Oh, bleep.' "

Blount's profile was sprinkled with valentines: "He's a beautiful person, says Giants outfielder Frank Johnson. 'I don't think anybody on the club dislikes him. If they do, they're crazy.' Bobby Bonds adds, 'He's the most nonchalant superstar you'll ever see. He acts just like he draws the minimum.' " But there were some spiders on the valentine. Blount dared to comment on some facts that few writers had previously noted. "Mays," he wrote, "would rather not have his significance probed and belabored in interviews with the press, with whom he is wary. The San Francisco writers give him his due as 'incomparable,' but many avoid him personally because 'He never says anything.' He is defensive towards writers he hasn't known for a long time. He can also be curt, and what American boy — or sportswriter — wants Willie Mays to have been curt with him?

"In Houston, a long-faced fan kept yelling, 'Hey, Willie!' at Mays from the stands, following him around, tonelessly demanding an autograph while Mays was conferring with his peers during batting practice. Finally the man threw his program and a pen onto the field at Mays's feet, without a word. Mays tossed them back at him without a word."[14]

While Willie was making headlines for his present, Mickey was making them for his past. In the summer of 1970, the sports world was rocked by the publication of what has come to be called the best-selling and most influential sports book ever written, Jim Bouton's *Ball Four.*

Other books, most notably Jim Brosnan's *The Long Season,* had revealed the less glamorous side of the game. But Bouton's book opened the public's eyes to things the baseball press, through a gentleman's agreement, simply didn't write about: drinking parties, skirt chasing, the often irresponsible and childish behavior of the players off the field, and even their cheating on it. (Bouton revealed how Yankee catcher Elston Howard scuffed baseballs for his pitcher Whitey Ford.)

More than forty years later, *Ball Four* remains a great read and one of the best insights into the life of a professional ballplayer ever written, but it's hard for today's fans to understand why it was so shocking at the time, and why Mantle, in particular, was deeply embarrassed, especially since his children had come of age and could read about their father's antics. In the early 1970s, there had been no public discussion of Mantle's many bad habits and often shameful personal life: his betting on horse races and golf matches (though Willie Mays might have had something to say on the latter) or the impact of his drinking and nightlife on his injury problems. Would he have healed more quickly, Bouton asked rhetorically, "if he'd been sleeping more and loosening up at the bar with the boys less?"[15]

Ball Four also eroded forever the vision of Mantle as a smiling, all-American model for youth: "There were times when he'd push little kids aside when they wanted his autograph, and the times when he was snotty to reporters, just about making them crawl and beg for a minute of his time. I've seen him close a bus window on kids trying to get his autograph. And I hated that *look* of his when he'd get angry at somebody and cut him down with a glare. Bill Gilbert of *Sports Illustrated* once described that look as flickering across his face 'like the Nictitating membrane in the eye of a bird.' And I don't like the Mantle that refused to sign baseballs in the clubhouse before games. Everybody else had to sign, but [clubhouse man] Little Pete [Previte] forged Mantle's signature."[16]

The funny thing, though, on rereading *Ball Four* many years later, is that the book does not mock Mantle but humanizes him. The picture Bouton painted was of a flawed but complex human being, a man of generosity to his teammates and opponents alike. Bouton relates a story that Mickey loved to tell about Yankees manager Johnny Keane, the man who was hired from the St. Louis Cardinals after Yogi Berra was fired in 1964. Bouton wrote that Mantle's story would invariably go like this:

> How do your legs feel today, Mick?
>
> Not too good.
>
> Yes, but how do they feel?
>
> It hurts when I run, the right one especially. I can't stride on it or anything.
>
> Well, do you think you can play?
>
> I don't know. I *guess* I can play. Yeah, hell, what the hell. Sure, I can play.
>
> Good, great, we need you out there. Unless you're hurt — unless it really hurts you. I don't want you to play if you're hurt.
>
> No, it's okay, I hurt, but it's okay. I'll watch it.
>
> Good, good. We sure need you.

After a while, Bouton wrote, they had a routine in the outfield:

> Mick, how does your leg feel?
> Well, it's severed at the knee.
> Yes, but does it hurt?
> No, I scotch-taped it back into place.
> And how's your back?
> My back is broken in seven places.
> Can you swing the bat?
> Yeah, I can swing. If I can find some scotch-tape.
> Great. Well, then get in there. We need you.*[17]

Bouton represented a new generation of ballplayers who were college-educated, hip, and socially conscious. He loved Mickey, but he saw him without illusion and noted how immature and downright juvenile he could be at times. Fifteen years after the publication of *Ball Four*, Mickey was doing Bouton one better and telling outrageous stories about himself. In his 1985 memoir, he related incidents he never would have talked about years before — or at least not before the publication of *Ball Four* — like the night he and Billy Martin were drunk, crawled out onto a ledge outside their hotel room window, and had to circle the hotel on their hands and knees to get back into their rooms.

For the next fifteen or so years, Mickey would transform himself into a professional Mickey Mantle storyteller, grinning and telling self-deprecating tales to Dick Cavett, David Letterman, or any other talk show host who invited him to appear. A story spread that Mantle and Bouton were enemies; some even said that it was Mantle who asked the Yankees to ban Bouton from Yankees' old-timers games.

---

* Mantle, though he never openly rebelled against him, never got along with Keane. "After all those years in the major leagues," he said, "I was too old to knuckle under to Keane's regimentation and his silly little high school rules" (Mantle and Gluck, *The Mick*, p. 214). Keane was fired in 1966 after the Yankees won just four of their first twenty games. Ralph Houk replaced him.

None of it was true. The Yankees had plenty of reason to be angry at Bouton without Mickey's assistance, and the reason they never got together was that their paths never crossed. They lived in different worlds. Bouton went on to write more books, start a bubblegum brand and personalized trading cards company, and even act on TV and in films.

In 1996 I interviewed Bouton for a story that appeared in the *Village Voice*. Bouton told me that when Mickey's son Billy died in 1994, he had written him a letter of condolence. One day when he arrived at his office in Teaneck, New Jersey, he found a message on his answering machine that began, "Hey, bud."

"It was so great to hear his voice," Bouton told me. "He thanked me for my letter and said he was 'cool' with *Ball Four* — 'Don't let it bother you.' He also wanted me to know he had nothing to do with the Yankees black-balling me from the old-timers games. I still have the tape."

If there was a kicker to the story, it's that as a boy Bouton was a Willie Mays, not a Mickey Mantle, fan. "I was always a Giants fan when I was a kid," he wrote in *Ball Four*. "Whenever we played stick ball as kids, we'd take turns being the Giants and Dodgers. I pitched to Willie Mays hundreds of times, only it was my brother, batting righthanded even though he was lefthanded so he'd look as much like Willie as possible."[18]

I n spite of being a good baseball book, *Ball Four* depressed me when I read it in the summer of 1970. I felt as if something had been taken away. One day shortly after I finished the book I went to a newsstand and, for some reason, stopped to look at a comic-book rack. It occurred to me that I had not bought a comic book since 1962, the first year Bouton pitched for the Yankees and the last time Mantle and Mays played against each other in the World Series. My eye was drawn to the June issue of *Action Comics*, which showed Superman being struck out by a Little League pitcher. "Ha! Ha!" read a caption balloon. "He's got muscles, but he's no Super-Mantle!" *Well, good,*

I thought. *He's been out of the game for two years, but they haven't forgotten him.*

Mickey's post-baseball career was little more than one long series of regrets. By 1985, he was finally able to "admit to myself that I gave Merlyn everything she wanted except having me around enough. I was no better father than I was a husband. I've been to my kids just about like what I've been to Merlyn." And here was the key admission: "I didn't spend the time with them that my dad spent with me."[19]

The Yankees gave him a job as a batting instructor. It was a disaster; Mickey had no idea how to instruct young players. What could he tell them? He had been playing baseball since he could walk and by the last few years of his career was playing on sheer willpower. He had long ago forgotten the details and fine points of baseball, and even if he hadn't, he had no idea how to articulate them.

The year 1971 saw Willie's last flash of greatness. At the relatively old age of forty, he learned some new tricks. He still hit with some power — 18 home runs and 24 doubles, the most he had hit in five seasons — but the Giants thought he would be useful batting in the leadoff spot, and Willie responded with remarkable efficiency. Like Mickey in his later years, he proved adept at getting on base without a hit; he batted just .271 but actually led the NL in both walks and on-base percentage, the first time he had led in the first category and only the second time he'd led in the second. He also stole 23 bases. And like Mickey, he learned to play first base and played it well for 44 games. Willie's season ended, though, in the playoffs. The Giants, winners of the NL's Western Division, faced the Pittsburgh Pirates for the pennant; the Pirates won and went on to win the World Series over the Baltimore Orioles. Willie had to face facts: it wasn't likely he would ever get into the World Series again.

Willie had always been one to keep his personal life private. In the 1950s and 1960s, this was easy, as the mainstream press, exclusively white, paid little attention to what black athletes did off the field. Sportswriters who had known Willie since his rookie season, particularly Einstein and Hano, knew the particulars of his unfortunate first marriage to Marghuerite but wrote little or nothing about it. And so the baseball world was caught by surprise when, in November 1971, it was announced that he had married Mae Louise Allen. His friends thought that she was the best thing ever to happen to him.

Mae Allen had seen Willie play when she was a young girl and her father, a chauffeur, had taken her to see the Pirates at Forbes Field. Years later, Willie met her almost by accident. Wilt Chamberlain knew her, liked her, and told Willie she was a nice girl, "though kind of a square," which happened to be exactly what Willie was looking for. He called her the next time he was in Pittsburgh; they went to dinner (Mays brought his teammate Willie McCovey along), and they liked each other. Allen, a graduate of the University of Pittsburgh with a graduate degree in social work from Howard, soon moved to San Francisco, where she got a job as a child-welfare worker and saw Willie on a much more regular basis. James Hirsch quoted a friend: "She thought Willie was her soul mate from the first time they met. She never dated another person, and needless to say, she had tons of admirers."[20]

In 1974, during an appearance on *The Merv Griffin Show*, Mays was asked what he thought a woman's role should be. "Women," Willie replied with a straight face, "should be in the kitchen." The remark caused a commotion in the press. But as Hirsch points out, "the irony was that Willie loved a woman who did not stay in the kitchen but seemed to satisfy the feminist ideal — a financially independent professional who was not tethered to a man for her own happiness."[21]

By 1972, National League managers were no longer saying, "Oh [bleep]," when Willie Mays came to bat. Watching Willie bat through the first nineteen games of the season was torture; his batting average was just .184, the worst beginning to a season he had had since his rookie year. Three years earlier, watching Mays on a hit-less weekend against the Braves, the *Atlanta Constitution*'s Furman Bisher wrote, "Willie Mays wasn't supposed to grow old. He was sup-posed to go on forever, his cap flying off as he broke the sound barrier on foot, face bright and two eyes twinkling like stars. Willie Mays was born for eternal youth. Age is acting in direct violation of that code."

Before the season, Mays asked Horace Stoneham for a ten-year, $750,000 contract. Obviously Willie had plans to stay with the Giants in some sort of front-office position for years after his playing days were over. He found out with a shock that, as John Matuszak's foot-ball player says to Charles Durning's coach in *North Dallas Forty*, "when we call it a game, you call it a business. When we call it a business, you call it a game." Stoneham called it a business — loyalty in baseball was a one-way street. The player was expected to give it to the team, but the team could reject the player for whatever reason it chose. Despite Mays's twenty-one years of service with the Giants, Stoneham double-talked Willie, telling him that the Giants' board of directors was authorized to offer him only a five-year deal. It was the first time Willie had ever heard Stoneham say that important team decisions were made by the board of directors. He decided to turn down Stoneham's offer and settled for a two-year contract as a player for $165,000 a season — not bad money for a player who had not hit over .300 in six seasons or more than 28 home runs in the last five.

The season began horribly for the Giants, and the team was scarcely out of the gate when communications problems developed between Willie and Giants manager Charlie Fox. Before the first game of a doubleheader, Willie handed the lineup card to the home plate umpire and, apparently miffed because he was not in the lineup, left the stadium without telling Fox. Fox fumed. A few days later, the Giants suffered three ugly losses to the New York Mets. They then traveled to Philadelphia. On May 5, while Mays was resting for a game with the Phillies, he took a phone call from a New York reporter he knew who told him of a red-hot rumor: the Giants had been talk-ing to the Mets about a trade.

Willie was in shock. His first thought was not that the Giants had traded him but that Stoneham hadn't told him. When he reached the ballpark, he found reporters not just from Philadelphia but from New York and other major league cities. He seemed subdued. "I'm not mad at anybody," he told them. "They're mad at me." And, "When your time is up, they tell you to go? That's not fair." After two decades of benefiting from benevolent paternalism, Mays had discovered what professional baseball was like for all other players.

The New York sports pages were once again alive with Willie Mays headlines: Willie was coming back to New York. Though he had played in the city for only a little more than five full seasons, many veteran sportswriters were proclaiming him the most popular ballplayer in the city's baseball history. There was something to be said for their argument.

The actual terms of the deal were hidden in the stories. The Giants received some cash — some reported the sum was $100,000, but the Giants never confirmed that, implying that the actual amount was much less — and a pitcher named Charlie Williams, who would last eight years in the big leagues. Williams spent the rest of his career with San Francisco, winning 23, losing 22, and gaining his dollop of fame as the answer to a trivia question: who was the man traded for Willie Mays? Back in San Francisco, Horace Stoneham gave a teary press conference in which he blamed the trade on the Giants' financial woes and their financial difficulties on having to compete with another team in the Bay Area. (At the same time, the other team, Charlie Finley's Oakland A's, was poised in 1972 to win the first of three consecutive World Series, so the economy must have been doing a bit better on the eastern side of the Bay.)

It didn't take Willie long, though, to understand that there was an upside to the trade: New York wanted him back with a passion. The *Daily News*'s Dick Young, perhaps the one writer in New York who was the biggest cheerleader for both Mays and Mantle, expressed the city's sentiments when he wrote, "When there's a chance to get Willie Mays, don't quibble about a decade or two."[22] The wave of emotion that greeted Willie upon his return was unlike anything seen in New York sports history.

Yankees fans had regarded Mickey Mantle with unconditional love only from 1961 through the end of his career, but no baseball fan in New York withheld anything from Willie. Joe DiMaggio had alienated fans for a while when he held out for more money during the war; some who had followed Joe's career closely felt that it was only in his last few seasons that Yankee fans began to acknowledge his true greatness. In any event, as Roger Kahn put it, "what Yankee fans felt for DiMaggio was awe, not love." Lou Gehrig was booed occasionally for not being Babe Ruth, and Babe Ruth was often booed early in his Yankee years for *being* Babe Ruth — that is, for striking out too much, losing his temper with fans and his manager, and not being the kind of ballplayer John McGraw, New York's most revered manager, thought he should be.

But with Willie Mays, it was a matter of pure love from the first time they saw him step onto a ball field. Even Brooklyn Dodgers fans had cheered him just before he left for the Army. Many sportswriters around the country were indignant that the Giants had shown such lack of respect by trading him; they apparently forgot that Ty Cobb and Babe Ruth had been traded near the end of their careers and that the Dodgers had been willing to trade Jackie Robinson to the hated Giants.

Part of Mets fans' enthusiasm — they were, after all, mostly former Giants and Dodgers fans — stemmed from knowing that Willie had had a pretty good year in 1971 and a repeat performance would be a big boost to the team. (Mays's 18 home runs and 23 stolen bases from the season before could have been team highs for the '72 Mets, for whom John Milner paced the team in homers with 17 and Bud Harrelson led in stolen bases with just 12.)

Sportswriters and fans, however, were overlooking some cold, hard facts. The first was that the Willie Mays who came to the Mets in 1972 was light-years from the Say Hey Kid who had gone west with his team fifteen years before. Right after the trade was completed, the Giants manager, Charlie Fox, had told the *San Francisco Chronicle's* Glenn Dickey, "They should have traded him five years ago. I'm supposed to be the manager, but I f____g had to come to him every day and say 'Willie, can you play today?' "

The year before, Dickey had written in his column: "Mays is certainly the best and most exciting ballplayer of his generation. But he sheds his greatness like a cloak when he leaves the playing field, the Willie Mays myth not to the contrary. You know the myth, created by New York: Mays, the 'Say-Hey' Kid, a happy-go-lucky fellow with a kind word for everyone. Try that on an autograph-seeking kid who has been brushed off, a sportswriter who has been cursed, a manager who had tried to exercise authority, a black who had tried to get Mays to speak out against racial inequalities as Hank Aaron, Bill White, and Bob Gibson do.

"Mays always had an idolatrous press, but that has not made him cooperative. He talks only to the sycophants and those he thinks can help him. Questions from the others are met with obscenities or silence. . . . Giants managers are hardly more fortunate. They know they must give Mays preferential treatment or Willie will become fatigued or beset by one of his mysterious ailments."[23] New York sportswriters knew little of the bad humor that had festered in Willie during his last few months with the Giants, and the ones who did either ignored it or simply blamed the Bay Area sportswriting establishment, which the New York crowd had pretty much been hostile to since the Giants went west.

On May 12, Willie Mays came to bat to ecstatic applause from a Shea Stadium crowd against, of course, the San Francisco Giants. There were only about 35,000 in the stands because rain had threatened to cancel the game. It was the final game of a three-game set, and fans were already murmuring at, if not actually booing, manager Yogi Berra for not having played Willie earlier. (When a pinch-hitting opportunity came up in the first game, Berra went with the percentages and sent up the left-handed hitter John Milner.) The uniform looked odd on Mays — the Mets cap was Dodger blue with the Old English "NY" that the Giants had worn — but there was the number 24 on his back, and that's what mattered. (Outfielder Jim Beauchamp had been wearing number 24 but graciously turned it over to Willie, becoming number 5.)

Giants pitcher "Sudden Sam" McDowell smiled at his former teammate and then proceeded to walk him when a curve just missed on a 3-2 count. The second time around, McDowell fanned Mays. In the fifth inning, with the score tied at 4–4 and Don Carrithers on the mound as the drizzle turned into a hard rain, Willie connected with a curveball and drove it on a line into the left-field seats. Grinning, his old teammates blocked his path around the bases; after touching home plate, he instinctively headed toward the San Francisco dugout before realizing his mistake and trotting back. The Mets won, 5–4. It was the only bit of magic anyone would see in Shea Stadium that season.

Willie didn't do badly in 88 games with the Mets over the remainder of the 1972 season. He hit .250 with 8 home runs and 11 doubles in 244 at-bats. With or without him, the Mets were caught in a spiral of mediocrity that had begun the year after their 1969 "miracle" year, and they finished third in the NL East for the third consecutive year, thirteen and a half games out of first.

The major leagues' first players' strike, which began on April 1, 1972, gave Willie Mays an opportunity to have his one heroic moment as a union member, the only known time he stood up to baseball's authority figures.

Gaylord Perry was the Giants' rep, and Mays, because of his national fame and popularity, had been asked to be the number-two man and had accepted. Perry was suddenly unable to meet his obligations, for personal reasons, and Willie surprised his fellow reps by stepping up to bat. Many players feared that the veterans would not have the conviction or patience for a long work stoppage, and soon tensions were running high among the player reps. During one particularly emotional meeting, Willie surprised them all by asking to speak. Marvin Miller recalled that "the room was silent. Willie told everyone, 'I know it's hard being away from the game, and our paychecks and normal lives. I love this game, it's been my whole life, and I know I'm risking a chance to play in what might be my final season. But we made a decision in Dallas to stick together, and until we're satisfied we have to stay together. If we don't hang together, everything we've worked for will be lost." Miller said that Mays was eloquent, empathic, and unwavering. The player reps passed the word on, and the strike continued. On April 13, an agreement was reached.*

One of the most important victories in the 1972 strike was that it brought arbitrators into baseball for the first time. In 1976 that change would result in Peter Seitz overthrowing the reserve clause that had bound players to one team for life. Miller said that his greatest regret was that "I hadn't become the Player Association head ten or twelve years earlier" (he began in 1966). "I would have loved to have seen what Willie Mays, Mickey Mantle, Sandy Koufax, and Henry Aaron would have pulled in as free agents in their primes."[24]

Mickey tried a stint as a baseball color man for NBC, but it was short-lived. Curt Gowdy, a fellow Oklahoman, tried to help him prepare for talking on national TV, but "it was an embarrassment. To say Mickey's heart wasn't in it would be an understatement. In truth he had quite a lot to say about what happened on a baseball field, but he was hampered by what he regarded as lack of intelligence and was reluctant to say anything that might be interpreted as a criticism of other ballplayers. He once told me, 'Shit, man. By the time I was twenty, baseball was an easy game for me to play. I felt like I had already been playing my whole life. Maybe it ain't so easy for some-

---

* Nearly forty years later Miller told me, "I never heard Willie Mays speak with that kind of conviction, either before or after. One of my great regrets is that I did not have a tape recorder on for Willie's speech. I wrote it down afterwards as much as I could remember."

one else."[25] There was another problem: everyone knew he was often inebriated before going on the air.

Mickey spent most waking hours getting drunk or being hung–over. In December 1972, the Yankees sent out a letter to former play–ers. Bob Fishel, director of the business and ticket offices, cheerfully informed Mickey that "1973 marks the 50th anniversary of Yankee Stadium, and we are going to have a season-long Golden Anniversary celebration. We hope to mark the occasion on our Old Timer's Day, Saturday, August 11, as well as on individual dates during the season.

"We thought it would be interesting to learn from you what you consider your outstanding event at Yankee Stadium. In many cases the answer is obvious, but because we are writing a large number of your former team mates, we're asking you to answer this question for us."

Recipients of the letter were asked to complete this sentence: "I consider the following my outstanding experience at Yankee Sta–dium." Mickey's response, handwritten, was "I got a blow-job under the right field bleachers by [i.e., beside] the Yankee bull pen."

The form continued: "This event occurred on or about: (Give as much detail as you can)." Mickey responded, "It was about the third or fourth inning. I had a pulled groin and couldn't fuck at the time. She was a very nice girl and asked me what to do with the come after I came in her mouth. I said, 'Don't ask me, I'm no cocksucker.' "

Signed: "Mickey Mantle*The All American Boy."

Mantle's "outstanding event" was not mentioned at the Old-Timers' Day celebration. Collectors have offered up to $10,000 for his original note.

Willie showed up for the Mets' 1973 spring training a day late with so much tape around his knees that, according to Roger Kahn, "some of the writers thought he looked like Mickey Mantle."[26] He was eager to play, he told the writers, but added, "If I can do it my way." The Mets were managed by perhaps the only New York baseball leg-end who could have rivaled Mays in both respect and affection, Yogi

Berra. Yogi was, and remains to this day, the winningest player in New York, having played on more pennant winners (fourteen) and won more World Series (ten) than any other ballplayer. He had also won more MVP Awards than Willie, three to two. In the process, Yogi had transformed himself into a folk hero, largely through his own infectious good nature but also through the diligent work of sportswriters who rewrote much of what he said into "Yogisms."

That Berra was a disciple of the game who took playing, coaching, and managing very seriously escaped many players, especially Mays, who picked right up with Yogi where he had left off in San Francisco with Charlie Fox. In his 1974 book, the *San Francisco Chronicle*'s Glenn Dickey summed up what no New York writer would say about Willie: "As a Met, Mays's behavior toward manager Yogi Berra was the same as that towards the Giant managers. He left the club in spring training without consulting Berra. He was fined upon his return; half of the fine, said one writer, was for leaving, the other half for returning. During the regular season, he was on the disabled list early. When he came off — ironically against the Giants in San Francisco — he spent one game up in Giants broadcasting booth . . . instead of on the bench with his teammates. The next week Berra put his name on the lineup card without consulting Willie. Mays not only didn't play, he went home — again without permission."[27] Tug McGraw would later recall that Mays and Berra "had a tough time as far as the lineup went, and a lot of times Willie didn't want to come to the ballpark at all." *[28]

Winning, though, like love, covers a multitude of sins, and much to their surprise, the Mets rallied from a midseason slump and a near

---

* James Hirsch felt that "Berra resented Mays being there in the first place. Years later, he was discussing his problems as a Yankee manager when George Steinbrenner kept interfering with the roster. 'It was not just one guy like Willie Mays when he came to the Mets in 1973,' Berra said, 'it was four or five guys who Steinbrenner wanted and the coaches and I didn't' " (Hirsch, *Willie Mays: The Life, the Legend*, p. 517). "Resented" sounds like the wrong word here. I spent most of 2008 and 2009 working on a biography of Berra, and I never heard anyone use the word "resent" in connection with him. That Berra thought Mays couldn't help his team is more likely, and judging from the results, Berra's judgment was justified.

swoon in September to make it to the NL playoffs against the Cincinnati Reds. Few noticed that Willie, hitting .211 in 209 at-bats, had done almost nothing to put them there. He had lost nearly all his speed and range in the outfield, and his throwing arm was so bad that on one occasion he had to relay the ball back into the infield with an underhand toss. For the first time he failed to be voted onto the All-Star team or to be chosen by the NL manager, Sparky Anderson, for the additional roster. Chub Feeney, the NL president, made a special dispensation to include Willie on the team. Mays was at first indignant and declined, but after thinking it over for a day he decided to go.

The Mets prevailed against a superior Reds team for the pennant and then extended the powerful Oakland A's, led by future Hall of Famers Reggie Jackson, Catfish Hunter, and Rollie Fingers, to seven games in the World Series. Willie had one more crack at World Series greatness, and he made the most of it. In Game 2 at Oakland, Willie came to bat in the twelfth inning of a tie game with runners on first and third and two outs. Fingers tried to whip a slider past him in the late-afternoon shadows. Willie lashed a one-hopper over Fingers's outstretched glove; trying to hustle out of the box, he stumbled ingloriously and lost his cap on a major league ball field for the last time. He stayed on base and later scored on an error. The Mets won, 10–7. The A's fans — or at least Giants fans who had come to see an A's World Series game to get a final look at Willie Mays — gave him a standing ovation. Mays was just 2-for-7 in the Series, and the hit in Game 2 produced his only RBI.

It is one of the great statistical oddities in the baseball record books — for it is really no more than that, an oddity — that Willie Mays played in only 20 World Series games and batted 71 times without hitting a single home run. And in one of the oddest contrasts, Mickey Mantle, whose prime years paralleled Willie's, hit 18 World Series home runs, a record that still stands.

⚾ ⚾

The single off Rollie Fingers was satisfying, but one wishes there was something greater, more heroic, to the close of Willie's career. Unlike Mickey, Willie did not wait until the off-season to announce his retirement. On the morning of September 20, he made the announcement on NBC's *Today Show.* At 3:00 that afternoon he held a press conference at Shea Stadium's Diamond Club. "I thought I'd be crying by now," he said as he held back tears, "but I see so many people here who are my friends, I can't. Maybe I'll cry tomorrow." He enumerated his reasons for retirement, which were as negative as Mickey's had been five years earlier: "When you're forty-two hitting .211, it's no fun. . . . I just feel that the people of America shouldn't have to see a guy who can't produce." He squashed rumors that he might take a big league managing job: "Managing is hard work, and I don't want that." Then, stopping to nod at Yogi, "and I don't want to be a coach and just stand out there like an Indian."

Five days later, before a game with the Dodgers, Willie appeared at Shea for what Mayor John Lindsay proclaimed as "Willie Mays Day." With him were Cat, who flew in from Oakland, Mae, and Michael, who was so seldom seen with his father in public that even writers who had followed Willie for years were asking who he was. A handful of baseball greats such as Joe DiMaggio, Stan Musial, Larry Doby, Duke Snider, and Pee Wee Reese were there, as was a man whose name would forever be entwined with Willie's, Vic Wertz. Some Mets fans brought along pictures of Mays's catch in the '54 Series for Wertz to sign. The *Daily News*'s Vic Zeigel asked Wertz if he resented being asked to sign a picture in which he did not appear, one that commemorated a hit taken away from him. "Hell," replied a smiling Wertz, "it's the first time in 15 years anyone's asked me to sign anything."

There were enough gifts to stock a month of episodes of *The Price Is Right,* including a pair of Chryslers for Willie and Mae. More spectacular, though, was a Mercedes-Benz with a card from . . . Horace Stoneham. There were also bottles of champagne and scotch whiskey; no one had told Teacher's and Moet, both advertisers on Mets broadcasts, that Willie did not drink. The strangest gift was from heavyweight champion Joe Frazier, who presented Willie with a gorgeous new snowmobile.

Mays dabbed his eyes and made a few short dignified remarks to the sold-out crowd, ending with: "I see these kids over here, and I see how these kids are fighting for a pennant, and to me it says one thing: Willie, say good-bye to America." He then waved his cap, hugged his wife and son, and picked up a box of long-stemmed roses. Walking over to the first-base line, he presented them to the Mets' revered seventy-year-old owner, Joan Whitney Payson, seated in a wheelchair. Payson leaned over and kissed him on the cheek. Payson had done more than anyone else to bring Willie back to New York.

And yet, in surely one of the strangest endings to a great player's career, there was not a single gift or note from the New York Mets organization. No explanation for this has ever been given.

18

Burden of Dreams

I mourn the season of my youth
In which I revel'd more than most.
— FRANÇOIS VILLON

On August 10, 1974, a chartered bus left Manhattan for Coopers-town, New York; the passengers included Mickey Mantle, Phil Rizzuto, Carl Lombardi (a pal of Mickey's from their sandlot days in Oklahoma), Whitey Ford, and Lovell Mantle, who had come all the way from Oklahoma for the occasion. They were there to see Mickey and Whitey inducted into the Hall of Fame. Mickey's vote was impressive; 322 of 365 for slightly better than 88 percent. Still, it seems odd that forty-three baseball writers did not deem Mickey Mantle worthy of the Hall of Fame.

In his induction speech, Mantle thanked Commissioner Bowie Kuhn — who, in just nine years' time, would ban Mickey from major league baseball — not just for listing his accomplishments, "but for leaving out those strikeouts. He gave all those records but he didn't say anything about all those strikeouts. I was the world champion in striking out. . . . I don't know for sure, but I'm almost positive I must have that record in the World Series too." Mickey thanked his dad, his mom, his family, old high school and sandlot pals, and Barney Barnett, his manager on the Baxter Springs Whiz Kids, who had died two years before. Sticking to the legend, he thanked Tom Greenwade for discovering him. He also thanked Casey Stengel, who had ridden him hard, and Joe DiMaggio, who had all but ignored him during his rookie season. After the ceremony, he showed his mother his shining new Hall of Fame ring. Whitey Ford recalled that Lovell looked at Mickey and asked, "Who in hell is in the Hall of Fame?" Mickey looked at Whitey and grinned, "Well, that'll put you in your place, won't it?"[1]

The Hall of Fame induction was one of the few times in the decade that most of Mickey's family was together. Later, he could not remember where he was when he got the news that his son Billy, whom he had named for Billy Martin, was diagnosed with Hodgkin's disease. The news devastated Mickey and helped confirm his fatalistic view of life. Mickey had made it past the age when most of the men in his family had died of Hodgkin's, but now a new guilt weighed upon him: the disease had passed him up only to strike his nineteen-year-old son.

Mickey didn't pray for his son; he once confessed to a writer that he didn't even know how to say the Lord's Prayer. Hodgkin's did not get Billy, who, like his three brothers and both parents, was an alcoholic and developed heart disease. He was thirty-six when he finally succumbed to a heart attack in 1994. His father was in the Betty Ford Center when Billy died.

Mickey Mantle was always there for me, even in retirement. His image of eternal youth, grace, speed, and power was ingrained on my mind's eye whenever I saw baseball played. To the outside world in the 1970s, by contrast, it was as if he had ceased to exist. Now and then, though, he popped up in the most unlikely places.

In the spring of 1977, working on a story for the *Birmingham News*, I interviewed the diva of local theater, Margie Bolding. Margie was performing the one-woman show *I Don't Want to Be Zelda Anymore,* inspired by the wife of F. Scott Fitzgerald. We met at her century-old house on the crest of Red Mountain, with its panoramic views of the city and walls covered with family memorabilia. (The Rev. O. T. Bolding's five daughters — "the *Fabulous* Bolding Girls," Margie laughingly recalled — had moved to Birmingham as teenagers.) When I took off my jacket, revealing a navy blue Yankees spring training shirt with MANTLE on the back — the kind that wasn't used during Mantle's career — Ms. Bolding beamed. "Turn off the recorder," she said, "and I'll tell you about me and Mickey." And she did.

Margie was living in New York when she met Mickey at the Harwyn Club on East Fifty-Second Street in Manhattan. This was in the midst of Mickey's greatest season, 1956, when he was chasing Babe Ruth's home run record, the Triple Crown, and just about anything attractive in a skirt.* Margie, an aspiring actress, was tall, blond, and statuesque in 1956 — even as she was still in 1977. She was waiting for friends when the maître d' politely informed her that "Mr. Mantle requests that you join him." "I told him that I didn't know who Mr. Mantle was," but, she said in relating the story to me, "of course I knew who he was. That is, I certainly recognized the name. There wasn't anyone in New York and probably very few in America who didn't know who Mickey Mantle was. But I wasn't going to admit that to the maître d' or to 'Mr. Mantle.' "

Unlike Tallulah Bankhead, another actress from Alabama who had come to New York two decades before, Margie didn't know a thing about baseball. She did know, however, that a well-bred southern girl did not go to a strange man's table, even if that man was possibly the most famous man in the country. She told the messenger that she would be receptive toward Mr. Mantle joining her. Mantle did not. He did, however, follow her into the powder room, where, with

---

*In 2008, when my friend Jane Leavy was researching her biography of Mickey, *The Last Boy,* I hooked her up with Ms. Bolding. When she spoke to Leavy, Margie couldn't pinpoint the exact year she had met Mickey, but my memory is precise on the point — in 1977 she told me it was 1956.

a grin as big as the Oklahoma sky, he told her, "You got the prettiest blue eyes I've ever seen."

It became, she told me, a "unique relationship" that lasted for decades. There were high times, some of them in public. Once, in P. J. Clarke's while Mickey, Margie, and her sister Bonnie were eating hamburgers in a backroom, a customer shouted something abusive — or at least it sounded that way to Bonnie, who, blessed with what Margie called "that Fabulous Bolding Girl temper," picked up a bottle of ketchup from which the cap had been removed and threw it at the man, splattering ketchup all over him. Mantle immediately jumped up. The man said, "That's okay, Mickey. Any woman with Mickey Mantle who wants to cover me with ketchup is okay by me." (They invited him to join the party.)[2]

When I spoke to Margie again a few years ago, she offered few details about her and Mickey except to say that he had once bought her a pair of cowboys boots with red hearts at Billy Martin's country and western store. He got them tickets to Yankees games, both in New York and on the road; once, when Bolding was in Chicago with her son Ernie, Mickey called out, "Hi, kid!" and, as Margie recalled it, hit a home run for him. And when her mother, Gertha, was in the hospital, Mickey surprised her by dropping by her room with flowers. "He could really surprise you sometimes by being so thoughtful," she said.

Recently Bolding sat down and penned a posthumous letter to Mickey, drawing on years of memories. You can hear her reading it, at times in tears, online (Google "Margie Bolding Open Letter to Mickey Mantle"). The lines I like best: "You used people and allowed people to use you and you were generous to a fault," "You were kind to my family and my son," and "Life was too short, there never was enough time for you to discover the real you that I knew and loved."

When Commissioner Bowie Kuhn stood on a stage in Coopers-town on August 5, 1979, to introduce Willie Mays, no one could have had any idea that in a few months' time Kuhn would be the man who banished Willie Mays from baseball. "Willie Mays needs no embroidery," Kuhn told the raucous Cooperstown crowd. The excited fans chanted, "Wil-*lee*, Wil-*lee!*" so loudly that Mays's first words could scarcely be heard. Apparently casting aside the outline of his speech, Willie gave an impromptu history of his life, starting with "My uncle told me when I was ten, 'Boy, you have to be a ballplayer.' And my high school principal told me, 'We will put you out of school if you don't play sports.' " Curiously, Cat Mays, who was there, was not mentioned by his son, and Willie revised some history about his high school principal, who had actually told him he could get paid for playing baseball with the Black Barons if he played football for Fairfield Industrial. Willie thanked the Birmingham Black Barons: "We had twenty-five guys on the club, and all twenty-five would put me to bed every night. I didn't get to meet many girls that way, but I got plenty of sleep." (Actually, while Willie was there the Barons usually had an active roster of sixteen.) It was odd that he did not acknowledge Piper Davis, without whom he might never have made it to the major leagues.

He thanked Leo Durocher, who was in attendance, profusely, and called Giants owner Horace Stoneham "my backbone." He forgave the city of San Francisco for not appreciating him enough: "It took them about five years to get used to me there. They had another center fielder. His name was Joe DiMaggio" (though in fact DiMaggio had been gone from San Francisco nearly twenty-three years when the Giants moved there).

At least a couple of Willie's remarks were incomprehensible. "Baseball," he told the crowd, "means dedication. You have to sacrifice many things to play baseball. I sacrificed a bad marriage, and I sacrificed a good marriage. But I'm here today because baseball is my number-one love." One wonders, what good marriage did Willie sacrifice? Would Marghuerite have been any less a disaster for Willie if he hadn't been traveling? And he certainly didn't "sacrifice" his marriage to Mae, who turned out to be the best thing that ever happened to him. Was Mae perhaps a bit hurt to find out that baseball, not she, was Willie's "number-one love"?

The vote for Willie's induction was 409 of 432, just under 95 percent. That was higher than any of the post–World War II players whose careers overlapped Willie's, including Joe DiMaggio, Stan Musial, Ted Williams, and Mickey Mantle. In fact, it was the highest vote for any player since the initial five greats — Ty Cobb, Honus Wagner, Walter Johnson, Christy Mathewson, and Babe Ruth — were selected in 1936. And yet . . . when Willie Mays retired, he was second only to Babe Ruth on the all-time home run list, with 660. He had scored 2,062 runs and driven in 1,903, had batted over .300 ten times, had stolen 338 bases, was regarded by many as the greatest defensive outfielder of all time, won two MVP Awards (and should have won seven or eight), and played in twenty-four All-Star Games, more than anyone else . . . and there were still twenty-three cretins who called themselves baseball writers who did not think Willie Mays merited a plaque in the Hall of Fame. Just think about that.

A few months later, Willie would have his run-in with Commissioner Bowie Kuhn. The story began with Al Rosen, who had been a four-time All-Star third baseman and two-time home run champ with the Cleveland Indians in the 1950s — he had been a runner on first base when Vic Wertz hit the fly ball that Mays made into his immortal catch in Game 1 of the 1954 World Series. In 1979, Rosen had quit his job as president of the New York Yankees to become executive vice president of Bally's International. At the time, the most famous sports representative employed by Bally's — some would have called him a greeter — was longtime heavyweight champion Joe Louis, but by 1980 Louis was sixty-four and in failing health. (He would die the next year.)

Rosen had a flash: perhaps the most admired former athlete under the age of fifty was Willie Mays. Rosen offered Mays a ten-year, $100,000-a-year contract — an appealing offer, considering the job pretty much amounted to playing golf and being seen at the Atlantic City casino's public relations and charity events. Willie, who was working for the Mets as a batting coach, told Rosen he was interested.

Bowie Kuhn, one of the most ineffectual baseball commissioners ever, decided to interfere and told Mays he would have to choose between the Mets job and Bally's offer. If he chose Bally's, he would be banned from all future major league functions. Mae Mays told the *New York Times* that "Willie faced this trauma two other times in his life. First when he was traded, then when he retired. We sat around our apartment in Riverdale last night with Willie's lawyer and accountant, using them as a sounding board."[3] Mays pleaded with Kuhn, who wouldn't budge; Willie needed the money and took the job with Bally's.

Kuhn's pronouncement was the act of a pompous and uncompassionate man. Kuhn was supposedly worried about gambling infiltrating baseball, but as James Hirsch phrased it, "The reality was that Mays could in no way affect the outcome of a Major League Baseball game while schmoozing with patrons of a New Jersey casino. He wasn't working for a bookie. The casino had nothing to do with sports betting. All activities in the casino were legal, and under state law Mays wasn't even permitted to gamble there. Part of his job involved going to schools, where he would urge kids not to smoke and drink. He also told them not to gamble."[4]

At a press conference announcing his decision, Willie nearly broke into sobs. "What skills," he asked rhetorically, "do I have outside of baseball? Only public relations, dealing with people." Still, he would not try to challenge Kuhn's decision legally: "That's challenging baseball. I'm not here for that." Willie Mays was never a man to challenge authority. But then, authority had always worked pretty much in Willie's favor.

Nonetheless, the hiring of Mays proved to be a public relations bonanza for Bally's. The only question was why it took the Claridge Casino, which was right across the way from Bally's, three years to realize that Mickey Mantle could do a similar job — minus lecturing school kids on the evils of drinking, one assumes — for them. For Mickey, the decision to go with the casino was much less gut-wrenching than it had been for Willie. The only job Mickey had

had connected with baseball was as a Yankees batting coach, and as he was quick to tell any reporters who would listen, "I wasn't much of a batting coach."

The sports press was pretty much split down the middle on the issue. Murray Chass of the *New York Times* boldly pointed out that Warner Communications had recently invested in the Pittsburgh Pirates and that three of the company's executives had been either convicted of or pleaded guilty to stock-purchasing fraud, yet Kuhn had done nothing to block Warner's purchase of a piece of the Pirates. Chass was suggesting that Kuhn's actions banning Mays and Mantle indicated a double standard. At the *Daily News*, Phil Pepe, who was a good friend of Mantle's and friendly with Willie, also took their side: "The real pity is that there are no jobs in baseball for Mickey Mantle or Willie Mays that can pay them the amount of money they are getting from the casinos."[5] Pepe, though, wasn't being entirely honest. The truth was that Mays might have been able to handle several different jobs in Major League Baseball, but realistically, a job like the one at the casino — which involved mostly shaking hands, playing golf, and telling an occasional joke at a luncheon — was probably the only one Mantle was capable of doing at this point in his life.

Predictably, the eternally crabby Dick Young, then of the *New York Post*, sided with Kuhn: "Mantle is not a baseball leper. He can visit his buddies here or anywhere in baseball. He can play in old timers games, same as Willie Mays."[6] Nonetheless, Mickey told friends that the banishment chafed him; off the record, he told people that he *felt* like a leper. And there was another issue that went unmentioned in the press: unlike Mays, whose gambling was confined to a game of pool or a round of golf, Mantle was a heavy gambler, particularly on college football.

Early in March 1983, I was dispatched to Atlantic City for *Inside Sports* magazine to try to get Mickey and Willie together for a dual interview. This, not scoring a touchdown in the Super Bowl or hitting a home run to win a World Series game, was my ultimate sports fantasy. I touched base with Mickey at the Echelon Mall in southern

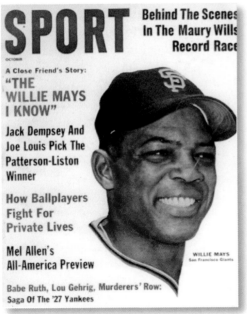

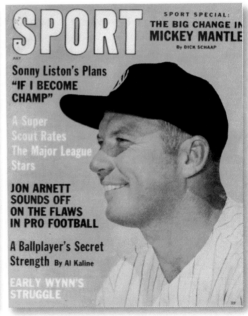

From the early 1950s through the early 1970s, *Sport* magazine set a standard for sports journalism that hasn't been approached before or since. The most popular cover boys were Mickey and Willie, who between them appeared on nearly 20 percent of the magazine's covers until Mantle's retirement in 1968.

SPORT MEDIA GROUP

Despite the title of this 1962 Topps card, Mickey and Willie were not always a manager's dream — Mickey never truly relaxed around Casey Stengel, though they won eight pennants together. Willie had at least some friction with every manager after Leo Durocher.

THE TOPPS COMPANY

Mickey and Willie at the 1962 World Series in San Francisco's Candlestick Park. Charles Einstein wrote, "As the players came in from the field, my eye fell on Mays and Mantle as they entered together, immersed in private conversation of the sort two consummate, tired professionals will have at the end of a day's work. There was no sense that one was black, the other white."

NATIONAL BASEBALL HALL OF FAME, COOPERSTOWN, N.Y.

"All you need are a family, a camera and Kodacolor Film." Mickey got the lion's share of the lucrative national endorsements. Top right with bat in hand is Mickey Jr.

COURTESY OF KODAK CORPORATION

"Little Mickey swings a big bat for a six-year-old. I never thought a shot like this could come out of my Brownie Camera. But leave it to Kodacolor Film!"

Mickey Mantle says: "You don't need any practice to take Kodacolor snapshots like these!"

All you need are a family, a camera and Kodacolor Film. You'll get beautifully lifelike pictures from the first time you try. May Time is Picture Time. Get out your camera.

"I'm no photographer," admits Yankee slugger Mickey Mantle, "but look at the color snapshots I got. Nothing special about *how* you take them—just so it's with Kodacolor Film. It sure gives pictures that look real!" (Use Kodacolor in *any* camera. It can be processed locally in many cities, or by Kodak. Ask your dealer.)

"Merlyn and Davey, he's four, both sport green thumbs. I've taped an 11x14 blow-up of this shot on the door of my locker. It's a real knockout!"

"The barefoot boy at our house is Davey. We mailed prints of this picture to the folks back in Oklahoma. They said it was almost like a visit!"

"The whole gang, even baby Billy, sat for this. The same roll of Koda-color works great with flash, too!"

See Kodak's "The Ed Sullivan Show" and "The Adventures of Ozzie and Harriet"

EASTMAN KODAK COMPANY, Rochester 4, N. Y.

Kodak

"**Here's the way to get a hot streak going at the dinner table**"

says **WILLIE MAYS**

BASEBALL'S HOTTEST STAR GOES FOR AMERICA'S HOTTEST SAUCE

There's only one Willie Mays. There's only one Frank's Red Hot Sauce. Both are the hottest in their fields. And Willie goes for Frank's Red Hot Sauce on ribs, chicken and greens with the same "Say-hey" enthusiasm that he goes for the fences in every ballpark in the league. "Try it", says Willie, "your appetite will have a real hot streak going for it."

WRITE FOR FRANK'S RED HOT SAUCE RECIPES.
The Frank Tea & Spice Co., Dept. WM, Cincinnati, Ohio 45202

Mickey got the endorsements for Kodak, Timex, and other big-name companies. Most of Willie's endorsements were for products targeted to the much smaller black audiences.

"The Champions Choice." In 1963 Mickey suggested to his agent, Mike Scott, that a product endorsed by both him and Willie might appeal to a wide audience. Scott, who also handled some endorsements for Mays, got them with Zipee, who made plastic balls and bats similar to those made by Wiffle. This modest little plastic ball may well have had the first interracial sports product promotion.

Mickey, Merlyn, and the boys on a vacation. To the public they were an ideal family, but later Mickey would openly lament he had been "a terrible father." His wife and all four of his sons became alcoholics. Billy died of a heart attack in 1994 at age thirty-six, while Mickey Jr. succumbed to non-Hodgkins lymphoma in 2000, age forty-seven. Left to right: Danny, Mickey Jr., Billy, and David.

PERSONAL COLLECTION OF THE MANTLE FAMILY

Willie and Marghuerite admire their adopted son, Michael. This is one of the rare photos of Willie and Michael, and little is known about their relationship.

AP/WIDE WORLD PHOTOS

Mickey is presented with two horses from a friend in Texas at the first Mickey Mantle Day, September 9, 1965. Mantle always loved horses; as a boy he rode Tony to school. (Tony was named after the famous steed of Mickey's cowboy movie idol Tom Mix.) CORBIS

In the mid-1960s Joe Namath supplanted Mickey as New York's number one sports idol. The two hit it off immediately, but not even the advertising genius of George Lois could save the short-lived employment agency the two stars fronted, Mantle Men and Namath Girls. COURTESY OF GEORGE LOIS

Mickey and Willie in *Esquire*, August 1968. Seventeen years later in Atlantic City, when they signed the picture for me, Willie told Mickey, "I sure look better than you." "Hell you do," said Mantle. "I look great in that suit. Yours looks off the rack." COURTESY OF PARS INTL.

Just a couple of country boys — Mickey and Willie share some corn and Blue Bonnet margarine in a 1983 commercial. COURTESY OF GEORGE LOIS

Willie and Mickey in a 1982 commercial for a new daily paper, *USA Today*. "I read it every day," sang Mickey, "just like my friend Say Hey." COURTESY OF GEORGE LOIS

Mickey, Duke Snider, and Willie on an unidentified TV show in 1981. Mays always seemed to be sharper dressed in public than Mantle. AP/WIDE WORLD PHOTOS

The Return of the Prodigal Sons. New commissioner Peter Ueberroth scored a big hit with fans by welcoming baseball's two most beloved stars back to the game; they had been banished by previous commissioner Bowie Kuhn for taking PR jobs with Atlantic City casinos. CORBIS

OUR GUEST   By Bill Gallo

MANTLE

MAYS

GIANTS

CUT OUT AND PLACE IN DOTTED LINES ON FIGURE ACCORDINGLY— IF MICKEY ADD PIN-STRIPES.

THE BEST

WE THINK IT'S A TOSS-UP, SO FOR THE BENEFIT OF ALL THOSE WHO WRITE IN AND ASK— "WHO'S BETTER?"— WE ASK YOU TO DRAW YOUR OWN CONCLUSIONS!

Left: The late great Bill Gallo eloquently addressed the "Who's the best?" question in this 1964 *New York Daily News* cartoon. COURTESY OF BILL GALLO

Below: New Mexico artist Thom Ross captured Willie's 1954 World Series feat in this installation and brought it to New York on the fiftieth anniversary of "The Catch." His efforts to make the diorama permanent have yet to produce results from the City of New York. The four figures, seen here at the former site of the Polo Grounds in Harlem, now reside with Ross's friend Rich Tarrant Jr., who mounts them in his front yard in Burlington, Vermont, during the baseball season. COURTESY OF THOM ROSS AND GUY WATKINS

New Jersey, where he was signing autographs. "Yeah, sure, day after tomorrow, right? Yeah, I'm on." He was in a good mood and handed me a button from his previous Echelon Mall appearance. (I still have the button.)

I saw Mays briefly at Bally's; he was brusque and seemed distracted, but he was game: "Yeah, sure, I'll get with Mickey. Will give me a chance to win back some of the money I lost to him on the golf course a couple of weeks ago." (I hadn't thought of that; maybe I could ask questions and record their answers while the two of them went head-to-head on the golf course. What a story that would make.)

I was so close. But I couldn't get Mickey and Willie together—for one reason or another—through 1983. The next year, I was promised by both that we'd get together for sure in the fall. It never came off.

It wasn't until eight years later, working with Marvin Miller on his autobiography, *A Whole Different Ballgame*, that I found out the details of what sabotaged my plan. Soon after Peter Ueberroth became commissioner in October 1984, he called the new head of the Players Association, Donald Fehr, and asked to set up a meeting with Miller, who, after all, had started the union. According to Marvin, "he asked to get together to become acquainted and to discuss ways to head off future problems." At their first meeting, over lunch, Ueberroth raised the idea of lifting Bowie Kuhn's ban on Willie Mays and Mickey Mantle. Miller told him that he was enthusiastic about the idea and that it would be a huge hit with baseball fans everywhere.

I found out about Ueberroth's decision the day before I was scheduled to meet Mickey and Willie in Atlantic City, and when they canceled their trip to New York for a photo shoot, I knew I'd probably never be able to get them together in the same spot again. A few days later, I passed a newsstand and saw three smiling faces gracing the cover of *Sports Illustrated*: Peter Ueberroth, Willie Mays, and Mickey Mantle.

The New York Mets had not given Willie a gift on the day he retired, and it took the Giants a long, long time to finally give him their own tribute. Their tardiness was an ongoing source of bafflement and irritation to Mays over the years. To be fair to the Giants, they had scheduled a Willie Mays Day a few years earlier, in 1979, but Willie had balked, asking to receive compensation for the extra seats he would fill that day. To be fair to Mays, his point was perfectly valid. The Giants weren't selling out home games that year, and a Willie Mays Day could certainly have been counted on to fill Candlestick Park. To be even fairer, by one account Willie wanted the money, or at least part of it, for his Say Hey Foundation. In any event, for reasons that remain a mystery to this day, Willie Mays had to wait more than twenty-five years to have a day with the San Francisco Giants.

The Mick, published in the spring of 1985, hit bookstores at precisely the right moment. Mickey had been almost completely out of the public eye for much of the 1970s, but the bad publicity — and then the *good* publicity — over his Atlantic City stint at the Claridge had put him back in the minds of fans who were now prepared to view him through the haze of nostalgia. Mantle had finally found a post-career job: being Mickey Mantle.

In later years, sportswriters often quipped, with some degree of truth, that Mickey Mantle and Willie Mays "invented nostalgia" — which is to say, they were the biggest draws on the autograph circuit. The truth was that Mantle was far more in demand than Mays; no one could say exactly why, but by the mid-1980s Mickey's rookie card was worth at least $30,000, while Willie's sold at about $5,000. Still, there was no prospect more exciting on the autograph circuit than Mantle and Mays appearing at the same show. I saw them together in 1985 in Atlantic City, right after their reinstatement; it took me more than an hour in line to reach them, but I had no thought of not staying the course. When my turn came, I asked them to sign the full-page color photo of them that had appeared in the 1968 *Esquire* in which they interviewed each other. They laughed and giggled like schoolboys. "Man, who took that picture?" Willie asked. "I sure look better than you." "Hell, you do," Mickey told him. "I look great in that suit. Yours looks off the rack." The photo now adorns the wall of the office where I wrote this book.

Mantle's new enterprise might not have been possible if he had not met Greer Johnson at the Claridge in 1983. A former elementary school teacher from Georgia, Johnson organized Mickey's business affairs and fielded offers. After a short time, both proclaimed that they were in love. After managing Mickey's business for a while, Johnson developed a good enough reputation to attract other clients, including Whitey Ford, Yogi Berra, Hank Bauer, and Bill Skowron. It didn't take her long to see "a real big need to protect Mickey. . . . He was like a little boy to me, he was very naive and totally inexperienced when it came to business." She was also more honest with him than anyone else had ever been: "When he'd screw up, and he did, I'd tell him. You know, if he'd been drinking and used foul language, I'd tell him. I wouldn't pull any punches, and I think that's what he respected and trusted. . . . Whenever he got out of line, whenever he did something, the person who felt worse was him."[7]

But even the money and freedom from financial pressure couldn't relieve Mickey's anxieties. At a 1986 card show at the Trump Plaza in Atlantic City commemorating the twenty-fifth anniversary of the great 1961 Yankees World Series champions, thirty-three of Mantle's teammates agreed to appear. There was a ceremony the night before the signing, and by dinnertime Mickey still hadn't shown. Allen Rosen (no relation to the Indians slugger and Claridge executive), who had put the event together, called him in his hotel room. According to Rosen, Mantle had a fit: "Fuck your mother," he screamed into the phone. "Fuck your show, and fuck Donald Trump!" (Trump was among the guests waiting for Mickey to appear.) When he finally did show up, someone approached him, pushing a crippled child in a wheelchair. The boy wanted Mickey to sign a bat. Astonishingly, Mantle refused. He had a long-established rule that he wouldn't sign bats. Sometime later, Bill Skowron brought him a bat that the other thirty-three Yankees from the 1961 team had signed. Mantle again refused to sign. Skowron, who had been buddies with Mickey since they broke into the Yankees' farm system in 1950, was flabbergasted.

Around this time, there was simply no anticipating Mantle's mood and behavior at a given moment. He was visibly irritated when people came up to him, particularly when he was getting on and off a plane, to ask for an autograph. He had Greer Johnson carry a stack of autographed photos to pass out in these circumstances.

There was another side of Mickey that no one wrote about and precious few were able to see. Bob Costas tells this story. "One night, in the late eighties — I don't remember exactly what year — it was January and very cold. We had gone out to eat and were walking back to the Regency, where we were both staying. It was windy, and we had our collars up, but I noticed Mickey had a paper bag jammed in his pocket. He asked me if I'd walk a couple of blocks out of the way with him; it wasn't the kind of night where you wanted to take a long walk, but Mickey seemed a little wobbly and I thought it best to stay with him. We got to Madison Avenue, and Mickey walked up to this cardboard box and rapped on it. This guy with a scraggly beard and a wool ski cap pulled low popped his head out, looking terrified. Then he noticed that it was Mickey, and he beamed, 'Hi, Mick.' Mickey grinned and handed the man his dinner. The homeless guy *knew* him. As we walked away, I thought that what was so amazing about this is that it could have happened only an hour after Mickey had told a stranger to go fuck himself for asking for an autograph."[8]

In August 1985, advertising genius George Lois recruited his old friends Mickey Mantle and Willie Mays for a *USA Today* campaign. Mickey and Willie, along with financial broker Charles Schwab, former Chicago mayor Jane Byrne, and TV weatherman Willard Scott, were filmed for a series of commercials celebrating the paper's third birthday. All contributed their time for free. ("I told Mickey and Willie it would be great national exposure," Lois told me.) In the TV spots, a grinning Mickey, his arm draped around a smiling Willie's shoulder, droned, "I read it every day, just like my pal Say Hey!" After the shoot, Lois, Mantle, and Mays grabbed a cab to go out to dinner. When they pulled up in front of the restaurant, Lois hopped out and then, noticing that Mantle was having a hard time getting out of the backseat, extended his hand for support. To his surprise, Willie seemed to be having nearly as much trouble as Mickey, groaning in pain as he struggled to get out. *Damn*, thought Lois, who worked out regularly, *I'm in better shape than my idols.*

In his *$ellebrity* book, Lois chose Mickey as his second favorite celebrity of all time, after Muhammad Ali. "I'm in awe of any man who can keep producing under the eyes of the world year after year. When he becomes a legend, like Mickey Mantle, there's a truth to the legend and usually a decency in the man. The Mick was no braggart. He once told me, 'George, when I was sixteen I was the best ballplayer who ever lived, and it scared me.' Then he stopped for a moment and drawled softly, 'But you take a guy like Hank Aaron — he's twice as good as I ever was.' " Curious that Mantle would say that about Aaron instead of Mays.

Lois saw Mickey at his best and worst, sometimes in the same day. One evening in the mid-1980s, Lois recalled, "I got a frantic call from his teammate, Billy Martin, begging me to collect Mickey at the bar at the nearby Pierre Hotel and 'Get his ass to JFK' where his concerned wife had booked a flight to Dallas so her philandering husband could be home for the holidays. I ran over to the Pierre, and sure enough, there was the great Yankee legend surrounded by adoring fans, charmingly unloading his repertoire of baseball stories — getting loaded. I pulled the tipsy Mickey off his stool and guided him to the checkroom to retrieve his suitcase. He peeled off a $100 bill to tip an attractive hatcheck lady. But she gave him back the hundred and handed him a blank sheet of paper and a pen. 'Please, Mr. Mantle,' she said, 'I don't want the money, but if I could have your autograph for my eight-year-old son that would be wonderful. His name is *Mickey*, and he idolizes you!' Mantle would much sooner part with the hundred than sign an autograph, and he reached out . . . and fondled her! I reprimanded him, he wrote a lovely note to her son, and the bewildered young mom gave America's superstar a kiss on the cheek. I was really pissed at his behavior as I grabbed his suitcase and pushed into the revolving door. I shoved it hard, following with his baggage. When I got outside, he was gone. Then I saw him. He was lying in the Fifth Avenue gutter, his cheek on the edge of the sidewalk, by the curb, with slush from a recent snowstorm on his face. I had pushed the revolving door too hard — he tripped on the way out and went into a dive, landing on his handsome puss. 'Holy shit, Mickey,' I said, leaning over him, 'are you hurt?' He sheepishly looked up at me and sweetly said, 'F-i-ine place to be for America's *heeero.*' " Mantle made it back to Dallas with a big Band-Aid on his cheek.[9]

I once asked Lois who he liked better, Mickey or Willie. "That's a tough one," he replied. "I spent a lot of time with both of them, and I got to know Mickey very well. But it was easy to know Mickey. For better or worse, and often for worse, what you saw was what he was. He was transparent. Willie? I have enormous respect for Willie, but I can't say that I ever really *knew* him. I don't know anyone who really did. If Mickey was transparent, Willie was opaque."

Roger Maris died on December 14, 1985. How close Mickey and Maris were has never really been established. Mickey Hersko-witz — who worked with Mantle on *All My Octobers* and with Merlyn on her 1996 memoir, *A Hero All His Life* — thought that Mickey "was closer to Billy and Whitey, but I don't think Mickey had any team-mate that he *respected* as much as Roger."[10] Mantle braved minus-eighteen-degree weather to go to Fargo, North Dakota, for Maris's funeral. Afterward, Ed Hinton, a baseball writer for the *Atlanta Journal-Constitution*, sat with Mickey and other members of the 1961 Yankees, including Ford, Clete Boyer, and Bobby Richardson. Hinton heard Mickey say, as if to himself, "I want to go back to Commerce, Oklahoma."

The Mick was a huge success and catapulted Mantle back into the public eye. He had been retired for more than seventeen years when the book hit the stores (aided, in large part, by a feature story and generous review in the same *USA Today* he had plugged for free on television).

What, though, of Willie? Mickey evoked nostalgia in this period, but it was difficult to say what feeling Willie evoked. For black and white fans alike, a generation of more vocal, forceful, and militant black athletes made Willie's story seem to be something from an earlier century. A friend of mine who worked as a publicist for Simon & Schuster told me that the sales figures on Mantle's memoirs were what inspired Willie to get his story out and rekindle the love affair he once had with his fans. But *Say Hey: The Autobiography of Willie Mays*, cowritten with Lou Sahadi, quickly fizzled after it appeared in the spring of 1988. By the following year, stacks of copies had been remaindered. Part of the problem, no doubt, was that Willie couldn't offer titillating details on his personal life like Mickey could. After all, there was no dirt to be had on Willie's private life, or if there was, no journalist had ever said so or written about it. There were no rumors to dispel, no confessions to make, no forgiveness to ask for.

Another reason, though, was the writing. Sahadi did a dutiful job and even got Willie to talk about some things from his childhood that he had never before revealed. But Sahadi did not know Willie like Arnold Hano and Charlie Einstein, the two men most responsible for creating Willie's legend in print. Willie had long since alienated both men. (Years later, when we were both working for the *Newark Star-Ledger*, I asked Einstein why he hadn't worked on the project with Mays. "Very simple," he replied. "When I write I have to get paid *something*. I got more money writing *My Life In and Out of Baseball* with Willie back in 1972 than he offered me to do the new book seventeen years later.")

Beyond the flatness of the prose and the lack of genuine excitement in the recollection of the great baseball moments, there were some real problems with *Say Hey* that Willie never addressed. The book was dedicated "To my father, who was there at the start; to Leo, who was there when it counted; and to Mae, who was there when it mattered most." On the following page, in the acknowledgments, Mae Mays was thanked again; so was Carl Kiesler, a businessman who had helped Willie with numerous investments but with whom he would have a bitter falling-out just a short time later; and Piper Davis, without whom he might not have had a baseball career at all. Missing from the ranks were Sarah and Ernestine, who had raised him; any of the other old Black Barons who had sheltered the teenage Willie in the crucial years before he was signed by the Giants; Horace Stoneham, against whom Willie was perhaps still harboring a grudge over the 1973 trade; and surprisingly, Monte Irvin, who had practically been Willie's big brother with the Giants.

But what was really missing from *Say Hey* was Mays himself. Unlike *The Mick*, which plunged right into heartfelt stories of Mantle's boyhood and his relationship with Mutt, frank admissions of his carousing with Billy Martin and others, and an honest account of his failures as a husband and father, Willie's book had a remote, secondhand feel, as if he were describing someone else's life — a life less interesting than his own.

Also missing was an explanation of Willie's position on the civil rights movement and why he had never made public statements in support of it. As a lifelong fan and a good liberal, I decided to give Willie a forum to explain his views. I asked my editor at the *Village Voice* about doing an interview; also an impassioned Mays fan, he said, go for it. Allen Peacock, the book's editor, promised to get me some time with Willie after a signing at a Barnes & Noble on the Upper East Side. When I finally sat down with Willie, he seemed exhausted and distracted. My heart pounding, I opened my copy of *Say Hey* for his signature. (I asked him to sign it for my father.) Then, determined to let him know I was on his side, I asked my first question: "Some people over the years have criticized you for lack of involvement in the civil rights movement. Could you set them straight on this issue?"

Mays pulled his chair back from the desk and glared at me: "I don't gotta tell you fuck about the civil rights movement." He got up and walked away. End of interview. Stunned, shocked, I staggered out of the store. Other employees who had overheard Mays were all silent. As I stumbled down the street toward the subway, it came to me what the feeling I had reminded me of: it was exactly like the time, boxing in the Police Athletic League, when I was caught by a short left hook and knocked down for the first time. Once again, it seemed I had caught Willie Mays on a bad day.

In 1988 filmmaker Dan Klores was shooting a video for the Paul Simon hit "Me and Julio Down by the Schoolyard," which was to be included on Simon's album *Negotiations and Love Songs*.* A major sports fan, Klores wanted to use a prominent athlete from each of the three major sports in the video; he finally settled on basketball player Spud Webb, football coach-turned-TV-commentator John Madden, and Willie Mays. He contacted Mays through the San Francisco Giants' front office, and much to his delight, Willie said yes. Willie asked for $1,500, cash, to be given to him in a brown paper bag.

Klores met with Willie beforehand and was enthralled by Mays's gossipy stories. "'There was only three guys I ever saw who were faster than me going from second to home or first to home,' he told me. 'One was Willie Davis =of the Dodgers, the second was Vada Pinson of the Reds.' Who was the other, I asked. 'Mickey,' he told me. 'Man, when he was young he was faster than me. He was the fastest I've ever seen.'

"I was happy to hear him say nice things about Mickey. 'Oh yeah, we're pals,' he said. 'He's always been great to me.'"

On the Friday before Labor Day weekend, as the film crew assembled for a Monday shoot at a schoolyard in Hell's Kitchen, Klores was dismayed when Mays called to say he couldn't make it. He offered no explanation.

Stuck for a replacement, Klores took a friend's suggestion that

---

* Klores would go on to create several acclaimed documentaries, including the Peabody Award–winning *Black Magic*, which told the story of the Historically Black Colleges and Universities (HCBUs) and their basketball teams, and *Crazy Love*, which won the 2008 Independent Spirit Award for Best Documentary.

he contact Mickey Mantle through a friend of his, Bill Liederman, at Mantle's restaurant. The idea of using Mickey greatly appealed to Simon, a former high school baseball player and a lifelong Yankees fan. Mickey agreed to appear in the video but had the following stipulations. First, he wanted to be put up in a suite, which he was — at the Plaza. He wanted a stretch limo to and from the shoot, and he didn't want to sign any autographs. Oh yes, and "he wanted $1,500 cash, in a brown paper bag."

"I picked him up," Klores recalled. "He was with Greer Johnson, who was handling most of his affairs by that time. And was he hungover. He was also in kind of a bad mood. It was the first week of the pro football season, and he apparently had dropped a bundle."

The script called for Paul, a lefty, to pitch a Spaldeen to Mickey, who would be batting right-handed. Mickey probably hadn't swung a stick-ball bat since his rookie year thirty-seven years earlier, when he'd played with some kids in the street in front of his hotel in the Bronx. He couldn't quite get the hang of it. "He hit a high pop-up," said Klores. "We edited it into a 565-foot Spaldeen home run."

Klores remembered that "Mickey and Paul had a really good afternoon together." He also recalled, though, that "Mickey wouldn't sign any autographs for the kids who asked him."

"These guys were my idols," Klores told me, "especially Willie. After I met them, they weren't my idols anymore. But, you know, I still love them." I know exactly how he felt.

By the end of the 1980s, Mantle was tormented by blinding headaches often accompanied by anxiety attacks and hyperventilation. Though he admitted to a severe drinking problem in his autobiography, it's clear he was not ready to admit he needed help. "In the last few years," *The Mick* reads, "my drinking has been confined to social occasions. Merlyn has been highly successful in reminding me if I forget. As a matter of fact, if it wasn't for her I probably would have wound up an alcoholic like so many other ballplayers who did come to a tragic end that way."[11] Actually, Mickey saw little of Merlyn by this time in their lives, and there was no question that he had been an alcoholic for years.

Some of his old friends were not so close as they had once been. He had cowritten a book with Whitey Ford, and the two were involved with a fantasy baseball camp for a while, but Ford was increasingly annoyed at Mickey's irresponsible attitude — even when a friend was depending on him. John Lowy, a business partner in Mickey Mantle's, his Fifty-Ninth Street restaurant at Central Park South, thought that Whitey "wasn't a hanging-out buddy the way Billy Martin was, not in the years that I knew Mickey."[12]

More devastating for Mickey was his falling-out with Billy Martin. The details are unclear, but Greer Johnson felt that Billy's new wife, Jill Lowery, was trying to help Billy by screening out his old drinking buddies, which is ironic, as so many people close to Mantle felt for decades that Billy was the bad influence on him. Martin died on Christmas Day 1989 when he drove his pickup truck into a ditch. (Or perhaps he was a passenger — the details are still not clear.) Shortly before the accident, Jill Martin had arranged for Mickey to appear and speak at a roast for Billy. (It was understood that Mantle was to be paid for this appearance, but he agreed to do it for Billy at a reduced fee.) The two men had not spoken for nearly a year, but they hugged and chatted as if they had never been apart.

I n March 1995, Lovell died, and Mickey went back to Commerce for the last time for her funeral. Mickey, the twins Ray and Roy, and Lovell's other living children, Larry, Ted, and Barbara, laid her to rest on March 19 next to Mutt — the cemetery lot had been awaiting her for nearly forty-three years. After the service, Lovell and Mutt's children posed for a final picture together, and Mickey told them, "Well, guys, I guess I'll see you at the next funeral." They probably all knew whose funeral Mickey was thinking about.

Mickey and Lovell were never particularly close. For years she had lived with her daughter Barbara in Oklahoma City. Mickey sent gifts and called her on her birthday, Mother's Day, and, of course,

Christmas. Aside from that, they had little to say to each other. She was a hard woman and lived a hard life, but whether or not Mickey was capable of appreciating the fact, she had been every bit as responsible for his success as his father.

Mickey spent most of his last years living in Georgia with Greer Johnson — there was no formal divorce from Merlyn. A few days after New Year's in January 1994, Mickey finally admitted what everyone around him had known for years — that he was an alcoholic. He checked into the Betty Ford Clinic.

Throughout his treatment and recovery, he astonished friends and family with his cheerfulness, courage, and newfound compassion for others. After the April 1995 Oklahoma City bombing, Mickey and fellow Oklahoman Bobby Murcer made appearances and signed autographs to raise money for the families of victims.

I saw Mickey and Willie together one last time in May 1995 when the two of them plus Duke Snider were presented with the "Mickey– Willie–The Duke" award by New York sportswriters. They were photographed for the last time with Snider, the three grinning with hands on top of one another's. The sports historian Bert Randolph Sugar whispered to me, "Who do you think looks the worst in that trio?" I whispered back, "Mickey." Sugar nodded. When I saw Willie in Birmingham eleven years later, his memory seemed to be slipping on a number of topics, but he remembered seeing Mickey that day. "It was the last time I saw him," he told me. "He was still smiling and as nice to me as ever, but he looked bad."

I remember exactly when I heard that Mickey Mantle had died. On August 13, 1995, I had gotten up early and driven from my home in South Orange, New Jersey, to the New York Giants training camp on the campus of Fairleigh Dickinson University in Madison. I was working on a profile of Herschel Walker for the *New York Times Magazine* and was about to knock on the door of head coach Dan Reeves. Walker cautioned me, "I don't think you want to talk to

Coach right now. He's feelin' poorly. He and Mickey Mantle were good friends." I was dumbstruck. I had been listening to music on the way over instead of the radio. A couple of days later, I sat in front of the television all day, watching the funeral as Bob Costas gave his lovely eulogy and country singer Roy Clark sang his rendition of Charles Aznavour's "Yesterday When I Was Young," one of Mickey's favorite songs. At the end of the service, I was surprised to find tears streaming down my cheeks.

Jane Leavy quotes a friend, Tom Molito, that "Mickey Mantle was not destroyed by alcohol. He was destroyed by celebrity."[13] Maybe, but alcohol got there first. Mickey was already practicing his drinking before he became famous. And Willie Mays, whose fame paralleled Mickey's and often equaled it, wasn't destroyed by the spotlight.

After Mickey's death — or at least after Joe DiMaggio died in 1999 — Willie Mays finally became, without doubt, "the greatest living ballplayer," as DiMaggio had once demanded that he be introduced at all public events. Willie also, finally, became the undisputed king of the autograph circuit.

Still, though, Willie was not content. "There was always something ill-tempered about Willie," T. S. O'Connell, a collector and columnist ("Infield Dirt") for *Sports Collectors Digest*, told me. "In 1995, maybe a month after Mickey died, I saw Willie at a signing event in the ballroom of the Statler Hotel across the street from Madison Square Garden. He started telling me how much he missed Mickey and how much Mickey had meant to him throughout the years. Then, maybe half an hour later, he looked at the price Mickey's cards were selling for and blew up. 'Damn! Why does his stuff sell for more than mine? I was better than him.' I was kind of embarrassed. I wanted to tell him that maybe the price had shot way up since Mickey's death, but I didn't say anything."

Arnold Hano, who had written the *Sport* magazine bio of Willie that thrilled me so much when I was a kid and who wrote *A Day in the Bleachers,* the second-best book about Willie (after Charles Einstein's *Willie's Time*), told me in 2011 that "it was sad to see Willie's gleeful quality fade away as he got older. By the time he was thirty, he was an embittered young man, jealous of the endorsement money Mickey Mantle was getting, bitter that society still discriminated against him as a black man, and, I suspect, secretly bitter at himself for not having made solidarity with other blacks who were discriminated against. Now he's an embittered old man. What else can I say?" Hano paused and said, "He was the greatest player I ever saw."

Perhaps some of Willie's longtime friends observing his bitterness failed to take into account that as the 1990s wore on, Mays had grown more and more isolated by the loss of friends and family. In 1997 he was dealt a double blow. In May, Piper Davis, the man who did more than anyone else to mold the teenage Willie into a big leaguer, died in Birmingham, just short of his eightieth birthday. According to Paul Hemphill, who was there, Willie did not attend the funeral but sent flowers. Mays was preoccupied by a tragedy closer to home. Mae, who was closer to him than any other woman in his adult life, was diagnosed with a form of dementia that was soon confirmed to be Alzheimer's. She was not yet sixty. According to friends in the Bay Area, Willie devoted himself to caring for Mae and for his father in a way he had never done before. Cat died in 1999; he was eighty-eight. A couple of Cat's old teammates from the industrial leagues flew out for the ceremony. Willie insisted on writing his father's eulogy himself. With the passing of Cat, Willie was now alone, most of his ties to Birmingham gone.

It's been said that baseball is the only thread that ties America together over three centuries. If so, as artist Thom Ross has discovered, it is a slender and fragile thread.

Ross is a Seattle-based artist whose passions are the frontier West and baseball. He re-creates events from both in installation art — life-sized re-creations of historical scenes.

In September 2004, Ross and his crew hauled a five-piece work to the site of the old Polo Grounds near West 155th Street and Eighth Avenue in upper Manhattan. Here they found a plaque marking the spot where the stadium's home plate was. What they didn't find was anything to commemorate the most famous event that happened there. They proceeded to step off about 460 feet toward the Hudson River, finding the approximate place where Willie Mays pulled down Vic Wertz's drive deep into the Polo Grounds' center field. In an empty lot behind an apartment building, the crew set up five painted plywood figures of Willie Mays depicting the five major stages of the play, from Willie's pursuit of the ball to his stopping, whirling around, and throwing it back to the infield.

Ross was two years old when Willie made that catch. He heard it described by his father in a reverential tone when he was five and grew up in awe of a play he had never seen. At age twelve, he read Arnold Hano's classic book on that game, A *Day in the Bleachers*, and became inflamed with the thought of capturing the moment in a work of art.

To Ross's disappointment, although a few older men stopped, pointed, and smiled at the five Willies, none of the teenagers — most of them in NBA shirts — recognized the man immortalized in the artwork. The next day Ross and his assistants moved the exhibit to Central Park, where he had a permit to display it. The reaction was a little better, but still mixed. Some young boys in baseball shirts who knew the name Willie Mays were surprised to learn that he had played in New York. Then Ross staged a "guerrilla raid" to set up the figures in Times Square. "Most people's response was appreciative but a bit puzzled," Ross recalled. "I thought almost everyone in New York would remember Willie and The Catch, but it was more like one person in twenty. I thought I'd light a fire, but it was more like a candle in the wind."

Ross spent more than $7,000 out of his own pocket to bring the installation across the country from his studio in Seattle to Coogan's Bluff. Before he left New York, he contacted Mayor Rudy Giuliani's office asking for permission to erect a permanent steel installation in the lot at 155th Street. He got no response.

Today Ross's "The Catch" resides at the home of a friend, Rich Tarrant, in Vermont. Tarrant sets up the installation on his lawn every September, "in tribute to the great Willie Mays." Tarrant said, "Reactions have been as varied as a honk of the horn as they drive past, to passersby stopping and ringing my doorbell to chat about Willie Mays, to a woman breaking down in tears on my lawn as she thanked me for installing it. When she saw the pieces, the memories of sitting on her mother's lap watching Mays play came flooding back to her. Mays was her mother's favorite baseball player."

T. S. O'Connell saw a Willie Mays a great deal different from the one known to most sportswriters — one, perhaps, that many of us did not want to see. "Willie Mays the ballplayer," he wrote in a 2008 column in *Sports Collectors Digest*, "doesn't reconcile well with Willie Mays the grumpy old man. For several generations of fans, the image of the Hall of Fame center fielder is wrapped in a shroud of misty-eyed recollections of stick ball games in the streets of Harlem, his cap flying off wildly as he flashes along the base paths, or simply the grainy black-and-white footage of the greatest catch (and throw) in World Series history.

"For those same generations of fans, Willie Mays will always be the player who seemed born to play the game, the man for whom baseball seemed to be part of his nature. His instinctive abilities were legendary, perhaps even to the point of fostering the notion that everything came easy for him. His knowledge and dedication to the game he loved was similarly other-worldly; he would often in the early sixties suffer from exhaustion as he led his ball club through extraordinary battles with downstate archrival Los Angeles.

"Matching up all that with his 35 years of retirement can be difficult for modern fans who may only know him from a card show autograph signing. If the vast center field expanse of the Polo Grounds was the perfect showcase for the 'Say Hey Kid,' the autograph table in a hotel ballroom or convention center is seemingly the natural habitat for the Hall of Famer in his retirement years."

But, wrote O'Connell, "it is widely thought within the hobby that once the baseball card boom took off in the late 1970s and early 1980s, Mays was dismayed at what he thought was the disproportionate value collectors held for Mantle."

Mickey's signature went for a higher price than Willie's, and when the two did an occasional show together, lines for Mickey were longer. "Mickey was very embarrassed about this," said O'Connell. "I heard him ask a promoter at an Atlantic City show if he could make it into a joint Mantle-Mays event with a fixed price that guaranteed both of them would sign. This took some frantic last minute renegotiation, but that's the way it was finally done. And Mickey lost some money on the deal because a lot of people there only wanted him."

To be fair, O'Connell told me, "there were a lot of people there from the New York area after Willie and the Giants moved to the West Coast. They grew up with stories of Mickey and didn't have the allegiance for Willie."[14]

O'Connell sent an interview Mantle had done with *Sports Collectors Digest* columnist Rich Marazzi. "I never felt a personal rivalry while it was going on. Mays had some great statistics. . . . As for me, Willie and the Duke, Willie was the greatest. But there were four or five years though when I was better than he was."[15]

I would see Willie again in 2008 when Bob Costas invited me to a taping of his HBO show, which, as it turned out, featured a special hour-long interview with baseball's two greatest living players, Willie Mays and Henry Aaron. Something about Willie seemed different that night; he was jovial and outgoing, talking almost incessantly — much to the amusement of both Aaron and Costas. He emphatically denied that there had ever been any hostility between himself and Aaron, and with Henry smiling and nodding in agreement, who was there to say otherwise? And so history was rewritten that night.

Mays showed a touch of irritation when Costas talked about Aaron besting Willie over their respective careers by 95 home runs. "But he had much better ballparks to hit 'em in," insisted a suddenly indignant Willie. "I must have lost a hundred home runs to my ballparks, especially that wind at Candlestick." Again Aaron chuckled and made no reply.

After the show, I waited to shake hands with Willie. For the first time in our face-to-face meetings, he was smiling. And this time I didn't mention civil rights.

You can't go home again, and Mickey and Willie seldom tried. Commerce continued to shrink, slowly, until by Mickey's death in 1995 the population was scarcely 2,500. The mines have been closed for decades, and the town no longer has a main industry. There are four sites of interest to outsiders. The first to greet visitors is a tall, handsome Route 66 sign that commemorates what was, until it was officially removed from the U.S. Highway System after fifty-nine years of service, the most famous road in America. There is a lovely restored Conoco gas station that has been turned into a museum of a bygone era before franchise gas stations and fast-food joints took over the highways. Then there is the Mantle home at 319 South Quincy Street, which probably doesn't look a great deal better now than it did when Mutt Mantle moved his family there. (Of course, to the baseball fan/tourist, that is its charm.) Finally, there is a handsome statue of Mickey at a small baseball field right off Mickey Mantle Boulevard — formerly Highway 69.

The *New York Daily News*'s Wayne Coffey visited Commerce in 1995, two months after Mickey's death, and called the boulevard named after Mantle "a two-lane strip of gas stations and churches, a desultory stretch of Dust Bowl dreariness, a few miles from Kansas and not much further from Missouri. It takes you past long-dormant mines, and near a downtown dotted with abandoned storefronts and empty lots."

There were once plans for a Mickey Mantle Museum, but never a plan for how to raise the revenue to build it. One idea that worked was to sell signs that read MICKEY MANTLE BOULEVARD for $20 apiece; the idea arose because it seemed as if everyone passing through town would steal the real sign. "We had 200 signs and sold out in the first week," a captain of the fire department told Coffey. Another idea, which did not work, was to sell prints and replicas of the proposed statue; Mantle's lawyer requested that they stop, saying Mickey "had a financial interest in another print."

Much of the resentment that locals had toward Mick back in 1957 over coming back home so seldom is long gone; most current residents never knew Mickey. Police Chief Robert Bain told Coffey, "When Mickey went on TV [with Bob Costas] and said he wasn't nobody's hero, admitting that he had let people down and asking for their forgiveness, everyone here loved him over that."

Picher, the town just a few miles away where Merlyn grew up, met an even sadder fate. It's now a ghost town with plaques in front of a couple of buildings deemed "historical." In 2006 the Army Corps of Engineers conducted a study that showed 86 percent of Picher's buildings, including the only school, to be "badly undermined and subject to collapse at any time."

Merlyn died in Plano, Texas, on August 10, 2009, from complications of Alzheimer's disease. She was seventy-seven. She was buried next to Mickey and their two sons, Mickey Jr. and Billy. In her *New York Times* obituary, she was quoted as saying, "I adored Mick. I thought I couldn't live without him. In many ways, he was very good to me, very generous."

The last remnant of Mickey's presence in Manhattan disappeared over the summer of 2012 when the restaurant bearing his name was padlocked and the contents auctioned off.

⚾   ⚾

On February 26, 2006, while Picher was on the verge of dying, a black limo with Willie Mays in the backseat drove through the area where Westfield used to be. "I went by there on the way over here," Mays said a few hours later, seated in the grandstand at Rickwood Field wearing a fur cap and wrapped in a blanket. "There's nothing left to look at." (Westfield, in the late 1960s, suffered the same fate as many communities, black and white, as the steel industry began to shut down in the wake of diminished demand and competition from Japanese companies. Some homes in the old neighborhoods were boarded up; others were vandalized or even targeted by arsonists. Many of the old stores pulled up stakes and moved to more prosperous neighborhoods.)

I had the good fortune of running into Mays that February because I was back home in Birmingham for a signing of my biography of Bear Bryant, *The Last Coach*, and also to see an old friend and mentor, journalist Paul Hemphill, who was publicizing his biography of Hank Williams, *Lovesick Blues*. As we wrapped up, Paul said, "Hey, if we hurry, we can make it out to Rickwood in time to catch the end of the Classic, and maybe talk to Willie Mays."*

Willie's appearance at the Classic caused no small stir in Birmingham, in part because he so seldom visited his hometown. In 1985 he had told *Sports Illustrated*, "I'd like to get involved with Alabama . . . this area is so open. Bear Bryant [who had died in 1983] was the king here for so long. Now there's nobody left to carry on the tradition."[16] Exactly what "tradition" Willie was speaking of wasn't clear; Bryant represented the rise of college football, which had become so popular since the late 1950s as to almost obliterate Birmingham's rich baseball past. As with so many remarks Willie made to journalists in this period, there seemed to be no easy interpretation.

---

* Rickwood hosts an annual classic game. That year, it was called the ESPN Classic and televised nationally. The game featured the Bristol Barnstormers in vintage uniforms, coached by former Yankees pitcher and *Ball Four* author Jim Bouton.

In any event, aside from visiting a few old friends such as Richard Arrington Jr., who became the city's first black mayor in 1979, there was very little for Willie to do in his old town. The rich black culture that had been centered on the Fourth Avenue North area was long gone, and most of the old shops and restaurants were boarded up.* (Bob's Little Savoy Café, Willie's favorite nightspot, did not survive the decline of the Negro Leagues and closed in 1954 — the same year Mickey's favorite joint in Commerce, the Black Cat Café, shut down.) The few friends Willie did have in Birmingham sometimes felt neglected. In his 1993 memoir *Leaving Birmingham: Notes of a Native Son*, Hemphill recalled dropping by to see Piper Davis to swap old baseball stories. "Tell me about Willie," Hemphill asked. "Which one?" asked Davis, meaning either the kid or the man who became the biggest star in baseball. Hemphill wanted to know about both. When it came to talk of "Willie the Star," Davis frowned. "He's still got a place, you know, up on Red Mountain. One time a few years ago I got a call from him. Says he was having some folks over, come on up. So I go up there and we greet each other and I don't see a single soul I know. Can't even find Willie anymore, so after a while I just walk out. Willie doesn't exactly stay in touch. He just left and got in with a different bunch of folks, I guess."[17]

At Rickwood that chilly February afternoon, Paul was skeptical that Willie would even talk to us. Mays was distant, as if lost in thought as he gazed out on the field where he had first played professional ball fifty-eight years before. Paul, too, sat looking out to the hand-painted advertisements on the fences; by his own count, he had seen more than five hundred games at Rickwood back in the days when baseball ruled. When we got him talking, Mays recalled being too shy to talk to Jackie Robinson, but how encouraging Jackie was about Willie's chances to make it in the big leagues. His own regret

---

* Adjacent to Birmingham's Civil Rights District, Fourth Avenue has gradually been rejuvenated. The historic Carver Theatre, the elite of the black movie houses, has been restored and is now the home of the Alabama Jazz Hall of Fame. In September 2011, Fourth Avenue hosted a jazz festival.

about playing with the Black Barons, he said, was that he had never gotten the chance to leave his "X" at the ballpark — long home runs hit by both Barons and Black Barons were customarily marked with a big white X at the spot where they landed or left the park. "I want to make a difference," he told me. "We're losing so many good athletes to football and basketball. I love football and basketball, but I want to try and get kids to stick with baseball. It's the greatest game."

Then, just as I had eighteen years earlier, I blew it. Was it possible, I wanted to know, that he had taken no public stance during the civil rights movement because his lack of formal education had left him feeling inadequate when it came to making speeches and giving interviews? Deadly silence followed. After what seemed like five minutes, a grim-faced Willie, his head turned toward the field, told me, "I don't gotta say nothin' to you about me and the civil rights." Paul put his hand on my arm and said, "I think maybe the interview is over."*

Mickey and Willie were back in the news in 2010 when James Hirsch's *Willie Mays: The Life, the Legend* and, later, Jane Leavy's *The Last Boy: Mickey Mantle and the End of America's Childhood* were published. Leavy's book, though it included little about Mantle's childhood and early life, is the frankest and most honest account of his late-career dissolution. Hirsch's book, at a whopping 628 pages, is the most detailed telling of Willie's life and career ever. Yet, at the end of it, there was still something of a hole in the center — namely, Willie himself. Mays cooperated so completely with Hirsch that when I called Mays's office in 2009, his personal assistant, Renee Anderson, informed me that "Willie regards this book as his memoir." But despite Hirsch's best efforts, Willie's real personality never coalesced in the book. As Bill James put it in a 1999 *Sports Century* profile of Mays on ESPN, "We don't

---

* But Willie did give me enough memories about the Negro Leagues to fill up two pages in my 2010 book on Rickwood Field.

really know Willie Mays. He's as much a puzzle to us as, say, Lou Gehrig."

Mickey's life, at least over the last twenty-five to thirty years, was a sad, open book; his honesty in admitting to his own failures will always color our remembrance of him. In some ways, it would become even sadder after his death. In the first decade or so of Mantle's career, he often seemed angry, usually at himself but often with fans and reporters; as he grew older he learned to relax, get past his shyness, and talk about the burden of being a flawed hero. He revealed his humanity. With Willie, it was the opposite; most of his early profiles in newspapers, magazines, and books were condescending, portraying him as an adolescent, or at least as a young man with an adolescent's mentality. We never knew of his marital problems, his anxiety over money, the drive to succeed that so often resulted in fainting spells. As he grew older he grew away from us, though in the last few years he seemed to like us all a little more. But Willie has never really let us inside.

Nonetheless, Willie's stature as a ballplayer has increased while Mickey's has declined. To many young baseball fans who study the game, they are no longer locked together as they were when Mickey was alive. In May 2010, on the MSG Network's series *The Lineup*, fans and a panel of sportswriters voted on New York's greatest baseball players. Mays was voted the all-time greatest center fielder, easily passing DiMaggio, Mantle, and Duke Snider, in that order.

What happened to Mickey's reputation? I suspect it has suffered because Mantle left no easily identifiable records or marks behind. Mays hit four home runs in a game; he hit 660 home runs, 54 behind Babe Ruth and second on the all-time list the year he retired. Aaron hit 755 career home runs, DiMaggio hit safely in 56 straight games, and Ted Williams hit .406 in 1941, the last hitter to reach the .400 mark. Every fan knows these numbers. But a generation of younger fans has to dig deeper to discover Mantle's true greatness. Some look at the .298 career average (and how Mickey grieved over his career batting average falling below .300 in his final season), the RBI totals (just *four seasons* with more than 100 RBIs?), and the relatively low (compared to players in the 1970s, 1980s, and 1990s) stolen base totals and consider them outside the context of Mantle's time and place. They wonder what the fuss was all about.* The only number associated with Mickey is 565, the distance of the famous home run in 1953, and no one knows whether that number is real.

Mickey was a miserable father whose sons all descended into alcoholism; nothing in Mantle's career became him so much as his admission near the end that he had been a bad father. In 2000 his oldest son, Mickey Jr., died of cancer at the age of forty-seven, the second of Mickey's sons to die tragically young. "If I could go back and do it over," Mickey said in 1985, "I would never have named my first son after me."

We know virtually nothing at all of Willie's feelings about fatherhood. Michael Mays is barely a shadow in his adopted father's story; Willie dedicated his 1966 memoir, *My Life In and Out of Baseball*, to him, but Michael is mentioned only a couple of times in the text. (He seems to disappear from Hirsch's massive biography practically at the midpoint.) Like his father, Michael has no biological children; no picture of Willie and a grown Michael has ever surfaced.

Does the knowledge of their shortcomings as men diminish my love for them as heroes? Yes and no. I will never be able to think

---

* Leaving aside the seasons when injuries kept him from accumulating enough at-bats for a 100-RBI season — such as 1962, when he batted just 377 times and drove in 89 runs — it does seem remarkable that Mantle had just four seasons when he drove in at least 100. One explanation is that for most of his career he batted behind some truly terrible leadoff hitters. For instance, in 1961, for no reason anyone has ever been able to figure out except that baseball analysis wasn't far enough along to understand such things, manager Ralph Houk had Bobby Richardson leading off for 162 games, and he responded with an OBP of .295. With Mantle batting two spaces behind him, and Roger Maris behind Mantle, Richardson had just 80 runs scored all season. Mickey finished with 128 RBIs. If he'd had a genuine leadoff hitter in front of him, he could have easily driven in 140 to 150 runs.

Willie's stats, too, suffered from a relative lack of good leadoff hitters; it seems odd that a player lauded by so many as the greatest of all time never once, in twenty-two seasons, led his league in RBIs. In truth, even trivia experts are hard-pressed to remember most of the Giants' leadoff hitters during Willie's best seasons.

of Mickey or Willie with the same unbridled admiration I felt for them when I was a boy. And yet, and yet . . . a part of me will always agree with Mark Linn-Baker in *My Favorite Year* when he says to Peter O'Toole, "Something in you had to be that hero that I saw on the screen or you couldn't have played him. You're not that good an actor — no one is." Yes. But now at a point when I look back and measure what I am against the person I wanted to be, I must forgive Mickey and Willie for not always being the heroes I wished them to be. No men — not even our heroes — should be expected to carry the burden of our dreams.

Acknowledgments

T his book could not have been written without the aid of a great many people, most of whom never knew one another and many who are no longer with us. There are so many people I want to thank for "planting seeds" that I scarcely know where to start.

In the mid-1990s, when I was a film critic for the *Newark Star-Ledger*, I met the late great Charlie Einstein, whose book *Willie's Time* might be the best baseball book I've ever read. Charlie was then playing out the string of a long and distinguished newspaper career by writing about lounge acts in Atlantic City. His numerous letters and phone conversations filled me in on a world and a time that I would have never otherwise known about—the New York that Willie Mays knew in the 1950s and the West Coast as it received the two New York teams, the Giants and the Dodgers, in the late 1950s. Charlie knew Willie Mays as, I believe, no one else ever has; he loved him, became disillusioned with him, then learned to reconcile that disillusionment. In the end, he could pay Willie no greater compliment than to say "I knew him as he was, and I'm still a fan."

The late George Plimpton was wonderfully encouraging in the 1980s when I was writing for the *Village Voice* and, once at Elaine's, told me the story of his attempt to pitch to the Willie Mays and Mickey Mantle All-Stars at Yankee stadium in 1958, the first indication I had that Mickey and Willie barnstormed together.

Dick Schaap, too, was always there for me when I was starting out, full of great stories about Mickey, some of which he would punctuate with "Please don't use that until I'm gone." A couple of them live in this book.

Piper Davis, the great player and manager of the Birmingham Black Barons, lavished me with hours of time talking about Willie, the Negro Leagues, and a bygone era in baseball. Nothing would make me happier than this book sparking a movement to get Piper into the Hall of Fame.

I wish I had known Frank Scott better. He died in Maplewood, New Jersey, a few blocks from where I write this, in 1998 and on more than one occasion I heard him speak at the Maplewood Library on his years of representing Mickey, Willie, and other players in commercial and endorsement deals. He never wrote a book and was full of wonderful anecdotes and stories; I'm happy I could include some of them in *Mickey and Willie* before they were lost to posterity.

Vic Ziegel, who died in 2010, always took a phone call, and each time I phoned him had two good stories on Mantle and Mays that I had never heard.

Rich Ashburn—that's what he asked me to call him, not Richie— was one of the finest gentlemen I've ever met. I had the pleasure of interviewing him twice, and in the course of our conversation he touched on his experiences playing for the Willie Mays All-Stars in the Mickey-Willie barnstorming tours. His recollections were one of the seeds that took years to bear fruit in this book.

Hank Bauer, who passed away back in 2007, was a brave and cheerful man who was always happy to take my calls and talk to me about both Yogi and Mickey. Both *Yogi Berra, Eternal Yankee* and this book are dedicated to his memory.

While I working on *Yogi Berra, Eternal Yankee*, Clete Boyer gave me a hot blast of great stuff about Yogi, Mickey, Ralph Houk, and the Yankees in the first half of the 1960s. The last thing I told him in our final conversation was that I thought he was a better third baseman than Brooks Robinson. I'm glad he got such a kick out of that and am delighted to say it again in this book.

Jim Hamilton was a dear friend, a lifelong union man, a fine scriptwriter, and a baseball fan who watched Willie from his barnstorming days on the West Coast through his career with the Giants.

The great artist Bill Gallo was a friend and supporter and a vital part of my life as a young fan. I'm proud to have done two books that included his cartoons, particularly my all-time favorite, his Mickey-Willie paper doll, the last image in this book. The only thing he asked in return was a donation to Juvenile Diabetes.

Paul Hemphill was a great journalist, a great sportswriter, and a great fan, and I treasure the moments we spent together at ball games and talking about baseball in Birmingham.

And finally, one of my greatest regrets is that Bert Randolph Sugar didn't live to see it. For twenty-eight years no writer or historian was more helpful or generous with his time, knowledge and wit than Bert. I had so looked forward to seeing Bert at the book party for *Mickey and Willie*. It just doesn't seem right living in a world without him.

John Hall, the historian for the Kansas-Oklahoma-Missouri League, not only wrote a wonderful little book on Mickey and his pre-Yankees years but was generous with his time in helping me track down the origins of many Mickey legends.

Bob Costas has been a great baseball talker since I first met him when I was writing for the *Village Voice* in the mid-1980s. I'll never be able to thank him enough for inviting me and my daughter for his HBO show featuring Willie Mays and Hank Aaron in 2008. It was a night neither she nor I will ever forget.

Margie Bolding, my college drama teacher, God bless you. Without you I would never have known about Mickey's secret life in New York in the 1950s. You've got a book in you, darlin,' and I hope you don't hesitate any more to write it.

Roger Kahn is the repository for more New York baseball knowledge than any man who ever lived, and I can never repay him for all the hours on the phone and at his home in upstate New York.

What Charlie Einstein didn't know about Willie, Arnold Hano did, and I thank him for being honest and opening up to me on the darker side of Willie Mays's personality.

Monte Irvin has now spent hours filling in background on two of my book subjects, Yogi Berra and Willie Mays. I thank him twice.

I also am most grateful to his cousin, Daniel McGriff, who shared photos of Monte and Willie that I've never seen before.

Mickey's son Danny was most helpful in untangling some of the myths that built up around his father over the years.

Bill James gave me carte blanche to quote from his writing and analysis of both Mays and Mantle. His first *Historical Abstract* lit a spark for me.

Kristi Jacobson, granddaughter of the legendary Toots Shor, brought me inside the smoke-filled rooms of the saloon that was Mickey's, Billy Martin's, and Whitey Ford's favorite hangout in the 1950s.

Ray Robinson has, over the years, been a wonderful friend when it came to talking about the New York sports world of the 1950s and 1960s. Whenever I speak to him I feel like I remember why I became a fan in the first place.

Rob Neyer took off a couple of days of his valuable time to dig out information on the Mantle-Mays barnstorming tours in Syracuse and Philadelphia. Sorry about Kansas in the NCAA final this year, Rob.

Alex Belth, host of the blog *BronxBanter* (bronxbanterblog.com), helped me track down many veteran sportswriters, most notably Arnold Hano.

Marty Appel, a fine historian and writer, had loads of Mickey and Willie stories and always gave whatever contact information I needed.

David Falkner, one of the most objective biographers of Mickey as well as Billy Martin, generously allowed me to quote from *The Last Hero*.

A mainstay in New Jersey journalism and a columnist I read for more than thirty years, Jerry Izenberg, knew both Mickey and Willie intimately and shared nearly half a century of history with me.

Thomas Barthel, whose book *Baseball Barnstorming and Exhibition Games, 1901–1962*, is definitive and was invaluable in filling in the background of baseball's last great barnstorming era.

I could not have written *Yogi Berra, Eternal Yankee* nor *Mickey and Willie* without the help of Jim Bouton, pitcher, bestselling author, entrepreneur, union rep, movie actor, and iconoclast supreme. Jim knew Mickey and Willie as they were and loved them both; no higher compliment can be paid.

Jane Leavy was wonderful about sharing Mickey stories while working on her own great biography of Mantle, *The Last Boy*.

Robert Creamer was the secret author of Mickey's 1964 book, *The Quality of Courage*, and knew the mid-to-late career Mickey as well as anyone.

My old friend Mickey Herskowitz has now given me able assistance on two books, *The Last Coach: A Life of Paul "Bear" Bryant*, and this one. No one knew the post-career Mantle as well as Mickey.

Our friend Steve Mavropoulus runs a heck of a tight ship at *Garden State News* in South Orange, where we moved, and just plain inspired me with his love for Mickey Mantle.

A special salute across the years to my friends from six years of my youth in Old Bridge, New Jersey, including Mark and Kevin Feely, Jamie and Brian O'Kane, Allan Nordstrum, Joe Casamento, Steve Irwin, Marty and Jimmy Bean, Frankie Mischetti, Peter Frechette, Mike Santiago, and Tony Pasqua. I can't think of Mickey and Willie without thinking of you. How many times were we Mickey and Willie when playing "Three flys and you're out" on William Street?

Marvin Miller is the wisest man I've ever known. Working with him on his memoirs, *A Whole Different Ball Game*, is the greatest honor I've had as a working writer, and my family's relationship with Marvin and his late wife, Terry, has been an unending treasure. As founder and director of the Major League Baseball Players Association, Marvin saw sides of Willie and Mickey that no one else did. His story about Mays's speech to the union reps during the 1972 strike preserves what I believe to be Willie's finest hour.

Over the years I've often wondered why writers thank their agents and editors in acknowledgments. With this book, I now understand. Andrew Blauner was a huge help on this book from the beginning, constantly finding articles and items concerning Mickey and Willie that were just the way I like 'em — way out of left field.

Regarding Julian Pavia, let me leave it at this: he's the best editor I've ever had.

Thanks again to my wife, Jonelle Bonta, who knows as much about baseball as I do and a hell of lot more about editing. Every paragraph of this book bears her imprint. And thanks to my daughter, Maggie, for giving me someone to tell these stories to.

And finally, I want to thank my father, Alfred, for loving Willie and Mickey so much and for taking me to see them play in so many different ballparks, but most especially for bringing home the tickets to my first game, that 1961 exhibition between the Yankees and the Giants.

Appendix A

Mickey vs. Willie—Who Was the Best?

So then, who was better?

For most of their careers, the debate had them pretty much neck and neck, with a nod generally going to Mays by about a nose. After their careers were over, Willie pulled ahead, and he remains so today. In the all-century voting, Willie Mays placed third on the list of best players to Mickey Mantle's thirty-second, and in *The Sporting News*'s top one hundred, Mays again left Mantle in the dust, placing second to Mantle's seventeenth.

Why did the experts in their own time regard Mays as superior? The case was summed up neatly in the 1962 *Sport* magazine Mantle-Mays issue: "He can do more things better. It is possible, some people say, that no player in history has ever been able to do so many things so well." According to the story, the Dodgers' chief, Alex Campanis — yes, *that* Al Campanis — set a point value rating system for all the things a player could do on a baseball field: "hitting for average, hitting for power, speed on the bases (stealing and going for the extra base), strength and accuracy of arm, and fielding." (How refreshing, by the way, to see the terms "hitting" and "fielding" used instead of "offense" and "defense.") The only one judged to have a perfect score in every category was Mays.

In his 1994 book *All My Octobers*, published a year before his death, Mickey Mantle finally came clean about who he thought was the greater player. With a refreshing lack of modesty, Mantle said to Mickey Herskowitz, "I have been asked the question a thousand times at card shows — Which of us was the best? All you have to do is open the record book and the answer, over a full career, is Willie. He played 22 years to my 18. He finished with more of everything, including homers. In my prime years, head to head, I think I had the edge. I was faster and a better base stealer and we were about even defensively, although Mays, with his basket catches, had more of a flair. I'll give him that."

I think Mantle's assessment is more accurate than not, though he rates himself a little too high when he says he and Willie were "about even defensively."

What does the record book say? A statistical comparison of Mickey Mantle and Willie Mays is a baseball analyst's dream. Their prime years occurred at exactly the same time, with park conditions and rules virtually the same for both leagues. The National League had more superstars in this period, almost all of them black, but as black players overall contributed about 8 percent of major league rosters in the 1950s, it really can't be said that, on the whole, Mays competed against better players than Mantle. In terms of what Mantle and Mays faced day to day, the competition and conditions are strikingly even. Here are the career lines from *Total Baseball*, the game's official encyclopedia:

	G	AB	R	H	2B	3B	HR
MANTLE, 1951–68	2,401	8,102	1,677	2,415	344	72	536
MAYS, 1951–73	2,942	10,851	2,062	3,283	523	140	660

	RBI	BB	SO	BA	OBP	SLG	SB/CS	SB%	FieldAvg
MANTLE	1,509	1,733	1,710	.298	.423	.557	153/38	.801	.982
MAYS	1,903	1,464	1,526	.302	.387	.557	338/103	.766	.981

I've looked at these numbers so many times over the years that I'd stopped *seeing* them. I'd always assumed, for instance, that Mantle was clearly a superior power hitter, but the record doesn't show it.

Mantle had a greater home run percentage — that is, Mickey averaged a home run every 15.1 times at bat, while Willie averaged one for every 16.4. But Mays hit doubles and triples with more frequency. Mantle's career stolen base percentage is actually better than that of Mays (who led the NL in stolen bases for four straight years from 1956 through 1959 and was regarded by many as the best base runner of his time). And Mantle's walk total is particularly impressive: he had 269 more walks despite playing in 541 fewer games.

It has always been argued that Mantle's career numbers would look much more impressive if not for his serious injuries, and of course they would, but how about Mays? It's always puzzled me that Mays was never given hypothetical credit for the 270 or so games he missed while in the service. Let's fantasize for a moment. As a twenty-year-old rookie in 1951, Mays hit 20 home runs in 121 games, scored 59, and drove in 68. As a twenty-three-year-old in 1954, he hit 41 home runs, scored 119, and drove in 110. He played only thirty-four games before going into the Army in 1952, with 4 home runs, 17 runs scored, and 23 RBIs. For the sake of argument, let's split the difference between Mays's 1951 and 1954 seasons and give him 31 home runs, 79 runs, and 79 RBIs for both 1952 and 1953, then subtract what he *did* do in 1952 before entering the Army. Here's what Mays's career numbers on the all-time chart really look like:

Home runs:	660
Runs:	2,062
RBIs:	1,903

Now let's add our hypothetical numbers and see how that would have changed the record book:

Home runs:	718
Runs:	2,163
RBIs:	2,061

There are already a great many people who consider Mays the greatest all-around player of all time, but think what it would have done for his career reputation if he could have been the first to break Ruth's career home run record.

Is there anything that would mitigate the career numbers for either Mantle or Mays? Were they particularly helped or hurt, for instance, by their home ballparks? In a home-road breakdown compiled for *The New Bill James Historical Baseball Abstract*, Mantle is shown to have hit .305 with 266 home runs and 743 RBIs at home, with a .291 average, 270 home runs, and 766 RBIs on the road; that's near-perfect balance. The same is true for Mays, who hit .302 with 335 home runs and 932 RBIs at the Polo Grounds and Candlestick Park, and .301, with 325 home runs and 971 RBIs, on the road. Mantle was a switch-hitter and thus was not hurt by Yankee Stadium's deep left-center-field power alley. Oddly enough, though, Mays, contrary to popular belief — and contrary to Willie himself, who constantly complained about the parks he had to hit in — lost nothing from the Polo Grounds' similar left-center configuration or from that famous but apparently mythical wind that was supposed to have cost him, in the familiar litany of his fans, "at least a hundred home runs." In fact, Mays actually hit *ten* more homers at home than he hit in all other NL ballparks.

But all this comes under the heading of "career value." We already know Mays lasted longer and performed at a quality pace longer than Mantle. The more important question for me is: Who was the *best* at his peak? And what do we mean when we say "peak"? Is fifteen years okay? Let's try their fifteen peak seasons, 1951 to 1965 for Mantle, 1951 and 1954 through 1967 for Mays. (And I'm going to toss in SLOB, slugging average times on-base percentage, a stat that I think gives a truer picture of a player's ability to produce runs than the popular OPS, which is OBP *plus* SLG.)

	G	AB	R	RBI	HR	BA
MANTLE, 1951–65	2,015	6,894	1,517	1,298	454	.306
MAYS, 1951, 1954–67	2,264	8,505	1,662	1,552	560	.310

	BB/SO	SB/CS	PCT	OBA	SLG	SLOB
MANTLE	1,463/1,424	145/34	81.0	.427	.567	24.21
MAYS	1,054/1,049	283/86	69.6	.386	.586	22.62

This brings them closer together in total numbers, but Mays still has an edge because Mantle missed so many games. In 1963, for instance, the year after winning his third MVP Award, he missed 89 games owing to injury. But note that Mantle's *quality* numbers are terrific; he led in the most important numbers, on-base percentage and slugging percentage, by wide margins, and even had a higher stolen base percentage, *81 percent* to *70 percent*. And though Mays batted more than 1,600 times more than Mantle, Mickey was only 106 home runs behind. Mays's only edge is in fewer strikeouts, but we have no real evidence that strikeouts hurt Mantle's ability to produce runs.

Let's try it another way: let's define "peak" as their twelve best seasons. Let's eliminate the rookie seasons for both, and Mantle's 1963 season, even though he hit .314 for the year. Here's how they compare:

	G	AB	R	RBI	HR	BA
MANTLE 1952–62, 1964	1,722	6,020	1,372	1,198	426	.321
MAYS 1954–65	1,850	7,003	1,421	1,311	481	.317

	BB/SO	SB/CS	OBA	SLG	SLOB
MANTLE	1,308/1,242	131/25	.433	.589	25.50
MAYS	876/816	264/81	.393	.556	21.85

At first this looks like another clear advantage for Mays; more home runs, more runs, more RBIs, more hits, more stolen bases. But it doesn't take long to see that Mantle was the superior hitter, and by a decisive margin. In their dozen best seasons, Mays played 128 more games, but the difference in their *total* production isn't that great. Let's use one more table:

	AB	BB	PA*	H + BB
MANTLE 1952–62, 1964	6,020	1,308	7,327	1,871 + 1,307 = 3,178
MAYS 1954–65	7,003	876	7,879	2,224 + 867 = 3,100

*PA = plate appearances

Though Mays was in 128 more games than Mantle in their twelve best seasons and had nearly 1,000 more official at-bats and 552 more plate appearances, *Mantle reached base 78 more times.* And in their fifteen best seasons, Mays batted 1,600 more times than Mickey, *but reached base just 121 more times.* Not only that, but measured over a fifteen-season or twelve-season span, Mantle's SLOB was superior to Mays's. Over a twelve-year span, Mantle had a superior on-base *and* slugging percentage.

I don't know how else to interpret these numbers except to conclude that Mickey in his prime was a superior hitter, at least if you interpret the term "superior hitter" as the hitter who does the most to produce runs. What does SLOB say? When you multiply slugging percentage and on-base percentage, Mantle jumps into a clear and resounding lead, 25.50 to 21.85.

Are there any factors that could possibly mitigate Mantle's superiority in batting statistics? Let's look at stolen bases. It was generally accepted when I was a kid that Mantle was the fastest runner in baseball — every biography and profile mentioned that he had been clocked running down to first base faster than any other player in history — but that Mays was a smarter and superior base runner. (In the 1962 *Sport* magazine special issue, Mantle was given by the panel of experts the nod for "speed," while Mays got the edge in "base running.") Mays was regarded as a dazzlingly "instinctive" base runner. (Black athletes were "instinctive" back then, while white athletes were "hardworking.") And Mays was beautiful to watch, rounding bases with a wide sweep that took him right out from under his cap. Mantle could probably have beaten Mays to first by a step, but I don't think any runner in baseball could have beat Mays from first to second. Mays led the National League in stolen bases for four straight seasons, from 1956 through 1959; in fact, from 1956 through 1958, he led *both* leagues in stolen bases.

This was an era when hardly anyone stole bases; Mays's total of 40 in 1956 was the highest NL mark of the decade and the highest in the major leagues until Luis Aparicio stole 56 in 1959. Nothing was more indicative of Willie's amazing versatility than his ability to lead the league in home runs one season and stolen bases the next. Think of it this way: from 1956 to 1959, while Mays was leading the National League in stolen bases, Aparicio was also leading the American League in stolen bases. For those four seasons, Mays had 136 steals, Aparicio had 134. But over those four seasons, Aparicio hit 14 home runs; Mays hit 134.

It's difficult for me to accept that Mickey Mantle was a better base runner — or at least a better base *stealer* — than Willie Mays. But the numbers say he was. Mantle's stolen base percentage is not only higher than Mays's, but higher than the average of such other stolen base champions as Jackie Robinson (78 percent), Luis Aparicio (79 percent), and Lou Brock (75 percent), and much higher than the average for Ty Cobb (65 percent) (though we don't have his stolen base records for every season). If I had to pick the most impressive display of power and speed in baseball history, I'd say this: from 1952 to 1964, including 1963 when he played in just 65 games, Mickey Mantle hit 443 home runs and stole 133 bases in 159 attempts, a success rate of 83.6 percent.

I see no rational reason why, if circumstances had demanded, Mickey Mantle couldn't have stolen more bases than Willie Mays. If you have a higher percentage of steals in, say, 190 attempts, I don't see any reason why you would have a lower rate of success in, say, 440 attempts. It might be argued that Mantle, playing on a better team, could be more selective as to when he attempted to steal. I disagree. I think it can be assumed that Mickey tried to steal only when games were close. Or why try at all?

There's another area concerning speed that Mantle shows up well in: GIDP, or grounded into double plays. Researcher Neil Munro did some eye-opening work for Bill James on the subject of great hitters and their GIDP totals; let's collect those numbers in a chart to compare Mantle with other Hall of Famers:

	Years	Games	GIDP
Mickey Mantle	1951–68	2,401	113
Willie Mays	1951–73	2,992	251
Johnny Bench	1967–83	2,158	201
Jackie Robinson	1947–56	1,379	113
Eddie Mathews	1952–68	2,391	123
Mike Schmidt	1972–86	2,107	122
Luis Aparicio	1956–73	2,599	184
Ted Williams	1939–60	2,292	197
Stan Musial	1941–63	3,026	243
Lou Brock	1961–79	2,616	114
Joe DiMaggio	1936–51	1,736	130
Duke Snider	1947–64	2,143	166
Roberto Clemente	1955–72	2,433	275
Hank Aaron	1954–76	3,298	328
Pete Rose	1963–84	3,371	235
Reggie Jackson	1967–86	2,705	180

That's quite a variety of players, including great all-around hitters, sluggers, and base stealers, and it spans more than six decades. Ted Williams, considered by many to be the greatest hitter who ever lived, played in 109 fewer games than Mantle but hit into 84 more double plays. Luis Aparicio, who is in the Hall of Fame precisely because of his speed, hit into 71 more double plays in 198 more games. Mantle drew a lot of criticism from writers who worshiped Joe DiMaggio because Mickey struck out far more often. But in 1,000 fewer games, DiMaggio hit into 17 more double plays than Mantle — and we don't even have the GIDP information for the first three years of DiMaggio's career.

And so, neither at bat nor on the bases can I make an objective case for Willie over Mickey. Perhaps Mays's best chance is in the outfield. There are, after all, many people who still regard Willie Mays as the best defensive center fielder in baseball history. There were a couple of writers who thought Mantle covered as much ground as Mays, but none I know of who thought that in their prime Mantle was better or had as good an arm as Mays — though everyone acknowledges that

Mantle had an excellent throwing arm. But what exactly was the difference between them in terms of *value*? For what it's worth, Mantle's career fielding average was a point higher than Mays's, but most baseball experts don't put much stock in fielding average. Throwing assists are also difficult to figure, if only because outfielders with truly great arms don't get challenged very often. In 1967, his sixth full season, Roberto Clemente gunned down 27 runners from right field; he never had more than 19 assists in the rest of his career. Al Kaline, in his fifth full season, 1958, had 23; he never had more than 14 again. Joe DiMaggio had 20 or more in his first three seasons, then never topped 16 again. It's a similar story with Mays. In 1955, his second season back from the Army, he had a career-high 23 assists; for the rest of his career, he topped 14 only once. Either these great players' arms got weaker as they matured, or the runners wised up. The problem is that there's no way to measure the runs prevented by an outfielder's *reputation*.

Mantle, too, may have developed an early reputation with his arm. In 1955 he had 20 assists; he never had more than 11 in any other season. For their careers, Mays averaged 10.6 assists per 154 games, while Mantle averaged 9.0. The difference between them might amount to a run per season.

What, then, of range in the outfield? For his career, Mays averaged 2.56 fly balls per game, while Mantle averaged 2.26. That means, roughly, that Mays got to about one fly every three-odd games that Mantle didn't get to. Both played in spacious center-field areas with plenty of room to move. Could the difference between them be accounted for by the Yankees' pitching staff allowing fewer fly balls? Yankee pitchers almost always struck out more batters than Giant pitchers, and Casey Stengel, you may recall, always had a fondness for selecting pitchers who could "throw ground balls." Maybe the other Yankee outfielders had more range than the other Giant outfielders and intruded upon Mantle's territory more and took away a fly ball or so every three or four games. I don't really think so. I don't think there's any reason to believe the difference represents anything other than Willie Mays being better — and probably, at their respective peaks, just a little better — at pulling down fly balls than Mickey Mantle.

What does that mean in terms of runs prevented? Bill James in his Mantle-Mays comparison thought the difference between Mantle and Mays in the outfield to be worth five or six runs a year. I'm content to leave it at that.

But even if, for the sake of argument, you allow Willie the value of, say, another five runs on the field, that's not going to make up the difference between Mantle and Mays as hitters. The only conclusion I can come up with is that all the objective evidence points to Mickey Mantle, in his prime, being a better ballplayer than Willie Mays in his prime. I may not have convinced anyone else, but at least, after all these years, there's no doubt in my own mind. Thank God my father isn't alive to read this.

Am I leaving something out? Should I consider all the qualities lumped together under the heading of "intangibles"? Willie Mays's attitude toward the game was infectious and inspiring, while Mantle's, we know, was childish and temperamental, at least until Roger Maris's arrival in 1960 took some of the focus off him. But if you take in Mantle's prime seasons — starting in his rookie year of 1951 and going through 1964 — the Yankees won pennants in '51, '52, '53, '55, '56, '57, '58, '60, '61, '62, '63, and '64. And one of the years they didn't win, 1954, they had their best regular-season record under Casey Stengel, winning 103 games. They won the World Series in '51, '52, '53, '56, '58, '61, and '62 — Mantle had more championship rings at a comparable age than Michael Jordan. Mays's Giants won pennants only in '51, '54, and '62, and went to the playoffs in '72. (Willie also put in a stint for the Mets in their pennant drive in '73.) Yes, I know, Mantle's Yankees were a better team than Mays's Giants. But when you win twelve pennants in fourteen years, how can you really say a guy's attitude is hurting his team? To hear Mickey's teammates in those years is to come away with the opposite impression.

Practically to a man, they say that Mickey's grit and determination to play while in pain inspired them.

The effects of Mantle's shoulder injury are usually overlooked by analysts. Let's do a quick review. Mantle was always better hitting from the right side than from the left. But in 1956, when he hit his peak, he became one of the best left-handed hitters in baseball, batting .342 (with a .375 BA right-handed). In 1957 he was still among the best lefties in the league at .339 (with an overall .365 BA, the highest of his career and an awesome .425 from the right side of the plate). After 1957, though, something changed: in 1958 Mickey hit .377 right-handed and just .282 left-handed. In seven of his eleven subsequent seasons, he batted higher as a righty than a lefty — in most of them substantially better, the righty Mantle out-hitting the lefty Mantle by 95 points in 1958, 98 points in 1960, 80 points in 1961, 52 points in 1963, 83 points in 1964, and 81 in 1967. From 1958 through the end of his career, Mickey batted 3,145 times from the left side and 1,557 from the right; his righty self out-hit his lefty self by nearly 50 points.

From 1958 through 1968, if Mickey had been able to hit left-handed with anything like the consistency he showed in 1956 and 1957, I think there's little doubt that he would not only have finished over .300 for his career but possibly at .310 or better, with similar boosts in other batting stats. Would 600 career home runs have then been out of reach? I don't think so.

But here's a really intriguing thought: What if by, say, 1959 or even 1960, Mickey Mantle had quit switch-hitting altogether? What if he had decided to just bat right-handed against *all* pitching? Suppose, for the sake of argument, he hit 25 points worse against right-handed pitchers than left-handed pitchers? He would still have been a healthy 25 points better than his left-handed self. What prevented him from doing so? It's hard to believe that somewhere in Mickey's psyche Mutt Mantle wasn't looking over his shoulder, reminding him to do it the way he was taught.

No matter what I write here, no matter what anyone writes, Mantle's career will always be perceived in terms of what might have been — and there's no doubt in my mind that if he had not contracted osteomyelitis after football practice back in Commerce, had he not stepped on the drain in the 1951 World Series chasing Willie Mays's fly ball, and if he had not injured his shoulder in the 1958 World Series, Mickey Mantle would have been the greatest player ever. Here are some epitaphs about Mantle I saved from newspapers: "could have been one of the truly greats," "never quite lived up to his enormous potential," "squandered so much of his enormous talent." Well, he *did* squander a lot of his talent.

But what about what Mickey *did* do? We spent so much of Mantle's career judging him from Casey Stengel's perception as the moody, self-destructive phenom who never mastered his demons, and we spent much of the rest of Mantle's life listening to a near-crippled alcoholic lament over and over about what he *might* have been able to accomplish. For an entire generation of fans and sportswriters who saw their own boyhood fantasies reflected in Mantle's career and their worst nightmares fulfilled by his after-baseball life, Mantle's decline became the dominant part of the story.

It's time to dispel this myth. Mickey Mantle played more games in a Yankee uniform than any other player in the history of baseball's greatest team before Derek Jeter, more than Ruth, Gehrig, DiMaggio, or Berra. He played more games than Ted Williams. *Potential?* He was a hitter with a terrific batting eye — as evidenced by one of the top twelve on-base percentages in this century, a better OBP than that of Stan Musial (seven batting titles), Wade Boggs (five), or Tony Gwynn (eight) — spectacular power, blinding speed, and superb defensive ability. He could do things none of his contemporaries could do — not Duke Snider, not Hank Aaron, not Ted Williams. He could switch-hit for high average and power, and he could bunt from either side of the plate, and no power hitter in the game's history was harder to catch in a double play. He was an All-Star center fielder for eleven straight seasons, he won three MVP Awards and should have

won several more, and he had seven championship rings. His life is a
cautionary tale on the dangers of success and excess to be sure, but as
a player he has a right to be remembered not for what he might have
been but for what he was.

I'm not going to make a proper argument about whether Mickey
or Willie was better than Babe Ruth, Honus Wagner, or the pre-Balco
Barry Bonds. But I do believe that if Mickey Mantle and Willie
Mays — in their prime — lined up together to compete against all
other players in the record books at the same age and under exactly
the same conditions, it would be obvious that they are the two greatest
players in the history of the game.

Appendix B

Mickey and Willie Ranked by Total Player Rating and Win Shares

O ver the last few decades, several advanced statistics have been invented that seek to boil all of a ballplayer's contributions to his team down to a single, easily compared number. I couldn't resist seeing how Mickey and Willie stack up according to two of the best-known such measures, Total Player Rating and Win Shares.

Total Player Rating, developed by sabermetrician Pete Palmer, is defined in *Total Baseball: The Official Encyclopedia of Major League Baseball* as "the sum of a player's Adjusted Batting Runs, Fielding Runs, and Base Stealing Runs minus his positional adjustment, all divided by the Runs Per Win factor for that year."

This calls for yet more explanation. Adjusted statistics, explains the "Glossary of Statistical Terms" in the *Baseball Encyclopedia*, "means that the statistic has been normalized to league average and adjusted for home park factor."

Fielding runs are defined as "the Linear Weights measure of runs saved *beyond* what a league-average player at that position might have saved. . . . This stat is calculated to take account of the particular demands of the different positions" — meaning that center fielders such as Mantle and Mays are rated as more valuable than the corner outfielders because they must cover more territory.

Positional adjustment is "a key factor in the Total Player Rating that addresses the relative worth to a ball club of the defensive positions. A man who bats .270, hits 25 homers, and drives in 80 runs may be an average performer in left field, no matter how good his glove; but credit those batting stats to a shortstop or second baseman and you have a star, because the defensive demands of the position are so much greater." And "normally center fielders need more fielding skill and therefore do not hit as well as left and right fielders." Which means that Willie and Mickey were rated as all the more valuable for their batting and base-running contributions because they were brilliant defensive players.

A detailed explanation of Total Player Rating can be found on the website of the Society for American Baseball Research (SABR).

I begin with 1954 because it's the first year that both Mantle and Mays played full seasons. I make the comparison only until 1964, Mickey's last great season, though *Total Baseball* does not rank him among the AL's top five players for 1963 and 1964 because he played too few games. (Though in 1963 he performed brilliantly for the 65 games that he did play, with a .441 on-base percentage and .622 slugging percentage, both numbers considerably higher than Willie's .384 and .582.)

	MAYS	MANTLE
1954	6.7 (1)	4.0 (4)
1955	7.8 (1)	6.2 (1)
1956	4.7 (1)*	8.7 (1)
1957	6.6 (1)	8.7 (1)
1958	7.2 (1)	6.5 (1)
1959	4.9 (4)	4.5 (1)
1960	6.0 (1)	4.5 (1)
1961	5.5 (2)	8.3 (1)
1962	6.7 (1)	5.2 (2)
1963	7.0 (1)	—
1964	6.7 (1)	—

NOTE: The number in parentheses indicates league ranking.
*tied for first with Henry Aaron

It should be noted that Mays was number one in the NL in Total Player Rating in 1965 at 7.5 and number four the following season at 4.5.

Before we talk about these Total Player Rating numbers, let's look at our other measure, Win Shares.

Win Shares was developed by Bill James. It attempts to make the same "total" measurement of a player's worth, but from the perspective of the wins the player contributed to his team that season. In the introduction to his 2002 book, James wrote, "What is a Win Share? Well, are you familiar with the concept of Runs Created? Runs Created is any formula by which we take the singles, doubles, triples, walks, etc. for each hitter and estimate from that how many runs the player has created.

"Win Shares are, in essence, Wins Created . . . or actually, thirds of a Win Created. Win Shares takes the concept of Runs Created and moves it one step further, from runs to wins. This makes it different in essentially two ways. First, it removes illusions of context, putting a hitter from Yankee Stadium on equal footing with a hitter from Colorado, and putting a hitter from 1968 on equal footing with a hitter from 2000. Second, the Win Shares system attempts to state the contributions of pitchers and of fielders in the same forum as those of hitters."

Readers searching for a more detailed explanation of James's method are urged to consult his book or go to his website, http://www.billjamesonline.com/.

	MAYS	MANTLE
1954	40 (1)	36 (1)
1955	40 (1)	41 (1)
1956	27 (7)	49 (1)
1957	34 (2)	51 (1)
1958	40 (1)	39 (1)
1959	32 (4)	30 (1)*
1960	38 (1)†	36 (1)

*tied for first with Nellie Fox
†tied for first with Eddie Matthews

Mays, by the way, was the NL's number-one player in Win Shares in 1965, with 43, and in 1966, with 37.

Two things: Willie's relatively lower standing in the National League compared to Mickey's in the American League is due in large part to his having to compete against better players — Henry Aaron, Eddie Mathews, Ernie Banks, Frank Robinson.

Second, Willie is number one in Total Player Rating an amazing nine times from 1954 through 1964; in Win Shares he's in the top spot five times (tied for first place in two of them). That's good enough for me: Willie Mays should have been the league's MVP — or co-MVP — five times from 1954 to 1964. And he should also have been MVP in 1965 and 1966.

Mickey finished number one in Total Player Rating seven times from 1954 to 1964. He finished number one in Win Shares an astounding ten times in eleven seasons; the only season he didn't finish first was 1963, when injuries held him to 65 games — and the way he was playing in 1963, he would almost certainly have been the best in that season too.

Again, that's good enough for me. Mickey Mantle should have had at least seven Most Valuable Player Awards.

From 1954 through 1966, Willie Mays and Mickey Mantle both should have been MVP seven times.

Notes

Introduction: My First Game Was Better Than Yours

1. Castro, *Mickey Mantle: America's Prodigal Son*, p. ix.
2. Halberstam, *The Fifties*, p. 693.
3. *The Definitive Story of Mickey Mantle* (DVD), HBO Sports, 2005.
4. Hano, *Willie Mays*, p. 12.

Chapter 1: Fathers and Sons

1. Robinson, *I Never Had It Made*, p. 172.
2. Mays and Einstein, *Born to Play Ball*, p. 22.
3. Piper Davis, interview with the author, 1987.
4. Einstein, *Willie's Time*, p. 12.
5. Ibid., p. 13.
6. Ibid., p. 12.
7. Hirsch, *Willie Mays: The Life, the Legend*, p. 13.
8. Mays and Sahadi, *Say Hey*, p. 19.
9. Ibid., p. 19.
10. Swearingen, *A Great Teammate*, p. 1.
11. Hano, *Willie Mays*, p. 36.
12. Mantle and Gluck, *The Mick*, p. 9.
13. Ibid., p. 7.

14. Ibid., p. 3.
15. Ibid.
16. Hall, *Mickey Mantle: Before the Glory*, p. 52.
17. Mays, *My Life In and Out of Baseball*, p. 43.

Chapter 2: Bred to Play Ball

1. Mays, *My Life In and Out of Baseball*, p. 51.
2. Hano, *Willie Mays*, p. 21.
3. Ibid., p. 38.
4. Mantle and Gluck, *The Mick*, p. 8.
5. Hank Bauer, interview with the author, 2006.
6. Mays, *My Life In and Out of Baseball*, p. 40.
7. Mantle, Herskowitz, et al., *A Hero All His Life*, p. 117.
8. Mantle and Gluck, *The Mick*, p. 37.
9. Falkner, *The Last Hero*, p. 28.
10. Mantle and Gluck, *The Mick*, p. 22.
11. Falkner, *The Last Hero*, p. 25.
12. Mantle, Herskowitz, et al., *A Hero All His Life*, p. 95.
13. Mantle and Gluck, *The Mick*, p. 15.

14. Ibid., p. 50.

15. Ibid., p. 52.

16. Mays and Sahadi, *Say Hey*, p. 173.

17. Barra, *Rickwood Field*, p. 136.

18. Hirsch, *Willie Mays: The Life, the Legend*, p. 36.

19. Sahadi, *Say Hey*, p. 19.

20. Ibid., p. 26.

21. Falkner, *The Last Hero*, p. 43.

22. Hall, *Mickey Mantle: Before the Glory*, p. 8.

23. Mays, *My Life In and Out of Baseball*, p. 40.

24. Ibid., p. 39.

25. Ibid., p. 59.

26. Dick Young, "Farewell to Mickey Mantle," *Sport*, April 1969.

27. Young, *Sport*, April 1969.

Chapter 3: No Other Enjoyment

1. Mays and Einstein, *My Life in and Out of Baseball*, p. 40.

2. Mays and Sahadi, *Say Hey*, p. 24.

3. Ibid., p. 62.

4. Mantle and Gluck, *The Mick*, p. 16.

5. Falkner, *The Last Hero*, p. 47.

6. Swearingen, *A Great Teammate*, p. 3.

7. Personal interview with Darell Royal for *The Last Coach*.

8. Falkner, *The Last Hero*, p. 35.

9. Mantle and Gluck, *The Mick*, p. 19.

10. Mays and Einstein, *My Life In and Out of Baseball*, p. 38.

11. Hano, *Willie Mays*, p. 20.

12. Mantle and Gluck, *The Mick*, p. 16.

13. Shahadi, *Say Hey*, p. 11.

14. Mantle and Gluck, *The Mick*, p. 19.

15. Ibid., p. 31.

16. Einstein, *Willie Mays*, p. 51.

17. Falkner, *The Last Hero*, p. 41.

18. Hall, *Mickey Mantle Before the Glory*, p. 11.

19. Falkner, *The Last Hero*, p. 34.

20. Mantle and Gluck, *The Mick*, p. 25.

21. Fullerton, *Every Other Sunday*, p. 67.

22. *Birmingham News*, September 13, 1936.

23. Fullerton, *Every Other Sunday*, p. 67.

24. Mays and Einstein, *My Life In and Out of Baseball*, p. 71.

Chapter 4: Pass-the-Hat

1. Mantle, *The Education of a Baseball Player*, p. 15.

2. Mays and Sahadi, *Say Hey*, p. 29.

3. Barra, *Rickwood Field*, p. 222.

4. Hall, *Mickey Mantle: Before the Glory*, p. 86.

5. Ibid., p. 66.

6. Mantle and Gluck, *The Mick*, p. 22.

7. Ibid., p. 24.

8. Hall, *Mickey Mantle: Before the Glory*, p. 79.

9. Mickey Mantle, speech at Baseball Hall of Fame,

Cooperstown, New York,
August 12, 1974.

10. Hall, *Mickey Mantle: Before the Glory*, p. 81.
11. Ibid., p. 47.
12. Mays and Sahadi, *Say Hey*, p. 26.
13. Hirsch, *Willie Mays: The Life, the Legend*, p. 51.
14. Barra, *Rickwood Field*, p. 230.
15. Mays and Sahadi, *Say Hey*, p. 23.
16. Ibid., p. 34.
17. Personal interview, 2009.
18. Mays and Sahadi, *Say Hey*, p. 32.

Chapter 5: A Dream Come True
1. Mays and Sahadi, *Say Hey*, p. 27.
2. Ibid.
3. Mays and Einstein, *Born to Play Ball*, p. 52.
4. Barra, interview with Rich Ashburn, *Philadelphia*, 1993.
5. Mays and Einstein, *Born to Play Ball*, p. 47.
6. *Joplin Globe*, May 23, 1949.
7. *Coffeyville Daily Journal*, May 26, 1949.
8. Hall, *Mickey Mantle: Before the Glory*, p. 117.
9. Mantle and Gluck, *The Mick*, p. 26.
10. Hall, *Mickey Mantle: Before the Glory*, p. 115.
11. *The Sporting News*, March 15, 1952.

12. Mantle and Gluck, *The Mick*, p. 27.
13. Hirsch, *Willie Mays: The Life, the Legend*, p. 57.
14. Ibid., p. 62.
15. Mays and Einstein, *Born to Play Ball*, p. 56.
16. Roger Kahn, interview with the author, January 2010.
17. *Birmingham World*, June 2, 1950.
18. Mays and Einstein, *My Life in Baseball*, p. 156.

Chapter 6: "This Is Your Chance"
1. Mantle and Gluck, *The Mick*, p. 30.
2. Ibid., p. 29.
3. Mantle, *The Education of a Baseball Player*, p. 13.
4. Ibid., p. 16.
5. Ibid., p. 19.
6. Ibid., p. 31.
7. Mantle and Gluck, *The Mick*, p. 31.
8. Falkner, *The Last Hero*, p. 52.
9. Mays and Sahadi, *Say Hey*, p. 46.
10. Hall, *Mickey Mantle: Before the Glory*, p. 25.
11. Einstein, *Born to Play Ball*, p. 52.
12. Ibid.
13. Falkner, *The Last Hero*, p. 65.
14. Interview with the author, 2007.
15. Ford, Mantle, and Durso, *Whitey and Mickey*, p. 1.

16. Mays and Sahadi, *Say Hey,* p. 53.
17. Ibid., p. 54.

Chapter 7: "You're Going to Eat Steak"

1. Mays and Einstein, *Born to Play Ball,* p. 35.
2. Mays and Sahadi, *Say Hey,* p. 56.
3. Mays and Einstein, *Born to Play Ball,* p. 55.
4. Mays and Sahadi, *Say Hey.*
5. Pietrusza et al., *Baseball, The Biographical Encyclopedia,* p. 261.
6. Ibid., p. 262.
7. Mays, *My Life In and Out of Baseball,* p. 58.
8. Interview with the author, 2006.
9. Interview with the author, 1995.
10. Interview with the author, 2007.
11. Interview with the author, 2007.
12. Falkner, *The Last Hero,* p. 81.
13. Ibid., p. 83.
14. Creamer, *Stengel: His Life and Times,* p. 267.
15. Ibid.
16. Interview with the author, 1987.
17. Falkner, *The Last Hero,* p. 83.
18. Castro, *Mickey Mantle: America's Prodigal Son,* p. 49.
19. Ford and Pepe, *Slick,* p. 41.

20. Durso, *The Legend of Charles Dillon Stengel,* p. 61.
21. Personal interview with the author, 2006.
22. Ibid.
23. Mantle and Gluck, *The Mick,* p. 67.
24. Ibid., p. 70.
25. Creamer, *Stengel: His Life and Times,* p. 271.
26. Mantle and Gluck, *The Mick,* p. 61.
27. Castro, *Mickey Mantle: America's Prodigal Son.* p. 82.
28. Ibid., p. 61.
29. Personal interview with the author, 2009.
30. Mays and Sahadi, *Say Hey,* p. 59.
31. Personal interview with the author, 2009.
32. Personal interview with the author, 2006.

Chapter 8: "Is That Mickey and Willie?"

1. Trimble, *Yogi Berra,* p. 123.
2. Personal interview with the author, 2007.
3. Mays and Sahadi, *Say Hey,* p. 63.
4. Mays and Einstein, *My Life In and Out of Baseball,* p. 68.
5. Mays and Einstein, *Born To Play Ball,* p. 21.
6. Hano and Schaap, "Mickey Mantle & Willie Mays," p. 92.

7. Interview with the author, 2009.
8. *Time*, July 26, 1954.
9. Ibid.
10. Interview with the author, 2009.
11. Ford, Mantle, and Durso, *Whitey and Mickey*, p. 68.
12. Durocher and Linn, *Nice Guys Finish Last*, p. 272.
13. From a panel discussion at the Yogi Berra Museum, October 3, 2011: Neil Lanctot, Allen Barra, and Marty Appel.
14. Mantle and Gluck, *The Mick*, p. 63.
15. Ibid., p. 65.
16. Ibid., p. 67.
17. Mantle, *Education of a Baseball Player*, p. 56.
18. Mantle and Gluck, *The Mick*, p. 67.
19. Personal interview with the author, 2008.
20. Hirsch, *Willie Mays: The Life, The Legend*, p. 119.
21. Mays and Einstein, *My Life In and Out of Baseball*, p. 97.
22. Mays and Sahadi, *Say Hey*, p. 92.
23. Kahn, *The Era*, p. 143.
24. Mays and Einstein, *Born to Play Ball*, p. 93.

Chapter 9: "Greetings"
1. Mays and Sahadi, *Say Hey*, p. 100.
2. Hirsch, *Willie Mays: The Life, the Legend*, p. 144.

3. Lundquist, *Baseball: The Fan's Magazine,* June 1952.
4. Falkner, *The Last Hero,* p. 95.
5. Mantle and Gluck, *The Mick,* p. 84.
6. Mantle, *A Hero All His Life,* p. 60.
7. *New York Herald Tribune,* May 29, 1952.
8. *New York Herald Tribune,* May 28, 1952.
9. Mays and Einstein, *Born to Play Ball,* p. 100.
10. Ibid.
11. Schaap, *Mickey Mantle: The Indispensable Yankee*, p. 54.
12. *Sport*, April 1953.
13. Schaap, p. 90.
14. Ibid.
15. Mays and Einstein, *My Life In and Out of Baseball*, p. 148.
16. Ibid., p. 149.
17. Ibid., p. 149.
18. Irvin and Riley, *Nice Guys Finish First*, p. 94.
19. Mays and Sahadi, *Say Hey*, p. 102.
20. Hirsch, *Willie Mays: The Life, The Legend*, p. 37.

Chapter 10: "Right Up There with the Babe"
1. Schaap, *Mickey Mantle: The Indispensable Yankee*, p. 99.
2. Ibid., p. 124.
3. Interview of Jenkinson by the author, 2010.

4. Allen Barra, "Tripping Over Greatness," *Wall Street Journal*, October 21, 2010.
5. Interview with the author, 1987.
6. Schapp, *Mickey Mantle: The Indispensable Yankee*, p. 100.
7. Falkner, *The Last Hero*, p. 109.
8. Interview with the author, 2008.
9. *Time*, June 15, 1953.
10. Ibid.
11. Mantle and Epstein, *The Mickey Mantle Story*, p. 88.
12. Schaap, *Mickey Mantle: The Indispensable Yankee*, p. 100.
13. Personal interview with the author at the Yogi Berra Museum and Learning Center, April 4, 2010.
14. Falkner, *The Last Hero*, p. 110.
15. Schaap, *Mickey Mantle: The Indispensable Yankee*, p. 104.
16. Ibid., p. 105.
17. Interview with the author, 2009.
18. Hano, *Willie Mays*, p. 87.
19. Interview with the author, 2010.
20. Mays and Sahadi, *Say Hey*, p. 105.
21. Hano, *Willie Mays*, pp. 91–92.
22. *New York World-Telegram and Sun*, March 3, 1954.
23. Mays and Einstein, *Born to Play Ball*, p. 47.
24. Hano, *Willie Mays*, p. 92.
25. Einstein, *Willie's Time*, p. 145.
26. Hano, *Willie Mays*, p. 90.
27. Personal interview with the author, 2010.
28. Mays and Sahadi, *Say Hey*, p. 110.
29. Cannon, *New York Post*, April 14, 1954.
30. *The Sporting News*, July 7, 1954.
31. Mays and Sahadi, *Say Hey*, p. 111.
32. *Time*, July 26, 1954.

Chapter 11: "In Here, It's 1954"
1. Einstein, *Willie's Time*, p. 201.
2. Hano, *A Day in the Bleachers*, p. 1.
3. Ibid., pp. 119–21.
4. Hano, *Willie Mays*, p. 115.
5. Mays and Einstein, *Born to Play Ball*, p. 112.
6. *Toots* (film), directed by Kristi Jacobson.
7. Mantle and Herskowitz, *All My Octobers*, p. 47.
8. Berra and Kaplan, *Ten Rings*, p. 147.
9. Einstein, *Willie's Time*, p. 125.

Chapter 12: "A Whole Different Ball Game"
1. Falkner, *The Last Hero*, p. 106.
2. Young, *Sport*, May 1962.
3. Interview with author, 2008.
4. Letter from Charles Einstein to the author, 2003.

5. Dick Young, "The Man Who Handles Maris and Mantle," *Sport*, May 1962.
6. Letter to the author, 1998.
7. Interview with the author, March 2010.
8. Falkner, *The Last Hero*, p. 107.
9. Interview with the author, March 2010.
10. Durocher and Linn, *Nice Guys Finish Last*, p. 287.
11. Hirsch, *Willie Mays: The Life, The Legend*, p. 245.
12. Povich, *Washington Post*, April 4, 1956.
13. Golenback, *Dynasty*, p. 276.
14. Snide, *Sport*, August 1959.
15. *New York Daily News*, July 22, 1956.
16. Personal interview with the author, March 2010.
17. Mantle and Pepe, *My Favorite Summer*, p. 156.
18. Personal interview with the author, 2008.
19. Personal interview with the author, 2009.
20. Mantle and Herskowitz, *All My Octobers*, p. 76.
21. Mays and Einstein, *My Life In and Out of Baseball*, p. 168.
22. Mantle and Herskowitz, *A Hero All His Life*, p. 90.

Chapter 13: "Exactly the Same Ballplayer"

1. Personal interview with the author, 2010.

2. Hano, *Willie Mays*, pp. 131–32.
3. Einstein, *Willie's Time*, p. 111.
4. *San Francisco Chronicle*, November 14, 1958.
5. Hirsch, *Willie Mays: The Life, The Legend*, p. 280.
6. *Parade*, February 16, 1958.
7. Frimrite, *Sports Illustrated*, March 25, 1985.
8. Mantle and Herskowitz, *All My Octobers*, p. 84.
9. Mantle and Gluck, *The Mick*, p. 199.
10. Young, Ibid.
11. Ibid., p. 155.
12. Ibid., p. 171.
13. Barthel, *Baseball Barnstorming and Exhibition Games*, p. 4.
14. Ibid., p. 8.
15. *New York Times*, October 13, 1958.
16. Ibid.
17. Plimpton, *Out of My League*, pp. 44–45.
18. Ibid., p. 45.
19. Personal interview with the author, 1993.
20. Barthel, p. 184.
21. Hirsch, *Willie Mays: The Life, The Legend*, p. 307.
22. Castro, *Mickey Mantle: America's Prodigal Son*, p. 183.
23. Ibid.

Chapter 14: "Neither One of Us Was Joe DiMaggio"

1. "Mantle Fans Mays, Mays Fans Mantle," *Esquire*, August 1968.

2. Letter to the author, 1997.

3. Letter to the author, 1997.

4. Hano, *Willie Mays*, p. 177.

5. Ibid., p. 161.

6. *Mickey Mantle and Willie Mays*, produced by the editors of *Sport*, 1962.

7. Ibid.

8. *Esquire*, August 1968.

9. Mantle and Gluck, *The Mick*, p. 193.

10. Personal interview with the author, 1983.

11. Bob Costas, Studio 42, MLB Network, February 9, 2010.

12. Ford, Mantle, and Durso, *Mickey and Whitey: An Autobiography of the Yankees Years*, p. 177.

13. Mantle and Herskowitz, *All My Octobers*, p. 150.

14. Falkner, *The Last Hero*, p. 153.

15. Murray, *The Best of Jim Murray*, p. 77.

16. Ibid., p. 132.

17. Letter to the author, 1996.

18. Mantle and Herskowitz, *All My Octobers*, p. 148.

19. Mays and Sahadi, *The Autobiography of Willie Mays*, p. 181.

20. *Newark Evening News*, October 17, 1962.

21. Mantle and Herskowitz, *All My Octobers*, p. 161.

22. Mays and Sahadi, *Say Hey*, p. 212.

23. Ibid., p. 198.

24. Einstein, *Willie's Time*, p. 71.

Chapter 15: "Flash, Dash, and . . . a Nervous Rash"

1. Mays and Sahadi, *Say Hey*, p. 200.

2. Mantle and Gluck, *The Mick*, p. 199.

3. Falkner, *The Last Hero*, p. 164.

4. Ibid., p. 163.

5. Kahn, *The Best of Sport, Sport Magazine Library*, 1961, p. 25.

6. John Devaney, *Sport*, "The Ballplayers Reveal 'My Favorite Mickey Mantle Stories,'" October 1964.

7. Ibid.

8. Personal interview with the author, 2008.

9. Mantle and Herskowitz, *All My Octobers*, p. 173.

10. Mays and Sahadi, *Say Hey*, p. 208.

11. Issacs, *Newsday*, July 31, 1961.

12. Mantle and Herskowitz, *All My Octobers*, p. 176.

13. Interview with the author, 2008.

14. Mantle and Herskowitz, *All My Octobers*, pp. 204–5.

Chapter 16: The Boys of Summer in Their Ruin

1. Mays and Sahadi, *Say Hey*, p. 235.

2. Falkner, *The Last Hero*, p. 165.

3. James, *New Historical Baseball Abstract*, p. 729.

4. *Cleveland Plain Dealer*, January 17, 1969.

5. Letter to the author, 1966.

6. Mays and Sahadi, *Say Hey,* p. 235.
7. Hirsch, *Wille Mays: The Life, The Legend,* p. 467.
8. Castro, *Mickey Mantle: America's Prodigal Son,* p. 220.
9. Ibid.
10. Mays and Sahadi, pp. 256–57.
11. Ibid.
12. Lois, *$ellebrity.*
13. *New York Post,* January 8, 1968.
14. Interview with the author, March 2010.
15. Mantle and Gluck, *The Mick,* p. 137.
16. Ibid., p. 206.
17. *Sport,* "The Players' Favorite Willie Mays Stories," June 1967.
18. Interview with the author, June 2, 2010.
19. Smith, *Women's Wear Daily,* September 21, 1968.
20. *Sports Illustrated,* March 25, 1985.
21. Miller, *A Whole Different Ball Game,* p. 100.

Chapter 17: Say Good-Bye to America

1. Falkner, *The Last Hero,* p. 184.
2. Young, *Sport,* July 1969.
3. Falkner, *The Last Hero,* p. 184.
4. Bryant, *The Last Hero: A Life of Henry Aaron,* p. 364.
5. Ibid., p. 369.
6. Ibid.
7. Ibid., p. 366.
8. Ibid., p. 160.

9. Letter to the author, 1993.
10. Falkner, *The Last Hero,* p. 197.
11. Interview with the author, 2010.
12. Flood, *The Way It Is,* p. 70.
13. Hirsch, *Willie Mays: The Life, The Legend,* pp. 489–90.
14. *Sports Illustrated,* July 27, 1970.
15. Bouton, *Ball Four,* p. 212.
16. Ibid., p. 209.
17. Ibid., pp. 51–52.
18. Ibid., p. 64.
19. Mantle and Gluck, *The Mick,* p. 200.
20. Hirsch, *Willie Mays: The Life, The Legend,* p. 453.
21. Ibid.
22. Young, *New York Daily News,* May 12, 1972.
23. Dickey, *San Francisco Chronicle,* August 5, 1971.
24. Personal interview, 2011.
25. Personal interview, January 2005.
26. Dickey, *The Jock Empire,* p. 32.
27. Golenbock, *Amazin',* p. 308.

Chapter 18: Burden of Dreams

1. Personal interview, 2008.
2. Personal interview.
3. *New York Times,* September 12, 1980.
4. Hirsch, *Willie Mays: The Life, The Legend,* p. 537.
5. Pepe, *New York Daily News,* February 20, 1983.
6. Young, *New York Post,* February 22, 1983.

7. Falkner, *The Last Hero*, p. 214.
8. Personal interview, 2008.
9. Lois, *$ellebrity*, "Heroes" section.
10. Interview with the author, 2009.
11. Mantle and Gluck, *The Mick*, p. 197.
12. Falkner, *The Last Hero*, p. 223.
13. Leavy, *The Last Boy*, p. 326.
14. Personal interview, 2009.
15. Ibid.
16. Ron Frimrite, *Sports Illustrated*, March 25, 1985.
17. Hemphill, *Leaving Birmingham*, p. 84.

Bibliography

Books

Allen, Maury, *Roger Maris: A Man For All Seasons*, Donald I. Fine, Inc., New York, 1986.

Barra, Allen, *The Last Coach: A Life of Paul "Bear" Bryant*, W. W. Norton and Company, New York, 2005.

Barra, Allen, *Rickwood Field: A Century in America's Oldest Ballpark*, W. W. Norton and Company, New York, 2010.

Barthel, Thomas, *Baseball Barnstorming and Exhibition Games,1901–1962: A History of Off-Season Major League Play*, McFarland and Company, North Carolina, 2007.

Berger, Phil, *Mickey Mantle*, Park Lane Press, New York, 1998.

Berra, Yogi, with Dave Kaplan, *Ten Rings: My Championship Series*, William Morrow, New York, 2003.

Borelli, Stephen, *How About That!: The Life of Mel Allen*, Sports Publishing, Inc., Champaign, Illinois, 2005.

Bouton, Jim, *Ball Four: The Final Pitch*, Bulldog Publishing, North Egremont, Massachusetts, 2000.

Bryant, Howard, *The Last Hero: A Life of Henry Aaron*, Pantheon Books, New York, 2010.

Castro, Tony, *Mickey Mantle: America's Prodigal Son*, Potomac Books, Dulles, Virginia, 2002.

Creamer, Robert W., *Stengel: His Life and Times*, Simon & Schuster, New York, 1984.

Durocher, Leo, and Ed Linn, *Nice Guys Finish Last*, Simon & Schuster, New York, 1976.

Durso, Joseph, *Casey: The Legend of Charles Dillon Stengel*, Prentice-Hall, Englewood Cliffs, New Jersey, 1967.

Einstein, Charles, *Willie's Time: A Memoir*, J. B. Lippincott Company, New York, 1979.

Falkner, David, *The Last Hero: The Life of Mickey Mantle*, Simon & Schuster, New York, 1995.

Falkner, David, *The Last Yankee: The Life of Billy Martin*, Simon & Schuster, New York, 1992.

Flood, Curt, with Richard Porter, *The Way It Is*, Trident Press, New York, 1971.

Ford, Whitey, Mickey Mantle, and Joseph Durso, *Whitey and Mickey: An Autobiography of the Yankee Years*, Viking Press, New York, 1977.

Ford, Whitey, with Phil Pepe, *Slick: My Life In and Around Baseball*, William Morrow, New York, 1987.

Forker, Dom, *Sweet Seasons: Recollections of the 1955–64 New York Yankees*, Taylor Publishing Company, Dallas, 1990.

Forker, Dom, *The Men of Autumn*, Taylor Publishing Company, Dallas, 1989.

Frommer, Harvey, *New York City Baseball, 1947–1957*, University of Wisconsin Press, Madison, Wisconsin, 2004.

Fullerton, Chris, *Every Other Sunday: The Story of the Birmingham Black Barons*, R. Booker Press, Birmingham, Alabama, 1999.

Gallagher, Mark, and Neil Gallagher, *Mickey Mantle* (Baseball Legends series), Chelsea House Publishers, New York, 1991.

Gittleman, Sol, *Reynolds, Raschi and Lopat: New York's Big Three and the Yankee Dynasty of 1949–1953*, McFarland & Company, Inc., Jefferson, North Carolina, 2007.

Golenbock, Peter, *Amazin'*, St. Martin's Press, New York, 2002.

Golenbock, Peter, *Bums*, Simon & Schuster, New York, 1984.

Golenbock, Peter, *Dynasty: The New York Yankees 1949–1964*, Prentice-Hall, Englewood Cliffs, New Jersey, 1975.

Grabowski, John, *Willie Mays* (Baseball Legends series), Chelsea House Publishers, New York, 1990.

Graham, Frank, *McGraw of the Giants*, G. P. Putnam, New York, 1944.

Graham, Frank, *The New York Giants*, G. P. Putnam, New York, 1952.

Graham, Frank, *The New York Yankees*, G. P. Putnam, New York, 1947.

Graham, Frank, Jr., *Casey Stengel*, John Day Co., 1958.

Halberstam, David, *October 1964*, Villard Books, New York, 1994.

Halberstam, David, *The Fifties*, Villard Books, New York, 1993.

Hall, John G., *Mickey Mantle: Before the Glory*, Leathers Publishing, Leawood, Kansas, 2005.

Hano, Arnold, *Willie Mays*, Grosset & Dunlop, New York, 1966.

Hano, Arnold, and Dick Schapp, "Mickey Mantle & Willie Mays," produced by the editors of *Sport*, 1962.

Heinz, W. C., *Once They Heard The Cheers*, Doubleday & Company, Garden City, New York, 1979.

Henrich, Tommy and Bill Gilbert, *Five O'Clock Lightning*, Carol Publishing Group, New York, 1992.

Hirsch, James, *Willie Mays: The Life, The Legend*, Scribner's, New York, 2010.

Honig, Donald, *Mays, Mantle, Snider: A Celebration*, Macmillan Publishing Company, New York, 1987.

Howard, Arlene, with Ralph Wimbish, *Elston and Me: The Story of the First Black Yankee*, The University of Missouri Press, Columbia, Missouri, 2001.

Irvin, Monte, with James A. Riley, *Nice Guys Finish First*, Carroll & Graf Punishers, Inc., New York, 1996.

James, Bill, *The New Bill James Historical Baseball Abstract*, Free Press (Simon & Schuster), New York, 2001.

James, Bill, with Jim Henzler, *Win Shares*, Stats, Inc., Illinois, 2002.

Kahn, Roger, *Beyond The Boys of Summer*, McGraw-Hill, New York, 2005.

Kahn, Roger, *The Era: 1947–1957*, Tichenor and Fields, New York, 1993.

Klima, John, *Willie's Boys: The 1948 Birmingham Black Barons, The Last Negro League World Series, and the Making of the Baseball Legend*, John Wiley and Son, Inc., New Jersey, 2009.

Lally, Richard, *Bombers: An Oral History of the New York Yankees*, Crown Publishers, New York, 2002.

Lang, Jack, and Peter Simon, *The New York Mets: Twenty-Five Years of Baseball Magic*, Henry Holt, New York, 1987.

Larsen, Don, with Mark Shaw, *The Perfect Yankee: The Incredible Story of the Greatest Miracle in Baseball History*, Sagimore Publishing, Champaign, Illinois, 2001.

Leiderman, Bill, and Maury Allen, *Our Mickey: Cherished Memories of an American Icon*, Triumph Books, Chicago, 2004.

Lois, George, *$ellebrity: My Tangling with Famous People*, Phaidon Press, New York, 2003.

Madden, Bill, *Pride of October: What It Was to Be Young and a Yankee*, Warner Books, New York, 2004.

Madden, Bill, and Moss Klein, *Damned Yankees: A No-holds Barred Account of Life with "Boss" Steinbrenner*, Warner Books, New York, 1990.

Mann, Jack, *The Decline and Fall of the New York Yankees*, Simon & Schuster, New York, 1967.

Mantle, Merlyn, Mickey Jr., David, and Dan, with Mickey

Herskowitz, *A Hero All His Life*, HarperCollins, 1996.

Mantle, Mickey, *The Education of a Baseball Player*, Simon & Schuster, New York, 1969.

Mantle, Mickey, *The Quality of Courage: True Stories of Heroism and Bravery*, Bantam Books, New York, 1964.

Mantle, Mickey, and Louis Early, *Mickey Mantle: The American Dream Comes to Life*, Sports Publishing, LLC, Champaign, Illinois, 2002.

Mantle, Mickey, as told to Ben Epstein, *The Mickey Mantle Story*, Henry Holt and Company, New York, 1953.

Mantle, Mickey, and Herb Gluck, *The Mick*, Doubleday and Company, New York, 1985.

Mantle, Mickey, with Mickey Herskowitz, *All My Octobers: My Memories of 12 World Series When the Yankees Ruled Baseball*, HarperCollins, New York, 1994.

Martin, Billy, and Peter Golenbock, *Number 1: Billy Martin*, Delacourt, New York, 1980.

Masterson, Dave, and Timm Boyle, *Baseball's Best: The MVPs*, Contemporary Books, Chicago, 1985.

McGraw, John, *My Thirty Years in Baseball*, Boni and Liveright, New York, 1923.

Mays, Willie, as told to Charles Einstein, *Born to Play Ball*, G. P. Putnam's Sons, New York, 1955.

Mays, Willie, as told to Charles Einstein, *Willie Mays: My Life In and Out of Baseball*, E. P. Dutton and Company, New York, 1972.

Mays, Willie, and Jeff Harris, *Danger in Centerfield*, J. Lowell Pratt & Company, New York, 1963.

Mays, Willie, with Lou Sahadi, *Say Hey: The Autobiography of Willie Mays*, Simon & Schuster, New York, 1988.

McWhorter, Diane, *Carry Me Home: Birmingham, Alabama — The Climactic Battle of the Civil Rights Revolution*, Simon & Schuster, New York, 2001.

Meany, Tom, *The Magnificent Yankees*, Grosset & Dunlap, New York, 1957.

Miller, Marvin, *A Whole Different Ball Game: The Inside Story of the Baseball Revolution*, Ivan Dee, Chicago, 2004.

Neft, David, Richard Cohen, and Michael Neft, *The Sports Encyclopedia Baseball 2005*, St. Martin's Griffin, New York, 2005.

Neyer, Rob, and Eddie Epstein, *Baseball Dynasties: The Greatest Teams of All Time*, Norton, New York, 2000.

Neyer, Rob, *Big Book of Baseball Blunders*, Fireside Books/

Simon & Schuster, New York, 2006.

Okrent, Daniel, and Harris Lewine, eds., *The Ultimate Baseball Book*, Houghton Mifflin, Boston, 1979.

Olderman, Murray, "Say Hey at the Golden Gate," *Baseball—Sports All-Stars*, 1959.

Olen, Ben, ed., *Big-Time Baseball*, Hart Publishing Company, Inc., New York, 1960.

Pietrusza, David, Matthew Silverman, and Michael Gresman, *Baseball: The Biographical Encyclopedia*, Total Sports Publishing, Kingston, New York, 2000.

Plimpton, George, *Out of My League*, Pocket Books, 1967.

Powers, Jimmy, *Baseball Personalities*, Rudolph Field, New York, 1949.

Richards, Paul, *Modern Baseball Strategy*, Prentice-Hall, New York, 1955.

Rickey, Branch with Robert Riger, *The American Diamond: A Documentary of the Game of Baseball*, Simon & Schuster, New York, 1965.

Rizzuto, Phil, with Tom Horton, *The October Twelve: Five Years of Yankee Glory 1949–1953*, Forge/Tom Doherty Associates, New York, 1999.

Robinson, Jackie, *I Never Had It Made: An Autobiography*, Putnam, New York, 1972.

Robinson, Ray, *Baseball's Most Colorful Managers*, G. P. Putnam, New York, 1969.

Robinson, Ray, and Christopher Jennison, *Pennants & Pinstripes: The New York Yankees 1903–2002*, Viking Studio/Penguin, New York, 2002.

Smith, Curt, *The Voice: Mel Allen's Untold Story*, Lyons Press, Guilford, Connecticut, 2007.

Smith, Red, *Red Smith on Baseball*, Ivan R. Dee, Chicago, 2000.

Smith, Red, *Strawberries in the Winter Time*, Chicago. Quadrangle Books, 1974.

Smith, Red, *The Red Smith Reader*, Random House, New York, 1982.

Stanton, Tom, *Hank Aaron and the Home Run That Changed America*, William Morrow, New York, 2004.

Stark, Jayson, *The Stark Truth: The Most Overrated and Underrated Players in Baseball History*, Triumph Books, Chicago, 2007.

Stengel, Casey, with Harry T. Paxton, *Casey at the Bat: The Story of My Life in Baseball*, Random House, New York, 1962.

Stout, Glenn, ed., *Top of the Heap: A Yankees Collection*, Houghton Mifflin Company, New York, 2003.

Sugar, Bert Randolph, *Rain Delays,* St. Martin's Press, New York, 1990.

Swearingen, Randall, *A Great Teammate: The Legend of Mickey Mantle,* Sports Publishing LLC, Champaign, Illinois, 2007.

Thorn, John, ed., *The National Pastime,* Warner Books, New York, 1987.

Thorn, John, and Pete Palmer, *The Hidden Game of Baseball,* Dolphin Books/Doubleday and Company, Garden City, New York, 1985.

Thorn, John, Peter Palmer, and Michael Gershman, *Total Baseball,* Total Sports Publishing, Kingston, New York, 2001.

Vincent, Fay, *It's What Inside the Lines That Counts: Baseball Stars of the 1970s and 1980s Talk About the Game They Loved,* Simon & Schuster, New York, 2010.

Ward, Geoffrey C., and Ken Burns, *Baseball,* Alfred A. Knopf, New York, 1994.

Whitt, Timothy, *Bases Loaded with History,* R. Boozer Press, Birmingham, Alabama, 1995.

Magazines

Allen, Maury, "Why Mickey Mantle Must Keep Playing," *Sport,* January 1967.

Anderson, Dave, "Willie Mays: Is the Pressure Getting to Him?" *Dell Sports,* July 1965.

Barra, Allen, "An Embarrassment of Richies," *Philadelphia,* August 1995.

Carley, Clyde, "The Mickey Mantle Nobody Knows," *Inside Baseball — The Big League Magazine,* August 1953.

Devaney, John, "The Ballplayers Reveal: My Favorite Mickey Mantle Stories," *Sport,* September 1964.

Donnelly, Joe, "Mickey Mantle's Fight to Play Baseball," *Sport,* July 1966.

Donnelly, Joe, "Mickey Mantle: My Ten Greatest Baseball Memories," *Sport,* May 1967.

Einstein, Charles, "What Willie Mays Still Means to the Giants," *Sport,* May 1968.

Graham, Frank, "The MVP of The Yankees," *Sport,* October 1955.

Hano, Arnold, "Orlando Cepeda: I Am Always Against the Wall," *Sport,* July 1966.

Hano, Arnold, "The Willie Mays Decade," *Sport,* June 1961.

Irvin, Monte, "What Willie Mays Really Wants," *Sport,* June 1965.

Jupiter, Harry, "The Players Tell Their Favorite Willie Mays Stories," *Sport,* June 1967.

Kahn, Roger, "Sports Column," *Esquire,* May 1971.

Katz, Fred, "Is Wills Really More

Valuable Than Mays?" *Inside Baseball*, produced by the editors of *Sport*, 1963.

Leggett, William, "Trouble Sprouts for the Yankees," *Sports Illustrated*, March 2, 1994.

Lundquist, Carl, "Broken Bones Take A Heavy Toll," *Baseball — The Fan's Magazine*, June 1952.

Mays, Willie, "Willie Mays' Diary — The Season as He Lived It," *Sport*, October 1964.

Meaney, Tom, "From DiMaggio to Mantle: Epic of the Greatest Yankee Era," *Sport*, September 1961.

O'Day, Joe, "Willie Mays' Greatest Day," *Sports Cavalcade*, November 1963.

Olderman, Murray, "Mickey Mantle, What's Holding Him Back," *Baseball — Sports All Stars*, 1959.

Olderman, Murray, "Say Hey at the Golden Gate."

Reichler, Joe, "Living Hall of Famers Pick the Greatest Centerfielder Ever," *Sport*, August 1964.

Schaap, Dick, "The Big Change in Mickey Mantle," *Sport*, July 1962.

Schoenstein, Ralph, "A Giants Fan's Lament: My Heart Is a Yo-Yo," *Sport*, September 1961.

Silverman, Al, "What the Players Think of Mickey Mantle," *Inside Baseball*, produced by the editors of *Sport*, 1963.

Weil, Robert, "Mickey Mantle — Interview," *Penthouse*, September 1986.

Young, Dick, "The Man Who Handles Maris and Mantle," *Sport*, May 1962.

Authors Not Listed

"Has Success Spoiled Mickey Mantle?" *Dell Sports Baseball Stars*, 1959.

"Mantle Fans Mays/Mays Fans Mantle — Willie and Mickey Appraise Each Other," *Esquire*, August 1968.

"Mickey Mantle's Season of Personal Crisis," *Sport Annual* (produced by the editors of *Sport*), 1963.

"San Francisco Steals the Pennant," *Sport Annual* (produced by the editors of *Sport*), 1963.

Stats All-Time Major League Handbook, Second Edition, Stats Publishing, 2000.

"The Private Mickey Mantle," *People Weekly*, August 28, 1995.

Index